Snap-on® Tools

Greetings!

Once again, we've put another great year behind us, thanks to the fine efforts of all of our Dealers and employees. I can't adequately convey the personal gratitude I feel at our having achieved such an important sales milestone in my last full year as a Snap-on employee. It's the best retirement gift I can imagine.

But more than a year of sales records, 1987 has been a year in which all that we stand for as a Company came into sharper focus than ever: Quality and Service. We all rededicated ourselves to those important hallmarks this year, and proved that staying on top is a challenge we can accomplish.

Since 1920, our growth and success have been uniquely American. Nowhere else in the world could such a success story have evolved, and nowhere else could Snap-on have found the caliber of employees and Dealers to make it happen.

This book, "America," captures in words and pictures the essence of our country, north to south, east to west, better than any atlas I've seen. Considering that 1987 was important in another regard for the United States--the 200th anniversary of the signing of our Constitution--this book takes on added significance for all of us.

I truly hope you enjoy it as much as I have. And once again, please accept my warmest personal thanks for your outstanding efforts this year, along with my best wishes for a safe and happy holiday season.

Sincerely,

William B. Rayburn
Chairman and Chief Executive Officer

Rand McNally's

America

Rand McNally's

America

Photographs by David Muench

Maps by Rand McNally

Rand McNally & Company

Chicago • New York • San Francisco

PHOTOGRAPHY OF AMERICA BY DAVID MUENCH

Jacket, title page spread, 10-35, 51, 60-86, 101, 109-135, 136 bottom, 141, 143, 151, 162-212, 219, 231, 234-253, 256-257.

Map Credits:

49 *Population* Dr. Klaus J. Bayr, Keene State College, New Hampshire. 103 *Small-Town Growth* Dr. Charles T. Zier, Dept. of Geography and Planning, East Carolina University, North Carolina. 161 *Ethnic Diversity* Bulletin of the University of Wisconsin, October 1942.

Map Section Photo Credits:

36 top James Blank/FPG; bottom Anthony Morganti/FPG. 39 Tom Algire/FPG. 41 DuPont Co. 43 J. Randklev/FPG. 45 Chuck Feil/FPG. 47 top J. Blank/FPG; bottom Marcus Brooke/FPG. 49 N. Groffman/FPG. 53 Grant Heilman Photography. 55 Grant Heilman Photography. 57 top Alastair Black/FPG; bottom A. Griffin/ H. Armstrong Roberts. 59 G. Hampfler/H. Armstrong Roberts. 87 W. Metzen/H. Armstrong Roberts. 89 Chevron U.S.A., Inc. 91 Grant Heilman Photography. 93 NASA. 95 A. McGee/FPG. 97 Southern Living/Geoff Gilbert. 99 E. Cooper/FPG. 103 William Felger/ Grant Heilman Photography. 105 Dick Dietrich/FPG. 107 Tennessee Tourist Development. 136 top Grant·Heilman Photography. 139 Illinois Dept. of Transportation. 145 Grant Heilman Photography. 147 H. Armstrong Roberts. 149 Grant Heilman Photography. 153 Grant Heilman Photography. 155 North Dakota Tourism Promotion Division. 157 Bernard G. Silberstein/FPG. 159 Courtesy of South Dakota Division of Tourism. 161 Edgar G. Mueller. 213 Kent Dannen. 215 Richard C. Towlen/FPG. 217 James Blank/FPG. 221 L. Burton/ H. Armstrong Roberts. 223 J. Messerschmidt. 225 Ray Nelson. 227 W. Metzen/H. Armstrong Roberts. 229 Grant Heilman Photography. 233 Ron Thomas/FPG. 258 Ray Atkeson. 259 Chuck O'Rear/West Light. 261 Ed Cooper/H. Armstrong Roberts. 263 Chuck O'Rear. 265 E. Nagele/FPG. 267 Jim Hosmer. 269 G. Schwartz.

Second printing 1988

Copyright © 1986 by Rand McNally & Company.
From *This Great Land* and *Atlas of the United States*
© 1983, Rand McNally & Company.
Library of Congress Catalog Card Number: 86-62390
ISBN 0-528-81143-6

Printed in Italy

Contents

The States

The United States is a composite of the cultures, economies, political tendencies, and environments of its fifty states. In the country today, numerous trends are at work, serving to alter the character of the states and thus the nation as a whole. In this section of the atlas, the individual states are examined through reference maps; special-topic maps, graphs, and diagrams; land use maps; photographs; economic graphs; text; and fact blocks.

Reference Maps

The reference map for each state shows in detail cities, highways, railways, rivers, lakes, and, through shaded relief, the terrain. The maps allow easy location of places and examinations of relationships among settlements, transportation routes, and topography. Accompanying each reference map is a place-name index.

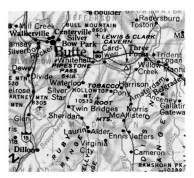

Maps, Graphs, and Diagrams

The special-topic maps, graphs, and diagrams provide a close-up analysis of an outstanding aspect of each state. Vital statistics and historical, cultural, and geographical information are portrayed in visual form to describe past, present, and future trends and situations. Each map, graph, or diagram has been selected to give insight into an idea that is important in defining the state's character.

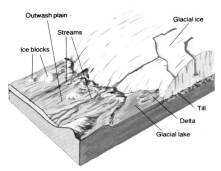

Land Use Maps

The land use maps depict the character of the land, whether natural or modified by humans. The land is classified into nine major categories in terms of its nature and use.

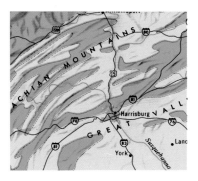

Photographs

Each state is a result of the interaction of the land and the people that are principally found within its boundaries. Color photographs capture significant physical and human geographical aspects of the states — landforms and vegetation, the population, or the way in which people have altered the earth.

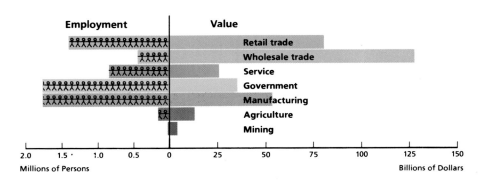

Economic Graphs

The economic graphs describe employment and the value derived from major activities. Created on a variable scale, the graphs allow comparison among economic categories within each state. The data presented here are supplemented by The Economy table on page 272, which allows further comparisons.

Data for mining shipments and receipts is taken from the United States Bureau of the Mines; government employment data is from the United States Bureau of Labor Statistics; the source for all other data is the United States Bureau of the Census. Dates of information and category descriptions are as follows.

- Retail and wholesale trade, 1977 data: Employment reflects paid employees, exclusive of proprietors of and partners in unincorporated businesses. Value includes all sales by establishments whose primary activity is either retail or wholesale trade.
- Services, 1977 data: Employment has been determined in the same way as that for trade. Value is a total of the receipts of establishments whose primary activity is services, such as hotels, advertising agencies, and auto-repair facilities.
- Government, 1980 data: Employment excludes armed forces; value indicates total revenue from federal, state, and local governments.
- Manufacturing, 1977 data: Employment has been determined in the same way as that for trade. Value is value added by manufacture, or the dollar value added to a good in the process of its manufacture.
- Agriculture, 1980 data: Farm labor reflects all farm population. Value displays farm marketings, or the dollar value of the agricultural products sold at the market.
- Mining, 1977 data: Employment includes all persons employed in mining. Value reflects mine shipments and receipts.

Text

Many patterns established in the past continue to influence current situations, even though those patterns may not remain obvious. The text provides the background necessary to understanding these cause-and-effect relationships of the past and the present. And because a state's development is an ongoing process, the articles point to what these current events may mean in terms of the future.

Fact Blocks

The fact blocks at the top of the right-hand pages relate basic information essential to understanding the people, economy, and land of the states. In conjunction with the tables at the back of the book, they describe each state's general character.

These various components provide basic comprehensive information on the fifty states. Many conclusions and interpretations about each state may be drawn from the information presented in The States, and as a whole, the section presents a concise description of America.

Map Symbols

CULTURAL FEATURES

Political Boundaries

International
Secondary (State)
County

Populated Places

Cities, towns, and villages

• • • • ● ● ● Symbol size represents population of the place

Chicago
Gary
Racine
Glenview
Edgewood

Type size represents relative importance of the place

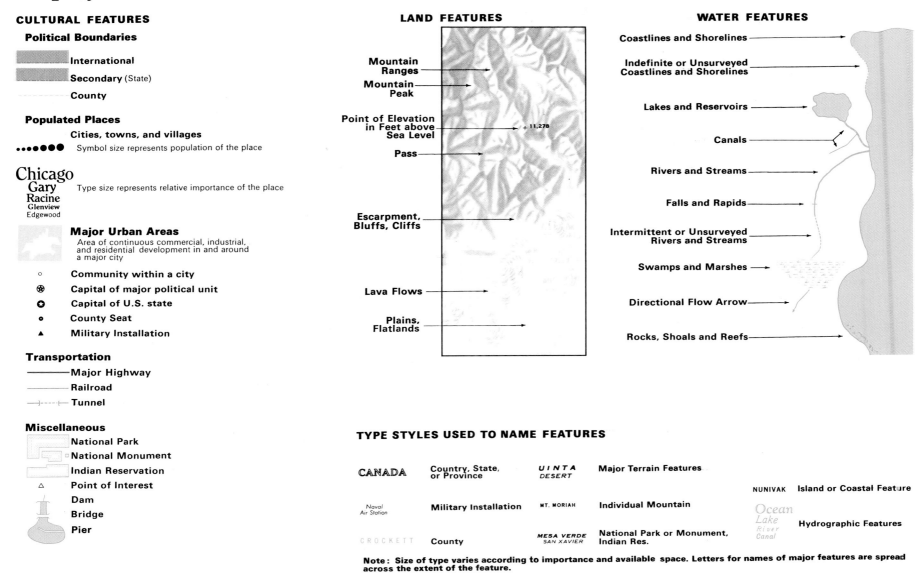

Major Urban Areas
Area of continuous commercial, industrial, and residential development in and around a major city

○   Community within a city
⊛   Capital of major political unit
⊙   Capital of U.S. state
○   County Seat
▲   Military Installation

Transportation

———— Major Highway
———— Railroad
—┼--·--┼— Tunnel

Miscellaneous

National Park
National Monument
Indian Reservation
△   Point of Interest
Dam
Bridge
Pier

LAND FEATURES

Mountain Ranges
Mountain Peak
Point of Elevation in Feet above Sea Level   + 11,278
Pass
Escarpment, Bluffs, Cliffs
Lava Flows
Plains, Flatlands

WATER FEATURES

Coastlines and Shorelines
Indefinite or Unsurveyed Coastlines and Shorelines
Lakes and Reservoirs
Canals
Rivers and Streams
Falls and Rapids
Intermittent or Unsurveyed Rivers and Streams
Swamps and Marshes
Directional Flow Arrow
Rocks, Shoals and Reefs

TYPE STYLES USED TO NAME FEATURES

CANADA	Country, State, or Province	*U I N T A* *DESERT*	Major Terrain Features
		NUNIVAK	Island or Coastal Feature
Naval Air Station	Military Installation	MT. MORIAH	Individual Mountain
			Ocean *Lake* *River* *Canal* Hydrographic Features
CROCKETT	County	*MESA VERDE* *SAN XAVIER*	National Park or Monument, Indian Res.

Note: Size of type varies according to importance and available space. Letters for names of major features are spread across the extent of the feature.

The Map Reference System

The indexing system of this atlas is based upon the conventional pattern of parallels and meridians used to indicate latitude and longitude. The city of **Amherst** is located in **B2.** Each index-key letter, in this case **B,** is placed between degree numbers of latitude along the vertical borders of the map. Each index key number, in this case **2,** is placed between degree numbers of longitude along the horizontal borders of the map. The parallels above and below the index letter cross the meridians on each side of the index number to form a box in which the place is located. The location of the place may be anywhere within this box.

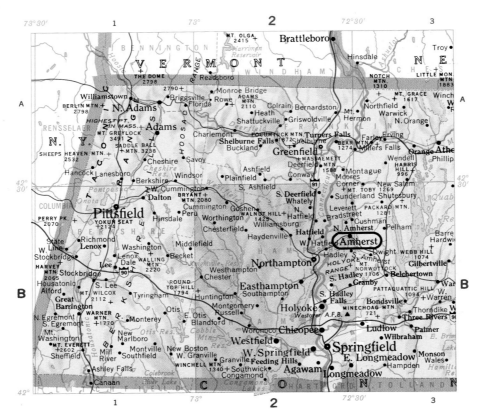

Lambert Conformal Conic Projection
SCALE 1:12,000,000 1 Inch ≈ 189 Statute Miles

DAWN, NAUSET MARSH, CAPE COD NATIONAL SEASHORE / MASSACHUSETTS

The Northeast

A Stubborn, Enduring Corner of America

BY CASKIE STINNETT

THE POWERFUL BEAUTY OF WOODS AND shore sweeps across this vast continent, but in the Northeast it seems to have a redolence, a pastoral strength of its own, especially in that corner of America known as New England. Stormy seas pound the worn boulders of the coast of Maine, tossing spray high into the air, where it is caught by the fitful sea wind and blown across the tops of the spruce and pine. Across the rolling meadows of Vermont and New Hampshire, ancient fences of fieldstone create strange geometric patterns, and in the low areas there are great thickets of alder, birch, and goldenrod. Curtains of snow move down the rocky shore of the North Atlantic, shrouding the coastlines of Massachusetts, Rhode Island, and Connecticut, and bringing a premature darkness to a winter day. But in late April, the voice of the whippoorwill sounds in the evening air, a flutelike announcement that spring has arrived, that life endures, that the fields and the woods will become youthful again, and that the sunshine will once more warm the earth. There is an excitement, a stimulation to be found in the seasons of New England that I think exists nowhere else in this country.

It has been said that landscapes form the character of the people they shelter, and there is a great deal to recommend this theory. Lawrence Durrell once expressed the belief that you could exterminate the French at a blow and resettle the country with Tartars, and within two generations discover, to your astonishment, that the national characteristics of the French were prevalent once again. Human beings, he was convinced, are expressions of their landscape. When I think of the New Englander, I detect traces of the original Massachusetts Bay colonist in his flinty manner, his frugality, his determination to strip away nonsense from fact, his ability to deal competently with hardship.

When Ralph Waldo Emerson dropped by the Concord jail to visit his friend Henry David Thoreau, who had refused to pay taxes of which he disapproved, he inquired, "Why are you here?" There was a moment's silence, and Thoreau replied: "Why aren't you?" I once spent a quiet afternoon talking with Rachel Carson, and she told me that at her home on the coast of Maine she would bring small samples of

Connecticut
Delaware
Maine
Maryland
Massachusetts
New Hampshire
New Jersey
New York
Pennsylvania
Rhode Island
Vermont

seawater up from the tidal pools to examine under her microscope, but, she added, she always returned the sample to the sea when she had finished with it. When I laughed and said I hardly thought the balance of nature would be upset by a spoonful of seawater, she said, "Then you will think I'm crazy when I tell you that if those small creatures are going to survive they must be returned to the sea at the same tide level from which I took them." She was silent a moment. "This means," she went on slowly, "that sometimes I must set my alarm clock and put on a robe in the middle of the night and walk to the sea and put them back."

The spirit of Thoreau and Miss Carson lingers in New England; what appears to be self-sufficiency is really a recognition of the need for mutual forbearance. The landscape of New England is rich, with its rivers, lakes, forests, mountains, and seashore, but the New Englander is frugal by nature and will not exhaust them. Large areas of the United States have been thoughtlessly laid bare, but deep in the heart of the New Englander is the belief that nature's primal capacity to renew and to continue to provide is not unlim-

ited, and that man will ultimately have to reduce his demands upon the earth.

Character moderates and softens as one moves south. New York and Pennsylvania can have cold winters, but autumn lasts longer and spring comes earlier and the cruel sting of the New England winter is lacking. If there is truly an alliance between character and climate, the Northeast states would seem to prove it. The clean church spires and village greens of the New England states persist through New York, northern New Jersey, and Pennsylvania, but are seldom seen farther south. And the stringent austerity of the early Calvinists and the Shakers, still an influence in New England, is mellowed by the German Catholics. The Amish of Pennsylvania struggle to retain the purity of the simple life in defiance of contemporary thought and fashion.

City and country too often coexist on uneasy terms. In America, as in other countries, it is the rural population that remains the force that binds human beings to the earth and to the climate. Although the states of the Northeast are heavy with industry, they all possess large rural areas that cushion

the impact of industrial assault upon the environment and preserve the sometimes precarious balance between economy and ecology.

Since the first place that the morning sun shines upon the continental United States is Mount Katahdin in Maine, that state makes a logical point from which to begin a ramble across the sometimes bucolic, often rugged, enduring Northeast. The coast of Maine is a magnificent sight, a landscape of exalted expectancy. No other land, except perhaps Norway and Finland, possesses the same character. Spruce and fir trees grow in a dark green shadow to the sea's edge; waves break against wild ledges, sending spray high into the air, where rainbows are spun for a brilliant second from spume. Bleak headlands of sheer rock quiet the winter seas, and in the silent coves and reaches blue herons stand in the water searching for minnows or some other sea creature venturing out on the low tide at twilight.

Tides control the life of coastal Maine, as the heartbeat maintains life in the body. Under spring tide conditions, they rise and fall 35 feet or more, especially where Nova Scotia curves around to the east of Maine to form the Bay of Fundy. Some of these tidal flows create a witch's broth that can be disastrous to inexperienced sailors. Great, turbulent "northeasters" bear down upon coastal Maine in winter, lashing the villages with sleet and snow, while gale winds tear at anything that is not tightly secured. On clear winter nights

the temperature plunges and the whole country seems to be lying frozen in the moonlight. But in late March or early April, cakes of ice suddenly break off and begin to move on the full, outgoing tide, docks come alive with lobstermen and fishermen, and by June the icy grip of winter is just a memory as summer visitors begin to appear.

A place of extremes, Maine is seldom the same—sometimes shadowy and obscure, sometimes splendidly sunlit. I know this land well because I live on a small island in Casco Bay for five months or more every year, and I've seen the great fluctuations in its weather, from the humid haze that enshrouds the coast in summer to the cruel cold of winter. There are the heavy fogs, which can enfold the world in a gray blanket for days on end while dismal foghorns echo endlessly across the water; and the summer storms, which roll in with jagged forks of lightning and crashing thunder, only to subside, with fury spent, in a gentle drizzle of rain through which the afternoon sun shines with a strange chartreuse glow.

A still twilight on the Maine coast is a time of beauty, especially when the tide is flowing, covering the dark secrets of the seaworld and creeping across the low stones, invading the crevices in the rocks. A few mussel shells will float on the incoming swell, but the slightest ripple in the surface will cause them to sink. A dark grotto under a rock will begin to fill, giving off a strange clapping sound, as though ap-

Overleaf–SUNRISE, CAPE COD NATIONAL SEASHORE / MASSACHUSETTS

Left– COASTLINE, CAMDEN HARBOR / MAINE

Below– STONINGTON HARBOR / MAINE

plause is coming for some unseen performance. The wind springs up, shifts quickly, and the rich, moist odor of salt marsh grass is borne on the evening air. When the moon is full, it rises in the east while the western sky is still light, laying down a path of gold in the sea. That is a breathtaking sight, made all the more overwhelming by the silence that has seized the stage. There is only the sound of the incoming tide slapping gently on the rocks as the immense copper ball turns slowly to burnished gold and rises in the sky. In the shallows a clump of rockweed bobs gently, and from somewhere far away comes a blue heron's complaint, hoarse and solemn and sad. Here on these rocks there is something marvelously infectious, something sensual and profound. So much of the coast of Maine is as it always has been.

From Kittery, in southern Maine, to Calais, where the state first touches New Brunswick, Canada, the coastline is less than 250 miles for an airborne creature, but the coves, reaches, bays, and inlets provide the state with 3,478 miles of waterfront—one-half of the tidal line of the entire eastern littoral of the United States.

Inland, the Maine countryside changes abruptly. Gone are the coastal plains; first the country is rolling and then it becomes rough, even primitive. The landscape is dominated by wilderness and lakes, with deep forests and bogs. Here the dark recesses of woodland are difficult to reach, at times inaccessible except by foot; and although the hunting and fishing are unrivaled, the black flies and mosquitoes of summer can be brutal, and only the most dedicated sportsmen can withstand their attack for long. Wildlife abounds. Moose are now so plentiful in this country that in the fall of 1982 the state reopened a long-closed moose hunting season. The north woods is one of the few places in the nation where land-locked salmon still can be found.

The first escarpments of the massive Appalachian Mountain range rise in western Maine, New Hampshire, Vermont, and New York. The Appalachians are to the East what the

Rockies are to the West. They constitute a nearly continuous chain of mountains stretching all the way to Alabama, running roughly parallel to the Atlantic Seaboard. First formed by catastrophic upheavals in the earth's crust, then molded by eroding action of glaciers and rivers, the Appalachians are among the oldest mountains on earth.

Although the Appalachians pervade the Northeast and provide rural areas and even remote wilderness, there also exists in this corner of the nation that anomaly known as the Megalopolis. The pattern of human settlement that it entails cannot be ignored. Historically, the density of settlement in America has depended upon the agricultural capacity of the land to support its population, although the length of time a region has been settled also plays an important part. How, then, did the Northeast become the country's first great center of commerce and urban sprawl? Why has the seaboard region extending from Portland, Maine, to Washington, D.C., grown to be the third greatest population center in the world,

with about 45 million people? If it cannot be explained in terms of physical terrain, of landscapes, of convenient rivers and harbors, and temperate climate, perhaps one has to fall back upon the historical concept that this was the first landfall of the major European colonists, the first center of urbanization. From here the country grew to the south and the west as threats from unfriendly Indians and other external dangers diminished. Whatever explains the Megalopolis theory, one thing is certain. The rural areas of the Northeast are hospitable to this high density population; extensive agricultural areas serve the needs of the region's urban dwellers, with fresh vegetables, fruit, and milk, and the forested areas of the central and northern Appalachians satisfy many of their recreational needs.

Vermont and most of New Hampshire are largely divorced from the dense urban concentration found closer to the Atlantic Coast. Here the land sweeps westward toward Lake Ontario in a series of neat meadows, rolling hills, and

Left– VIEW OF LITTLE RIVER VALLEY, FROM MOUNT MANSFIELD / VERMONT

Above– QUARTZ LEDGE IN GREAT GULF WILDERNESS, PRESIDENTIAL RANGE / NEW HAMPSHIRE

the taller peaks of Vermont's Green Mountain range. The mountains are accurately named; there is a greenness here—even in the lowlands—that one seldom encounters. The meadows stretch across the landscape and enclose the brooks and streams and hedgerows. In the late afternoon, a pale sky fades above the misty trees of the low meadows, the willows and birch and beech, and only in densely forested mountain ranges are there the hazy green and blue and purple for which the region is famous. In the winter, snow drifts across the farther mountains, now hiding, now revealing those forests of spruce and pine that grow so densely in the Green Mountains. Basically, this is rural country with few cities, and because it is a rugged, inland area its people are inclined—indeed forced—to be self-reliant and individualistic. This does not mean that they are antisocial; rather their rural outposts become the sanctuary for their own way of life, which differs markedly from that of the industrial and coastal towns.

On countless hillsides between the sea and the Adirondack Mountains, and even on the low ranges of the Green Mountains, are America's great maple forests, which glow in autumn like a forest fire, and produce what many consider the most spectacularly blinding foliage in the entire nation. These forests also produce a large part of the country's maple syrup. Sugaring was a lesson the early settlers of this region learned from the Indians, who had long known how to boil the sap of the maple and convert it into sugar and syrup.

The Indians induced the flow of sap by cutting a V-shaped slash in the bark, letting it flow into a wooden trough. The white settler modified the technique by inserting a spout in the tree and catching the sap in a wooden bucket. Today, this improvement has generally been discarded in favor of plastic tubing, which carries the sap all the way to the modern collecting tank.

In the deep valley between the Green Mountains and the Adirondacks, where the land drops off to form Lake Champlain and Lake George, is some of America's most majestic country. I first saw Lake George many years ago and was stunned by the beauty of its blue surface reflecting the sunlight of a bright October morning, while to the west of me on a hillside the forest blazed in its autumn coat. South of Lake George, the Hudson River Valley commences, threaded by the Hudson River, which flows from Lake Tear of the Clouds in the Adirondacks all the way to the Atlantic Ocean at New York Bay. The Hudson's channel is said to extend more than 100 miles into the ocean to the end of the continental shelf.

New York's beautiful and fertile river valleys form a gigantic geographical Y, the Hudson being the right arm and the Mohawk River the left. With the opening of the Erie Canal in 1825, the Hudson River was linked to the Great Lakes, and eastern New York had, for the first time, a water route to the west. The Hudson River Valley and, to some

Left– FIRST SNOW, MOUNT GREYLOCK / MASSACHUSETTS

Below– LAKES OF THE CLOUDS AND RIDGES FROM TOP OF MOUNT WASHINGTON / NEW HAMPSHIRE

extent, the Mohawk Valley are now inhabited by ghosts of an earlier and grander era, their great mansions taken over by preservation groups, their ancient canals silted up, their small river towns slumbering and forgotten. But in the Hudson Valley lie some of America's oldest vineyards, which still produce many New York State wines. Like the Rhine, whose mountainous banks are dotted with castles, and the Loire, which flows through the region of France's great chateaux, the Hudson attracted some of America's greatest fortunes, and the mansions that were built on its scenic bluffs are still among the grandest in the country.

New York's most famous vineyards are in the Finger Lakes region, on the slopes between Lake Canandaigua and Lake Keuka, where the country—now clear of the mountains—sweeps spaciously toward that strange 36-mile-wide isthmus that is divided by the Niagara River. Here a freakish drop in the river of 326 feet, most of it in a single, roaring plunge, creates Niagara Falls, still considered one of the wonders of the world.

Of the three falls that make up Niagara Falls, the American Falls and Horseshoe (Canadian) Falls are perhaps the most scenic, but many insist that Bridal Veil Falls is the most spectacular. Although the heyday of Niagara Falls was a half-century ago, there is magnetism in the cascade's grandeur yet. One of the nation's greatest scenic attractions before the days of widespread international air travel, and the honeymoon destination of countless newlyweds, the falls do not seem to have suffered from the pallor and torpidity that often result when popularity wanes. Visitors still board *The Maid of the Mist*, a sightseeing boat, and sail within yards of the roaring falls, gazing upward at the awesome sight of tons of water hurtling through the air.

In the St. Lawrence River, which sweeps from Lake Ontario to the Gulf of St. Lawrence and the Atlantic Ocean, forming what is in effect another coastal area for New York State, lie the Thousand Islands. The islands actually number more than 1,700; some are hardly larger than an exposed rock ledge while others contain homes and some even accommodate small villages. In the summer the islands seem to come alive, and the residents have the superb river for their playground. The channels and small inlets are at their door. For miles, motorboats, sailing vessels, sleek cruisers, tankers, and freighters cruise up and down the waterway, twisting around islands and promontories, looping around buoys and channel markers, and sending small waves against the docks. Dozens of little launches ferry islanders to the mainland to do their marketing, visit the post office, or do other household errands. But in winter the great river turns silent, and the islands are seldom free of snow. Then a deeply rooted cold sweeps in from Canada, numbing everything it touches, turning the islands into abandoned outcroppings in the frozen landscape.

Still largely untouched by the spreading Megalopolis are the Berkshires in Massachusetts, the salt smell of the wharves at Gloucester and Marblehead, the ancient sea captains' mansions of Newburyport, the paradox of shifting sand dunes, cranberry bogs, and rich meadowland known as Cape Cod, the gently rolling sea islands of Nantucket and Marthas Vineyard, and the gentle charm of the old villages of Cape Ann. Cape Cod, that gaunt and twisted arm of the Massachusetts coastline that reaches northward before curving in again upon itself, still possesses long, isolated beaches bordered by bayberry and beach plum. In the spring, before the great throngs of tourists arrive at the Cape, and in the fall, after they leave, the villages shed the veneer of tourism, the sand dunes are largely deserted except for an occasional wanderer, clouds drop low over the horizon, and there is a stark wildness to the oceanfront. The Outer Cape is the most remote part of the area, and here one finds the Cape Cod National Seashore, set up by the National Park Service in 1961 to protect more than 44,000 acres of beaches and sand dunes.

About 10 miles offshore from Point Judith, Rhode Island, lies Block Island, a tiny sea island of high bluffs and moors. Its gentle hills and stone-walled pastures, its freshwater ponds, and its simple homes give Block Island an English atmosphere; more than anything it resembles one of the Channel Islands. The houses sparkle white in the summer sunlight, and the harsh Atlantic scours the island's beaches. In the village where the ferries dock there are a handful of small hotels, boarding houses, and restaurants, which rely mostly on the visitors who come over from Point Judith during the brief summer season. Throughout the major part of the year, Block Island remains a quiet and peaceful place, seemingly as detached emotionally from the mainland as it is physically.

Where the flat countryside of Massachusetts becomes the rolling hills of Connecticut, there is a serene landscape of small lakes, tiny patches of woodland, tobacco fields, and brooks meandering through meadows enclosed by stone fences. Upland game is plentiful in the forested hills around Litchfield, where fine cover is available, and ruffed grouse, partridge, and woodcock are common. Partridge and woodcock like the alder thickets, creek bottoms, and damp wooded areas where earthworms are plentiful, but grouse cling to high ground. There is a mellowness to the land, as opposed to the stony and defiant country farther north. One can stand on a hillside here, away from the ceaseless traffic thundering down the throughways, and see what a beautiful country this is, an enormous garden sloping gently down to Long Island Sound. Here the forests in the evening, gray with ground mist, stand out starkly against the sky; the stone fences, crumbling and picturesque, wind across the landscape dividing land for purposes long since forgotten; gloomy poplars stand sentinel beside the brooks; and a church spire rises on the horizon, a solitary reminder of the pervasive New England conscience. There is nobility here in the very air, a benignly autocratic feeling that makes one understand the passion for freedom that nourished the American Revolution and turned these fields into the battleground that they became.

The closer one gets to New York City, the more one is sucked into the vortex of the Megalopolis. But beyond the suburban cities, beyond the John Cheever country of swimming pools and tennis courts, beyond the reaches of the Merritt Parkway and the tollgates and shopping malls, beyond the coach houses and barns converted into expensive

Top– MOHAWK RIVER AT SCHENECTADY / NEW YORK

Bottom– SALT MARSH, POINT JUDITH BAY/ RHODE ISLAND

restaurants, lies rural Connecticut, and this is a different place. Here the wind blows off the sea, the rivers thread their way from the high ridges in the west through the rocks and valleys of a peaceful countryside, and the very texture of life changes. A combination of individualism and duty takes possession of the soul here, where an eccentric is more likely to be tolerated than feared, where discontent is as freely aired as agreement.

To the south a new region opens up, a region embracing the flatlands and marshes of New Jersey and Delaware, the Chesapeake Bay country of Maryland, and the mountains and plains and coalfields of Pennsylvania. Here the culture is more casual, more easygoing than that to the north. The hardships suffered by the Massachusetts Bay colonists seem to have settled into the lifestyle and personality of the New Englander, but their effect is not noticeable south of the Hudson. Instead, the people here seem to reflect more the spirit of Virginia's Jamestown Colony, where the settlers grew tobacco—hardly an essential crop—and many intermarried with Indian women. One seldom encounters the extremes of climate here, or the isolated farmhouses, the wilderness areas, the ice-gray skies of winter, or the great woodlands of the north, although there are vast forests in Pennsylvania, especially in the Pocono Mountain range.

In that great expanse of country that reaches westward across the Appalachian and Allegheny Mountains there is something for everyone. Everyone but beach lovers; this is landlocked country. It is a world of mostly unspoiled countryside. In the east along the Delaware River there are small

Left– NIAGARA FALLS / NEW YORK

Above– BUTTERMILK FALLS STATE PARK / NEW YORK

but prosperous towns scattered throughout a predominantly agricultural area, with barns decorated with hex emblems, streams running with trout, and fields of corn and wheat. Farther west are the coalfields that fire the great steel mills, where the towns are scruffier, the barns rotting, the earth more hostile; a fragmented sense of country prevails.

The Pocono Mountains, in eastern Pennsylvania, offer some of the state's most stunning scenery. To take advantage of its most pleasing prospects one should wander about in the area of Canadensis, Mount Pocono, Bushkill, and Stroudsburg. Although there are no truly magnificent, lofty peaks, as there are in the high Alleghenies, there are some rugged ranges, eventually dipping down to the Delaware Valley. There are places in Pennsylvania where the country is totally flat, totally empty, yet astonishingly beautiful. Above all else, this is a green country; nearly 2 million acres of Pennsylvania lie in protected state forests. The Susquehannock Trail System winds through 85 miles of unspoiled forest, over 2,500-foot-high mountains, across meadows strewn with wild flowers, and along rushing mountain streams.

Along Pennsylvania's eastern boundary, where the Delaware River breaks through the foothills of the Poconos at the narrow cleft known as the Delaware Water Gap, is a wooded land that reveals itself only to those who search it out. But if you travel past the motels and small inns that dot the river road and climb into the small mountains above the Delaware River, you will be rewarded by an incredible sight as the river, now broad and slow-moving, pushes its way through the last barrier before reaching the great plain that slopes to the Atlantic Ocean.

The great beaches and sand barriers all lie to the east of this country, beginning at the mouth of the harbor of New York and continuing southward as far as the Virginia capes, broken only by the natural indentations of Delaware Bay and Chesapeake Bay. Beachfronts shift, sandbars disappear, hurricanes alter dunelands, but the New Jersey, Delaware, and Maryland shorelines remain remarkably stable. Just inland from the broad sand beaches of New Jersey are the famous Pine Barrens, a desolate area of stunted and tangled pine growth, where few people live and where forgotten ghost towns were long ago swallowed up by the pine forests. Highways from Philadelphia and Trenton skirt the barrens, but no roads penetrate the isolated, still depths of this forest region. It is a lost land, and one that seems to offer no reward to a discoverer.

The large peninsula jutting into the Atlantic Ocean, bordered by Delaware Bay on the east and Chesapeake Bay on the west, is divided by Virginia, Delaware, and Maryland, with Maryland getting the lion's share. A low, ridgeless area, it is extremely hot in summer and uncomfortably cold in winter, but the soil is rich and it is a prosperous vegetable and poultry center. At Assateague Island, a barrier land in the Atlantic Ocean just off the coast of Maryland and Virginia, the Assateague Island National Seashore has been created to preserve the fragile dunes and primitive nature of this Atlantic spit. The Chesapeake Bay landscape is rural, tranquil, clean, flat. There is a tameness in the shoreline not found on the ocean coast, with small creeks emptying and filling with the tide, and the smell of fish in the air.

The sea dominates the Chesapeake Bay country, and seafood is its primary staple. Crabs, fish, and oysters crowd out all other dishes on restaurant menus. Nowhere in the world do oysters thrive so extensively as on the East Coast of the United States and the Chesapeake Bay. The Chesapeake oyster beds are among the finest, with the Chincoteagues, Lynnhavens, and smaller Rappahannocks among those favored most.

Spring comes explosively in this country. The geese go north in great droves, the ice breaks up in the freshwater ponds, and suddenly the fruit trees in the tiny orchards turn white with blossoms. Cold, rainy weather frequently comes with the end of winter, rain clouds drift in from the Atlantic Ocean, and mist and thin fog blanket the cheerless coast of the Bay. Then one day the showers end, the early summer sun appears, and a new season arrives. The woods are filled with bloodroot and May apples, skunk cabbage grows profusely in the low places, and in meadowland violets appear.

Away from the lowlands of the Chesapeake Bay, the country is flat, but soon small ridges begin to appear and behind them loom the foothills of the Blue Ridge Mountains. To the north, the meadows and small forests of Maryland climb into the Tuscarora Range and eventually into the high Alleghenies of Pennsylvania's anthracite country. There is a wild grandeur to this area, contrasting to the great plains of the upland region to the east, the latter as spectacular in its way as the former, with green fields and pasture land running away to the horizon.

This is the Northeastern corner of America, a stubborn, enduring land, where the continent rises out of the stormy North Atlantic and spreads south and west in majestic mountain ranges, green valleys, and plains. It possesses the priceless gift of variety, which it bestows extravagantly. The landscape offers the sea and rivers, great sand dunes and forests and lowlands. Four distinct seasons offer nearly every kind of weather a temperate land can provide. While the winter sea crashes upon the coast of Maine with the roar of thunder, darkness comes quietly a few hundred miles to the west, the only sound shattering the silence the voice of one loon calling to another over a waste of water. Fog may lie thick on the ocean's coast and across marshland, but elsewhere the sun shines brightly, and somewhere else it will rain; in winter snow will blanket the whole area. There is always something different to observe, to feel, to sense.

One night I heard a freight train laboring across the high Kennebec River bridge in Maine, its engine thumping and its whistle echoing mournfully in the night air. The sound would have been more mournful in other places perhaps, because it would be mourning the passage of things that were gone: the lost space, the simple life, the innocence of people turned materialistic, the great trails in the deep woods. But the mountains and the forests and the coast of the Northeast have not been spoiled. The nation began here, our government was invented here, and if landscapes can be reconciled to events, there is reason to believe that this glorious land was required for the events that transpired here.

BALD CYPRESS, TRUSSUM POND / DELAWARE

Left– ALLEGHENY RIVER FROM TIDIOUTE OVERLOOK / PENNSYLVANIA

Above– HEART LAKE, ADIRONDACK MOUNTAINS / NEW YORK

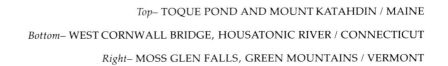

Top– TOQUE POND AND MOUNT KATAHDIN / MAINE

Bottom– WEST CORNWALL BRIDGE, HOUSATONIC RIVER / CONNECTICUT

Right– MOSS GLEN FALLS, GREEN MOUNTAINS / VERMONT

FARM ROAD THROUGH FLATLANDS, ALLEGHENY MOUNTAIN COUNTRY / PENNSYLVANIA

Left– BASS HARBOR HEAD, ACADIA NATIONAL PARK / MAINE

Above– BRENTON POINT, NEAR NEWPORT / RHODE ISLAND

Left– AUTUMN REFLECTIONS, CATOCTIN MOUNTAIN PARK / MARYLAND

Top– METAMORPHIC ROCK AND HARDWOOD FOREST, CONNECTICUT RIVER VALLEY / CONNECTICUT

Bottom– AUTUMN ALONG MULLICA RIVER, PINE BARRENS / NEW JERSEY

Maps of the Northeast

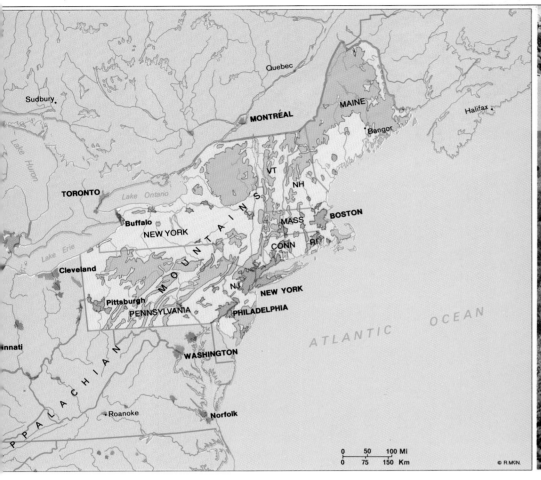

Land Use The major urban-suburban areas of Philadelphia, New York, and Boston form an almost continuous zone along the coast of the Northeast. The region's generally hilly terrain limits large expanses of pure farmland, and most agricultural areas contain woodlots. Extensive forests are found in the Allegheny and Appalachian mountains in Pennsylvania, the Adirondacks in New York, and the White Mountains in New Hampshire and Maine.

The forests of New Hampshire's White Mountains stand in striking contrast to the heavily urbanized sections of the Northeast. Wild regions such as this were able to preserve their natural beauty because their terrain was too rugged for settlement, and many were later set aside as national parks and forests. Because of the Northeast's relatively small area, these scenic regions are usually located within easy reach of urban dwellers.

The varied nature of the Northeast is reflected in the Niagara River and Niagara Falls in New York. Not only does this world-famous landmark draw thousands of tourists each year, but it also provides a significant portion of the Northeast's energy. Hydroelectric plants located along the Niagara River generate power to fuel industries and cities up to 350 miles away. The potential generating power of the river and its falls is among the greatest of any hydroelectric source in the world, and the area has attracted many industries.

The Northeast exerts an influence far out of proportion to its small size. Without this region, the land area and agriculture of the United States would be little affected. But the commerce, industry, and finance of the country would be crippled.

Not only does this region contribute significantly to manufacturing output and commercial traffic, but it also acts as a control center for the coordination of the nation's cultural, social, and economic activities. The Yankee culture gleaned from New England and the industrial and urban power contributed by New York, Pennsylvania, and New Jersey combine for a unique blend of cultural and economic prosperity. It is a tribute to American ingenuity that from a region of such small size and rather limited natural potential have come the innovations of literature, philosophy, technology, and economy that shaped an entire nation. As far away as Oregon and Wisconsin, towns of a distinctively northeastern character can be found, a result of the direct migration of people from this region. In a sense, the heritage of the Northeast is shared by all Americans—even southerners, whose agriculture was transformed by the Connecticut-born cotton gin.

As is often the case, historical accident accounted for much of the region's development. Upon arriving in the New World, the British found themselves limited in their expansion by French and Spanish claims, and the coastlines of other territories proved too treacherous, and their land too agriculturally demanding, for the available technology. All settlement efforts were therefore concentrated upon a single area, strengthening early attempts at colonization that would have been weakened by a more widespread population distribution. In addition, these early pioneers were a diverse mix of people coming from all walks of life, each with a special skill to contribute to the developing nation. Upon finding the land of the Northeast to be similar to that they had left, they quickly adapted, remaking the area in the image of

Population Distribution The urban fabric of the Northeast is intimately associated with transportation nodes, located in protected Atlantic harbors, along the Great Lakes' margins, and major river valleys. These nuclei, together with their surrounding metropolitan areas, comprise a vast urban system that dominates several hundred miles of the Atlantic Coast and the transportation corridors around and through the Appalachian Highlands. The rural hinterlands include extensive areas of agriculture as well as vast expanses of empty, or uninhabited, areas, which are highly prized for recreation and scenic splendor.

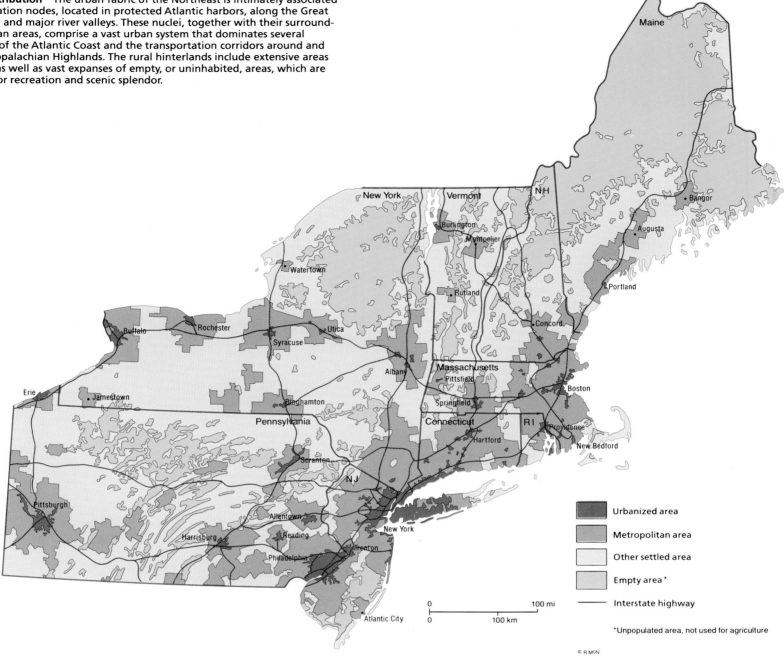

Urbanized area
Metropolitan area
Other settled area
Empty area *
Interstate highway

*Unpopulated area, not used for agriculture

© R.MCN.

their home. And they succeeded, establishing an agriculture, industry, and commerce suited to the country this territory would become. As the small country grew, the region maintained its grasp on the reins of growth. Initial opportunity became a lasting advantage, and the Northeast was able to exchange money and know-how for the wealth of newer, less-developed regions.

And from the Northeast have come innovations of every kind. To the arts, the region contributed the first generation of American writers, poets, artists, and composers, whose works expressed uniquely American values and ideals. In drawing upon their spiritual heritage and vision of natural harmony, these artists created a new philosophy, which in many ways continues to define America's cultural life. Although California can claim control over much of the entertainment industry, New York City is still the national center for the arts. And the region's economic influence, too, has shaped America's development. In science and technology, industry and manufacturing, the Northeast became a national and international leader.

Because of an early start strengthened by continued effort, the Northeast has capitalized on its initial advantage to exert influence over the development of nearly every other region of the United States. But early development has its drawbacks as well, and the Northeast has had to face many difficult problems resulting from its long-established urban-industrial character, such as pollution and urban decay. But although the region is more immediately faced with these problems than some of its counterparts, it will not necessarily lose its advantage. Despite great fluctuations in growth patterns—favoring rural areas, cities, and suburbs, each in turn—the Northeast continues to exhibit slow but steady growth. Exceedingly resilient, quick to change and innovate as needed, the Northeast should be able to maintain its footing among the larger, often faster-growing, regions.

The Urban Corridor In a relatively small area, covering less than 1.5 percent of the United States, is concentrated enough economic and financial power, corporate potential, commercial and manufacturing might, and educational prowess to run the nation. The population, which is principally urban-suburban, exceeds 23 million, and its diversity is apparent in its ethnic, linguistic, and religious traditions. This wealth of economic power and people is tied together by a complex transportation and communication structure.

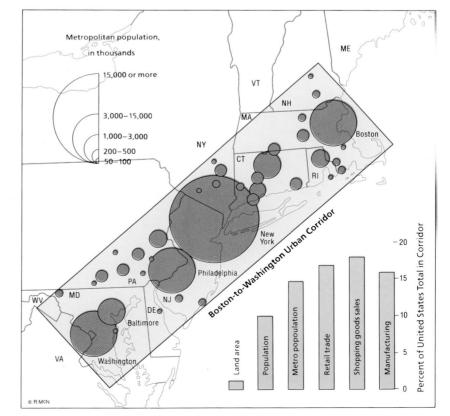

Metropolitan population, in thousands

15,000 or more

3,000–15,000

1,000–3,000

200–500

50–100

Boston-to-Washington Urban Corridor

Percent of United States Total in Corridor

Land area
Population
Metro population
Retail trade
Shopping goods sales
Manufacturing

© R.MCN.

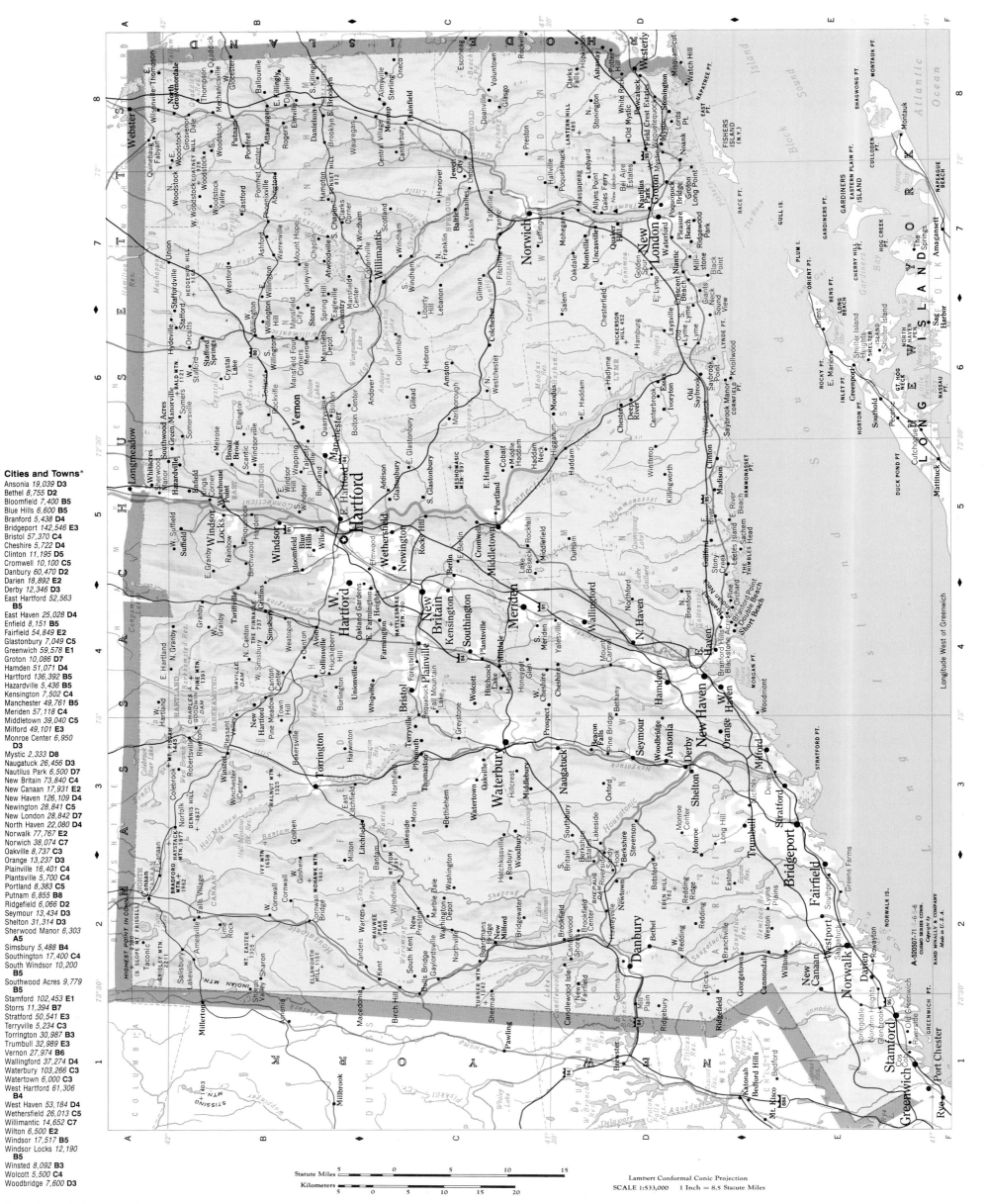

Cities and Towns*

Ansonia 19,039 D3
Bethel 8,755 D2
Bloomfield 7,400 B5
Blue Hills 6,600 B5
Branford 5,438 D4
Bridgeport 142,546 E3
Bristol 57,370 C4
Cheshire 5,722 D4
Clinton 11,195 D5
Cromwell 10,100 C5
Danbury 60,470 D2
Darien 18,892 E2
Derby 12,346 D3
East Hartford 52,563 B5
East Haven 25,028 D4
Enfield 8,151 B5
Fairfield 54,849 E2
Glastonbury 7,049 C5
Greenwich 59,578 E1
Groton 10,086 D7
Hamden 51,071 D4
Hartford 136,392 B5
Hazardville 5,436 B5
Kensington 7,502 C4
Manchester 49,761 B5
Meriden 57,118 C4
Middletown 39,040 C5
Milford 49,101 E3
Monroe Center 6,950 D3
Mystic 2,333 D8
Naugatuck 26,456 D3
Nautilus Park 6,500 D7
New Britain 73,840 C4
New Canaan 17,931 E2
New Haven 126,109 D4
Newington 28,841 C5
New London 28,842 D7
North Haven 22,080 D4
Norwalk 77,767 E2
Norwich 38,074 C7
Oakville 8,737 C3
Orange 13,237 D3
Plainville 16,401 C4
Plantsville 5,700 C4
Portland 8,383 C5
Putnam 6,855 B8
Ridgefield 6,066 D2
Seymour 13,434 D3
Shelton 31,314 D3
Sherwood Manor 6,303 A5
Simsbury 5,488 B4
Southington 17,400 C4
South Windsor 10,200 B5
Southwood Acres 9,779 B5
Stamford 102,453 E1
Storrs 11,394 B7
Stratford 50,541 E3
Terryville 5,234 C3
Torrington 30,987 B3
Trumbull 32,989 E3
Vernon 27,974 B6
Wallingford 37,274 D4
Waterbury 103,266 C3
Watertown 6,000 C3
West Hartford 61,306 B4
West Haven 53,184 D4
Wethersfield 26,013 C5
Willimantic 14,652 C7
Wilton 6,500 E2
Windsor 17,517 B5
Windsor Locks 12,190 B5
Winsted 8,092 B3
Wolcott 5,500 C4
Woodbridge 7,600 D3

*Populations are for localities, not incorporated towns.

Statute Miles 5 0 5 10 15
Kilometers 5 0 5 10 15 20

Lambert Conformal Conic Projection
SCALE 1:533,000   1 Inch = 8.5 Statute Miles

Connecticut

POPULATION 3,107,576.
Rank: 25. *Density:* 638 people/
mi² (239 people/km²). *Urban:*
78.8%. *Rural:* 21.2%.
AGE *<20:* 30%. *20–40:* 31%.
40–65: 27%. *>65:* 12%.
ETHNIC GROUPS *White:* 90.1%.
Black: 7%. *Spanish origin:* 4%.
Native American: 0.1%.
Other: 2.8%.

INCOME/CAPITA $11,720. *Rank:* 2.
POLITICS 1948–1980 elections:
President: 3 Dem., 6 Rep.
Governor: 7 Dem., 2 Rep.
ENTERED UNION January 9, 1788,
5th state.
CAPITAL Hartford, 136,392.
LARGEST CITY Hartford.

AREA 5,019 mi² (12,999 km²).
Rank: 48. *Water area:* 147 mi²
(381 km²).
ELEVATIONS *Highest:* Mt. Frissell,
south slope, 2,380 ft (725 m).
Lowest: Long Island Sound
shoreline, sea level.
CLIMATE Cold winters, warm
summers; moderate rainfall.

Connecticut has managed something of an economic wonder—furthering its development without sacrificing its quality of environment. Among its leading products are a skilled labor supply and ideas, and as a result, Connecticut enjoys the second highest per capita income in the nation. At the same time, the state contains some of the country's most beautiful landscapes.

Although Connecticut's dairy products and vegetables are important to New England and New York City, for generations the state has exported ideas, patenting and marketing the inventions on which manufacturing growth has depended. These innovations spurred the development of the great urban-industrial regions along Long Island Sound and Connecticut's river valleys. And some of the inventions themselves, such as the cotton gin and the Winchester rifle, helped transform the economies of western and southern states.

Connecticut has also benefited from its location in the heart of the eastern megalopolis. Workers can easily commute back and forth along the complex network of transportation routes, and in this sense, New York City and Boston are Connecticut's largest cities. The state's close ties with these urban centers have led some to claim that Connecticut is simply a suburban and commercial satellite of its larger, more populous neighbors.

But there is far more to Connecticut than a commuting work force. The state appears to be anticipating the future pattern of urban life in America. Once almost completely rural, Connecticut's population has evolved over the years into a highly urbanized society. As elsewhere in the nation, the move to the cities was followed by a general shift in population from urban to suburban areas. And most recently, people have begun to move into exurban areas—regions between countryside and suburbs. This development may be a harbinger of the emergence of America's so-called postindustrial society—states with decentralized populations yet highly integrated economies. Connecticut is once again in the forefront of the newest trend, seeking to preserve both its environment and its tradition as an innovator.

As elsewhere in the East, the sea played a major role in the early development of Connecticut. Mystic Seaport, a reconstructed nineteenth-century village in southeastern Connecticut, recreates the days when shipbuilding was a major activity.

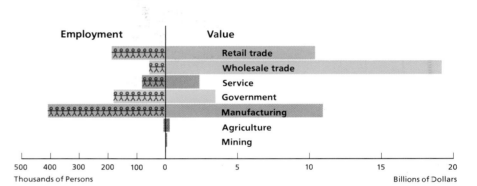

Economic Activities With a long history of manufacturing, Connecticut retains profitable and highly technical industries. Over the years, the state has also become identified with the insurance business.

Population Movement Like many highly urbanized states, Connecticut reflects the results of national population trends. Major metropolitan areas show the effect of population movement from central cities and the concurrent shift to the suburbs. Concentration in exurban areas—regions between suburbs and countryside that allow access to cities for jobs and recreation—is the most recent trend.

Population change, 1960–1980

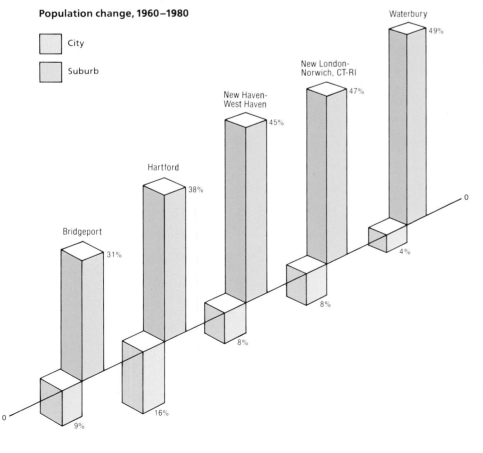

□ City

□ Suburb

Land Use Connecticut's scalloped coast and river valleys provided ample sites for settlement over wide areas. The result is a landscape dotted with an impressive collection of productive cities, of which no one alone seems dominant. Glacial scraping left little topsoil for agriculture, but much land of natural beauty attracts both tourists and nearby city residents.

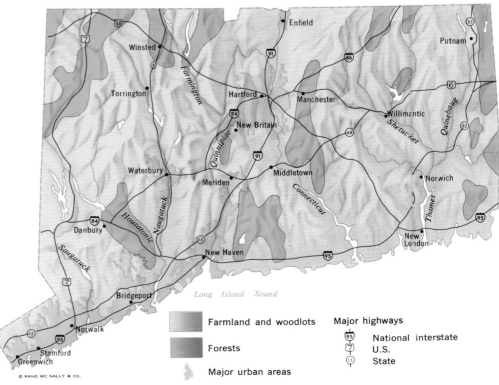

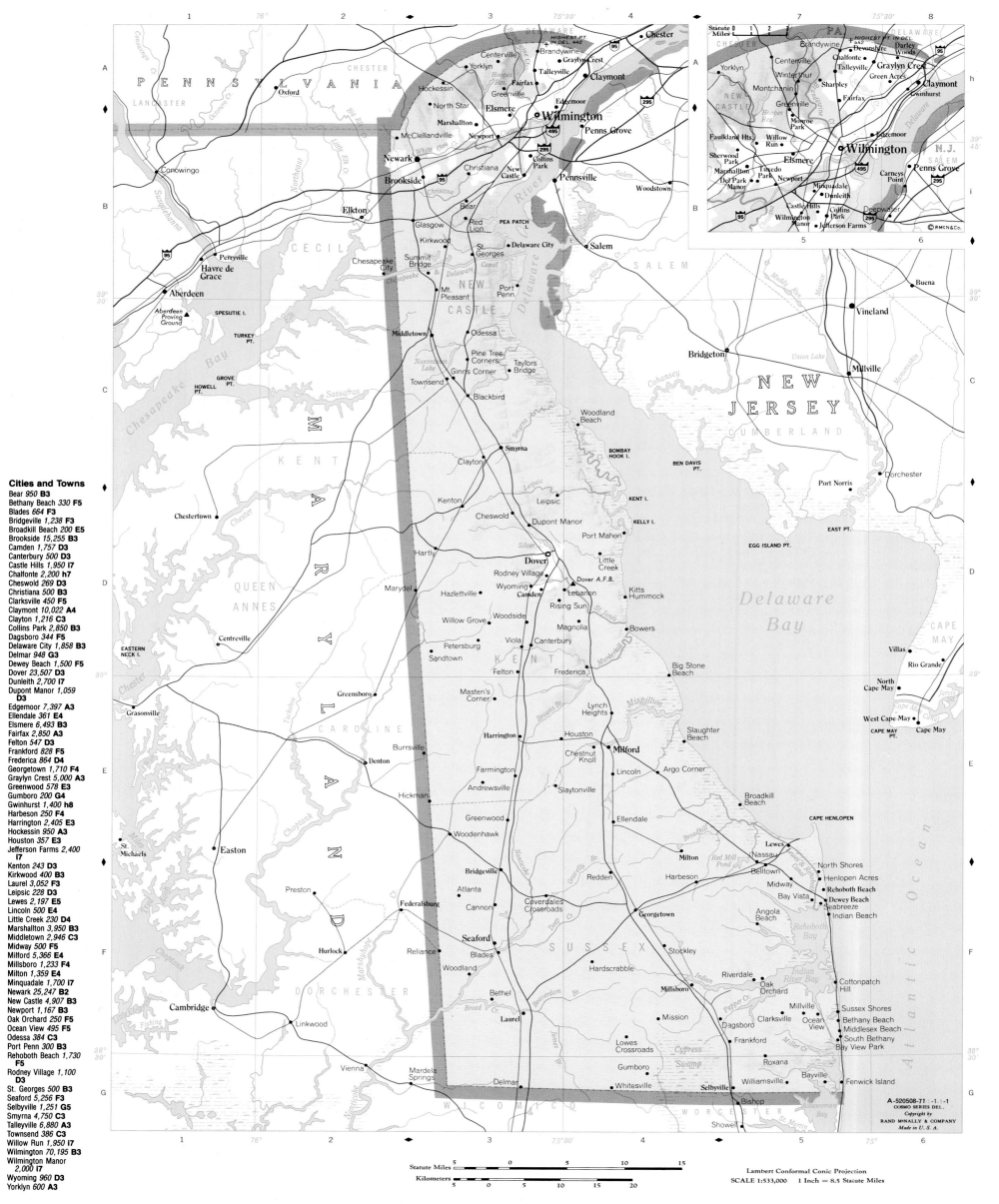

Cities and Towns

Bear *950* **B3**
Bethany Beach *330* **F5**
Blades *664* **F3**
Bridgeville *1,238* **F3**
Broadkill Beach *200* **E5**
Brookside *15,255* **B3**
Camden *1,757* **D3**
Canterbury *500* **D3**
Castle Hills *1,950* **I7**
Chalfonte *2,200* **h7**
Cheswold *269* **D3**
Christiana *500* **B3**
Clarksville *450* **F5**
Claymont *10,022* **A4**
Clayton *1,216* **C3**
Collins Park *2,850* **B3**
Dagsboro *344* **F5**
Delaware City *1,858* **B3**
Delmar *948* **G3**
Dewey Beach *1,500* **F5**
Dover *23,507* **D3**
Dunleith *2,700* **I7**
Dupont Manor *1,059*
    D3
Edgemoor *7,397* **A3**
Ellendale *361* **E4**
Elsmere *6,493* **B3**
Fairfax *2,850* **A3**
Felton *547* **D3**
Frankford *828* **F5**
Frederica *864* **D4**
Georgetown *1,710* **F4**
Graylyn Crest *5,000* **A3**
Greenwood *578* **E3**
Gumboro *200* **G4**
Gwinhurst *1,400* **h8**
Harbeson *250* **F4**
Harrington *2,405* **E3**
Hockessin *950* **A3**
Houston *357* **E3**
Jefferson Farms *2,400*
    I7
Kenton *243* **D3**
Kirkwood *400* **B3**
Laurel *3,052* **F3**
Leipsic *228* **D3**
Lewes *2,197* **E5**
Lincoln *500* **E4**
Little Creek *230* **D4**
Marshallton *3,950* **B3**
Middletown *2,946* **C3**
Midway *500* **F5**
Milford *5,366* **E4**
Millsboro *1,233* **F4**
Milton *1,359* **E4**
Minquadale *1,700* **I7**
Newark *25,247* **B2**
New Castle *4,907* **B3**
Newport *1,167* **B3**
Oak Orchard *250* **F5**
Ocean View *495* **F5**
Odessa *384* **C3**
Port Penn *300* **B3**
Rehoboth Beach *1,730*
    F5
Rodney Village *1,100*
    D3
St. Georges *500* **B3**
Seaford *5,256* **F3**
Selbyville *1,251* **G5**
Smyrna *4,750* **C3**
Talleyville *6,880* **A3**
Townsend *386* **C3**
Willow Run *1,950* **I7**
Wilmington *70,195* **B3**
Wilmington Manor
    2,000 **I7**
Wyoming *960* **D3**
Yorklyn *600* **A3**

Delaware

POPULATION 594,317.
Rank: 47. *Density:* 308 people/mi² (119 people/km²). *Urban:* 70.6%. *Rural:* 29.4%.
AGE *<20:* 32%. *20−40:* 32%. *40−65:* 26%. *>65:* 10%.
ETHNIC GROUPS *White:* 82.1%. *Black:* 16.1%. *Spanish origin:* 1.6%. *Native American:* 0.2%. *Other:* 1.6%.

INCOME/CAPITA $10,339. *Rank:* 9.
POLITICS 1948−1980 elections:
President: 3 Dem., 6 Rep. *Governor:* 4 Dem., 5 Rep.
ENTERED UNION December 7, 1787, 1st state.
CAPITAL Dover, 23,507.
LARGEST CITY Wilmington, 70,195.

AREA 2,044 mi² (5,294 km²). *Rank:* 49. *Water area:* 112 mi² (290 km²).
ELEVATIONS *Highest:* In New Castle County, 442 ft (135 m). *Lowest:* Atlantic Ocean shoreline, sea level.
CLIMATE Cool winters, hot summers; ample rainfall.

Delaware is a microcosm of the two contrasting sides of American economic life—industry and agriculture. North of the Chesapeake and Delaware Canal is one of the largest assemblies of chemical factories in the world. Yet south of the canal, manufacturing decreases, and the landscape takes on a gardenlike appearance, producing poultry, dairy, and truck-farm products for the East Coast.

While the industrial and agricultural division of Delaware often creates political friction between the two interest groups, liberal tax and incorporation laws continue to attract industry to the state. With these businesses has come considerable wealth, and the state has one of the highest per capita incomes in the nation.

Delaware's success can also be attributed to its favorable location. The state lies near four of the largest cities in the United States—Washington, Baltimore, Philadelphia, and New York—placing Delaware at the core of the eastern urban-industrial complex. The large population of this region guarantees a permanent, lucrative market for Delaware's ocean and farm products. And like other states, Delaware is taking advantage of a modern economy that is transcending state boundaries. Transport systems can easily connect the industrial and agricultural centers of several states into one commercial region.

Nevertheless, the consequences of a clear-cut division between industry and agriculture in so small a state are far-reaching, particularly in political terms. It is difficult at the state level to achieve an equitable distribution of representation between northern and southern regions. This situation is further complicated by the highly suburban nature of northern Delaware. Here, reapportionment has granted suburbanites political influence in proportion to their numbers; whereas in metropolitan areas in some states, the suburban vote is generally split among jurisdictions and thus rendered fairly ineffectual.

It will be interesting to see what effect reapportionment will ultimately have. It may be that Delaware is serving as a microcosm of a new political trend, placing its suburban population between the traditional industrial and agricultural interests.

This chemical plant is typical of many found in Delaware. The chemical industry employs a great number of Delaware's people, and with products such as drugs, synthetic fibers, and paints, it is one of the state's major sources of income.

Land Use Most of Delaware's land is part of the Atlantic Coastal Plain—a flat region, near sea level, with occasional swamps. In fact, a rise of the Atlantic of only a few yards would flood large sections of the state. Only the small area north of the Christina River, which is part of the higher Piedmont Plateau, would escape damage if such an event actually occurred.

Farmland and woodlots

Swampland and marshland

Major urban areas

Major highways

95 National interstate
40 U.S.
18 State

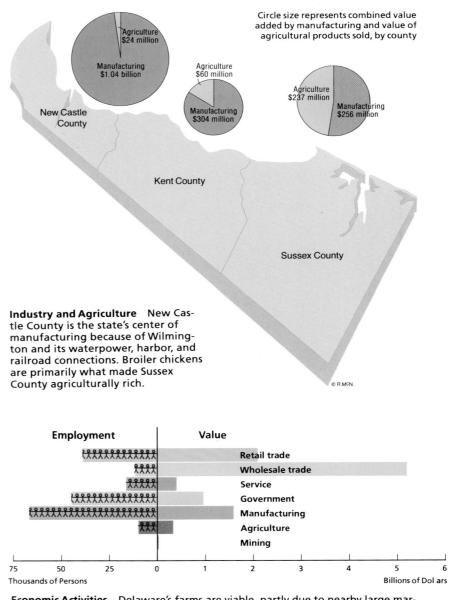

Circle size represents combined value added by manufacturing and value of agricultural products sold, by county

New Castle County
Agriculture $24 million
Manufacturing $1.04 billion

Agriculture $60 million
Manufacturing $304 million

Agriculture $237 million
Manufacturing $256 million

Kent County

Sussex County

Industry and Agriculture New Castle County is the state's center of manufacturing because of Wilmington and its waterpower, harbor, and railroad connections. Broiler chickens are primarily what made Sussex County agriculturally rich.

Employment	Value	
		Retail trade
		Wholesale trade
		Service
		Government
		Manufacturing
		Agriculture
		Mining

75 50 25 0 1 2 3 4 5 6
Thousands of Persons   Billions of Dollars

Economic Activities Delaware's farms are viable, partly due to nearby large markets where fresh produce and dairy and poultry products are always in demand. The state's identification with the chemical industry is warranted, because the manufacture and the distribution of chemical products, including gunpowder and synthetic fibers for textiles, are still the mainstays of its economy.

© RAND MC NALLY & CO.

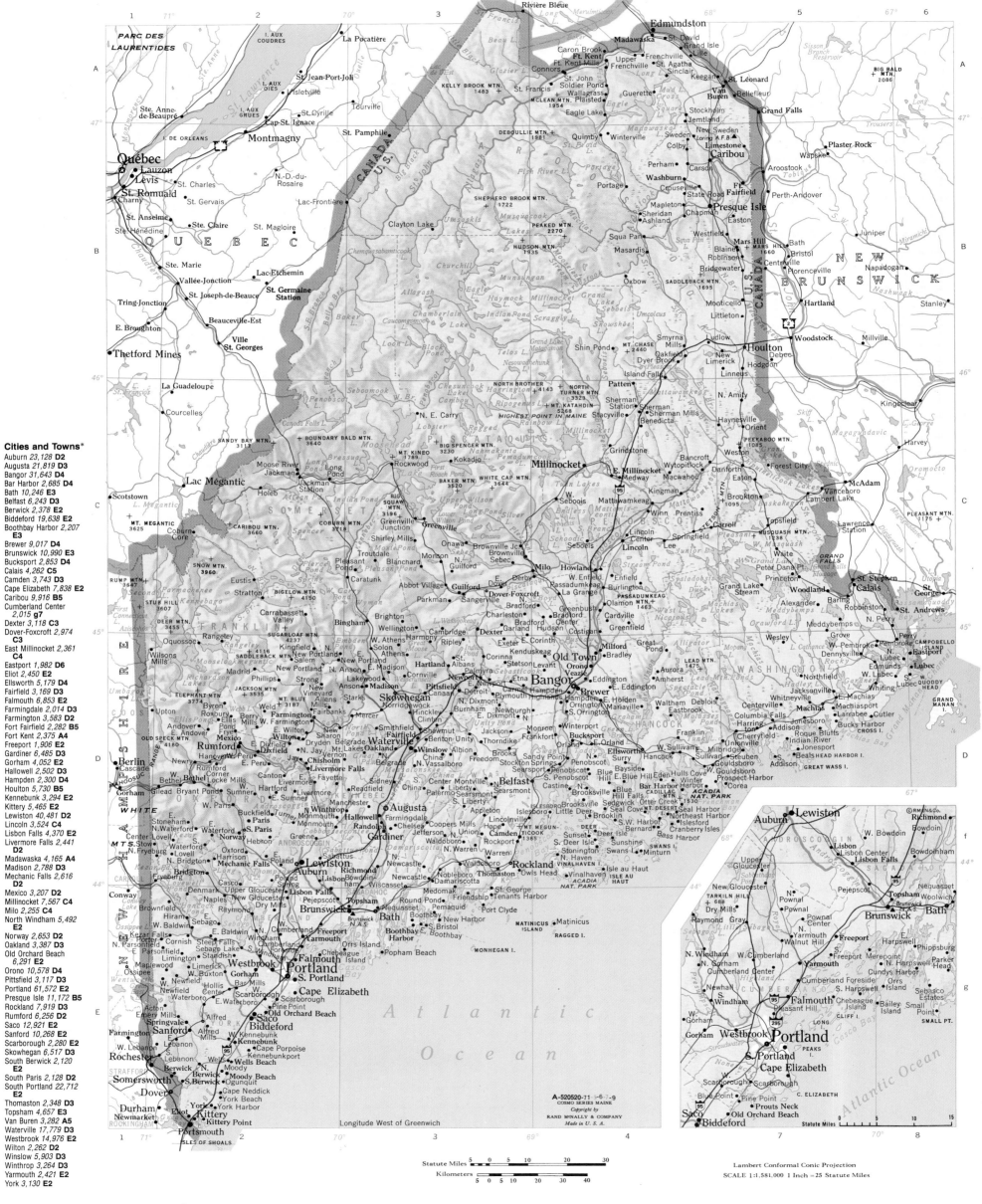

*Populations are for localities, not incorporated towns.

A-520520-71
COSMO SERIES MAINE
Copyright by
RAND McNALLY & COMPANY
Made in U.S.A.

Statute Miles

Kilometers

Lambert Conformal Conic Projection
SCALE 1:1,581,000 1 Inch =25 Statute Miles

Maine

POPULATION 1,125,027.
Rank: 38. *Density:* 36 people/mi²
(14 people/km²). *Urban:* 47.5%.
Rural: 52.5%.
AGE *< 20:* 32%. *20–40:* 31%.
40–65: 25%. *>65:* 12%.
ETHNIC GROUPS *White:* 98.7%.
Black: 0.3%. *Spanish origin:*
0.4%. *Native American:* 0.4%.
Other: 0.6%.

INCOME/CAPITA $7,925. *Rank:* 38.
POLITICS 1948–1980 elections:
President: 2 Dem., 7 Rep.
Governor: 6 Dem., 1 Inde-
pendent, 5 Rep.
ENTERED UNION March 15, 1820,
23rd state.
CAPITAL Augusta, 21,819.
LARGEST CITY Portland, 61,572.

AREA 33,265 mi² (86,156 km²).
Rank: 39. *Water area:* 2,270 mi²
(5,879 km²).
ELEVATIONS *Highest:* Mt.
Katahdin, 5,268 ft (1,606 m).
Lowest: Atlantic Ocean
shoreline, sea level.
CLIMATE Long, cold winters; short,
cool summers; moderate rainfall.

Maine's well-known rocky coasts are exemplified by those found in Acadia National Park, made up of a small area of the mainland and much of Mount Desert Island and Isle au Haut. The character of the Maine coast is a result of glacial action on an underlying granite formation.

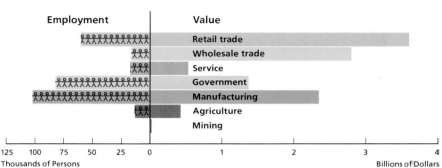

Employment | Value

Retail trade
Wholesale trade
Service
Government
Manufacturing
Agriculture
Mining

125 100 75 50 25 0 | 1 2 3 4
Thousands of Persons | Billions of Dollars

Economic Activities Maine's forests and rich fishing grounds once made the state a major part of America's economic life. This role was lessened substantially by the country's westward expansion, but the blend of agriculture, fishing, manufacturing, and commerce that best suits the state was never upset.

☐ Farmland and woodlots

▨ Forests

Major highways
🛡 National interstate
🛡 U.S.

© RAND MCNALLY & CO.

Land Use The lowlands along Maine's coast contain some of its most valuable land. Its harbors permit waterborne commerce, an aid to economic activity beyond the state's fishing industry. Despite the difficulty of transportation away from the coast to the north, the forests and farmlands of these mountains and valleys have attracted people who realize the land's potential for potato production and forestry.

aine's rocky coasts are an appropriate symbol for this enduring state. Over the past years, waves of people and the great economic centers of the United States have been moving to the West and most recently to the South, but Maine has preserved its rugged character and independence.

At one time, the state was an important part of the colonial maritime economy and more than once served as a battle site in the Revolutionary War. However, as settlers were attracted to the western frontiers, the mainstream of American life moved away from New England. Today, large areas of this region have returned to the heavily forested, lightly settled condition found before the coming of white settlers.

One reason for this gradual change is Maine's limited resources. To meet early colonial needs, the state's resources, especially timber, were rapidly developed, but this development slowed as western and southern territories quickly outproduced the state. Yet the people of Maine have learned to make the best use of their land and today continuously crop their forests by replanting after harvesting. The state is endowed with thickly forested areas that yield a steady harvest of timber, and the state's soil is carefully cultivated to support crops such as potatoes.

Although Maine has declined in overall importance to the nation's economy, it has made a rich contribution to American folklore. Here is the home of the legendary ''Down East Yankee,'' whose tales, songs, and folk humor uphold and satirize the tough, self-reliant side of American life. While not always elegant or polished, this Yankee is resourceful and adaptive to the situation at hand. Maine also enjoys a profitable tourist trade, with visitors attracted by the state's unique character, its scenic coastline, mountains, lakes, and brilliant fall display.

Compared with California and rapidly growing Sun Belt states, Maine is not experiencing spectacular economic or population growth. Yet the state continues to embody the essence of early America—its Yankee know-how, rugged self-reliance, and enduring ties with the land.

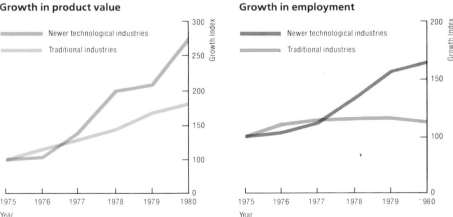

Growth in product value

━━ Newer technological industries
━━ Traditional industries

300
250
200
150
100

1975 1976 1977 1978 1979 1980
Year

Growth in employment

━━ Newer technological industries
━━ Traditional industries

200
150
100

1975 1976 1977 1978 1979 1980
Year

Industry Maine's traditional industries—lumber and wood, food, textiles, paper, and leather—have long provided the bulk of state income from manufacturing. Recently, the product-value and employee growth rates for new technological industries have risen much faster than those for these traditional industries, indicating that a change in Maine's economy may be under way.

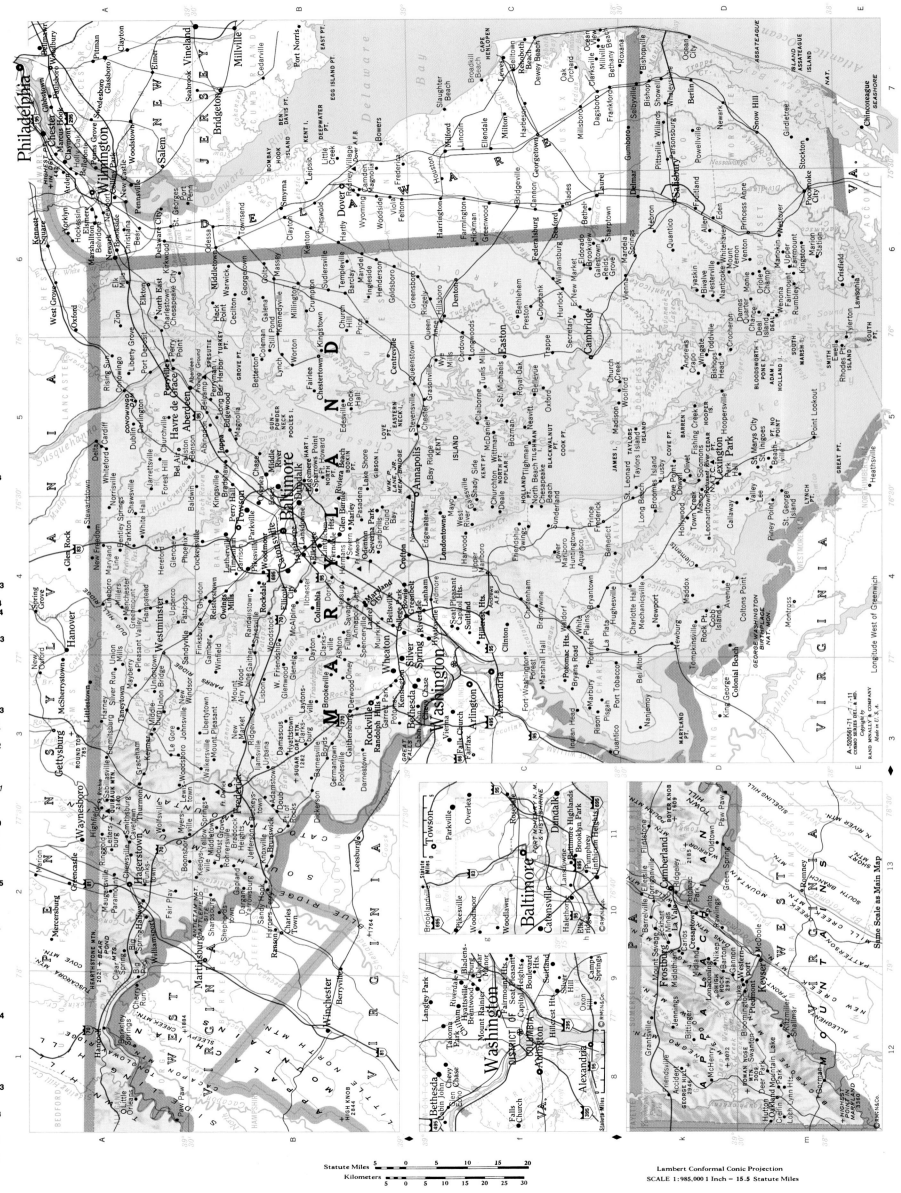

Cities and Towns

Aberdeen 11,533 A5
Annapolis 31,740 C5
Baltimore 786,775 B4
Bel Air 7,814 A5
Beltsville 12,760 B4
Bethesda 63,022 C3
Bladensburg 7,691 f9
Bowie 33,695 B4
Brunswick 4,572 B2
Cambridge 11,703 C5
Catonsville 33,208 B4
Chevy Chase 12,232 C3
Clinton 16,438 C4
Cockeysville 17,013 B4
College Park 23,614 C4
Columbia 52,518 B4
Crofton 12,009 B4
Cumberland 25,933 k13
Dundalk 71,293 B4
Easton 7,536 C5
Edgewood 19,455 B5
Elkton 6,468 A6
Essex 39,614 B4
Frederick 28,086 B3
Frostburg 7,715 k13
Gaithersburg 26,424 B3
Germantown 9,721 B3
Glen Burnie 30,000 B4
Greenbelt 17,332 C4
Hagerstown 34,132 A2
Halethorpe 20,163 B4
Halfway 8,659 A2
Havre de Grace 8,763
  A5
Hillcrest Heights 17,021
  C4
Hyattsville 12,709 C4
Joppa 11,348 B5
Langley Park 11,100 f9
Lansdowne 10,000 B4
Laurel 12,103 B4
Lexington Park 10,361
  D5
Lutherville-Timonium
  17,854 B4
Middle River 26,756 B5
Oakland 1,994 m12
Ocean City 4,946 D7
Olney 10,000 B3
Overlea 12,965 B4
Owings Mills 9,526 B4
Oxon Hill 8,100 f9
Parkville 35,159 B4
Perry Hall 13,455 B5
Pikesville 20,000 B4
Pocomoke City 3,558
  D6
Potomac 22,800 B3
Randallstown 20,500
  B4
Reisterstown 19,385 B4
Rockville 43,811 B3
Rosedale 19,956 g11
Salisbury 16,429 D6
Severn 20,147 B4
Severna Park 21,253
  B4
Sharpsburg 721 B2
Silver Spring 64,100 C3
Snow Hill 2,192 D7
Suitland 24,800 C4
Takoma Park 16,231 f8
Towson 51,083 B4
Waldorf 9,782 C4
Westminster 8,808 A4
Wheaton 48,600 B3
White Plains 5,167 C4
Woodlawn 8,000 g10
Washington D.C.
  638,432 C3

Statute Miles 5 0 5 10 15 20
Kilometers 5 0 5 10 15 20 25 30

Lambert Conformal Conic Projection
SCALE 1:985,000 1 Inch = 15.5 Statute Miles

Maryland

POPULATION 4,216,975.
Rank: 18. *Density:* 429 people/
mi² (166 people/km²). *Urban:*
80.3%. *Rural:* 19.7%.
AGE *<20:* 32%. *20–40:* 33%.
40–65: 26%. *>65:* 9%.
ETHNIC GROUPS *White:* 74.9%.
Black: 22.7%. *Spanish origin:*
1.5%. *Native American:* 0.2%.
Other: 2.2%.

INCOME/CAPITA $10,460. *Rank:* 8.
POLITICS 1948–1980 elections:
President: 5 Dem., 4 Rep.
Governor: 5 Dem., 3 Rep.
ENTERED UNION April 28, 1788,
7th state.
CAPITAL Annapolis, 31,740.
LARGEST CITY Baltimore, 786,775.

AREA 10,460 mi² (27,092 km²).
Rank: 42. *Water area:* 623 mi²
(1,614 km²).
ELEVATIONS *Highest:* Backbone
Mtn., 3,360 ft (12 m). *Lowest:*
Atlantic Ocean shoreline, sea
level.
CLIMATE Hot summers, cool
winters; warm summers, cold
winters in west. Ample rainfall

Maryland contains a great deal of economic and cultural diversity within its narrow borders. Its small size and its position on Chesapeake Bay would seem to indicate a relatively unified, even uniform, state. But Maryland is actually a composite of many areas, each reflecting a different tradition of American life.

East of Chesapeake Bay is the low-lying Delmarva Peninsula, shared by and taking its name from Delaware, Maryland, and Virginia. The section of the peninsula lying within Maryland is known as the Eastern Shore, and this area is a strong agricultural and fishing region, supplying products to large population centers to the north and west. But its culture still retains a prominent colonial flavor, reflected in its architecture and social customs. The beauty and seclusion of the peninsula make it attractive to both tourists and new residents.

Across Chesapeake Bay, on the Western Shore, lies Baltimore, one of the largest commercial and industrial cities in the country. Settled originally by members of the English upper class who preserved their customs for decades, Baltimore now has a large population of blue-collar workers, descendants of the many ethnic groups that migrated to the United States in the late 1800's and early 1900's.

The suburban counties of Maryland that border the District of Columbia form another distinct region. Expansion of the federal government has made this section of Maryland a center for military and civilian government installations.

And to the northwest, a narrow panhandle extends Maryland into the Appalachian hill country. The area acts as a haven for tourists, and many residents of this tri-state region identify with Pennsylvania and West Virginia as well as Delaware.

Each of Maryland's regions has its share of problems as well as assets. The rural Eastern Shore maintains a balance between agriculture and exurban development. Central Maryland, part of the corridor extending from Washington to Baltimore, is highly urbanized and thus increasingly plagued by problems common to cities. And the rural panhandle is a land of both tourism and poverty. But the regions also contain potential for development. Few states possess Maryland's cultural and economic variety with which to shape a future.

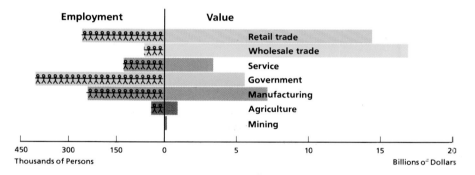

Farmland and woodlots

Forests

Swampland and marshland

Major urban areas

Major highways

National interstate
U.S.
State

Economic Activities Maryland's economy largely reflects the traditional importance of Baltimore as a commercial and manufacturing center. In contributing the District of Columbia to the nation, Maryland ensured many government jobs for its residents.

Employment	Value	
		Retail trade
		Wholesale trade
		Service
		Government
		Manufacturing
		Agriculture
		Mining

450 300 150 0
Thousands of Persons

0 5 10 15 20
Billions of Dollars

Land Use Although most of Maryland's income comes from manufacturing, much of the state contains good farmland. Vegetables are grown on the Eastern Shore; tobacco is found in the southwest; and the Piedmont area is a productive dairy-farming region.

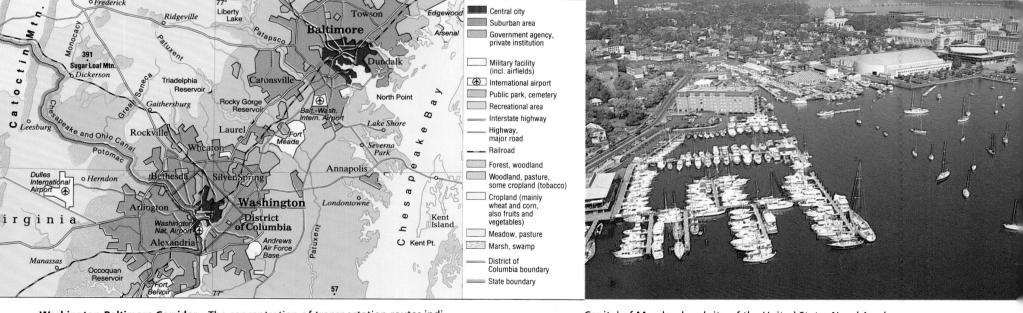

Washington-Baltimore Corridor The concentration of transportation routes indicates Washington's and Baltimore's importance to each other and to the nation and the world.

Central city
Suburban area
Government agency, private institution
Military facility (incl. airfields)
International airport
Public park, cemetery
Recreational area
Interstate highway
Highway, major road
Railroad
Forest, woodland
Woodland, pasture, some cropland (tobacco)
Cropland (mainly wheat and corn, also fruits and vegetables)
Meadow, pasture
Marsh, swamp
District of Columbia boundary
State boundary

Capital of Maryland and site of the United States Naval Academy, Annapolis played an important role in the early days of the United States. Today, the city retains a colonial atmosphere, with carefully preserved historical streets and buildings.

Washington, D.C.

POPULATION 638,432.
Density: 10,134 people/mi²
(3,917 people/km²).
AGE *<20:* 27%. *20–40:* 36%.
40–65: 25%. *>65:* 12%.

ETHNIC GROUPS *White:* 26.9%.
Black: 70.3%. *Spanish origin:*
2.8%. *Native American:* 0.2%.
Other: 2.6%.
INCOME/CAPITA $12,039.

POLITICS 1948–1980 elections:
President: 5 Dem., 0 Rep.
AREA 69 mi² (179 km²). *Water area:*
6 mi² (16 km²).

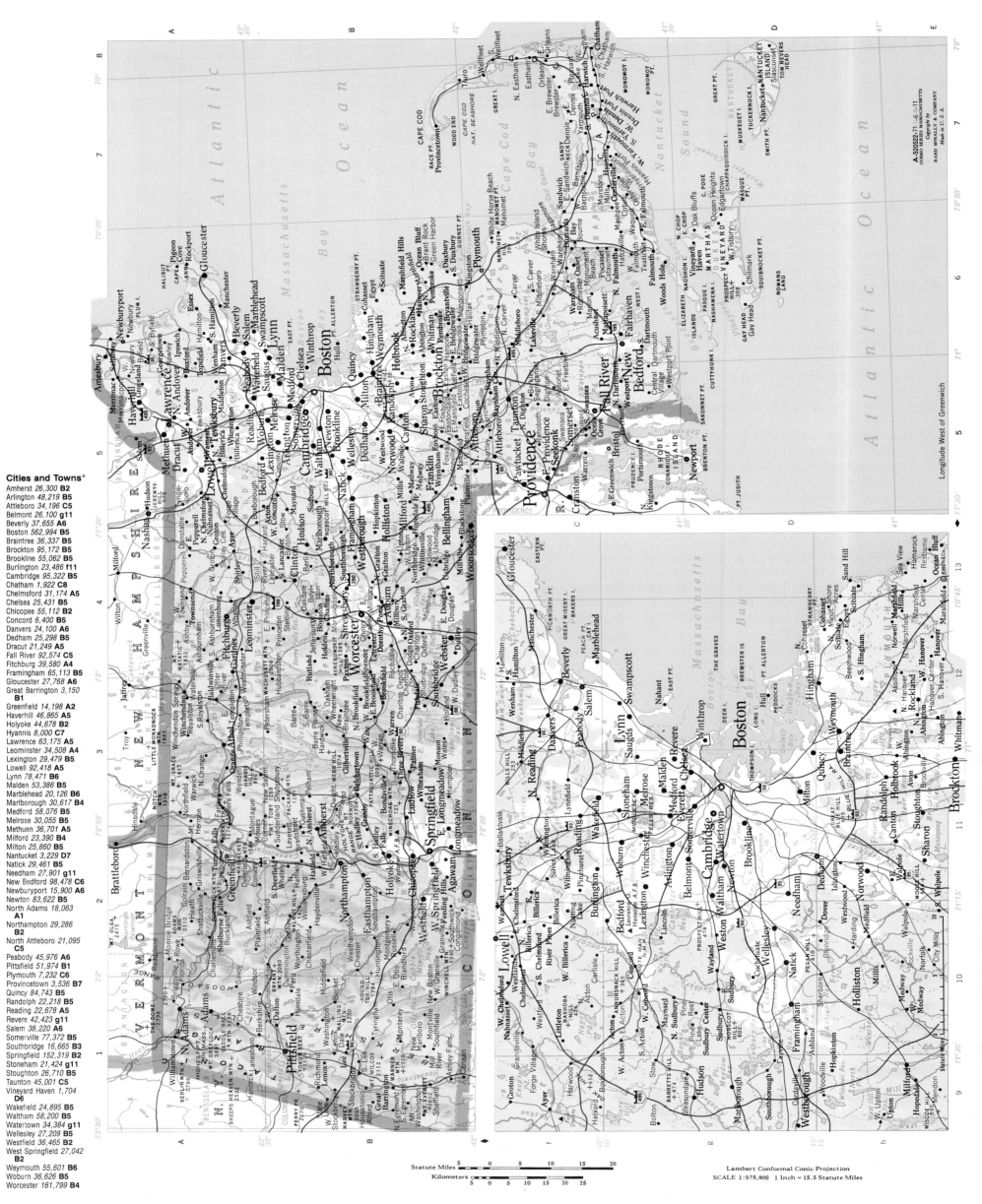

Cities and Towns*

Amherst 26,300 **B2**
Arlington 48,219 **B5**
Attleboro 34,196 **C5**
Belmont 26,100 **g11**
Beverly 37,655 **A6**
Boston 562,994 **B5**
Braintree 36,337 **B5**
Brockton 95,172 **B5**
Brookline 55,062 **B5**
Burlington 23,486 **f11**
Cambridge 95,322 **B5**
Chatham 1,922 **C8**
Chelmsford 31,174 **A5**
Chelsea 25,431 **B5**
Chicopee 55,112 **B2**
Concord 6,400 **B5**
Danvers 24,100 **A6**
Dedham 25,298 **B5**
Dracut 21,249 **A5**
Fall River 92,574 **C5**
Fitchburg 39,580 **A4**
Framingham 65,113 **B5**
Gloucester 27,768 **A6**
Great Barrington 3,150
   B1
Greenfield 14,198 **A2**
Haverhill 46,865 **A5**
Holyoke 44,678 **B2**
Hyannis 8,000 **C7**
Lawrence 63,175 **A5**
Leominster 34,508 **A4**
Lexington 29,479 **B5**
Lowell 92,418 **A5**
Lynn 78,471 **B6**
Malden 53,386 **B5**
Marblehead 20,126 **B6**
Marlborough 30,617 **B4**
Medford 58,076 **B5**
Melrose 30,055 **B5**
Methuen 36,701 **A5**
Milford 23,390 **B4**
Milton 25,860 **B5**
Nantucket 3,229 **D7**
Natick 29,461 **B5**
Needham 27,901 **g11**
New Bedford 98,478 **C6**
Newburyport 15,900 **A6**
Newton 83,622 **B5**
North Adams 18,063
   A1
Northampton 29,286
   B2
North Attleboro 21,095
   C5
Peabody 45,976 **A6**
Pittsfield 51,974 **B1**
Plymouth 7,232 **C6**
Provincetown 3,536 **B7**
Quincy 84,743 **B5**
Randolph 22,218 **B5**
Reading 22,678 **A5**
Revere 42,423 **g11**
Salem 38,220 **A6**
Somerville 77,372 **B5**
Southbridge 16,665 **B3**
Springfield 152,319 **B2**
Stoneham 21,424 **g11**
Stoughton 26,710 **B5**
Taunton 45,001 **C5**
Vineyard Haven 1,704
   D6
Wakefield 24,895 **B5**
Waltham 58,200 **B5**
Watertown 34,384 **g11**
Wellesley 27,209 **B5**
Westfield 36,465 **B2**
West Springfield 27,042
   B2
Weymouth 55,601 **B6**
Woburn 36,626 **B5**
Worcester 161,799 **B4**

*Populations are for localities, not incorporated towns.

Statute Miles

Kilometers

Lambert Conformal Conic Projection
SCALE 1:978,000   1 Inch = 15.5 Statute Miles

Massachusetts

POPULATION 5,737,037. *Rank:* 11. *Density:* 733 people/mi² (283 people/km²). *Urban:* 83.8%. *Rural:* 16.2%.
AGE *<20:* 30%. *20–40:* 32%. *40–65:* 25%. *>65:* 13%.
ETHNIC GROUPS *White:* 93.5%. *Black:* 3.9%. *Spanish origin:* 2.5%. *Native American:* 0.1%. *Other:* 2.5%.

INCOME/CAPITA $10,125. *Rank:* 12.
POLITICS 1948–1980 elections: *President:* 6 Dem., 3 Rep. *Governor:* 7 Dem., 6 Rep.
ENTERED UNION February 6, 1788, 6th state.
CAPITAL Boston, 562,994.
LARGEST CITY Boston.

AREA 8,284 mi² (21,455 km²). *Rank:* 45. *Water area:* 460 mi² (1,191 km²).
ELEVATIONS *Highest:* Mt. Greylock, 3,491 ft (1,064 m). *Lowest:* Atlantic Ocean shoreline, sea level.
CLIMATE Long, cold winters; warm summers; moderate rainfall.

B oston is often called the Hub, a description that could easily apply to Massachusetts as a whole. Since the beginning of the country's history, social, cultural, and economic changes originating in this state have radiated outward to the rest of the nation.

In the 1600's, Massachusetts served as the mother colony for many settlements that spread throughout New England. In the late 1700's, sparks struck by Boston radicals helped ignite the Revolutionary War, leading the country into its battle for independence. Later, the Boston area became a pioneer of the Industrial Revolution and the development of mass production. Throughout the 1800's, thousands of immigrants poured into the state, moving first into the hub of Boston, then spreading outward to the north, south, and west.

Today, the state's sea routes, roads, and rivers not only cover New England but reach out to the nation and the world. Centered on the Boston area, these transport systems, like spokes of a wheel, extend in all directions and distribute goods and services to regional, national, and international markets.

The educational institutions in the state, such as the Massachusetts Institute of Technology, have also made Massachusetts a center for ideas and, most recently, a focal point for the electronics and communication industries. The area outside Boston represents one of the most important concentrations of research and development facilities in the United States. From here, inventions and ideas flow to other institutions and regions in the country.

Since World War II, however, much of American industry has shifted from the Northeast and Midwest to the South and West, and Massachusetts no longer plays as central a role as it once did. Nevertheless, the state shows its leadership in the development of industries in line with the nation's high-technology future. This leadership, combined with the state's experience and ingenuity in marketing and distributing innovations, will keep the Boston-Massachusetts hub turning for quite some time.

Education The state's investment in education, as evidenced by the large number of institutions, has paid off in a greater-than-average participation in higher education. The educational history of Massachusetts includes many "firsts"—from the colonies' first public school to the nation's first college, Harvard.

Cape Cod is made up mostly of sand and gravel deposited by glaciers. To ensure its preservation, the Cape Cod National Seashore was established along the Outer Cape. This is one of the few remaining natural regions of the Atlantic Coast, with its landscape of sand dunes, forests, heath, and ponds.

Employment	Value
	Retail trade
	Wholesale trade
	Service
	Government
	Manufacturing
	Agriculture
	Mining

700 600 400 200 0
Thousands of Persons

0 5 10 15 20 25 30 35
Billions of Dollars

Economic Activities The economy of Massachusetts reflects the relative unimportance of agriculture and mining to this manufacturing and commercial state. Although manufacturing contributes to people's livelihoods throughout the state, Boston and its environs account for much of the state's income. Continued expansion in high-technology industries will ensure the state's manufacturing strength.

Land Use Whereas Massachusetts is fortunate that glaciers left the state with excellent harbors and landings, these ice sheets also stripped away much soil, leaving little fertile land. Despite the differing glacial inheritance of the state's coastal and inland areas, both express a beauty valued by residents and tourists alike.

Massachusetts 116
United States 64 (average)
Massachusetts 303,800
United States 171,276 (average)

Number of Colleges and Universities

Higher-Education Enrollment

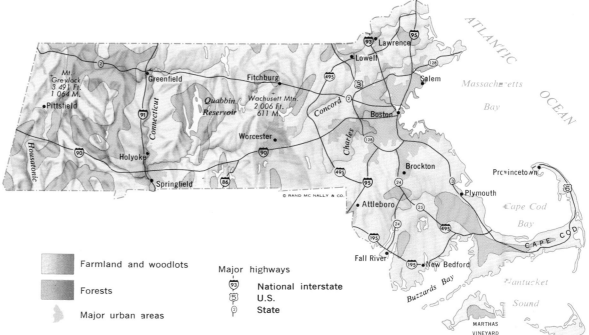

Farmland and woodlots

Forests

Major urban areas

Major highways
National interstate
U.S.
State

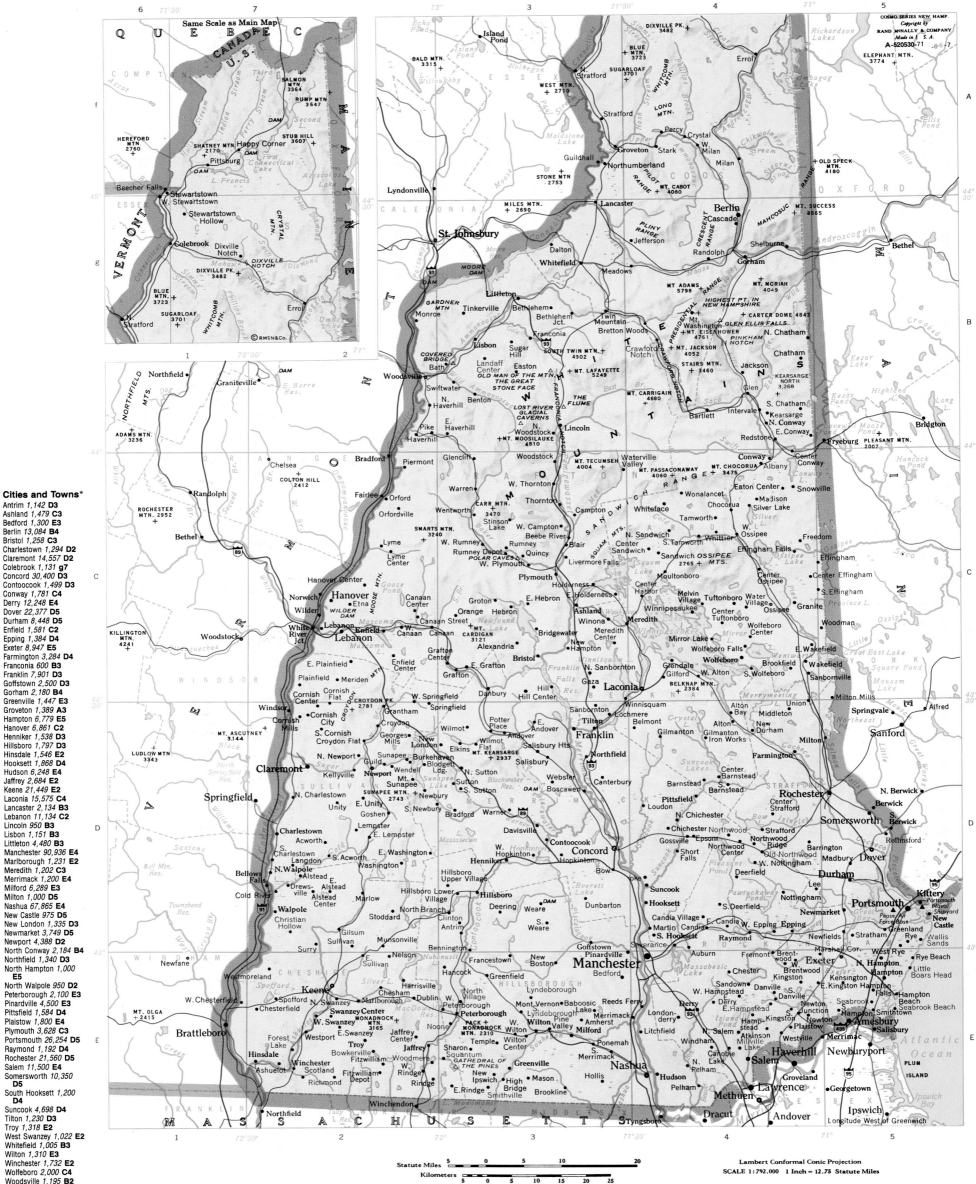

Cities and Towns*

Antrim 1,142 D3
Ashland 1,479 C3
Bedford 1,300 E3
Berlin 13,084 B4
Bristol 1,258 C3
Charlestown 1,294 D2
Claremont 14,557 D2
Colebrook 1,131 g7
Concord 30,400 D3
Contoocook 1,499 D3
Conway 1,781 C4
Derry 12,248 E4
Dover 22,377 D5
Durham 8,448 D5
Enfield 1,581 C2
Epping 1,384 D4
Exeter 8,947 E5
Farmington 3,284 D4
Franconia 600 B3
Franklin 7,901 D3
Goffstown 2,500 D3
Gorham 2,180 B4
Greenville 1,447 E3
Groveton 1,389 A3
Hampton 6,779 E5
Hanover 6,861 C2
Henniker 1,538 D3
Hillsboro 1,797 D3
Hinsdale 1,546 E2
Hooksett 1,868 D4
Hudson 6,248 E4
Jaffrey 2,684 E2
Keene 21,449 E2
Laconia 15,575 C4
Lancaster 2,134 B3
Lebanon 11,134 C2
Lincoln 950 B3
Lisbon 1,151 B3
Littleton 4,480 B3
Manchester 90,936 E4
Marlborough 1,231 E2
Meredith 1,202 C3
Merrimack 1,200 E4
Milford 6,289 E3
Milton 1,000 D5
Nashua 67,865 E4
New Castle 975 D5
New London 1,335 D3
Newmarket 3,749 D5
Newport 4,388 D2
North Conway 2,184 B4
Northfield 1,340 D3
North Hampton 1,000 E5
North Walpole 950 D2
Peterborough 2,100 E3
Pinardville 4,500 E3
Pittsfield 1,584 D4
Plaistow 1,800 E4
Plymouth 3,628 C3
Portsmouth 26,254 D5
Raymond 1,192 D4
Rochester 21,560 D5
Salem 11,500 E4
Somersworth 10,350 D5
South Hooksett 1,200 D4
Suncook 4,698 D4
Tilton 1,230 D3
Troy 1,318 E2
West Swanzey 1,022 E2
Whitefield 1,005 B3
Wilton 1,310 E3
Winchester 1,732 E2
Wolfeboro 2,000 C4
Woodsville 1,195 B2

*Populations are for localities, not incorporated towns.

Statute Miles 5 0 5 10 20
Kilometers 5 0 5 10 15 20 25

Lambert Conformal Conic Projection
SCALE 1:792,000   1 Inch = 12.75 Statute Miles

New Hampshire

POPULATION 920,610. *Rank:* 42. *Density:* 102 people/mi² (40 people/km²). *Urban:* 52.2%. *Rural:* 47.8%.
AGE <*20:* 32%. *20−40:* 33%. *40−65:* 24%. >*65:* 11%.
ETHNIC GROUPS *White:* 98.9%. *Black:* 0.4%. *Spanish origin:* 0.6%. *Native American:* 0.1%. *Other:* 0.6%.

INCOME/CAPITA $9,131. *Rank:* 27.
POLITICS 1948−1980 elections: *President:* 1 Dem., 8 Rep. *Governor:* 5 Dem., 12 Rep.
ENTERED UNION June 21, 1788, 9th state.
CAPITAL Concord, 30,400.
LARGEST CITY Manchester, 90,936.

AREA 9,279 mi² (24,033 km²). *Rank:* 44. *Water area:* 286 mi² (741 km²).
ELEVATIONS *Highest:* Mt. Washington, 6,288 ft (1,917 m). *Lowest:* Atlantic Ocean shoreline, sea level.
CLIMATE Short, mild summers; cold winters. Moderate rainfall, heavy mountain snows.

A small state with limited resources, a somewhat remote location, and a conservative outlook, New Hampshire has nonetheless kept up with changing economic times while retaining its independent Yankee character. The state has been able to capitalize on its long history of industrialization by supplanting shoemaking, woodworking, and textile industries with the manufacture of electrical and electronic products and equipment. Its wilderness forests continue to be a source of lumber and wood pulp, while the Portsmouth Naval Station clearly indicates the federal government's ongoing interest in the state.

Although New Hampshire attracted early settlers, the westward growth of the country left the state in a distant corner of the Northeast. Nevertheless, New Hampshire has been able to benefit from its proximity to Boston, which is the northernmost metropolitan area of the East Coast megalopolis. Urban areas near New Hampshire provide cultural and recreational outlets, as well as excellent markets for the state's poultry, dairy products, and vegetables. Residents of the urban areas are, in turn, drawn by New Hampshire's famed natural beauty.

New Hampshire's conservative outlook has built a state with a strong tradition of self-reliance, but that tradition may need to bend under the pressures of change. The state, without a sales or earned-income tax, has raised revenues through luxury taxes, sweepstakes, and legalized racetrack betting that draws heavily on the tourist trade. The modest income generated leaves little money for state aid to education and to health and welfare services. While New Hampshire in the past has managed to support many schools, colleges, and cultural and health facilities, rising costs may force its citizens to abandon their historical resistance to the growth of state government.

Even though modern problems have touched this part of the country, it is almost certain that New Hampshire will deal with them in a way that will preserve its traditionally independent nature. In this way the state will once again legitimize its claim to Yankee ingenuity and endurance.

The White Mountains derive their name from their gray-white summits, which rise far beyond the green timberline. The heat and pressure involved in their formation, more than 200 million years ago, account for their folding and crumbling characteristics. Rugged terrain and lack of good farmland have kept people from settling in the mountain area, and since 1911, much of the area has been preserved in state and national forests. The mountains are excellent for both summer and winter sports, especially hiking and skiing.

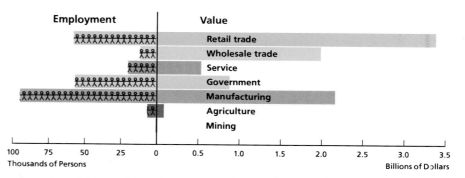

Employment	Value
	Retail trade
	Wholesale trade
	Service
	Government
	Manufacturing
	Agriculture
	Mining

100 75 50 25 0 0.5 1.0 1.5 2.0 2.5 3.0 3.5
Thousands of Persons   Billions of Dollars

Economic Activities Although New Hampshire is often considered a rural state, most of its work force is employed in manufacturing, a traditionally urban pursuit. Technologically advanced industries have become especially important.

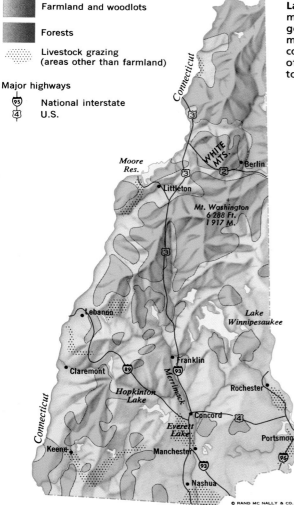

Farmland and woodlots

Forests

Livestock grazing (areas other than farmland)

Major highways
🛡 National interstate
🛡 U.S.

Land Use With New Hampshire's many mountains and its small amount of good farm soil left by the last glacier, most of the state remains in the forest cover best suited to its land. The beauty of the forests helps sustain the state's tourism industry.

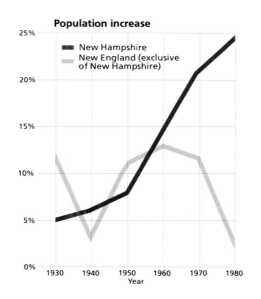

Population increase

- New Hampshire
- New England (exclusive of New Hampshire)

25%
20%
15%
10%
5%
0%
1930 1940 1950 1960 1970 1980
Year

Population New Hampshire's low income taxes and lack of a general sales tax have made the state an attractive location for many new businesses. The southeastern portion has been especially appealing because of its proximity to the East Coast megalopolis.

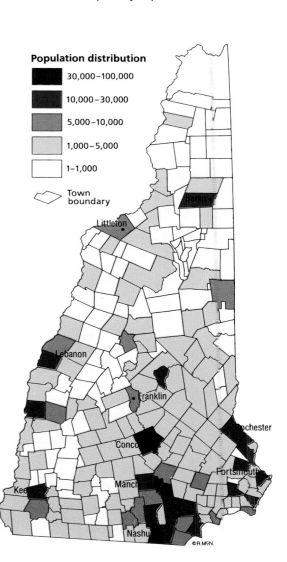

Population distribution

- 30,000−100,000
- 10,000−30,000
- 5,000−10,000
- 1,000−5,000
- 1−1,000
- Town boundary

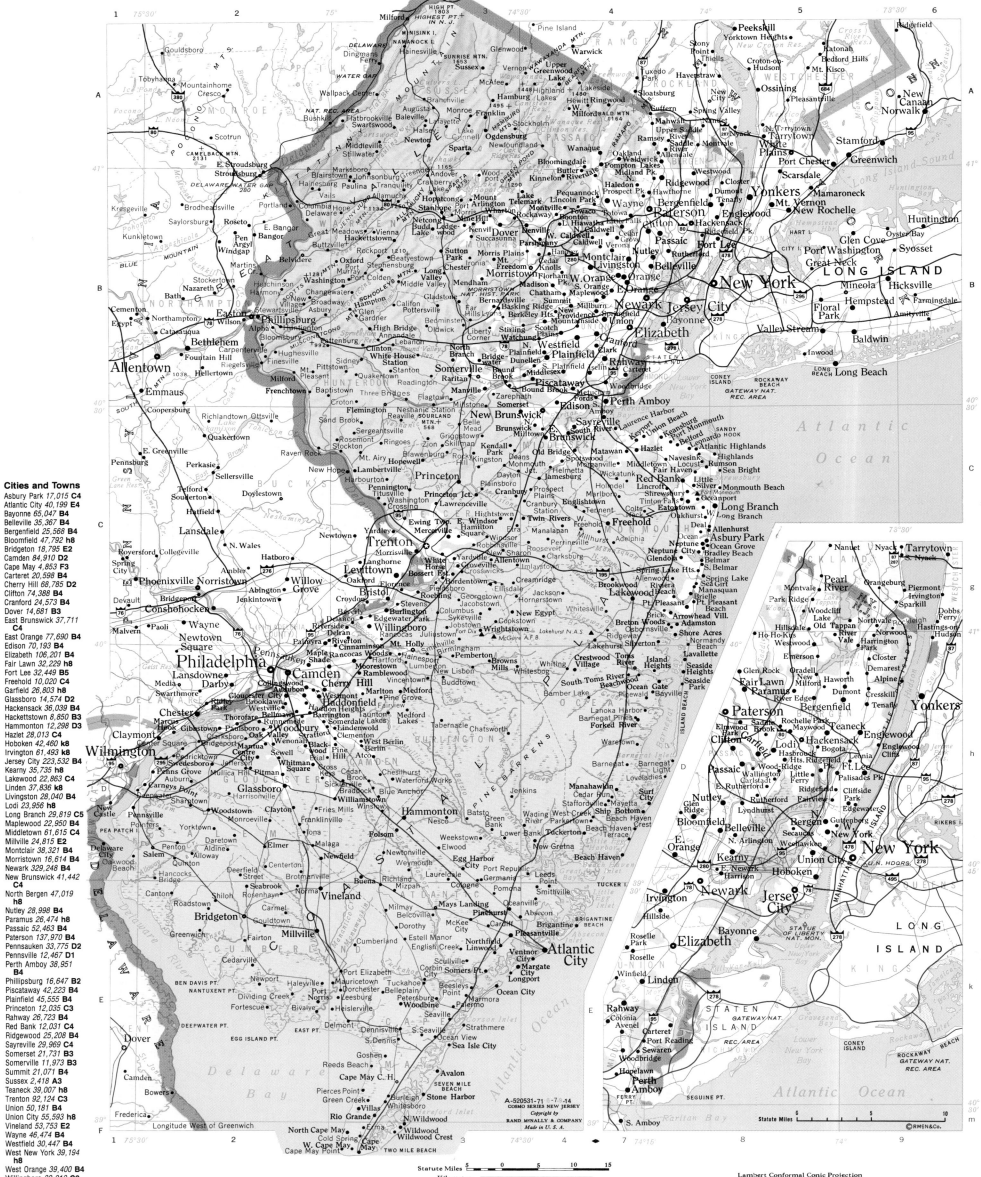

New Jersey

POPULATION 7,364,823.
Rank: 9. *Density:* 986 people/mi²
(381 people/km²). *Urban:* 89%.
Rural: 11%.
AGE *<20:* 31%. *20–40:* 30%.
40–65: 27%. *>65:* 12%.
ETHNIC GROUPS *White:* 83.2%.
Black: 12.6%. *Spanish origin:*
6.7%. *Native American:* 0.1%.
Other: 4.1%.

INCOME/CAPITA $10,924. *Rank:* 4.
POLITICS 1948–1980 elections:
President: 2 Dem., 7 Rep.
Governor: 6 Dem., 3 Rep.
ENTERED UNION December 18,
1787, 3rd state.
CAPITAL Trenton, 92,124.
LARGEST CITY Newark, 329,248.

AREA 7,787 mi² (20,168 km²).
Rank: 46. *Water area:* 319 mi²
(826 km²).
ELEVATIONS *Highest:* High Point,
1,803 ft (550 m). *Lowest:* Atlantic
Ocean shoreline, sea level.
CLIMATE Warm summers, cool
winters along coast;
considerable snow in highlands.
Ample rainfall.

The Great Swamp National Wildlife Refuge, filled with ancient oak and beech trees, is the site of more than two hundred kinds of birds and animals. Located near Morristown, it also serves as a refuge for residents of surrounding urban areas.

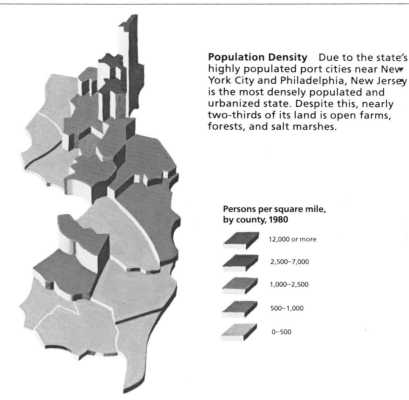

Population Density Due to the state's highly populated port cities near New York City and Philadelphia, New Jersey is the most densely populated and urbanized state. Despite this, nearly two-thirds of its land is open farms, forests, and salt marshes.

Persons per square mile, by county, 1980

12,000 or more

2,500–7,000

1,000–2,500

500–1,000

0–500

New Jersey's extraordinary role in American life is often overlooked. The state is an industrial leader with total and per capita incomes that rank among the highest in the country. Its urban population can take advantage of nearby New York City and Philadelphia, as well as enjoy miles of sandy beaches along the Atlantic and explore the rolling Appalachian wilderness to the north. New Jersey's investment in industry, its proximity to the East's great cultural centers, and its tradition of research and invention, established by such pioneers as Thomas Edison, ensure the state's future vitality.

Even so, America's modern economy shows little respect for old colonial boundaries. Perhaps if the Hudson and Delaware rivers actually surrounded New Jersey, turning it into an island like Long Island, the state would have a pronounced identity of its own. As it stands, the New York and Philadelphia metropolitan areas cast their long shadows over New Jersey, drawing thousands of commuters into these cities each day. While few people from New Jersey would choose to live in either of these urban giants, their allegiance is divided between their place of work and their residence. The growth of suburbs and slow decline of urban areas intensify New Jersey's problem of identity. As in other states, many residents feel justified in putting their local towns and villages ahead of state or urban needs—a trend that militates against developing a unified sense of statehood.

New Jersey is not alone in facing the challenge of preserving its identity, but its choices are limited by the eastern metropolitan growth that is transcending state boundaries and undermining New Jersey's attempts to unify its population. Still, the state remains a vital part of the great eastern megalopolis. And although in many ways New Jersey depends on this area, the megalopolis, in turn, depends on New Jersey's industrial strength for future growth.

Land Use The urban character of New Jersey's industrial and commercial corridor running from Paterson and Newark to Camden greatly contrasts with the lightly populated hill country to the northwest and the rolling pine forests to the south.

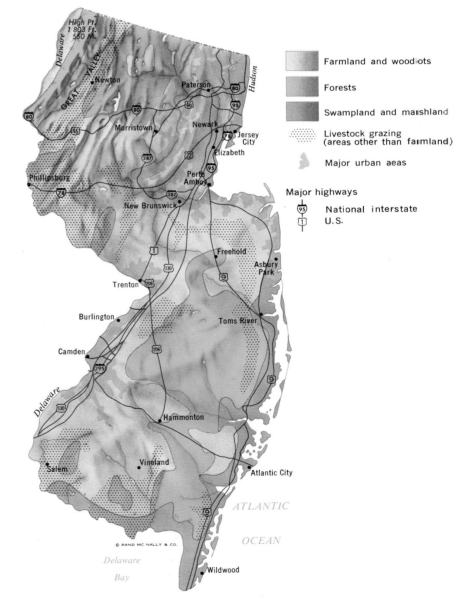

Farmland and woodlots

Forests

Swampland and marshland

Livestock grazing (areas other than farmland)

Major urban areas

Major highways

National interstate

U.S.

Economic Activities In addition to having manufacturing and commercial strength, New Jersey is a major center of industrial and scientific research and development. Its tourism industry contributes to its retail and service trades.

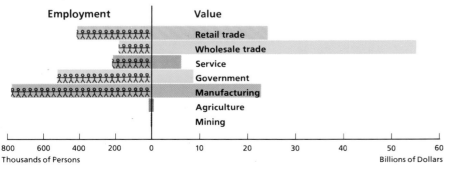

Employment	Value
	Retail trade
	Wholesale trade
	Service
	Government
	Manufacturing
	Agriculture
	Mining

800 600 400 200 0   10 20 30 40 50 60
Thousands of Persons   Billions of Dollars

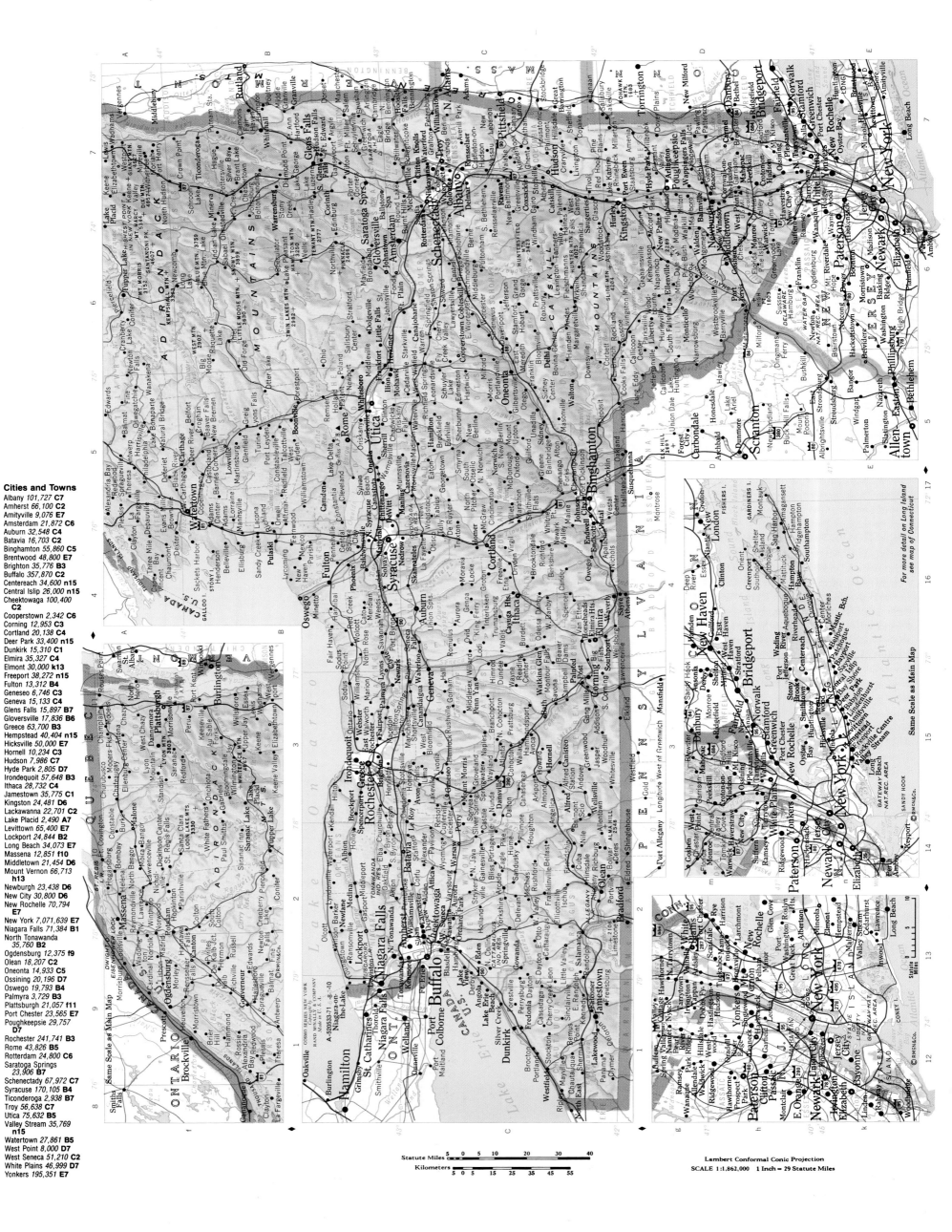

Cities and Towns

Albany 101,727 **C7**
Amherst 66,100 **C2**
Amityville 9,076 **E7**
Amsterdam 21,872 **C6**
Auburn 32,548 **C4**
Batavia 16,703 **C2**
Binghamton 55,860 **C5**
Brentwood 48,800 **E7**
Brighton 35,776 **B3**
Buffalo 357,870 **C2**
Centereach 34,600 **n15**
Central Islip 26,000 **n15**
C2
Cheektowaga 100,400
C2
Cooperstown 2,342 **C6**
Corning 12,953 **C3**
Cortland 20,138 **C4**
Deer Park 33,400 **n15**
Dunkirk 15,310 **C1**
Elmira 35,327 **C4**
Elmont 30,000 **k13**
Freeport 38,272 **n15**
Fulton 13,312 **B4**
Geneseo 6,746 **C3**
Geneva 15,133 **C4**
Glens Falls 15,897 **B7**
Gloversville 17,836 **B6**
Greece 63,700 **B3**
Hempstead 40,404 **n15**
Hicksville 50,000 **B7**
Hornell 10,234 **C3**
Hudson 7,986 **C7**
Hyde Park 2,805 **D7**
Irondequoit 57,648 **B3**
Ithaca 28,732 **C4**
Jamestown 35,775 **C1**
Kingston 24,481 **D6**
Lackawanna 22,701 **C2**
Lake Placid 2,490 **A7**
Levittown 65,400 **E7**
Lockport 24,844 **B2**
Long Beach 34,073 **E7**
Massena 12,851 **f10**
Middletown 21,454 **D6**
Mount Vernon 66,713
h13
Newburgh 23,438 **D6**
New City 30,800 **D6**
New Rochelle 70,794
E7
New York 7,071,639 **D7**
Niagara Falls 71,384 **B1**
North Tonawanda
35,760 **B2**
Ogdensburg 12,375 **f9**
Olean 18,207 **C2**
Oneonta 14,933 **C5**
Ossining 20,196 **D7**
Oswego 19,793 **B4**
Palmyra 3,729 **B3**
Plattsburgh 21,057 **f11**
Port Chester 23,565 **E7**
Poughkeepsie 29,757
D7
Rochester 241,741 **B3**
Rome 43,826 **B5**
Rotterdam 24,800 **C6**
Saratoga Springs
23,906 **B7**
Schenectady 67,972 **C7**
Syracuse 170,105 **B4**
Ticonderoga 2,938 **B7**
Troy 56,638 **C7**
Utica 75,632 **B5**
Valley Stream 35,769
n15
Watertown 27,861 **B5**
West Point 8,000 **D7**
West Seneca 51,210 **C2**
White Plains 46,999 **D7**
Yonkers 195,351 **E7**

Statute Miles 5 0 5 10 20 30 40
Kilometers 5 0 5 10 15 25 35 45 55

Lambert Conformal Conic Projection
SCALE 1:1,862,000   1 Inch = 29 Statute Miles

New York

POPULATION 17,558,072. *Rank:* 2. *Density:* 371 people/mi² (143 people/km²). *Urban:* 84.6%. *Rural:* 15.4%. **AGE** *<20:* 30%. *20–40:* 31%. *40–65:* 27%. *>65:* 12%. **ETHNIC GROUPS** *White:* 80%. *Black:* 13.7%. *Spanish origin:* 9.5%. *Native American:* 0.2%. *Other:* 6.1%.	**INCOME/CAPITA** $10,260. *Rank:* 11. **POLITICS** 1948–1980 elections: *President:* 3 Dem., 6 Rep. *Governor:* 3 Dem., 5 Rep. **ENTERED UNION** July 26, 1788, 11th state. **CAPITAL** Albany, 101,727. **LARGEST CITY** New York, 7,071,639.	**AREA** 52,735 mi² (136,583 km²). *Rank:* 30. *Water area:* 5,358 mi² (13,877 km²). **ELEVATIONS** *Highest:* Mt. Marcy, 5,344 ft (1,629 m). *Lowest:* Atlantic Ocean shoreline, sea level. **CLIMATE** Cool winters, hot summers in south. North and west, cold winters, short summers.

New York truly deserves its reputation as the Empire State. Its considerable influence extends from neighboring states to nations far beyond the shores of North America. As a result, New York City is more than America's largest urban area; in many ways it is the capital of the world's economy.

Yet surprisingly, New York State's economic potential was not realized until the nineteenth century, well after other colonial states had established a thriving commerce. New York's swift rise to fortune began with the settlement of the Great Lakes region and the upper Mississippi River valley. As these western territories grew, they found themselves separated from the markets and shipping routes of the East by the Appalachian Mountains. Because only New York had established river, canal, and rail routes through these mountains, the state quickly became the funnel through which foodstuffs, manufactured goods, and raw materials of the western regions poured into the East and beyond to overseas markets. The state not only served as the Midwest's gateway to the Atlantic, but rose to become North America's major port for world trade.

Today, New York is still a powerful presence in the nation. Its financial resources, evident in its bank holdings and stock exchanges, help to buffer the state during times of economic recession and industrial decline. No matter where in the United States a major factory or business is built, its owners are likely to turn to New York City for financing.

But New York's very size and strength has created special problems. As the capital of an economic empire, New York City attracts thousands of immigrants each year, many of whom are poor. The strain of assimilating so many newcomers adds to the city's already overburdened resources and, in turn, creates further tension between city and state administrators. Several times the federal government has been called in to help the city weather its financial crises. Longer-term solutions must be found if the city and state are to remain the symbol of what is best in the country. Because of the drive and energy of the people of New York, it is likely that the state will maintain its status as the capital of the empire.

The interdependence of New York's urban and rural areas is apparent in the state's agriculture. Heavily populated urban centers demand certain products, and New York's rural regions support their needs. The rich soils of the country's agricultural states are not to be found here, but much of the state's more productive land is intensively cultivated. Shown here, the Hudson Valley in southeastern New York provides dairy products and also ranks high in apple production.

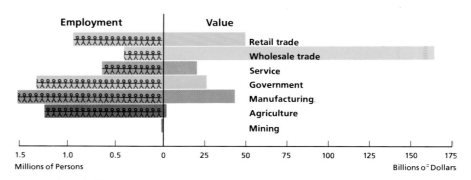

Employment	Value	
		Retail trade
		Wholesale trade
		Service
		Government
		Manufacturing
		Agriculture
		Mining

1.5   1.0   0.5   0   25   50   75   100   125   150   175
Millions of Persons   Billions of Dollars

Economic Activities   New York's importance to national and international trade and commerce is apparent in the value of wholesale trade, although other very valuable sectors employ more people.

Land Use   New York's cities trace the important Atlantic-to-Great Lakes corridor that established the state's empire. These cities remain the home of most of the population and the site of major industries. Outside the cities lies farmland, and beyond this land are the recreation areas of the Applachian Highlands, including the Catskills and the Adirondacks.

- Farmland and woodlots
- Forests
- Livestock grazing (areas other than farmland)
- Major urban areas

Major highways
- National interstate
- U.S.
- State

— Canal

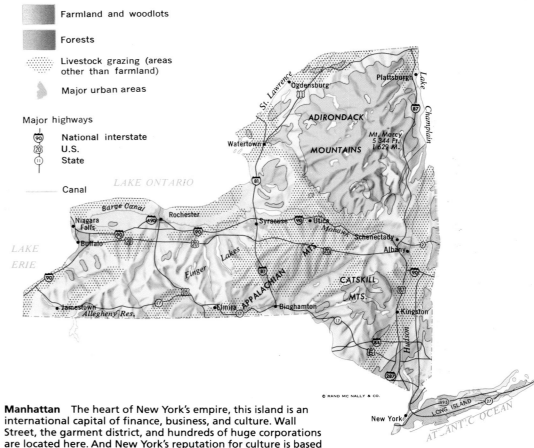

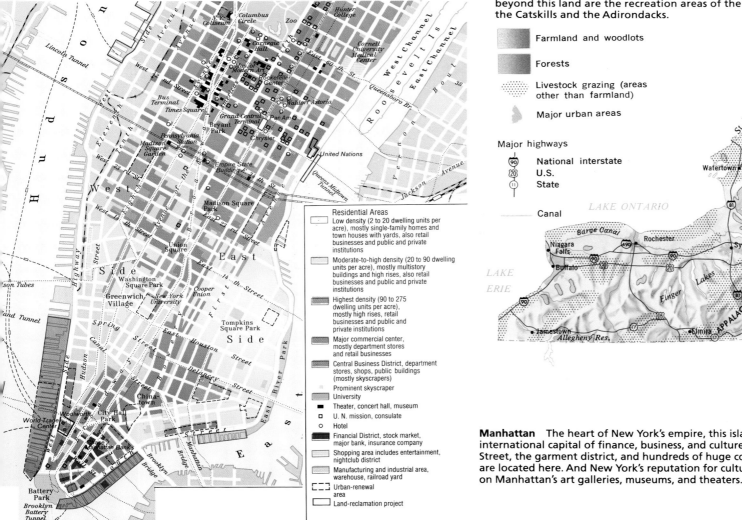

Residential Areas
- Low density (2 to 20 dwelling units per acre), mostly single-family homes and town houses with yards, also retail businesses and public and private institutions
- Moderate-to-high density (20 to 90 dwelling units per acre), mostly multistory buildings and high rises, also retail businesses and public and private institutions
- Highest density (90 to 275 dwelling units per acre), mostly high rises, retail businesses and public and private institutions
- Major commercial center, mostly department stores and retail businesses
- Central Business District, department stores, shops, public buildings (mostly skyscrapers)
- Prominent skyscraper
- University
- Theater, concert hall, museum
- U. N. mission, consulate
- Hotel
- Financial District, stock market, major bank, insurance company
- Shopping area includes entertainment, nightclub district
- Manufacturing and industrial area, warehouse, railroad yard
- Urban-renewal area
- Land-reclamation project

Manhattan   The heart of New York's empire, this island is an international capital of finance, business, and culture. Wall Street, the garment district, and hundreds of huge corporations are located here. And New York's reputation for culture is based on Manhattan's art galleries, museums, and theaters.

Cities and Towns

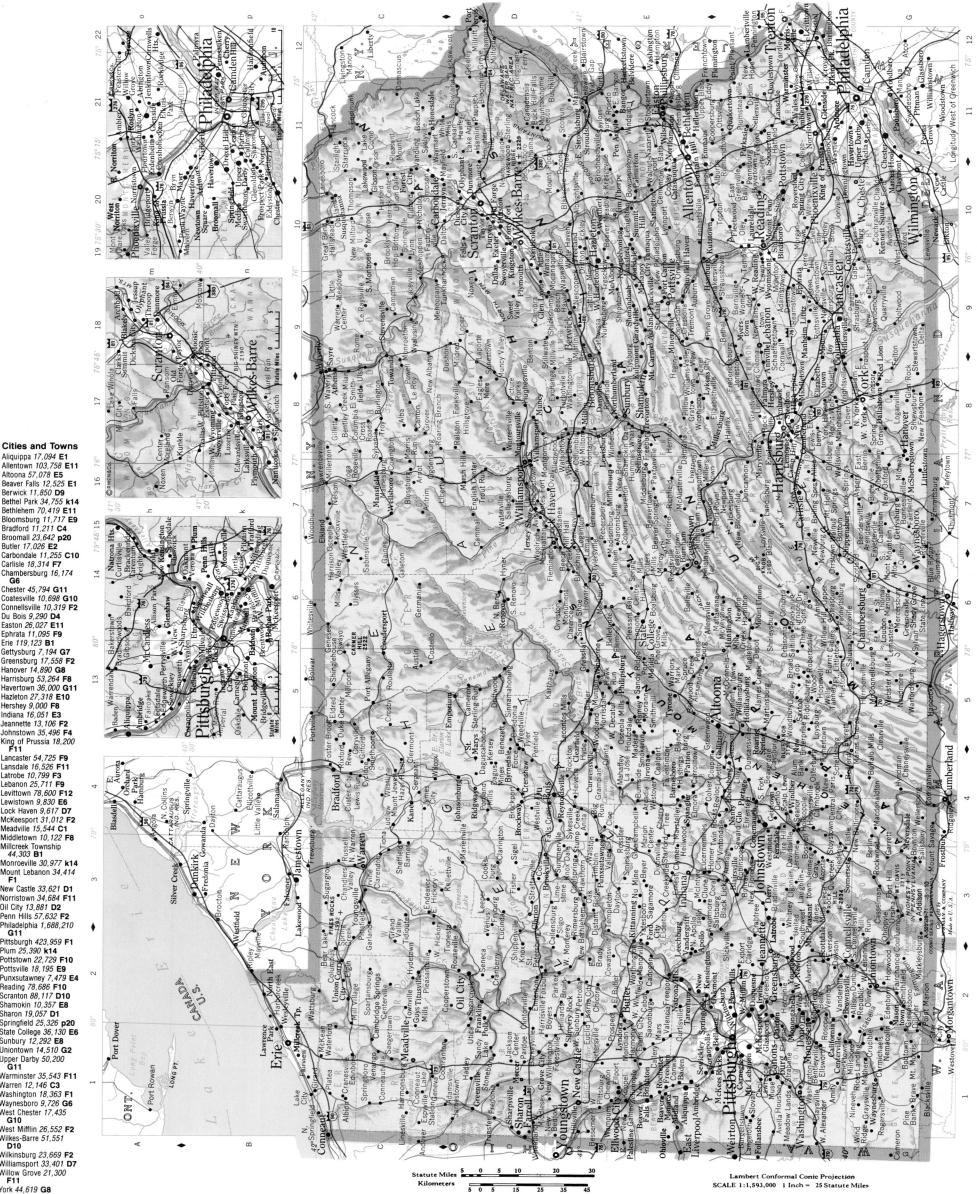

Statute Miles
Kilometers

Lambert Conformal Conic Projection
SCALE 1:1,593,000   1 Inch = 25 Statute Miles

Pennsylvania

POPULATION 11,863,895.
Rank: 4. *Density:* 264 people/mi² (102 people/km²). *Urban:* 69.3%. *Rural:* 30.7%.
AGE <20: 30%. 20–40: 30%. 40–65: 27%. >65: 13%.
ETHNIC GROUPS *White:* 89.8%. *Black:* 8.8%. *Spanish origin:* 1.3%. *Native American:* <0.1%. *Other:* 1.4%.

INCOME/CAPITA $9,434. *Rank:* 21.
POLITICS 1948–1980 elections: *President:* 4 Dem., 5 Rep. *Governor:* 4 Dem., 4 Rep.
ENTERED UNION December 12, 1787, 2nd state.
CAPITAL Harrisburg, 53,264.
LARGEST CITY Philadelphia, 1,688,210.

AREA 46,043 mi² (119,251 km²). *Rank:* 32. *Water area:* 1,155 mi² (2,992 km²).
ELEVATIONS *Highest:* Mt. Davis, 3,213 ft (979 m). *Lowest:* Along Delaware River, sea level.
CLIMATE Warm summers, cold winters; moderate rainfall, heavy snow in mountains.

Pennsylvania, the Keystone State, occupies its key location in two ways. First, it has long been the keystone in the north-south coastal arch formed by the original colonies. Second, it bridges the Appalachian Mountains between the coastal states and the vast interior lowland of America's midwestern heartland. These key roles are reflected in the character of its two largest cities.

Philadelphia, once the largest city in North America, played an important role in the Revolutionary War and in the unification of the colonies following independence; it remains the capstone of an entire era of American political and economic history. Although now a major port and part of the almost continuous urban-industrial belt extending along the northeastern seaboard, it is still sometimes called the "Athens of America." In contrast, Pittsburgh is the "Steel City," and its factories are a monument to the industrialization of America in the nineteenth and twentieth centuries. Its resources and leadership were used to turn the East North Central states into an industrial power-house.

Despite their location in one state, Philadelphia in the east and Pittsburgh in the west exist in relative independence, with their own markets and spheres of influence. This independence developed in part because the Allegheny and Appalachian mountains long posed a barrier to east-west communications. Today, railroads and highways cross the state, but the effects of the division remain.

Nevertheless, the two cities have come to support the entire commonwealth, and their commerce and industry have been associated with a prosperous and diversified agriculture. Culturally, too, the state has displayed rich diversity, including groups such as the Amish, the Quakers, the Mennonites, the Appalachian Highlanders, the Eastern Europeans of the cities and mining towns, and the black communities of the largest cities.

Today, Pennsylvania remains a wealthy and important state. Well endowed with human and natural resources, it can be expected to play a key role in solving the problems it shares with its neighbors—high unemployment, the declining quality of the urban environment, ethnic and racial conflict, and other issues that confront the industrial northeastern United States.

Pennsylvania's farmlands and forests provide examples of environmental conservation. Unlike settlers elsewhere, early Pennsylvanian farmers practiced crop rotation, keeping the soil productive. Conservation of forests, however, came later. Rapid early development destroyed almost all Pennsylvania's woodlands. At the end of the nineteenth century, conservation programs were enacted, restoring the forests that now cover over half the state. This south-central area near Kingwood consists of the rich farmland and forests that make up much of Pennsylvania.

Economic Activities   Known for its steel industry, Pennsylvania is less dependent on that activity than might be expected. The state's steady economic growth is the result of a diversified industry that is skilled at processing raw materials into a wide variety of products, from chocolate to machinery.

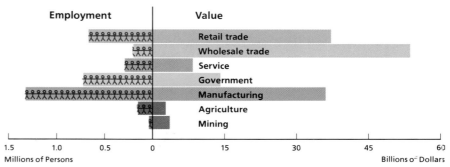

Employment   Value

Retail trade
Wholesale trade
Service
Government
Manufacturing
Agriculture
Mining

1.5   1.0   0.5   0   15   30   45   60
Millions of Persons   Billions of Dollars

Manufacturing   Pennsylvania plays a key role in manufacturing, forming a major part of the industrial coastal megalopolis and linking it with the western portion of the nation's principal manufacturing region.

Number employed in manufacturing by county

- Over 100,000
- 50,000-100,000
- 20,000-50,000
- 10,000-20,000
- 2,000-10,000
- 0-2,000

0   50   100 Mi.
0   50   100   150 Km
Copyright © by Rand McNally & Co.

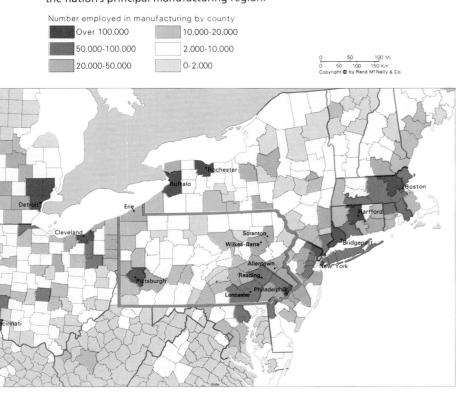

Land Use   Pennsylvania's land patterns are shaped by the Appalachian Mountains and the Allegheny Plateau. Forests generally follow the mountain crests, outlining a natural maze, while urban industrialized areas and agricultural activities fill the valleys in a complex but effective mix.

- Farmland and woodlots
- Forests
- Major urban areas
- Major highways
- National interstate
- U.S.

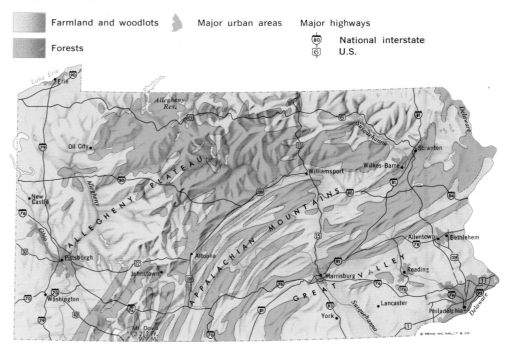

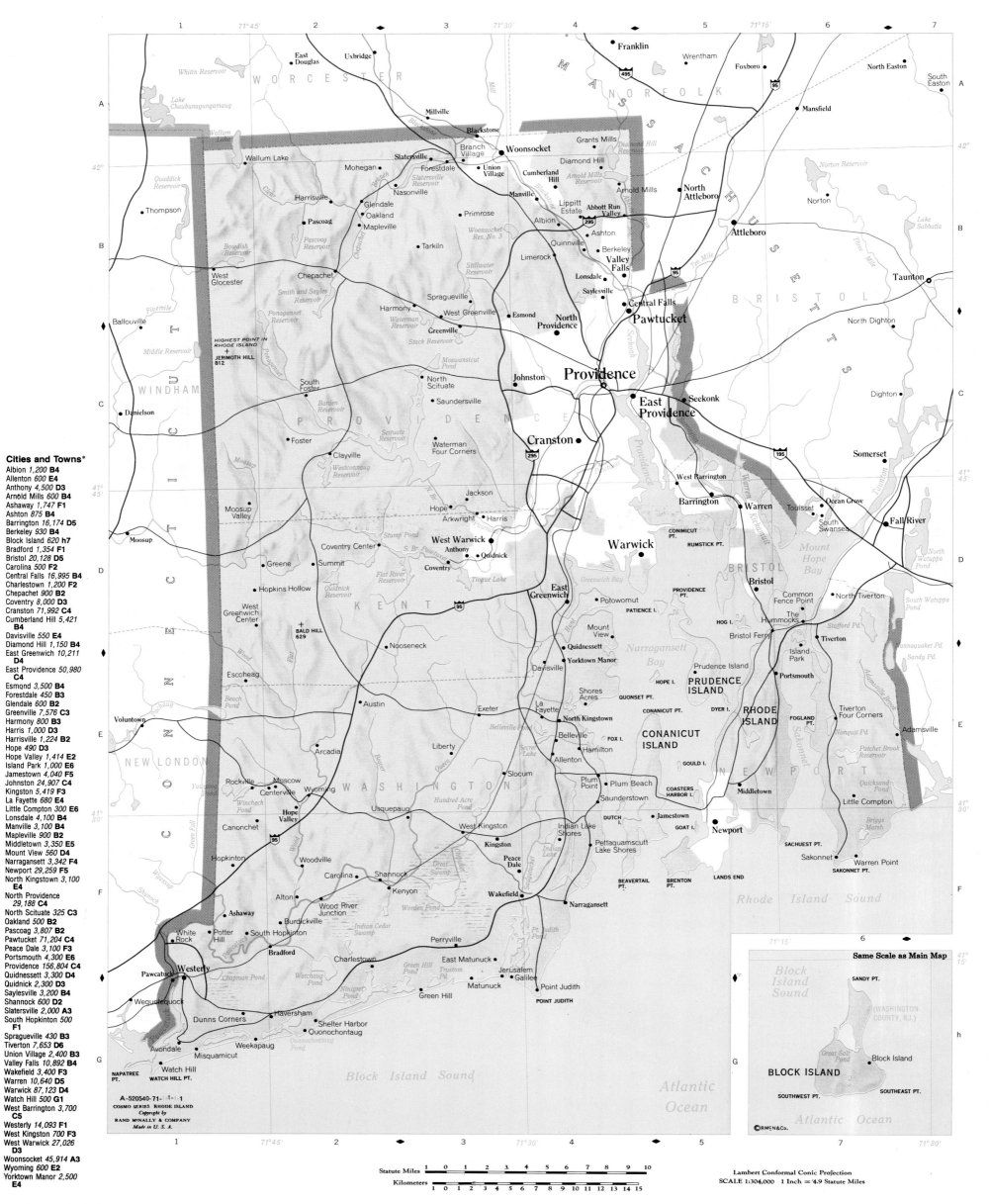

Cities and Towns*

Albion 1,200 **B4**
Allenton 600 **E4**
Anthony 4,500 **D3**
Arnold Mills 600 **B4**
Ashaway 1,747 **F1**
Ashton 875 **B4**
Barrington 16,174 **D5**
Berkeley 930 **B4**
Block Island 620 **h7**
Bradford 1,354 **F1**
Bristol 20,128 **D5**
Carolina 500 **F2**
Central Falls 16,995 **B4**
Charlestown 1,200 **F2**
Chepachet 900 **B2**
Coventry 8,000 **D3**
Cranston 71,992 **C4**
Cumberland Hill 5,421
B4
Davisville 550 **E4**
Diamond Hill 1,150 **B4**
East Greenwich 10,211
D4
East Providence 50,980
C4
Esmond 3,500 **B4**
Forestdale 450 **B3**
Glendale 600 **B2**
Greenville 7,576 **C3**
Harmony 800 **B3**
Harris 1,000 **D3**
Harrisville 1,224 **B2**
Hope 490 **D3**
Hope Valley 1,414 **E2**
Island Park 1,000 **E6**
Jamestown 4,040 **F5**
Johnston 24,907 **C4**
Kingston 5,419 **F3**
La Fayette 680 **E4**
Little Compton 300 **E6**
Lonsdale 4,100 **B4**
Manville 3,100 **B4**
Mapleville 900 **B2**
Middletown 3,350 **E5**
Mount View 560 **D4**
Narragansett 3,342 **F4**
Newport 29,259 **F5**
North Kingstown 3,100
E4
North Providence
29,188 **C4**
North Scituate 325 **C3**
Oakland 500 **B2**
Pascoag 3,807 **B2**
Pawtucket 71,204 **C4**
Peace Dale 3,100 **F3**
Portsmouth 4,300 **E6**
Providence 156,804 **C4**
Quidnessett 3,300 **D4**
Quidnick 2,300 **D3**
Saylesville 3,200 **B4**
Shannock 600 **D2**
Slatersville 2,000 **A3**
South Hopkinton 500
F1
Sprague ville 430 **B3**
Tiverton 7,653 **D6**
Union Village 2,400 **B3**
Valley Falls 10,892 **B4**
Wakefield 3,400 **F3**
Warren 10,640 **D5**
Warwick 87,123 **D4**
Watch Hill 500 **G1**
West Barrington 3,700
C5
Westerly 14,093 **F1**
West Kingston 700 **F3**
West Warwick 27,026
D3
Woonsocket 45,914 **A3**
Wyoming 600 **E2**
Yorktown Manor 2,500
E4

Populations are for localities, not incorporated towns.

Rhode Island

POPULATION 947,154.
Rank: 40. *Density:* 898 people/
mi² (347 people/km²). *Urban:*
87%. *Rural:* 13%.
AGE <20: 30%. 20–40: 31%.
40–65: 26%. >65: 13%.
ETHNIC GROUPS *White:* 94.7%.
Black: 2.9%. *Spanish origin:*
2.1%. *Native American:* 0.3%.
Other: 2.1%.

INCOME/CAPITA $9,444. *Rank:* 20.
POLITICS 1948–1980 elections:
President: 6 Dem., 3 Rep.
Governor: 13 Dem., 4 Rep.
ENTERED UNION May 29, 1790,
13th state.
CAPITAL Providence, 156,804.
LARGEST CITY Providence.

AREA 1,213 mi² (3,141 km²).
Rank: 50. *Water area:* 158 mi²
(409 km²).
ELEVATIONS *Highest:* Jerimoth H II,
812 ft (247 m). *Lowest:* Atlantic
Ocean shoreline, sea level.
CLIMATE Cold winters, warm
summers; temperature range
modified by proximity to ocean.
Moderate rainfall.

Tiny Rhode Island has often exerted an influence far out of proportion to its size, forecasting many national trends and problems. Size has been no handicap in developing innovative approaches to issues that other states have eventually had to face.

Rhode Island started its tradition as a forerunner early in its history. A charter in 1633 guaranteed the colony full religious freedom, and throughout colonial times, Rhode Island served as a haven from persecution for dissenters from less tolerant settlements. It was also the first colony to declare its independence from England and the first to prohibit the importation of slaves.

In its economy, too, Rhode Island has anticipated future trends. The state has few natural resources besides Narragansett Bay, with its fishing and the waterpower derived from its tributaries. With limited opportunities in agriculture, Rhode Islanders chose livelihoods first based in commerce, then in manufacturing. The state developed one of the earliest industrialized regions and experienced both the blessings and the burdens of industrial development, conditions that the nation would later share in the nineteenth and twentieth centuries. The great influx of foreign labor needed to work new factories strained the state's fundamental commitment to tolerance, and in 1842, that commitment was put to the test. The urban population, denied voting rights because they owned no property, fought for and eventually won equal representation in the state government.

Rhode Island today is meeting the challenges of industrial decline common to its neighbors by diversifying its economy into technologically innovative industries, such as electronics and jewelry design and manufacture. This diversification has integrated Rhode Island into the East Coast megalopolis, and in this respect, Rhode Island may still be considered a forecaster of national trends and problems. As urbanization has come to reflect the American norm, the significance of state boundaries is declining, and the need for regional solutions to urban problems is increasing. One thing, however, is certain—small Rhode Island should be able to hold its own among its larger neighbors.

Founded in 1639, Newport soon developed into a prosperous port city. Its proximity to New York led to its rediscovery in the 1800's, when wealthy urbanites found it the perfect site for the summer mansions that now grace its landscape.

Employment		Value
		Retail trade
		Wholesale trade
		Service
		Government
		Manufacturing
		Agriculture
		Mining

150 100 50 0   0.5 1.0 1.5 2.0 2.5 3.0 3.5
Thousands of Persons   Billions of Dollars

Economic Activities Rhode Island is primarily a manufacturing state, with small contributions from agriculture and fishing. But wholesale trade and manufacturing are more specialized here than in some of the state's larger neighbors; and light, rather than heavy, industry is the rule, producing products such as jewelry, silverware, and precision instruments.

Urbanization Rhode Island's role as a forecaster is evident in the character of its population. The state's early industrialization and the resulting urban growth prefaced the urbanization of the country. And Rhode Island's population shift of the past decades appears to foretell the national trend of movement from city to suburb.

Land Use Rhode Island can be divided into two natural regions. In the east lie the lowlands of the New England seaboard, and to the west are the hills of the New England uplands. But Rhode Island's most remarkable feature is Narragansett Bay, a deep inlet of the Atlantic Ocean. The bay's many natural harbors provided sites for cities well equipped for commerce and industry, with easy access to markets. Together with the bay, limited cropland helped Rhode Island maintain political and economic independence, despite its small size and proximity to states with greater quantities of resources.

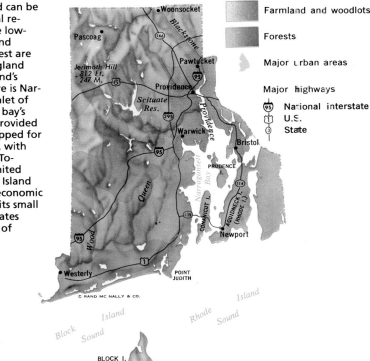

Farmland and woodlots

Forests

Major urban areas

Major highways

95 National interstate
U.S.
State

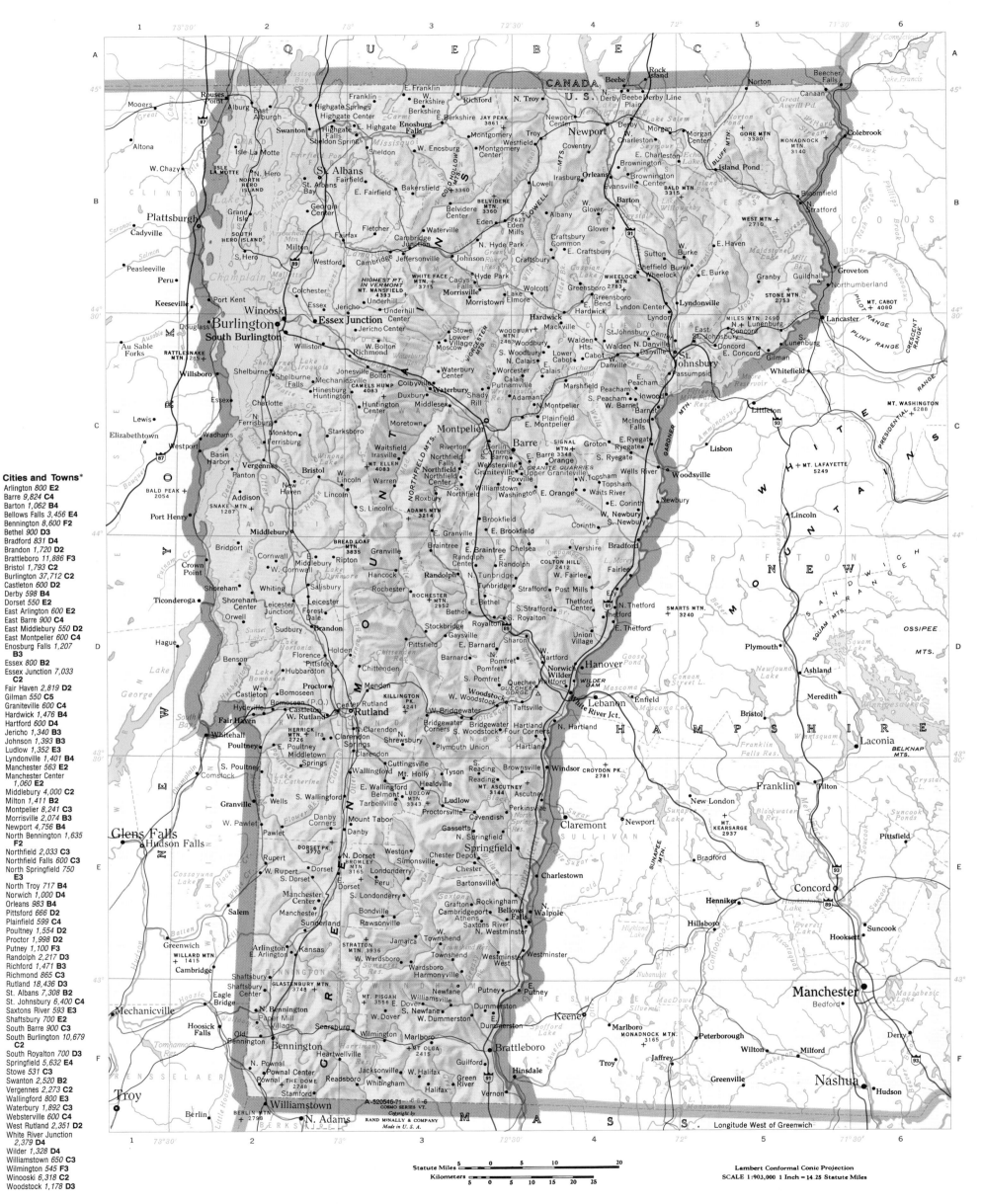

*Populations are for localities, not incorporated towns.

Vermont

POPULATION 511,456.
Rank: 48. *Density:* 55 people/mi² (21 people/km²). *Urban:* 33.8%. *Rural:* 66.2%.
AGE < 20: 33%. 20–40: 33%. 40–65: 23%. >65: 11%.
ETHNIC GROUPS *White:* 99.1%. *Black:* 0.2%. *Spanish origin:* 0.6%. *Native American:* 0.2%. *Other:* 0.5%.

INCOME/CAPITA $7,827. *Rank:* 40.
POLITICS 1948–'1980 elections: *President:* 1 Dem., 8 Rep. *Governor:* 5 Dem., 12 Rep.
ENTERED UNION March 4, 1791, 14th state.
CAPITAL Montpelier, 8,241.
LARGEST CITY Burlington, 37,712.

AREA 9,614 mi² (24,900 km²).
Rank: 43. *Water area:* 341 mi² (883 km²).
ELEVATIONS *Highest:* Mt. Mansfield, 4,393 ft (1,339 m). *Lowest:* Along Lake Champlain 95 ft (29 m).
CLIMATE Long, cold winters with heavy snows; short, mild summers. Moderate rainfall.

Vermont is a rural state in a country where city dwellers far outnumber their rural counterparts. Nearly seventy percent of Vermont's people live outside towns or cities—the highest percentage of rural residents found in any state. Vermont's entire labor force is smaller than that of many large cities, and this helps explain the state's modest contribution to the nation's total productive output.

Although Vermont is actively pursuing development and new businesses, many residents are not anxious for change. Their way of life recalls another era in American history, one more dependent on the land and geared to a slower, more tranquil pace. Vermont's lifestyle and its natural, rustic beauty draw thousands of visitors annually. The state probably would win over many others as the ideal location for a second home; and indeed, second homes comprise a large portion of Vermont's total housing. Income from tourism is supplemented by that from specialized industrial, agricultural, and mineral products. The state's timber and dairy products and its maple syrup, marble, and granite are in demand throughout the country.

A small population enables Vermont's citizens to participate easily in local and state politics. Voters generally have ready access to elected officials and an opportunity to voice their opinions on important public issues. Their town-meeting style of government, in which local budgets, plans, and problems are discussed, is reminiscent of the democracy envisioned by the framers of the Constitution. Through this system, Vermonters have chosen to support education and other government services despite the resulting tax burden, and the state is among the leaders in expenditures for these activities.

Such investments reflect the emphasis the state places on the traditions that form the basis for its life-style. And most residents feel that these commitments are essential if Vermont is to continue as one of the last bastions of American rural life.

Topsham, Vermont, with its scenic beauty and quiet atmosphere, is typical of many communities found in the state. Although such towns are small in population, they reflect the traditional image of the New England countryside.

Economic Activities Whereas Vermont is a well-known mecca for tourists, it is also important for the production of a few specialized manufactured goods, such as machine tools. The computer, wood-products, and printing industries also have facilities here.

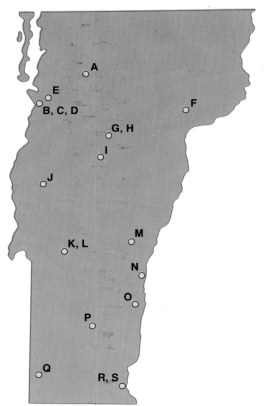

Art centers

A Johnson
　Johnson Friends of the Arts
B, C, D Burlington
　The Arts Source
　Church Street Center
　The George Bishop Lane Series
E Jericho
　Red Mill Arts Committee
F St. Johnsbury
　Catamount Film and Arts Company
G, H Montpelier
　Onion River Arts Council
　Vermont Council on the Arts
I Northfield
　Norwich Arts Forum
J Middlebury
　Frog Hollow Craft Association
K, L Rutland
　Crossroads Arts Council
　Moon Brook Arts Union
M Woodstock
　Tentangle Council on the Arts
N Windsor
　Windsor House
O Springfield
　Southeast Council on the Arts
P Stratton Mountain
　Stratton Arts Festival
Q North Bennington
　Park-McCullough House Association
R, S Brattleboro
　Brattleboro Museum and Arts Center
　Arts Council of Windham County

Commitment to the Arts The beauty of Vermont's landscapes has long inspired artists, and many of the nation's foremost creative personalities have sought the quiet refuge of the state. In order to encourage the development of the arts, Vermont has established many cultural centers that provide classes, workshops, and exhibitions. The centers shown above are just a few of those that foster artistic growth.

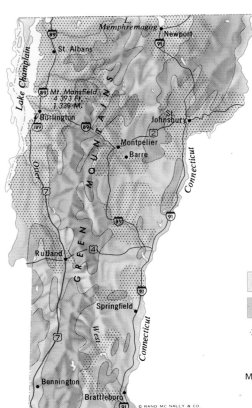

Land Use What Vermont lacks in variety of land use, it makes up for in the extreme beauty of its land. Much of the beauty is derived from the majestic Green Mountains, but a number of other ranges and many scenic rivers add to the state's appeal. Vermont's citizens learned long ago how to best appreciate these lands, and although some sections support a productive dairy industry and provide room for cities, these patterns of land use have stabilized and rarely threaten Vermont's natural splendor.

　Farmland and woodlots

　Forests

　Livestock grazing (areas other than famland)

Major highways
　National interstate
　U.S.

TIDELAND CHANNEL AND PINE HAMMOCK, CHINCOTEAGUE NATIONAL WILDLIFE REFUGE / VIRGINIA

The South

The Land Is Its Own Reward

BY CALEB PIRTLE III

THE SOUTH FOUND ISOLATION IN THE LENGTH and the breadth of its land: It has surrounded me down among the dunes of the Eastern Seaboard, and I have felt it reach back as a lonely spirit into remote, timbered pockets of Appalachian high country, finally tramping across the empty flatlands to hover like an autumn mist above the Mississippi River Valley. A wistful silence covers the landscape, broken only by the dull voice of the sea, a wind that plays its ruffles and flourishes among the magnolias, the far-off wail of a tugboat that pushes cotton from the fields to the factories. For me, the South is music, out of tune perhaps, but never out of time. The terrain is as tough as the granite in its rogue mountains, as fragile as a Piedmont wild flower that fights its way up from the mold and the mildew of the good earth. In the South I can stand alone and not be harassed by the multitudes. It is a land that tempted early settlers, then blanketed them with isolation. The land gave to them the only security they would ever have, which sometimes wasn't a lot, but it fed them and clothed them and even made a few of them prosperous.

The restless sands of the South's coastline beckoned. Mountains rose up in defiance, rewarding only those who were strong enough and stubborn enough to venture into the highlands that became home. Forests brought shade and shelter to a fruitful earth where harvests of cotton and tobacco, indigo and rice, peanuts and corn whiskey eventually broke some men and anointed others with aristocracy. Rivers became highways, quenching the thirst of the crops and giving life to settlements that begat new cities, which rose up like grand sculptures of steel and glass and chrome. Yet the soul of the South would forever lie buried deep among the roots and the riches of the land.

The Atlantic touches the beaches and the isles of the Eastern Seaboard, weaving together the heritage and the colonial traditions of Virginia, the Carolinas, Georgia, and Florida. The Gulf of Mexico sweeps gently onto the western coast of Florida, scattering spun-sugar white sands along the Miracle Strip, and its waters wash ashore among the sea oats and driftwood of Alabama and Mississippi, moving into the shifting marshes of Louisiana.

Alabama
Arkansas
Florida
Georgia
Kentucky
Louisiana
Mississippi
North Carolina
South Carolina
Tennessee
Virginia
West Virginia

Appalachia is the broad spine that links the Southern highlands. The Great Smoky Mountains keep North Carolina and Tennessee shoulder to shoulder. The Alleghenies and the Blue Ridge weld West Virginia, Virginia, and North Carolina inland from the Eastern Shore. Kentucky drops out of the Cumberland Mountains and basks in bluegrass. And Arkansas is crowned by the Ozarks' rugged peaks.

The South was settled, even tamed, by plows that broke new ground and sometimes spoiled it. In time, it belonged to the plantation lord, the farmer, the sharecropper. They fought to take the land, then fought to hold it. Wars left bloodstains upon the soil and a mournful legacy of unmarked graves strewn upon the hillsides. But the land and its promises, the Southerner has always believed, were worth the gambles and the calluses and the costs.

The Tidewater of Virginia reaches for the sea, sprawling across a low, swampy marshland that wades out among the splintered peninsulas toward the curve of Chesapeake Bay. On an April morning in 1607, the *Susan Constant,* the *Godspeed,* and the *Discovery* anchored off the Eastern Shore, and England landed its first colonists upon a narrow, vine-entangled cove that would be known as Jamestown. The colony would struggle, then prosper, then eventually decline. But the cultivation of tobacco as a money crop survived. Homesteads gradually spread out along the York, James, and Rappahannock rivers, built by men whose descendants would demand and die for independence, shouting for liberty at Williamsburg and winning it on the battlefield of Yorktown.

Throughout the Tidewater region, plantations nestle beneath the aging oaks. Thoroughbreds run the meadows. And just offshore, protected and undisturbed, lies Assateague Island, a National Seashore shared with Maryland, where wild ponies graze. Virginia Beach leaves its crowds on the boardwalk and follows its quest for seclusion down among the cypress lagoons that lead on to the sea.

In the Virginia Piedmont, tobacco has ruled the fertile land for more than 300 years, spreading northward from the North Carolina border and pointing toward the falls of the Potomac. The marshes of the Eastern Shore had offered little

hope to those who trusted the earth for their living, so pioneers trekked westward—using the James and Rappahannock rivers to guide them—to a forest wilderness, then axed the trees and sprinkled the Piedmont with farms. Upon it, Thomas Jefferson built Monticello amidst the tobacco and wheat fields of Charlottesville, the Confederacy flew the stars and bars above its capitol at Richmond, and Robert E. Lee rode sadly amongst the peach blossoms of Appomattox to lay down his sword and end the War Between the States.

The Piedmont plateau of North Carolina falls out of the Blue Ridge Divide and moves past Raleigh toward the Atlantic, laced by the Pee Dee, Roanoke, and Catawba rivers. The Uwharrie Mountains, once regal at 20,000 feet, now are merely mounds beneath the woodlands. For time has not been kind to the Uwharries, chiseling and sanding them down to less than 1,000 feet. As North Carolina flattens out to meet the Atlantic, its fields surrender cotton, tobacco, and peanuts. In the Piedmont, the winds frolic through meadows thick with grain, and along the coast, commercial fishing vessels crowd into the quaint harbors of Beaufort, Wilmington, and Morehead City, architectural remnants of colonial seafaring days.

The Outer Banks stand alone. On the northern tip, at Kitty Hawk, where the sands were soft, the Wright brothers, Orville and Wilbur, took an engine and a wooden crate and made an airplane, just beyond Jockey's Ridge, where hang gliders still play with the winds. These outer islands of North Carolina are restless, always moving uneasily, the graveyard of the Atlantic. For centuries they have been battered by an ill-tempered sea. On the far side of the dunes, twisted wooden skeletons poke their broken ribs out of the surf, shipwrecks that the sea had claimed, then tossed ashore, never quite buried, never quite free from the sand that is their tomb. The shoals off Cape Hatteras, shallow and grim, lie in wait, a vicious trap that gives no warning in a maddened Atlantic. For 2,000 ships, the beacon from the cape's lighthouse beamed in vain. Sadness rides with the winds of the Outer Banks. Loneliness is one neighbor who hasn't left.

The Atlantic beaches curve southward to the coast and the Up Country of South Carolina, sand and palmetto that separate Little River and Tybee Sound almost 200 miles away. Charleston is the grande dame of the Low Country coast, down along Oyster Point, where the Ashley and Cooper rivers meet to form the Atlantic Ocean, or so the bluebloods say. Tea olives, banana shrubs, thornless roses, and Confederate jasmine grow in gardens behind colonial walls of stone and iron. The whole countryside slips beneath aged oaks, their branches webbed with Spanish moss, and hangs onto the marshes that step warily out into the black, stained surface of the salt water.

The coastline of South Carolina is rooted with clumps of myrtles and yaupon that bend landward in the Atlantic winds, pointing back toward pine groves and dark lagoons brightened by water lilies and blue hyacinths. The Grand Strand is a frail ladyfinger of sand that runs recklessly from Myrtle Beach to Georgetown, tying together the lazy fishing villages of Murrells Inlet and Pawleys Island, where the salt marshes befriend the ocean.

In 1663, Captain William Hilton sailed toward the beaches of South Carolina and wrote in the log of his ship: "Facing the sea, it is most pines, tall and good. The ayr is clean and sweet; the land passing pleasant . . . the goodliest, best and frutefullest ile ever was seen." Upon those islands—Hilton Head and Kiawah—men have built their resorts, and golf balls now nestle amongst the sand dollars.

When George Washington rode into the Low Country in 1791, he wrote of its "sand and pine barrens," explaining that "a perfect sameness seems to run through all the rest of the country." In time, peach orchards, cotton patches, and tobacco fields would blanket the pine belt uplands.

Long ago, ships sailed with rice and indigo from Georgetown, perched on Winyah Bay. The fields were rich and flooded by the Pee Dee, Sampit, Waccamaw, and Black rivers. But along the coastal swamp, indigo died as a cash crop after the Revolution, and long-fibered sea island cotton seeds were imported from the Bahamas. French silk mills stood ready to buy the crops before they were ever even planted. Upon the Sand Hills surrounding Columbia, blackjack oak and scrub pines are knotted together around flatland bald patches. Melons, tomatoes, and pecan orchards cover ground that was once white with cotton, back before the boll weevil broke both the farmer and his land. That soil, always washing away, has finally been lined with rows of California peas, Tennessee corn, Texas oats, white Dutch clover, Jerusalem artichokes, and Russian sunflowers. Man is fighting to heal his mistakes.

Down in the Georgia Piedmont, between Columbus and Macon, the land suffered the same fate. Before the turn of the century, cotton sapped the soil, and erosion left deep ugly scars in farmland that had been abused. Much of it would become pasture for horses and cattle. But back in the azalea and dogwood ravines, too deep for either man or sawmill to deface, nestles a tiny pocket of Appalachia creased with valleys that have developed what may be the largest number of plant species in the world. Some would feel more at home in the tropics, and others deserve to be out in the arid Southwest. Yet they live in harmony, outcasts in a land that didn't desert them.

The Georgia Piedmont tumbles eastward past great fields of tobacco and peanuts toward the Golden Isles, preserved through so many years by poverty and neglect, shattered by the sounds of war, reshaped at last by the influence of money. Sea Island, a playground for the rich, is separated from the mainland by the storied Marshes of Glynn. St. Simons is at rest beneath its lighthouse, guarded, as always, by the guns of Fort Frederica, a National Monument.

Just inland, Georgia is blessed—or cursed—with the Okefenokee Swamp, once described to me as "one of the quietest, most peaceful places on earth, especially about sundown." The Okefenokee unfolds below Waycross, gripped by lily pads and water lilies and sawgrass that turns brown, out among the cypresses that rise up starkly from a peat bog that, long ago, was part of the ocean floor. Springs feed the swampland. Boat trails cut through its 412,000 acres. And the blue herons, pileated woodpeckers, the white and wood ibis, and red-shouldered hawks are always on the move. It's never wise to hang around too long within reach of the bear,

Overleaf– NEW RIVER VALLEY, BLUE RIDGE PARKWAY / NORTH CAROLINA

RHODODENDRON IN SUNSET, BLUE RIDGE PARKWAY / VIRGINIA

bobcat, and gator, back in that unruly vestige of real estate that can be neither conquered nor civilized.

The Appalachian Mountains have always been the cornerstone of the South, ascending from the Virginias and North Carolina, hiking westward into Kentucky and Tennessee, and knifing down at last into the burly northern heights of Alabama and Georgia. They have long seemed aloof to me, proud, and maybe even haughty. I have often wondered if they looked upon man as an intruder—lost or just passing through—seldom paying much attention when he arrives and never missing him at all when he's gone.

Sweeping away from the slopes of the Blue Ridge in far western Virginia, rolling on down to the foothills of the Alleghenies, is Shenandoah, a valley and a river, whose landscape is dotted with the stone barns, split-rail fences, and gray, weathered cabins of settlers who dared journey beyond a mountain wall to find unspoiled farmland. The Indians quietly referred to the Shenandoah as "the daughter of the stars," there amidst the honeysuckle and Scotch broom that clung to those hillsides of hickory, hemlock, and birch.

A haze wrapped itself like a soft white gauze across the meadows the day I followed the bloody footsteps of Robert E. Lee, Stonewall Jackson, and Philip Sheridan across this valley, a valley too beautiful for battle, but one that had heard the cries of the dying as it changed hands 72 times during the Civil War. The smoke of powdered gunfire must have looked much like the haze that seized the northern funnel of the Shenandoah that morning, as I found myself among the apple blossoms of Winchester. They smelled of spring and peace, and lay against the sky like pink lace. The shadows of seven natural chimneys fell to the earth near Mount Solon, needles against the sun, ragged beneath ramparts that rose tall and defiant as the walls of a medieval castle. Once they had been labeled "The Cyclopean Towers," so reminiscent of the place that sheltered the mythological Cyclopes when they weren't out making thunderbolts for Zeus, or so I was told. Legends grow as often and as tall as the pines in Shenandoah.

We drove southward down the Blue Ridge Parkway, a paved tightrope that runs across the spine of the high country from Waynesboro, Virginia, to Cherokee, North Carolina. The mountains echoed the hardship of those who had transferred their tribulations to the names of the peaks that jutted up before us: Poor, Purgatory, Devil's Backbone.

The Blue Ridge Parkway leads on into the highlands of North Carolina, where old-time mountaineers found it virtually impossible to haul a load of corn over bad roads and rugged terrain. Besides, they discovered that a bushel of corn only sold for $1.50, while a bushel of distilled corn brought $53. So the high-country farmers became moonshiners, and the land brought them a wealth that they never expected. Most of the time it wasn't much. From cornshucks they wove dolls, fashioned rugs and scrub mops, and braided harnesses for mules. From river cane and split oak came baskets. And cowhide was used for shoes, vests, hats, chair bottoms, and even hinges for wooden doors.

Sometimes, however, the land gave more than it promised. In 1799, a 12-year-old boy stumbled across a 17-pound gold nugget near Concord. Having no idea what it was, his family used it as a doorstop for three years, finally selling it for $3.50. Not long afterward, one New York journalist reported he saw "at least one thousand persons at work panning for gold along the banks of Meadow Creek." Within 30 years, they had shoveled more than $10 million worth of the precious metal out of those mountains.

Left– ROCK BRIDGE, RED RIVER GORGE / KENTUCKY

Right– NATURAL BRIDGE / ALABAMA

When Christian Reid gazed out upon the peaks of North Carolina's Blue Ridge in 1876, he prayed, "Dear Lord, I thank Thee for this, Thy gift, the land of sky." He had been smitten by the mountain laurel, rhododendron, and flame azaleas that rose up, as a velvet cloak of red, from the great granite backbone. Above him climbed Mount Mitchell, at 6,684 feet the highest peak east of the Mississippi River, and around him loomed the broad shoulders of the Great Smokies, the Blacks, and the Nantahalas, with more than 45 peaks stretching up toward the clouds at 6,000 feet.

On the western rim of the North Carolina high country, above Asheville, hang gliders dive for the wind that boils up alongside Grandfather Mountain. A rocky trail snakes down past crags and foliage to the Linville Gorge Wilderness Area, and the hardwood thickets of the Pisgah National Forest shut out the sun. In winter, snow ventures back into the ridges, dancing among ashen timber and sitting upon limbs that have been coldly deserted by their leaves. Some of it is even manmade. Boone, Blowing Rock, and Banner Elk find their riches on the slopes of the land as skis leave wayward tracks down mountains whose timbered walls have, at last, been conquered.

The Blue Ridge withers away in the northwest corner of South Carolina, with Sassafras Mountain the last granite outcropping to wedge itself into the red clay plateau. Table Rock and Caesar's Head drop sharply, the outer edges of a high country that has nowhere else to go. It was upon the summit of King's Mountain, near York, that British troops lost their fragile hold on South Carolina soil. The highlands fade quickly. They seem lost and out of place in a land that feels infinitely more comfortable with the sea.

Appalachia for years formed a dense barrier that denied early settlers a chance to journey inland to uncrowded land.

The high country of eastern Kentucky was virtually impregnable until 1775, when Daniel Boone and his men eased through the Cumberland Gap; and cleared a passage west for the Wilderness Road. Boone knew the mountains about as well as anyone, and he called this "the most extraordinary country on which the sun has ever shone."

The Breaks of Kentucky, outside Elkhorn City, slash their way down canyon walls that drop 1,600 feet from the Towers to the Russell Fork of the Big Sandy River, the largest gorge east of the Mississippi. Some call it the Grand Canyon of the South. Not far away is Hazard's Lilley Cornett Woods, holding within it the last remnant of a prehistoric forest—the Mixed Mesophytic—an untrammeled survivor that has successfully dodged the imprint of civilization. Beneath the earth, encompassing 51,000 acres is, as one old-timer said in awe, "the greatest cave that ever was." The famed evangelist Billy Sunday once crawled out of Cave City's Mammoth Cave and explained, "I felt smaller today than I ever did in my life, for I've just returned from exploring caverns that God has scooped out underneath the green hills of Kentucky." Near Corbin, Cumberland Falls roars through the forest, thunder without ceasing, a drumroll of sound that hasn't been silenced for more than 30 million years. It plunges for 68 feet, a broad skirt of water that fans out for 150 feet, the largest waterfall east of the Rockies and south of Niagara. At night, the cascading mist is a mirror for the moonlight, and a curious moonbow rises up out of the falls, a spectre in the darkness.

Tennessee hides its legends within the Great Smoky Mountains, cloaked by a thin will-o-the-wisp mist that entangles itself around the muscled peaks of a fragile highland. The Cherokee Indians know why the haze came. The chiefs from two tribes smoked the pipe of peace, then argued and fought for seven days and nights. The Great Spirit wasn't

pleased and turned the old men into gray flowers called Indian pipes, and he made them grow wherever friends have quarreled. He made the smoke of the pipe hang over the mountains until all people learned to live in peace.

Great Smoky Mountains National Park, spilling from North Carolina into Tennessee, covers 800 square miles with wizened peaks that have been watching over Appalachia for more than 200 million years. The slopes are quilted with wild flowers. Pine, oak, hemlock, and yellow poplar hug to the hideaway refuge for white-tailed deer, ruffed grouse, and Russian boar. The ridges are so steep, it is said, that farmers once climbed up mountainsides across the narrow valley from their gardens and blasted seeds into the ground with shotguns. The summers find shade. October's frosts paint the leaves of sweet gum and sumac purple, fire cherry and hawthorn red, persimmon and butternut yellow. Winter is the gray time of year. Snow. Pale skies. Trees that have undressed for the cold.

More than 1,300 different kinds of flowering plants run rampant in those highlands. In the late 1700s, William Bartram rode into the Smokies and wrote of the azaleas, "The clusters of the blossoms cover the shrubs in such incredible profusion on the hillsides that . . . we were alarmed with apprehension of the hill being on fire." Among the hardwood forests, mountain laurel and rhododendron remain as the bramble brush of the high country, so thick and tangled that old settlers called them "hells."

The Appalachian ridge crawls southward past Knoxville to Chattanooga's Lookout Mountain—leaning into Georgia—where North and South fought their Battle Above the Clouds, 1,700 feet above the Moccasin Bend of the Tennessee River, above Chickamauga Creek, known as "the river of blood." The Georgia mountains are bound in a solitude that comes when no one disturbs a land far from the beaten path. For it has been a long time since greed elbowed its way into the foothills of Dahlonega. The gold in its red clay afflicted men. It was as if someone had sprinkled the rivers and hillsides with tiny grains of gold from a huge salt shaker, tough to find, tougher to hold. From 1828 to 1838, the U.S. Mint at Dahlonega fashioned 1,378,710 coins worth more than $6.1 million from those tiny specks in the clay.

Across the top of Georgia, broad meadows separate the hills. Lakes spread among the valleys, their fingers reaching back into hidden coves that once felt the footsteps and heard the drumbeats of the Civil War. Brasstown Bald climbs highest of all, more than 4,000 feet. Cloudland Canyon hides away a rich lead mine, or so the Cherokees said. Across the summit of Kennesaw Mountain came the army of Gen. William T. Sherman, as he lit the torch to Georgia. Tallulah Gorge plummets as though the earth had forgotten it, a 2,000-foot-deep gash that is tempered by the outpouring of five waterfalls. And the angry Chattooga River surges with whitewater fury, pounding the rock cliffs of its narrow canyons, threading the back-country needle of Appalachia. Just outside Atlanta stands Stone Mountain, the world's largest granite monolith, rising 825 feet above the plain. Into its face the ghostly images of the South's Confederate heritage have been carved: likenesses of Jefferson Davis, Stonewall Jackson, and

Robert E. Lee on horseback. The sculptures are 36 stories high, larger than the figures on Mount Rushmore and the Sphinx at Giza.

Westward, the highlands of north Alabama are sometimes a little mysterious, as though each nook and cranny conceals a world of its own. Old farmsteads spill across broad meadows that chain together the steep bulkhead of the Blue Ridge. DeSoto Falls, near Mentone, tumbles wildly for 80 feet, dropping in a cloud of spray down Little River Canyon, hanging desperately to the strong ridges of Lookout Mountain. Along the walls of the ravine are traces of ancient Indian cave shelters, raided by Hernando DeSoto when he searched for gold in the 1500s but found only heartache and the long way home.

Ragged canyonlands crease the upper brow of Alabama. Hurricane Creek Gorge, near Cullman, ambles amiably, almost lazily, along a clear, spring-fed stream that slices through the last foothills of Appalachia, lost beneath a thick umbrella of mountain laurel, hickory, and pine. Rock Bridge Canyon, outside Hackleburg, is nothing more than a forbidding rock and flora garden where boulders and strange formations were created eons ago by sliding, wayward glaciers. And the Dismals, an untamed and sunken forest misplaced among the mountains, is haunting, secreted behind sheer rock walls and stitched together with trees that don't belong, waterfalls, and tunnels that are staggered throughout the high country. The early settlers of Phil Campbell, Alabama, didn't trust the Dismals at all. The sanctuaries, it seemed, lit up and glowed at night. But the phenomenon is only the dismalites, tiny, turned-on, phosphorescent worms that climb the rocks and appear blue, like the stars, when it's pitch dark. They have never been found anywhere but in the Dismals, in the summertime, when it rains.

The western slopes of the South's high country climb down from the mountains and ease across a gentle rolling plain that flattens out as it finds kinship with the Mississippi River Valley. In Kentucky, old fields range beyond the stone fences of Lexington, topped with the broad leaves of burley, of air-cured Green River dark tobacco, and Western dark-fired leaf tobacco, the kind that winds up in snuff cans. In older times, it was not merely a cash crop, it was cash itself, regarded as legal tender. Why, 26 pounds of good tobacco could buy a pretty fast horse. And Kentucky has had its share of pretty fast horses. More than 20,000 of them—proud and pampered—graze upon pastures of bluegrass. Standardbreds trot the Red Mile in Lexington. Thoroughbreds run for the roses in Louisville's Kentucky Derby. They are millionaires, born under the sign of the dollar. Upon those rich pastures of Kentucky bluegrass, men put white plank fences around their legends. Horses have always been royalty here, at least for a mile and a quarter.

Cotton and tobacco once ruled rural Tennessee, but those crops have turned the meadows over to cattle and walking horses. Much of the old farmland now lies buried beneath lakes, created primarily when the Tennessee Valley Authority harnessed the rivers and transformed the state's economy from agriculture to industry. Some say Tennessee is the home

SPANISH MOSS ALONG SOUTH RIVER / NORTH CAROLINA

of the Great Lakes of the South: Chickamauga and Nickajack at Chattanooga. Fort Patrick Henry at Kingsport. Fort Loudin at Lenoir. Pickwick near Savannah. Percy Priest at Nashville. And, of course, the Land Between the Lakes (Kentucky and Barkley) is a patch of well-protected wilderness that drops out of Kentucky toward Paris, Tennessee.

In the southwestern corner of the state Memphis reigns over the part of the Mississippi where cotton is still king. Old Man River, the Mississippi itself, washes up on the muddy banks of Memphis, then churns on past levees and plantations on its somnolent journey to the sea at New Orleans. The whistle of the steamboat has faded, but barges hitch a ride and dodge the sandbars that lie in wait, sometimes treacherous, always a nuisance.

The western shoreline of the Mississippi nudges Arkansas, described by the Spanish explorer DeSoto as "a fair and pleasant land." Peach orchards huddle together at the base of Red Lick Mountain near Clarksville. The Wiederkehr vineyards drape themselves around the winemaking hamlet of Altus. Throughout Arkansas, the pine forests and mountains hold such bass fishing kingdoms as Bull Shoals, Beaver Lake, Greer's Ferry, Nimrod, Lake Ouachita, and Dardanelle. At Gulpha Gorge, outside Hot Springs, gray boulders hang onto the mountainside like bricks from a wind-chiseled fireplace, embroidered by the delicate pink lady slipper and spider flower, sheltered by a dense oak and hickory forest. Down in the flatlands, below Little Rock, the power of cotton has at last wilted on the vine. Rice fields slosh across the Grand Prairie around Stuttgart, as ducks come winging through the dawn and men who don't trust nature create their own floods, making money from the wet, seemingly worthless plain that God gave them.

Arkansas' hill country lies northward. We found a scrapbook of hopes and disappointments in the Boston Mountains, all written on the weathered sidings of abandoned towns that struggled for a while, then gave up the ghost. In Winslow, an old-timer told me that Satan himself could feel right at home at Devil's Den State Park. When early-day settlers stumbled across that dragon-mouthed cavern, they were convinced that they had found the final resting place of the evil old archangel. The Ozark Mountains stand tall, and the land is insolent and harsh, a hard-scrabble slice of plow-scarred rocks and unmarked graves among the scrub oaks. The mountains dared man to survive, and he cursed the beauty that he revered. The Buffalo River brings relief to the rugged, isolated terrain, twisting along massive rock cliffs that cluster across the top of Arkansas, moving past the old abandoned zinc mining country around Yellville, and flowing on to Ponca's Lost Valley, sealed off by a natural bridge that ties the stark limestone bluffs to a gentle, sloping hillside. It hides at the end of a small tunnel that winds like a corkscrew between sheer cliffs for nearly a mile to the cave of Crystal Springs, leading on to Clark Creek and a ravine that is dotted, like a well-used pincushion, with tiny caves. Not far away, the valley abruptly ends, and Crystal Eden Falls pours from a little cavern, splashing downward over a sandstone draw to the creek, 200 feet below. The sun touches the water, and the water blesses the earth, and, for a mo-

ment, the Ozarks don't feel so harsh anymore.

The muddy, slow-moving Mississippi River leaves Arkansas behind and ambles toward the Gulf of Mexico, clutching the western edge of Louisiana firmly in its grasp. It has long been the major highway for the South to ship its crops to the market center of New Orleans, heavy laden with flatboats and keelboats of tobacco and cotton, of rice and sugar cane from the moist soil of Louisiana itself. The abundance of river traffic once prompted Thomas Jefferson to say, "The position of New Orleans certainly destines it to be the greatest city the world has ever seen." Today New Orleans leads North American ports in tonnage handled annually, ahead of New York and Houston.

Louisiana has always depended on its waterways, especially back among the live oak illusions of its Cajun country, that strange blend of French, Indian, Spanish, and Creole culture that blossoms amongst the swamps and levees below Lafayette and Baton Rouge. The bayous of south Louisiana curl through palmetto and cypress knees, cast upon the land like the thin, broken strands of a wind-blown spider web, wet, brackish roadways for log pirogues that, Cajuns swear, can ride on a heavy dew. Bayou Teche, sliding past New Iberia, is the most majestic of all, a place created, the Indians say, by the writhing of a huge silver snake that wore deep grooves in the soft, decaying dirt, then waited for the water to fill the cuts where it had passed by. The earth continually shifts down where alligator grass and salt cane form a walking prairie across the marshlands. Earthen levees push back the sea, and gnarled oaks bitterly fight for life upon the

MISSISSIPPI RIVER AT NATCHEZ / MISSISSIPPI

chênières, ridges of sand on a barrier beach where salt water slowly and ultimately sucks the life away, leaving the trees to lean like gray, shrunken crosses upon the sands that doomed them.

The pines of Louisiana crowd the sandhills around Shreveport, leading southeast to the Kisatchie National Forest and the logging industry of Winnfield. Monroe found itself rooted to a vast pool of natural gas. And Lake Charles acquired wealth from oil and gas that lingered deep beneath the tides of the Gulf. The old crops faded, and columned mansions became rotting, abandoned hulks, keeping watch over a land that plantation lords had owned and lost.

Behind the chênières, the moss-woven innards of the Atchafalaya Swamp are home for fish and wildlife. One of America's last great river swamps, the Atchafalaya seethes with crawfish; it floods when it loses its temper. The Atchafalaya, ranging from Lafayette to Morgan City, is unpredictable and fickle. Old men live back in the swamp, and they've never owned automobiles. No need to, they say. "There ain't no roads back in there." A pirogue gets them around just fine. One of them said of the Atchafalaya: "Take almost any acre of land you want, and—during a single year—you can trap otter, raccoon, mink, oppossum, skunk, and nutria on it. You can hunt deer, rabbit, squirrel, woodcock, or ducks on it. And you can catch bass, perch, catfish, sacalait, buffalo, and crawfish on it. It just depends on whether that acre is wet or dry."

Beyond the eastern banks of the Mississippi River lies a land where plantation owners and sharecroppers alike based their lone hope on the success of the cotton boll. Since 1917, the world's largest long staple cotton market has been tucked away in downtown Greenwood, Mississippi. And the first cotton crop in the world produced entirely by machinery came out of Mississippi's Coahoma County. Now rice, corn, pecans, wheat, oats, and soybeans—even oil and gas wells—occupy that delta dirt where cotton no longer is royalty.

Mississippi is a land that has known the best of times and the worst. Antebellum millionaires built the white-columned mansions of Natchez beneath magnolias and on the front doorstep of Old Man River. Civil War gunfire splintered the pineland thickets of Tupelo and brought starvation to the steep bluffs of Vicksburg.

Sawmill towns like Hattiesburg have been thrust into Mississippi's long leaf pine belt, which wraps itself in the DeSoto National Forest. And Columbus surrounds the grandeur of its antique homes with the Tombigbee National Forest. Pine and hardwood knit the states of the South with a bond as common as grits and redeye gravy. Nowhere is the beauty of the woodland more prevalent than along the Natchez Trace Parkway as it rambles through Tennessee and Mississippi. From the tracks of wild animals it originally came, a pathway through canebrakes and unruffled meadows, a vital link in the early 1800s between Nashville and Natchez. The road through the wilderness has been eulogized in pavement by the National Park Service, a 306-mile memorial to the men and women who carted their hopes, dreams, and fears westward. The parkway doesn't pretend to travel the exact route of the Natchez Trace, but it never strays far

from that early path, paralleling at times the historic ruts that wagon wheels and horses' hooves trampled deep into the tender loess soil.

The forests are a dark shelter upon the face of Mississippi. The Gulf Coast is free and open, reaching past its own beach toward the dunes, low marsh grass, and sea oats of Ship Island. Along with the isles of Horn, Cat, and Petit Bois, Ship Island is an unadorned link in the Gulf Islands National Seashore chain, where the ruins of Fort Massachusetts are the last sentry, a wasted sentry, built in 1856 to protect the coast from a Spanish invasion that never came. The sands of the Gulf drift eastward, a barefoot world where there's a beach for every mood. Dauphin Island is the orphan scape of Alabama, in the mouth of Mobile Bay, wrapped in a warm, wrinkled blanket of solitude, a place to be lonely, to laugh, to catch the sun that no one ever holds for long.

From the coves and inlets of its chiseled coastline, Alabama stretches northward into the black agricultural soil of its midlands, where peanut vines cover the fields of Dothan, primarily because George Washington Carver discovered that the peanut could be a commercially profitable crop in soil that had been depleted by planting too much cotton and was plagued by too many boll weevils. Only the antebellum homes of Montgomery reflect the heritage of cotton. The land had to find its fortune from some other source. In time, it did. Around the foothills that one day would harbor Birmingham, Creek Indians used iron ore for war paint. That hematite intrigued the white man, drawing him into the bowl between the mountains where he found a valley of limestone, buttressed on one side by a massive hill of red iron ore and on the other by a mighty coal range. It turned out to be the only place in the world where the three ingredients for making steel are in such close proximity. Soon the furnaces of Birmingham fired Alabama with a new kind of wealth, but wealth taken, as always, from the goodness of the land.

The northern crest of Florida weds itself to the piney woods of lower Alabama, a rural panhandle that is checkered with farms and weather-beaten cabins. It exudes a down-home kind of charm, mirrored by the Suwannee, the river Stephen Foster wrote about but never saw. In central Florida, cattle graze the ranges of Kissimmee, just as they have ever since Ponce de Leon first brought cows ashore in 1521. There amidst the palms, the sun nurtures citrus crops that grow thick and ripe in an eden that is forever drenched by the artificial rains of irrigation. More oranges are grown on the ridge of Polk County alone, for example, than in any other state. And sugar cane nails its tall stalks to the black dirt surrounding Lake Okeechobee, just beyond the seemingly endless fields of beans and corn.

On the southern tip of Florida the Everglades tremble, a land of 'gators and gardens, trapped amidst moss and quicksand, wallowing in bogs and mangrove thickets. For some, the swamps are pristine, a world that captures the holy essence of life in chaos and transition. The fragile river of grass sprawls over 5,000 square miles, wild and shallow, its nearly 1.4 million acres protected by the National Park Service. One day an airboat skimmed the sawgrass, carrying me back into the mysterious heart of the mangrove and cypress swamp-

land, back where alligators lie like logs in the sun, deer run free, panthers prowl, bears stalk, and the bald eagle is among the 326 species of birds that circle overhead. I sped past egrets and the roseate spoonbills, huge pink birds with crimson splashes, creatures we almost lost because man slaughtered them to make feathered plumes for women's hats. At times, the water was barely two inches deep beneath the boat as it barreled down narrow sloughs, cutting around the hammocks, islands of trees without soil. An otter chased a frog. A deer scooted back on dry land with suspicious eyes. An ibis strutted into the green shadows. The swamp is beautiful, I said. Yes, I was told, but then, so is a snake.

Florida's coast has long been the land of great expectations. Facing the Atlantic, eight flags have flown above Fernandina Beach, waving proudly over the sweep of salt marshes and mud flats that are left naked when tidal waters sneak away into the night. Amelia Island has become a resort that blends luxury into oak, palmetto, and sunken forests that creep to the feet of dunes and bend before the spray of ocean winds. Upon the hard-packed beaches of Daytona and Ormand, Fred Marriott drove his famed Stanley Steamer Rocket to a world record of 127.6 miles an hour, piloting the first auto to ever travel faster than two miles a minute. A scientific magazine of the day proclaimed that such speeds "caused harmful chemical reactions in the body, producing temporary insanity." Thus was born the term "speed demon." From the sands of Cape Canaveral, other rockets climbed to the moon and beyond, while not far away, upon the shallow Indian River, brown pelicans nest safely in the first national wildlife refuge ever established in America. Miami has built huge hotels and land-grabbing condominiums atop the sands where man once walked, then tried to create his own beaches—only to see them destroyed by the sea.

Somewhere just south of the Florida Keys, the Atlantic and the Gulf of Mexico become as one, out where the tarpon explode from turquoise waters and sailfish cut into an alley that bears their name. Coral reefs bare their beauty at John Pennekamp, the nation's first underwater park. Birds rise in great winged curtains, filling the sky and blotting out a sur-

Left– TUPELO AND CYPRESS ALONG SUWANNEE RIVER / GEORGIA

Above– BALD CYPRESS, BAYOU GRAND / LOUISIANA

prised sun above the Florida Bay rookeries of Tavernier. And tiny key deer, each the size of a collie dog, bounce into the brush, sliding past the bored white herons of Big Pine Key.

The Gulf shovels white sands up on the west coast. Crescent-shaped Sanibel and Captiva islands, off Fort Myers, are known worldwide for the shells that are deposited on their beaches. They are the last holdouts: a land where seashells and driftwood still outnumber the footprints. Marco Island has been overrun by tourists and developers. And up along the coast of Florida's panhandle drift the sands of the Miracle Strip, crisp, the texture of new-fallen snow, linked by the dunes of Panama City, Destin, Fort Walton Beach, and Pensacola. The sands. They are solitude or soaked with suntan lotion. They hear the lonely cry of a seagull or the white-knuckled scream of a roller coaster. They are at peace or in panic. Across the kindly waters of Escambia Bay, Pensacola Beach is the mute legacy of Spanish soldiers who trekked upon the sands in 1559 and tried to build a future. But, alas, a hurricane chased them away. Now, only the hollow eyes of crumbling Fort Pickens remain, the hermit of the dunes.

I have always felt a close kinship with the South. It is a place where I have lost myself for a while and felt a little sad when I found my way out again. The mountains, no matter how aloof, could make me forget my troubles. Or the oceans, no matter how angry, could wash them away. Somewhere through the years, the South became a friend, or perhaps it has always been family. Its isolation became my escape, the solitude my home. The land was good to the South. It provided opportunity, and it promised wealth. And sometimes, the beauty and the sanctity of the land were the only rewards it had to offer. Most times, that was enough.

Above– FALL CREEK LAKE, FALL CREEK FALLS STATE PARK / TENNESSEE

Right– DAWN, CADES COVE, GREAT SMOKY MOUNTAINS NATIONAL PARK / TENNESSEE

Left– NEW RIVER GORGE, GRANDVIEW STATE PARK / WEST VIRGINIA

Right– CEDAR ON LEDGE RIM, MAGAZINE MOUNTAIN / ARKANSAS

Left– CUMBERLAND FALLS STATE PARK / KENTUCKY

Below– DOGWOOD, TABLE ROCK STATE PARK / SOUTH CAROLINA

Top– PINNACLE OVERLOOK, CUMBERLAND GAP NATIONAL
HISTORIC PARK / TENNESSEE-KENTUCKY-VIRGINIA

Bottom– CASH LAKE, DESOTO STATE PARK / ALABAMA

Left– NATIVE GRASSES, PEA RIDGE NATIONAL MILITARY PARK / ARKANSAS

Above– SEA OATS, SANIBEL ISLAND / FLORIDA

Left– COCO PALMS, KEY WEST / FLORIDA

Right– POND CYPRESS AND LILY PADS, COOKS HAMMOCK / FLORIDA

Maps of the South

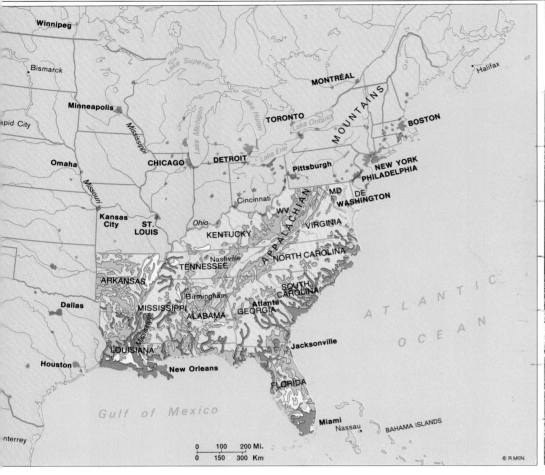

Land Use Swamps and forests edge the extensive coastline of the Southeast, extending inland along rivers that penetrate the rolling terrain of the interior. Farmland with woodlots characterize many inner regions, although rich, almost treeless expanses of agricultural land can be found—especially along the Mississippi River. Large expanses of forests occupy the steeper slopes and higher elevations of the Appalachian Mountains.

The Appalachians cover much of the Southeast from West Virginia to Alabama. Parallel northeast-to-southwest mountains and valleys have influenced transportation, with east-west communication routes funneled through valleys and relatively few gaps in the terrain. Settlement and cultivation, too, are restricted to valleys. But at the same time, the mountains contribute an abundant mineral and forest resource and great natural beauty for a growing tourist trade. The picture shows a typical ridge-and-valley area near Spruce Knob in West Virginia.

Few regions have drawn their legends and heroes in such fine detail as has the Southeast. With the cultural inheritance of the Old South, these states evoke images of a life-style and landscape as unique and vivid as those cherished by the Yankees of New England. Although the region's tradition suggests an origin of common heritage, the rich imagery of the Southeast springs from the diversity of its land and people more than from their similarity. The region may lack the geographic extremes of rugged mountain and desert, but here is just as dramatic a cultural landscape.

The Southeast expresses a pattern, set long before the Civil War, that differentiates between the upland and lowland South. The former is a region of small farms; the latter was originally dedicated to plantation agriculture. These two different regions are splintered even further. The lowlands are composed of the Atlantic Sea Islands, the Coastal Lowland, and the Piedmont. Waves of settlers emanating from the East, the North, and the Gulf Coast swept across the region to compound cultural fragmentation. A community's distance from coastal-area cities—such as Baltimore, Richmond, Wilmington, Charleston, and New Orleans—often accentuated existing differences. Discord was more common than harmony; upland farmers often allied themselves politically against the lowland planters.

The Southeast still reflects the strain of its cultural fragmentation, especially at its geographic extremes. Florida contrasts so sharply with the rest of the Southeast in character and demography that it could almost belong to a different region. Parts of Maryland and Virginia are included in America's northeastern megalopolis, and both these states are tied to the national government in Washington, D.C.

These differences make it difficult to generalize about population growth and change in the Southeast. Even patterns of migration into, around, and out of the region are complicated. As a consequence,

while the area is growing in population, the age, racial, and educational profiles of its states are changing at different rates. Rural blacks tend to leave the region or move to its cities, and their white counterparts remain in the region, also moving primarily to its cities. Retirees and vacationers continue to seek out inland areas, such as the Arkansas Ozarks, and Atlantic and Gulf Coast communities. Meanwhile, cities such as Miami and Tampa have attracted immigrants from Caribbean nations; and other rapidly growing cities, exemplified by Atlanta, now draw northern business people and professionals in large numbers. Manufacturing and construction industries also more frequently attract workers from the North.

Forecasting the region's economic future is similarly problematic. The industrial accomplishments of certain Southeast states rival those of their northern counterparts. Activities such as the production of chemicals are found in the factories of Delaware and in the plants of the Louisiana-Texas Gulf Coast.

Low literacy rates, rural poverty, and other barriers to economic progress are being overcome. The Southeast is also overcoming its prolonged reliance on agriculture and its general failure of the past to build a manufacturing base commensurate with its size. However, this one-time drawback can act as an asset. Unencumbered by a large amount of heavy industry, the Southeast is in an excellent position to diversify into today's light and high-technology industries.

In truth, there are many Southeasts, reflecting the traditional difference between upland and lowland and the unique way each state's economy is diversifying. States such as Georgia have launched themselves into the mainstream of current American economic trends; others, such as Florida, have been sought out by the rest of the nation. Thus, behind the evocative images of the Old South lie many New Souths, and the features of each are early in the making.

Contributors to a Growing Economy In the past decades, the basis of the Southeast's economy has shifted from agricultural to industrial. Manufacturing growth has been facilitated by an influx of high-technology industries. But outside influences, such as government and tourism, have also had economic impact. Federal facilities can be found in every state; and history, hospitality, transportation routes, and recreational facilities are credited for growing tourist expenditures. In addition, an amenable climate and a perceived low cost of living are attracting an increasing number of retirees.

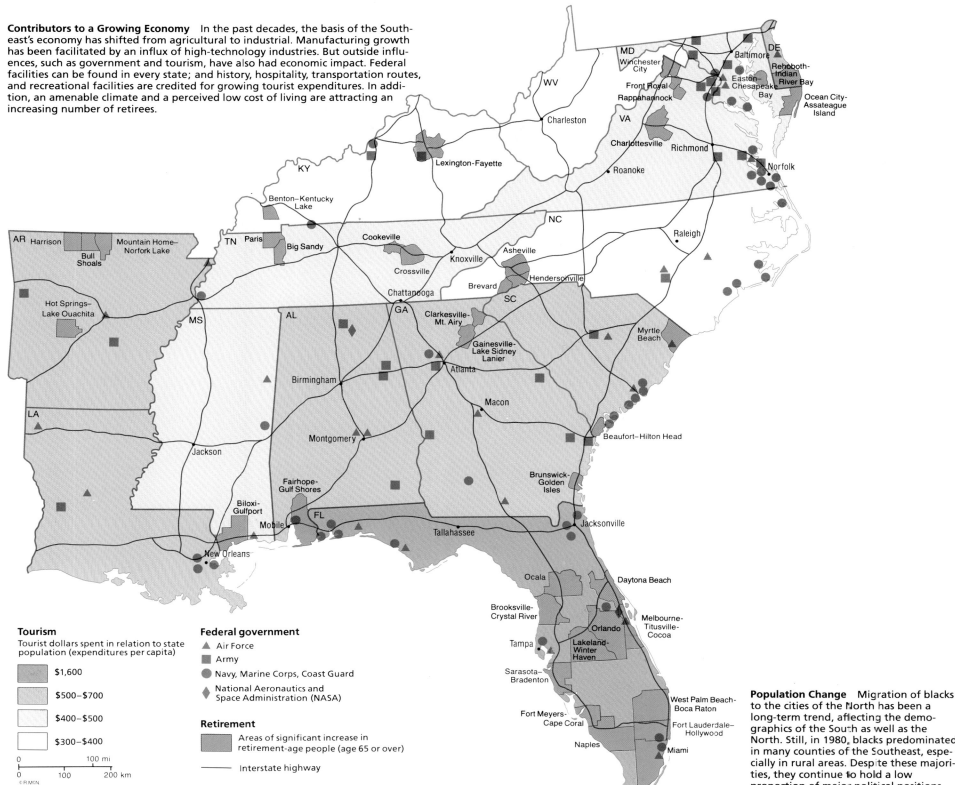

Tourism
Tourist dollars spent in relation to state population (expenditures per capita)

- $1,600
- $500–$700
- $400–$500
- $300–$400

0   100 mi
0   100   200 km
© R.MℕN

Federal government
- ▲ Air Force
- ■ Army
- ● Navy, Marine Corps, Coast Guard
- ♦ National Aeronautics and Space Administration (NASA)

Retirement
- Areas of significant increase in retirement-age people (age 65 or over)
- —— Interstate highway

Barrier islands lie off many coastal areas of the Southeast, serving to protect the mainland from certain ocean effects. The natural forces of tides, storms, climate, and shifting sea level—as well as human intervention—make these islands unstable landforms, with constantly changing shapes. In their natural state, the barrier islands provide a sanctuary for fish and wildlife, and many have been preserved as parts of national seashores. Shown here, Horn Island off the coast of Mississippi is part of the Gulf Islands National Seashore.

Population Change Migration of blacks to the cities of the North has been a long-term trend, affecting the demographics of the South as well as the North. Still, in 1980, blacks predominated in many counties of the Southeast, especially in rural areas. Despite these majorities, they continue to hold a low proportion of major political positions. Voter-registration campaigns aimed at black communities may help to alter this reality.

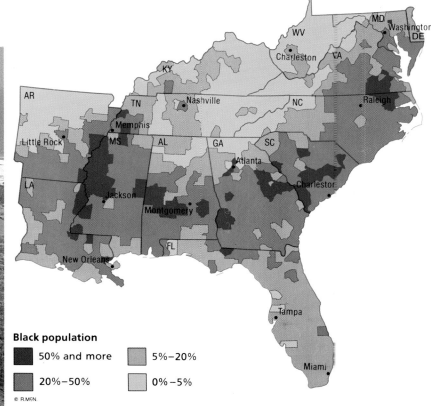

Black population
- 50% and more
- 20%–50%
- 5%–20%
- 0%–5%

© R.MℕN

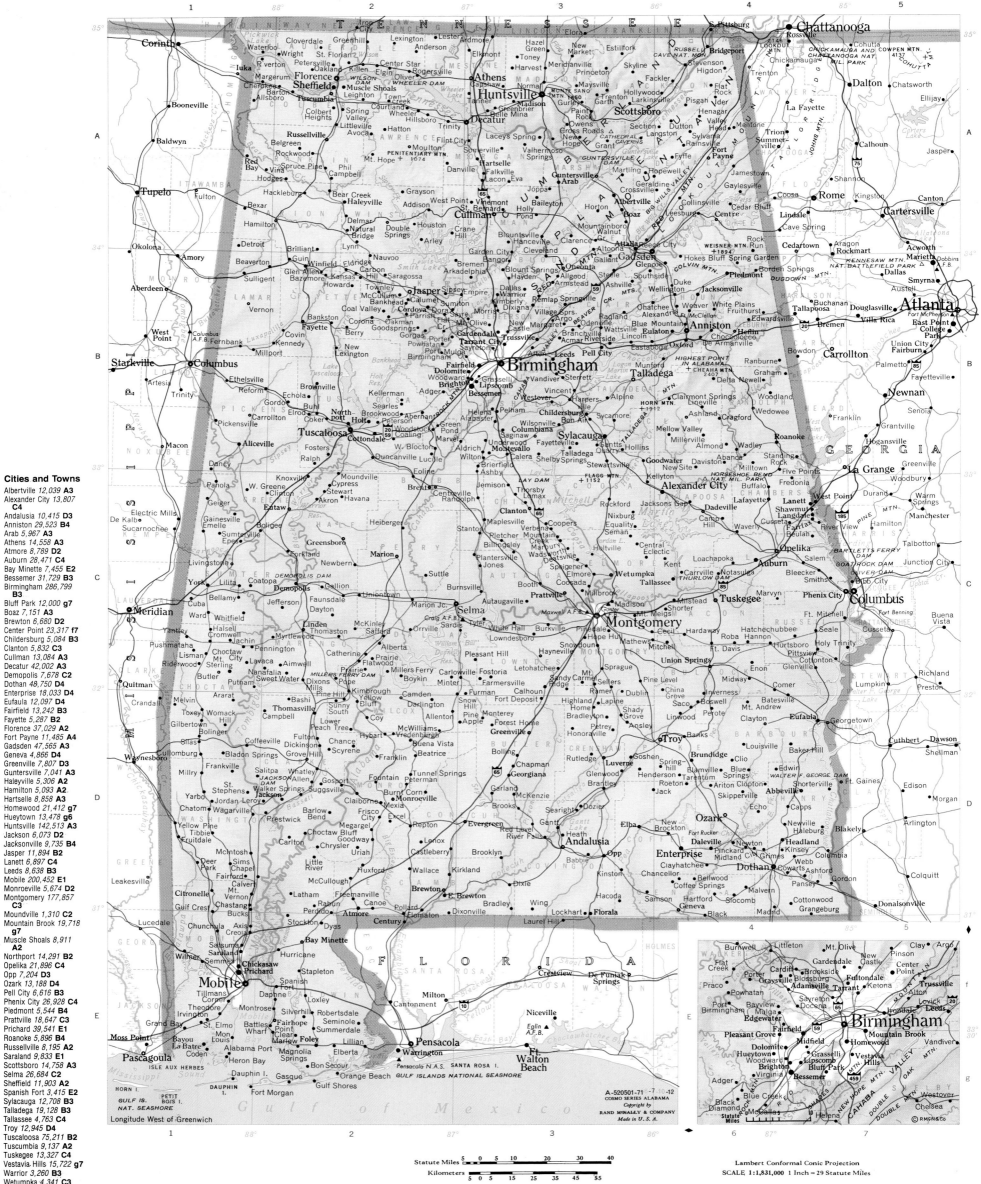

Alabama

POPULATION 3,893,888.
Rank: 22. *Density:* 77 people/mi²
(30 people/km²). *Urban:* 60%.
Rural: 40%.
AGE *< 20:* 34%. *20–40:* 31%.
40–65: 24%. *>65:* 11%.
ETHNIC GROUPS *White:* 73.8%.
Black: 25.6%. *Spanish origin:*
0.9%. *Native American:* 0.2%.
Other: 0.4%.

INCOME/CAPITA $7,488. *Rank:* 47.
POLITICS 1948–1980 elections:
President: 1 Am. Independent, 4
Dem., 3 Rep., 1 States' Rights
Dem. *Governor:* 8 Dem., 0 Rep.
ENTERED UNION December 14,
1819, 22nd state.
CAPITAL Montgomery, 177,857.
LARGEST CITY Birmingham,
284,413.

AREA 51,705 mi² (133,914 km²).
Rank: 28. *Water area:* 938 mi²
(2,429 km²).
ELEVATIONS *Highest:* Cheaha Mtn.,
2,407 ft (734 m). *Lowest:* Gulf of
Mexico shoreline, sea level.
CLIMATE Humid with long, hot
summers; short, mild winters.
Long growing season, heavy
rainfall.

In heavy industry, Alabama is a powerhouse of the Deep South. Its principal manufacturing city, Birmingham, is sometimes called the Pittsburgh of the South. Alabama is often held up as an example of how the agricultural South of the past is changing into a new industrial region, better integrated into the national trend away from farming and toward industry.

Like many other southern states, Alabama once depended on a single crop, cotton, as the basis for its economy. Fortunately, deposits of iron ore, coal, and limestone—rarely found together in a single southern state—helped spur development of heavy manufacturing. Thus, even though cotton remains an important crop, Alabama has diversified into sectors that other states lacked the resources to enter.

Today, Alabama's coal and oil not only power the steel mills and metal-fabrication plants near Birmingham but also fuel its petrochemical and plastics industries. Linked northward to Tennessee's TVA-inspired industrialization and southward to the manufacturing growth along the Gulf of Mexico from Florida to Texas, Alabama is in a position to tap two sources of development and change. This potential should not be underestimated, for Alabama is also well equipped with transportation systems that can support new growth. These systems include waterways, railroads, and the modern seaport of Mobile.

However, Alabama's progress has not been solely in the industrial sector. The state's one-crop agriculture has also diversified in ways that serve to stabilize the economy. Alabama has reforested timberland to ensure lumber harvests in the future. Dairy farming, poultry and cattle raising, and soybean production have all increased substantially and contribute to national as well as regional markets. Moreover, Alabama's race relations have improved since the days when Martin Luther King focused national attention on racial problems.

However, the shift to a prosperous industrial economy supplemented by agriculture is not complete. As elsewhere in the South, per capita income is relatively low, and much of the population lives in rural areas. Yet, while Alabama is still in a state of transition, the outlines of a successful future have been established.

Alabama's natural resources are not confined to its land area. Like many other Gulf Coast states, Alabama contains offshore natural-gas deposits. Rising gas production is a result of recent drilling operations taking place at the mouth of Mobile Bay and other areas.

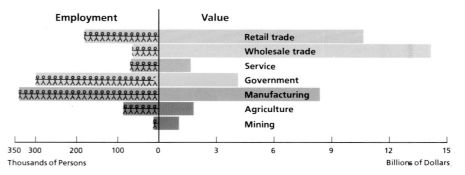

Economic Activities   Alabama's status as an industrial powerhouse is reflected in the state's manufacturing, processing, and wholesaling industries. The production of primary metals, paper and pulp, food products, textiles, rubber, and many other goods contributes to the state's reputation in industry.

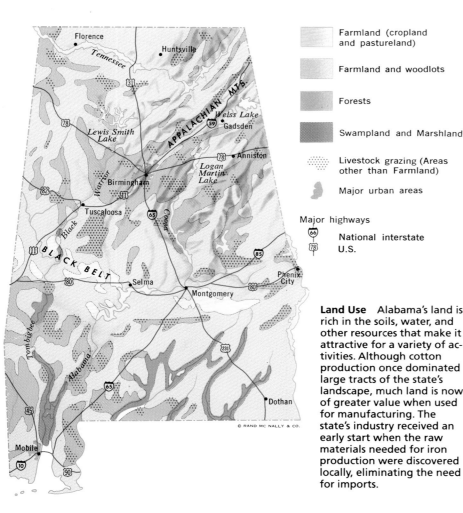

Land Use   Alabama's land is rich in the soils, water, and other resources that make it attractive for a variety of activities. Although cotton production once dominated large tracts of the state's landscape, much land is now of greater value when used for manufacturing. The state's industry received an early start when the raw materials needed for iron production were discovered locally, eliminating the need for imports.

Legend for Land Use map:
- Farmland (cropland and pastureland)
- Farmland and woodlots
- Forests
- Swampland and Marshland
- Livestock grazing (Areas other than Farmland)
- Major urban areas

Major highways
- National interstate
- U.S.

Major forest types
- Longleaf pine, slash pine
- Loblolly pine, shortleaf pine
- Oak, pine
- Oak, hickory
- Oak, gum, cypress
- Less than 10% forest

Southern Forests   Almost two-thirds of Alabama's land is covered with forests, and these constitute an important natural resource for the state. Most of this forest area is used for private commercial enterprises; thus, forestry is one of Alabama's major industries. Lumbering in the state depends upon the widespread pine forests, which contain loblolly, shortleaf, slash, and other pines that are common throughout the Southeast. Over the past decades, conservation practices have been introduced to ensure the future success of activities based upon this resource.

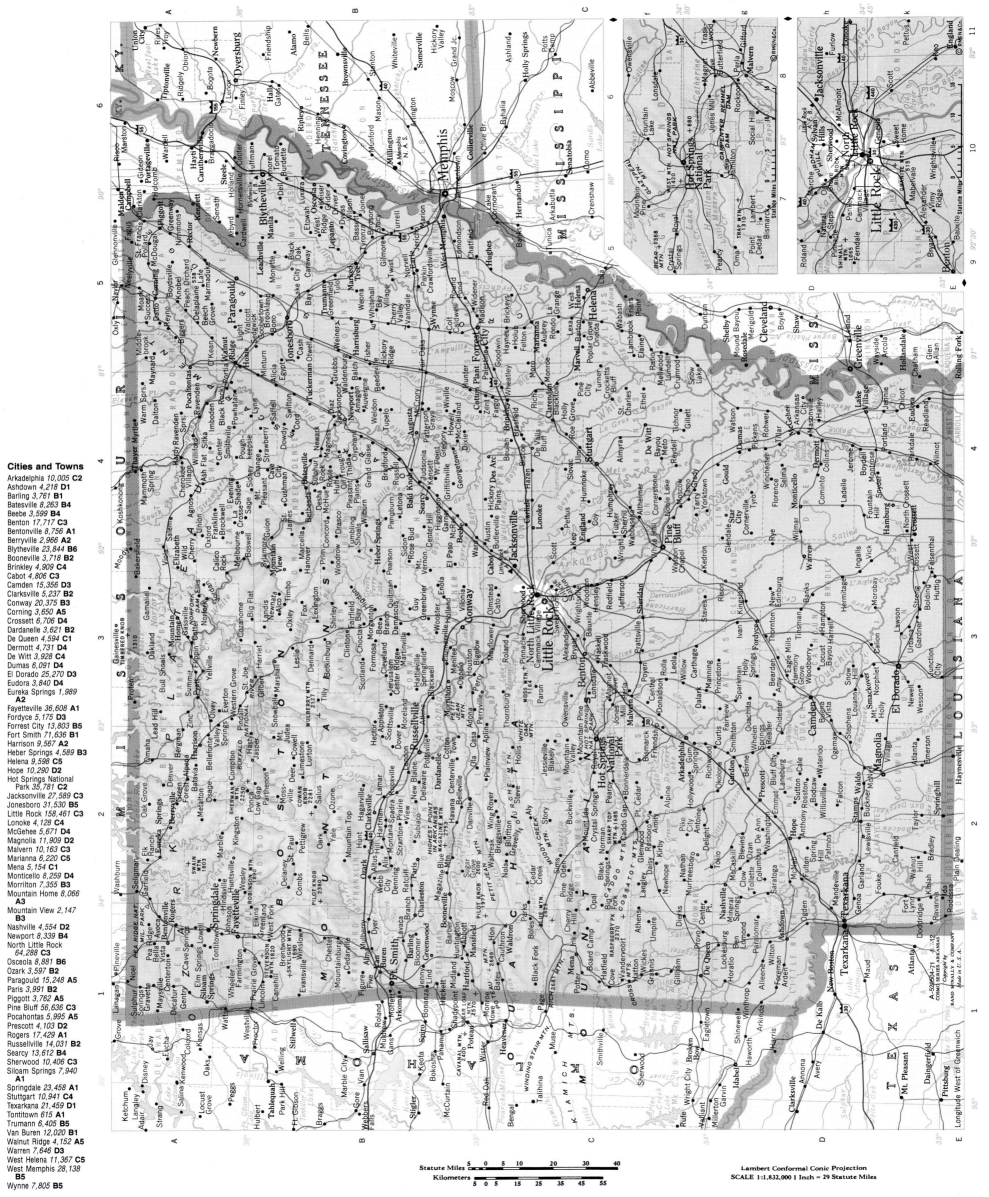

Cities and Towns

Arkadelphia 10,005 **C2**
Ashdown 4,218 **D1**
Barling 3,761 **B1**
Batesville 8,263 **B4**
Beebe 3,599 **B4**
Benton 17,717 **C3**
Bentonville 8,756 **A1**
Berryville 2,966 **A2**
Blytheville 23,844 **B6**
Booneville 3,718 **B2**
Brinkley 4,909 **C4**
Cabot 4,806 **C3**
Camden 15,356 **D3**
Clarksville 5,237 **B2**
Conway 20,375 **B3**
Corning 3,650 **A5**
Crossett 6,706 **D4**
Dardanelle 3,621 **B2**
De Queen 4,594 **C1**
Dermott 4,731 **D4**
De Witt 3,928 **C4**
Dumas 6,091 **D4**
El Dorado 25,270 **D3**
Eudora 3,840 **D4**
Eureka Springs 1,989
 A2
Fayetteville 36,608 **A1**
Fordyce 5,175 **D3**
Forrest City 13,803 **B5**
Fort Smith 71,626 **B1**
Harrison 9,567 **A2**
Heber Springs 4,589 **B3**
Helena 9,598 **C5**
Hope 10,290 **D2**
Hot Springs National
 Park 35,781 **C2**
Jacksonville 27,589 **C3**
Jonesboro 31,530 **B5**
Little Rock 158,461 **C3**
Lonoke 4,128 **C4**
McGehee 5,671 **D4**
Magnolia 11,909 **D2**
Malvern 10,163 **C3**
Marianna 6,220 **C5**
Mena 5,154 **C1**
Monticello 8,259 **D4**
Morrilton 7,355 **B3**
Mountain Home 8,066
 A3
Mountain View 2,147
 B3
Nashville 4,554 **D2**
Newport 8,339 **B4**
North Little Rock
 64,288 **C3**
Osceola 8,881 **B6**
Ozark 3,991 **B2**
Paragould 15,248 **A5**
Paris 3,991 **B2**
Piggott 3,762 **A5**
Pine Bluff 56,636 **C3**
Pocahontas 5,995 **A5**
Prescott 4,103 **D2**
Rogers 17,429 **A1**
Russellville 14,031 **B2**
Searcy 13,612 **B4**
Sherwood 10,406 **C3**
Siloam Springs 7,940
 A1
Springdale 23,458 **A1**
Stuttgart 10,941 **C4**
Texarkana 21,459 **D1**
Tontitown 615 **A1**
Trumann 6,405 **B5**
Van Buren 12,020 **B1**
Walnut Ridge 4,152 **A5**
Warren 7,646 **D3**
West Helena 11,367 **C5**
West Memphis 28,138
 B5
Wynne 7,805 **B5**

Statute Miles 5 0 10 20 30 40
Kilometers 5 0 15 25 35 45 55

Lambert Conformal Conic Projection
SCALE 1:1,832,000 1 Inch = 29 Statute Miles

Arkansas

POPULATION 2,286,435.
Rank: 33. *Density:* 44 people/mi²
(17 people/km²). *Urban:* 51.6%.
Rural: 48.4%.
AGE *<20:* 33%. *20–40:* 29%.
40–65: 24%. *>65:* 14%.
ETHNIC GROUPS *White:* 82.7%.
Black: 16.3%. *Spanish origin:*
0.8%. *Native American:* 0.4%.
Other: 0.6%.

INCOME/CAPITA $7,268. *Rank:* 48.
POLITICS 1948–1980 elections:
President: 1 Am. Independent, 6
Dem., 2 Rep. *Governor:* 14 Dem.,
3 Rep.
ENTERED UNION June 15, 1836,
25th state.
CAPITAL Little Rock, 158,461.
LARGEST CITY Little Rock.

AREA 53,187 mi² (137,753 km²).
Rank: 27. *Water area:* 1,109 mi²
(2,872 km²).
ELEVATIONS *Highest:* Magazine
Mtn., 2,753 ft (834 m). *Lowest:*
Along Ouachita River, 55 ft
(17 m).
CLIMATE Moderately long, hot
summers; short, mild winters.
Abundant rainfall.

Over the past two decades, Arkansas has been recharting its course in order to meet the future. For much of its history, Arkansas was a one-crop state, dominated by cotton. The focus on one crop meant that other resources remained undeveloped.

For generations, however, Arkansas had little reason to change. Cotton was a lucrative business in the south and east regions; and cotton growers, shippers, and manufacturers could easily wrest political control of the state from farmers living in the forested uplands to the north and west. The only early pretender to cotton's throne arose from the development of Arkansas's vast bauxite deposits, which still account for much of the total United States supply. In time, however, the people came to realize that their land could be put to more productive use.

Today, Arkansas's fortunes are changing. King Cotton has been deposed, and Arkansas is at last putting to use the full range of its natural and human resources. Soybeans, poultry, and rice share the limelight with cotton in the state's diversified agriculture. The production of oil, gas, and coal has boosted the state's revenues. Pine and hardwood forests, blanketing about half the state, supply timber for furniture and wood products. Arkansas's mineral waters, believed to be beneficial in treating certain illnesses, and the scenic beauty of the Ozark Mountains attract thousands of tourists and retirees each year. And as a state that once caused controversy in its opposition to school desegregation, Arkansas has since worked hard to build a more pluralistic, balanced society.

These changes have resulted in a dramatic rise in the state's per capita income, and its population, once tied to the land, is now concentrated in the cities, reflecting the pattern of urban growth experienced in other states. Moving from a one-crop state to a thriving, highly diversified region, Arkansas has chosen a new direction for itself, one that sets it firmly on the road to the future.

Unlike most crops, lowland rice grows best when its roots are submerged in water, and flooding a rice field also eliminates weeds. Arkansas's lowlands are especially suitable for rice production; the state provides much of the nation's supply.

Employment / Value

Employment		Value
	Retail trade	
	Wholesale trade	
	Service	
	Government	
	Manufacturing	
	Agriculture	
	Mining	

200 150 100 50 0
Thousands of Persons

0 1 2 3 4 5 6 7 8
Billions of Dollars

Land Use In the northern and western uplands of the Ouachita and Ozark mountains, livestock, hay, fruit, and vegetable production is common. On the southern and eastern lowlands, soils support a still broader variety of cash and staple crops.

- Farmland (cropland and pastureland)
- Farmland and woodlots
- Forests
- Swampland and marshland
- Irrigated areas
- Livestock grazing (areas other than farmland)
- Major urban areas

Major Highways
- (15) National interstate
- (15) U.S.

Economic Activities The major manufacturing and agricultural goods of Arkansas are also specialties of neighboring states. Perhaps more exceptional is Arkansas's production of rarer items. The state contains much of the domestic bauxite supply, and bromine is an important by-product of state oil production.

Water Transport The Arkansas River navigation system enables ships to travel from the Mississippi River all the way to Tulsa, Oklahoma. By connecting with the Mississippi River–Gulf of Mexico intercoastal waterway, the system makes Arkansas an integral part of United States water transport, with ports along the Arkansas River accessible to international trade.

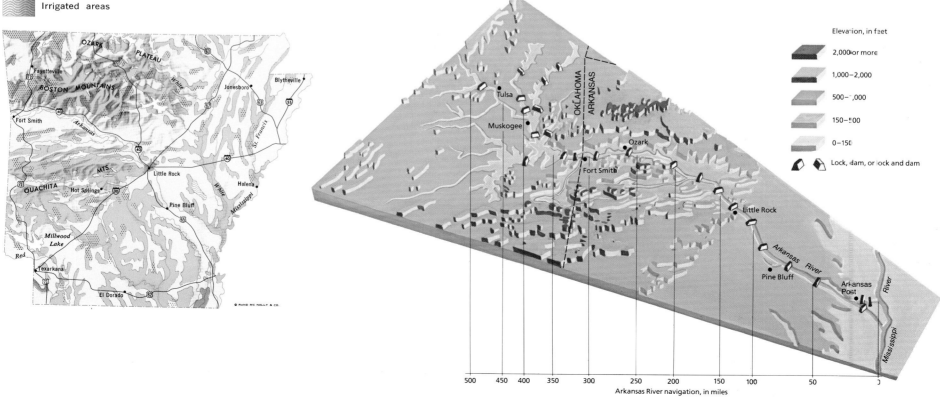

Elevation, in feet
- 2,000 or more
- 1,000–2,000
- 500–1,000
- 150–500
- 0–150
- Lock, dam, or lock and dam

500 450 400 350 300 250 200 150 100 50 0
Arkansas River navigation, in miles

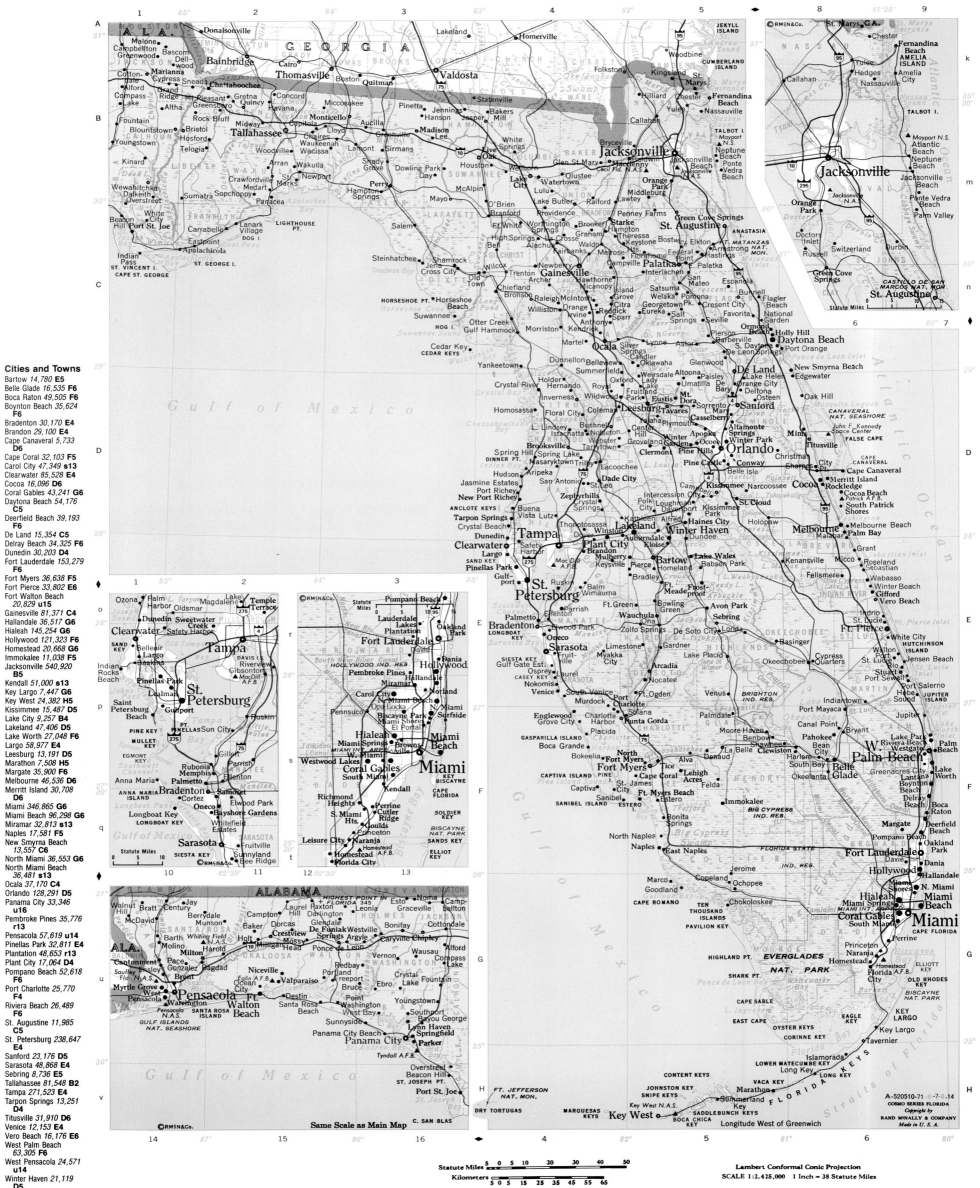

A-520510-71 -6-7-8-14
COSMO SERIES FLORIDA
Copyright by
RAND McNALLY & COMPANY
Made in U. S. A.

Same Scale as Main Map

Statute Miles 5 0 5 10   20   30   40   50
Kilometers 5 0 5 15 25 35 45 55 65

Lambert Conformal Conic Projection
SCALE 1:2,425,000   1 Inch = 38 Statute Miles

Georgia

POPULATION 5,463,105.
Rank: 13. *Density:* 94 people/mi² (36 people/km²). *Urban:* 62.4%. *Rural:* 37.6%.
AGE *<20:* 34%. *20–40:* 33%. *40–65:* 23%. *>65:* 10%.
ETHNIC GROUPS *White:* 72.3%. *Black:* 26.8%. *Spanish origin:* 1.1%. *Native American:* 0.1%. *Other:* 0.8%.

INCOME/CAPITA $8,073. *Rank:* 36.
POLITICS 1948–1980 elections: *President:* 1 Am. Independent, 6 Dem., 2 Rep. *Governor:* 8 Dem., 1 Rep.
ENTERED UNION January 2, 1788, 4th state.
CAPITAL Atlanta, 425,022.
LARGEST CITY Atlanta.

AREA 58,910 mi² (152,576 km²).
Rank: 21. *Water area:* 854 mi² (2,212 km²).
ELEVATIONS *Highest:* Brasstown Bald, 4,784 ft (1,458 m). *Lowest:* Atlantic Ocean shoreline, sea level.
CLIMATE Humid with hot summers, mild winters. Heavy rainfall in northeast.

Georgia has long been one of the economic and cultural leaders of the South. In the past, transportation routes and a prosperous agriculture contributed to Georgia's influence. Today, Atlanta, Georgia's largest city, is the hub of regional transportation networks, a center for business, and often called the Capital of the New South. In its successful transition from the agriculture of the Old South to the diversified economy of the New South, Georgia has become the focus of national as well as regional attention.

Yet in many ways, Georgia is still a state in transition. While Atlanta is a cosmopolitan area, drawing people and businesses from across the country, income in some nearby rural regions falls far below the national average. Many of these areas focus primarily on rural concerns, operating outside the state's current trend toward economic diversification. Yet the income disparities between city and rural dwellers, along with their regional differences, are slowly being recognized and overcome.

While Georgia's agriculture remains important, that agriculture has changed dramatically in the last hundred years. Cotton, formerly king here as in many southern states, now shares its throne with other important crops. Farming is diversified and mechanized, and in many areas, farms are run as businesses or corporations. As a result, more and more rural families have been leaving the land to move to the cities. Most still work in farm- or forest-related industries, such as poultry processing, lumber milling, and turning cotton into textiles and carpeting. These and other activities make industry rather than agriculture the prime source of revenue for the state. Economic and social changes resulting from the growth and spread of manufacturing are helping to unite regions that have been divided since the state's early history, and Georgia is also seeking ways to diminish divisions between whites and blacks in its society.

Industrial growth and regional and social integration will most likely continue as Georgia's transition from Old South to New South becomes complete. In working toward its economic and cultural goals, the state may well serve as a model for its neighbors, strengthening its traditional position as a leader of the South.

Atlanta symbolizes the successful city of the New South. In *Places Rated Almanac,* a publication ranking United States metropolitan areas, Atlanta scored the highest for general quality of life, which included factors such as education, housing, and recreation.

Employment | **Value**

Retail trade
Wholesale trade
Service
Government
Manufacturing
Agriculture
Mining

500 400 200 0 10 20 30 40
Thousands of Persons   Billions of Dollars

Economic Activities   Georgia's wholehearted development of its manufacturing potential allows it to vie with northern states in industries such as automobile assembly and with other Sun Belt states in high technology. Nonetheless, Georgia is most closely identified with the textile industry. The state's importance as a transportation center is reflected, partly, in the value of its wholesale trade.

Land Use   Although not the major activity it once was, agriculture is still important in Georgia. Soil erosion has long been a problem, however; and today, it is controlled by contour plowing, terracing, reforestation, and other conservation practices. In addition to reducing soil runoff, reforestation contributes to the growth of Georgia's forest-products industry.

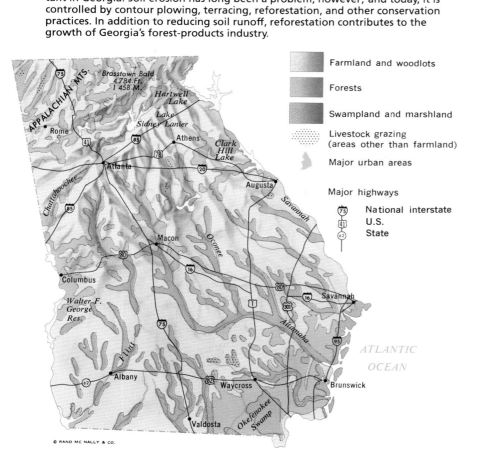

Farmland and woodlots

Forests

Swampland and marshland

Livestock grazing (areas other than farmland)

Major urban areas

Major highways
75 National interstate
41 U.S.
62 State

Employment Trends   Georgia's changing economy is evidenced by shifts in employment, and these reflect the transition from the agriculture of the Old South to the industry of the New South occurring throughout the Southeast. Once the state's major employer, agriculture has been overshadowed by manufacturing, and agricultural employment has dropped off dramatically. This is partially due to increased mechanization, but changing economic emphasis is the main cause. Manufacturing in the state is becoming more and more diversified, and future stability is ensured by the greater-than-average growth of high-technology industries. And as manufacturing increases in importance, other areas of the economy are affected. Wholesale and retail trade and service industries, for example, show the effects of growth in the manufacturing sector.

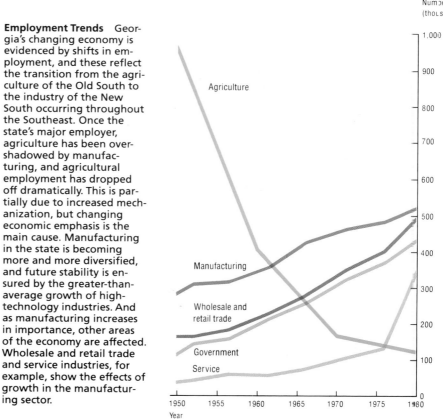

Number Employed (thousands of persons)

Agriculture

Manufacturing

Wholesale and retail trade

Government

Service

1950 1955 1960 1965 1970 1975 1980
Year

1.000 900 800 700 600 500 400 300 200 100 0

© RAND MCNALLY & CO.

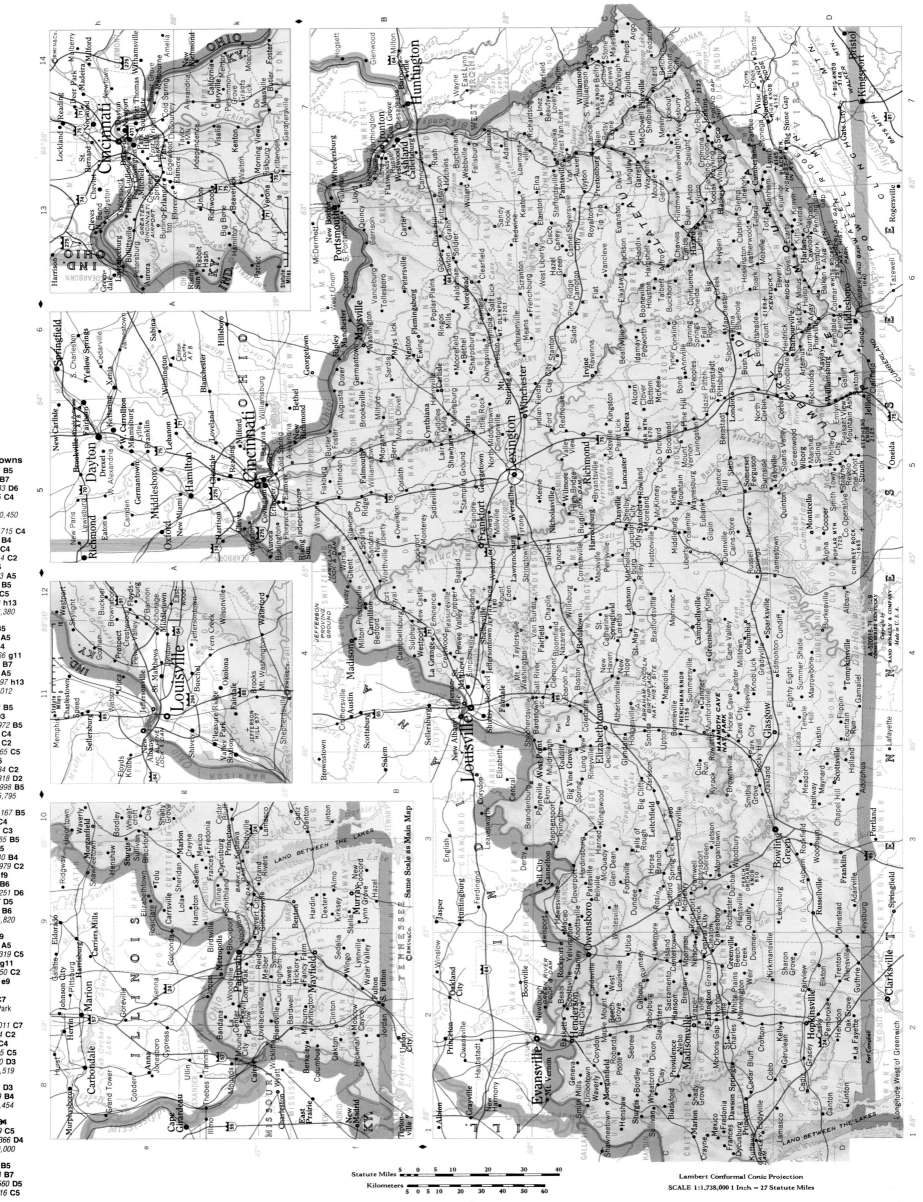

Cities and Towns

Alexandria 4,735 **B5**
Ashland 27,064 **B7**
Barbourville 3,333 **D6**
Bardstown 6,155 **C4**
Berea 8,226 **C5**
Bowling Green 40,450 **D3**
Campbellsville 8,715 **C4**
Carrollton 3,967 **B4**
Cave City 2,098 **C4**
Central City 5,214 **C2**
Corbin 8,075 **D5**
Covington 49,563 **A5**
Cynthiana 5,881 **B5**
Danville 12,942 **C5**
Edgewood 7,230 **h13**
Elizabethtown 15,380 **C4**
Elsmere 7,203 **B5**
Erlanger 14,433 **A5**
Fairdale 7,315 **B4**
Fern Creek 16,866 **g11**
Flatwoods 8,354 **B7**
Florence 15,586 **A5**
Fort Mitchell 7,297 **h13**
Fort Thomas 16,012 **h14**
Frankfort 25,973 **B5**
Franklin 7,738 **D3**
Georgetown 10,972 **B5**
Glasgow 12,958 **C4**
Greenville 4,631 **C2**
Harrodsburg 7,265 **C5**
Hazard 5,371 **C6**
Henderson 24,834 **C2**
Hopkinsville 27,318 **D2**
Independence 7,998 **B5**
Jeffersontown 15,795 **B4**
Lawrenceburg 5,167 **B5**
Lebanon 6,590 **C4**
Leitchfield 4,533 **C3**
Lexington 204,165 **B5**
London 4,002 **C5**
Louisville 298,840 **B4**
Madisonville 16,979 **C2**
Mayfield 10,705 **f9**
Maysville 7,983 **B6**
Middlesboro 12,251 **D6**
Monticello 5,677 **D5**
Morehead 7,789 **B6**
Mount Sterling 5,820 **B6**
Murray 14,248 **f9**
Newport 21,587 **A5**
Nicholasville 10,319 **C5**
Okolona 20,039 **g11**
Owensboro 54,450 **C2**
Paducah 29,315 **e9**
Paris 7,935 **B5**
Pikeville 4,756 **C7**
Pleasure Ridge Park 27,332 **g11**
Prestonsburg 4,011 **C7**
Providence 4,434 **C2**
Radcliff 14,519 **C4**
Richmond 21,705 **C5**
Russellville 7,520 **D3**
St. Matthews 13,519 **B4**
Scottsville 4,278 **D3**
Shelbyville 5,329 **B4**
Shepherdsville 4,454 **C4**
Shively 16,819 **B4**
Somerset 10,649 **C5**
Tompkinsville 4,366 **D4**
Valley Station 20,000 **g11**
Versailles 6,427 **B5**
Westwood 5,973 **B7**
Williamsburg 5,560 **D5**
Winchester 15,216 **C5**

Statute Miles 5 0 5 10 20 30 40

Kilometers 5 0 5 10 20 30 40 50 60

Lambert Conformal Conic Projection
SCALE 1:1,738,000 1 Inch = 27 Statute Miles

A-520518-71
© RAND MCNALLY & COMPANY
Made in U.S.A.

Kentucky

POPULATION 3,660,257.
Rank: 23. *Density:* 92 people/mi²
(36 people/km²). *Urban:* 50.9%.
Rural: 49.1%.
AGE <*20:* 34%. *20–40:* 31%.
40–65: 24%. >*65:* 11%.
ETHNIC GROUPS *White:* 92.3%.
Black: 7.1%. *Spanish origin:*
0.7%. *Native American:* 0.1%.
Other: 0.5%.

INCOME/CAPITA $7,613. *Rank:* 46.
POLITICS 1948–1980 elections:
President: 4 Dem., 5 Rep.
Governor: 7 Dem., 1 Rep.
ENTERED UNION June 1, 1792,
15th state.
CAPITAL Frankfort, 25,973.
LARGEST CITY Louisville, 298,840.

AREA 40,409 mi² (104,659 km²).
Rank: 37. *Water area:* 740 mi²
(1,917 km²).
ELEVATIONS *Highest:* Black Mtn.,
4,145 ft (1,263 m). *Lowest:* Along
Mississippi River, 257 ft (78 m)
CLIMATE Hot summers, short
winters with some snow;
moderate rainfall.

For stirring the romantic imagination, Kentucky has few rivals. The state's name conjures images of Daniel Boone, Abraham Lincoln, and Jefferson Davis; coal miners, moonshiners, and mountaineers; and white-suited colonels, bourbon whiskey, and the Kentucky Derby. Behind each image and legend lies a bit of truth about Kentucky and the historical diversity of its culture and landscape.

The legends of famous pioneers and statesmen reflect Kentucky's long history as a boundary state. It first marked the line between the eastern seaboard and America's great western frontier. During the Civil War, the state straddled the boundary between North and South, torn in the struggle that bitterly divided the nation, attempting to maintain neutrality.

Generations of coal miners have worked Kentucky's Appalachian Highlands and the coalfields east of the Tennessee River, two of the leading coal-producing regions of the country. Contrasts of wealth and poverty have plagued these regions for decades, and more recently, those who favor continued coal development have clashed with those seeking to save the land from the devastating effects of strip-mining.

The central Bluegrass basin brings to mind gentlemen farmers and colonels with their fine bourbon and prize thoroughbred horses. Like the neighboring Pennyroyal area and the far western corner of the state, this region is one of Kentucky's prime livestock and agricultural producers. In eastern upland Kentucky, timber is an important part of the economy, and this area is justly proud of its wood products and furniture. In addition, manufacturing has created a landscape of cities and industrial sites, particularly along the Ohio River, that are well known for tobacco products, whiskey, and a variety of industrial goods.

Throughout history, the special character of each of Kentucky's regions has contributed much of its romantic image. But today, economic stability requires regional integration, and distinctions are lost in working for the good of the state as a whole. Yet no matter how modern Kentucky may become, the legends of the past will continue to influence the nation's image of this diverse land.

Within the Bluegrass region of north-central Kentucky lies the state's most productive agricultural land, with its peaceful scenes of grazing horses, gently rolling meadows, and tobacco fields.

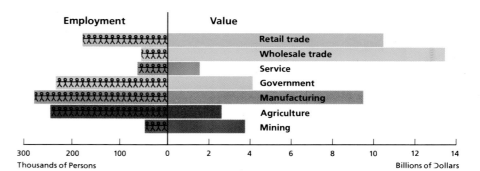

Economic Activities Kentucky is closely identified with its products—tobacco, bourbon, coal, and thoroughbred horses. But major products also include machinery, chemicals, and electrical equipment.

Income per capita, by county, 1979
- $7,000 or more
- $5,000–$7,000
- Less than $5,000

Per Capita Income The character of the land and the way humans use that land influence an area's quality of life. Urban development, productive soils, and coal and oil mean greater income, as evidenced by the income rankings of the northwestern and eastern mining counties and the Bluegrass, Pennyroyal, and far-western agricultural areas.

Land Use Early settlers were attracted by Kentucky's forest and soils, but the state's regions hold great mineral wealth as well, including coal, petroleum, and natural gas.

- Farmland and woodlots
- Forests
- Swampland and marshland
- Livestock grazing (areas other than farmland)
- Major urban areas

Major highways
- National interstate
- U.S.
- State

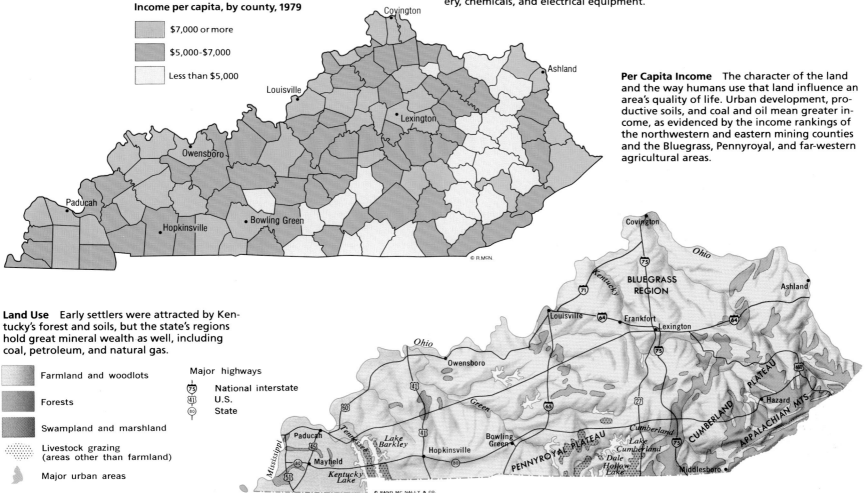

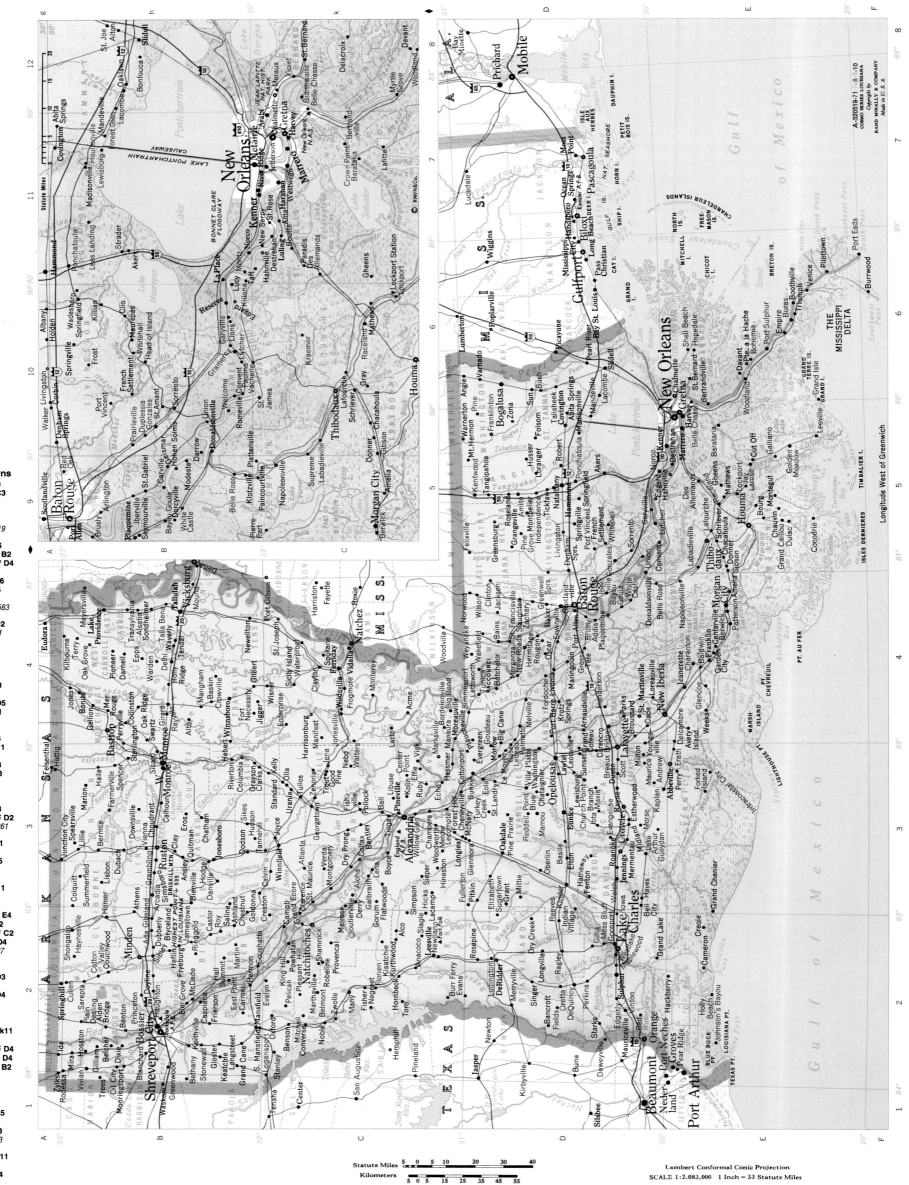

Cities and Towns

Abbeville 12,391 **E3**
Alexandria 51,565 **C3**
Arabi 10,248 **k11**
Baker 12,865 **D4**
Bastrop 15,527 **B4**
Baton Rouge 219,419 **D4**
Bogalusa 16,976 **D6**
Bossier City 50,817 **B2**
Breaux Bridge 5,922 **D4**
Bunkie 5,364 **D4**
Chalmette 33,847 **E6**
Covington 7,892 **D5**
Crowley 16,036 **D3**
Denham Springs 8,563 **D5**
De Ridder 11,057 **D2**
Donaldsonville 7,901 **D4**
Eunice 12,479 **D3**
Franklin 9,584 **E4**
Galliano 5,159 **E5**
Gonzales 7,287 **D5**
Grambling 4,226 **B3**
Gretna 20,615 **E5**
Hammond 15,043 **D5**
Harahan 11,384 **k11**
Harvey 15,000 **E5**
Houma 32,602 **E5**
Jeanerette 6,511 **E4**
Jefferson 15,550 **k11**
Jena 4,375 **C3**
Jennings 12,401 **D3**
Jonesboro 5,061 **B3**
Kaplan 5,016 **D3**
Kenner 66,382 **E5**
Lacombe 5,146 **D6**
Lafayette 81,961 **D3**
Lake Charles 75,226 **D2**
Lake Providence 6,361 **B4**
La Place 16,112 **h11**
Leesville 9,054 **C2**
Mandeville 6,076 **D5**
Mansfield 6,485 **B2**
Marrero 36,548 **E5**
Metairie 164,160 **k11**
Minden 15,084 **B2**
Monroe 57,597 **B3**
Morgan City 16,114 **E4**
Moss Bluff 7,004 **D2**
Natchitoches 16,664 **C2**
New Iberia 32,766 **D4**
New Orleans 557,927 **E5**
Oakdale 7,155 **D3**
Opelousas 18,903 **D3**
Pineville 12,034 **C3**
Plaquemine 7,521 **D4**
Raceland 6,302 **E5**
Rayne 9,066 **D3**
Reserve 7,288 **h10**
River Ridge 17,146 **k11**
Ruston 20,585 **B3**
St. Martinville 7,965 **D4**
Scotlandville 15,113 **D4**
Shreveport 205,820 **B2**
Slidell 26,718 **D6**
Springhill 6,516 **A2**
Sulphur 19,709 **D5**
Tallulah 11,634 **B4**
Thibodaux 15,810 **E5**
Vidalia 5,936 **C4**
Ville Platte 9,201 **D3**
West Monroe 14,993 **B3**
Westwego 12,663 **k11**
Winnfield 7,311 **C3**
Winnsboro 5,921 **B4**
Zachary 7,297 **D4**

Statute Miles 5 0 5 10 20 30 40
Kilometers 5 0 5 15 25 35 45 55

Lambert Conformal Conic Projection
SCALE 1:2,083,000 1 Inch = 33 Statute Miles

Louisiana

POPULATION 4,206,312. *Rank:* 19. *Density:* 94 people/mi² (36 people/km²). *Urban:* 68.6%. *Rural:* 31.4%.
AGE *< 20:* 36%. *20–40:* 32%. *40–65:* 23%. *>65:* 9%.
ETHNIC GROUPS *White:* 69.2%. *Black:* 29.4%. *Spanish origin:* 2.4%. *Native American:* 0.3%. *Other:* 1.1%.

INCOME/CAPITA $8,458. *Rank:* 35.
POLITICS 1948–1980 elections: *President:* 1 Am. Independent, 3 Dem., 4 Rep., 1 States' Rights Dem. *Governor:* 7 Dem., 1 Rep.
ENTERED UNION April 30, 1812, 18th state.
CAPITAL Baton Rouge, 219,419.
LARGEST CITY New Orleans, 557,927.

AREA 47,751 mi² (123,675 km²). *Rank:* 33. *Water area:* 3,230 mi² (8,366 km²).
ELEVATIONS *Highest:* Driskill Mtn., 535 ft (163 m). *Lowest:* New Orleans, 5 ft (2 m) below sea level.
CLIMATE Humid with long, hot summers; short, mild winters. Moderately heavy rainfall.

Much of Louisiana's history and culture has been shaped by the Mississippi River and the state's Spanish and French heritage. Even its legal system is based on French civil law rather than English common law, found in all other states. New Orleans, near the head of the river delta, is one of America's great ports, serving as the main entryway into the central part of the country.

But Louisiana's prime location did not always guarantee prosperity. At one time, the state was greatly dependent upon agriculture, and not until World War II did Louisiana experience real growth. The wartime demand for port facilities set Louisiana on its present course of rapid diversification and expansion, and soon manufacturing surpassed agriculture in importance. The discovery of land-based oil and gas spurred further development in establishing chemical industries. And when petroleum reserves were found in the Gulf of Mexico, southern Louisiana became important for offshore drilling.

Although agriculture no longer dominates Louisiana's economy, it is still important. The state's near-tropical climate and rich delta soil are ideal for crops such as soybeans, rice, cotton, and sugarcane. The Mississippi River is both creator and destroyer, however, since the floods that renew the delta soil also devastate nearby cities and towns. Much of the state lies close to sea level, and the banks of the river continue to build up because of flooding. As a result, drainage in crop fields is a chronic problem for farmers.

The river has also fragmented the geography and population of the state. The southern area is dominated by New Orleans, whose French Quarter is a charming reminder of the early French and Spanish presence. Coastal waterways and winding channels of the Mississippi Delta cut the southern region into enclaves, isolating one group of people from another. Partially due to this isolation, the Cajuns, who resettled from Nova Scotia in the eighteenth century, have preserved their culture and French dialect for over two hundred years.

Like many southern states, Louisiana has experienced rapid economic development in the past decades. And in maintaining its unique blend of old and new, the state still looks to the Mississippi River and a colorful and varied past.

Louisiana's heritage is reflected in the architecture of the French Quarter in New Orleans. Originally settled by the French, the Louisiana area was under Spanish rule when fires swept through New Orleans in the late 1700's. The Spanish style of architecture used in rebuilding can be seen today in the intricate iron grillwork gracing the balconies of many buildings.

Land Use The Mississippi River sets Louisiana apart from many of its neighbors on the Coastal Plain of the Gulf of Mexico. The river deposits valuable alluvial soil along its banks and delta channels but always threatens the state with destructive flooding. The Mississippi Delta contains the most fertile land in the state due to riverine deposition, but when the Mississippi tops its banks, most of the region faces flooding that can result in great loss of life and property.

Farmland (cropland and pastureland)

Farmland and woodlots

Forests

Swampland and marshland

Livestock grazing (areas other than farmland)

Major urban areas

Major highways

National interstate

U.S.

Canal

Bird Migration Over half the known North American bird species have been recorded in Louisiana, and one reason is the Mississippi Flyway that crosses the state. This is the longest and most heavily traveled of the four major American flyways. Each year millions of migrating birds pass through Louisiana, some stopping only for a short time, others remaining for a season before moving on.

Migration routes

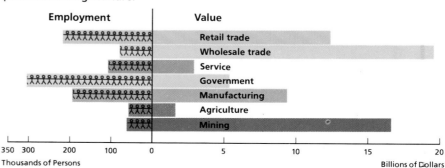

Forest

Swamp or marsh

Wildlife refuge

Bird Habitats Louisiana is a natural bird aviary, with forests, swamps, rivers, and plains providing homes for many types of birds. But the wetlands especially play a major role. In addition to migrating birds, over ninety species live in the marshes year-round. Conservation activities ensure the continued presence of wildlife.

Economic Activities Louisiana is one of the few states in which the value of mineral production surpasses that of manufacturing. Petroleum, natural gas, sulfur, salt, and their conversion into chemicals are central to the state's economy. And fertile soils and a warm climate allow Louisiana to remain productive in agriculture.

Employment	Value
Retail trade	
Wholesale trade	
Service	
Government	
Manufacturing	
Agriculture	
Mining	

350 300 200 100 0   0 5 10 15 20
Thousands of Persons   Billions of Dollars

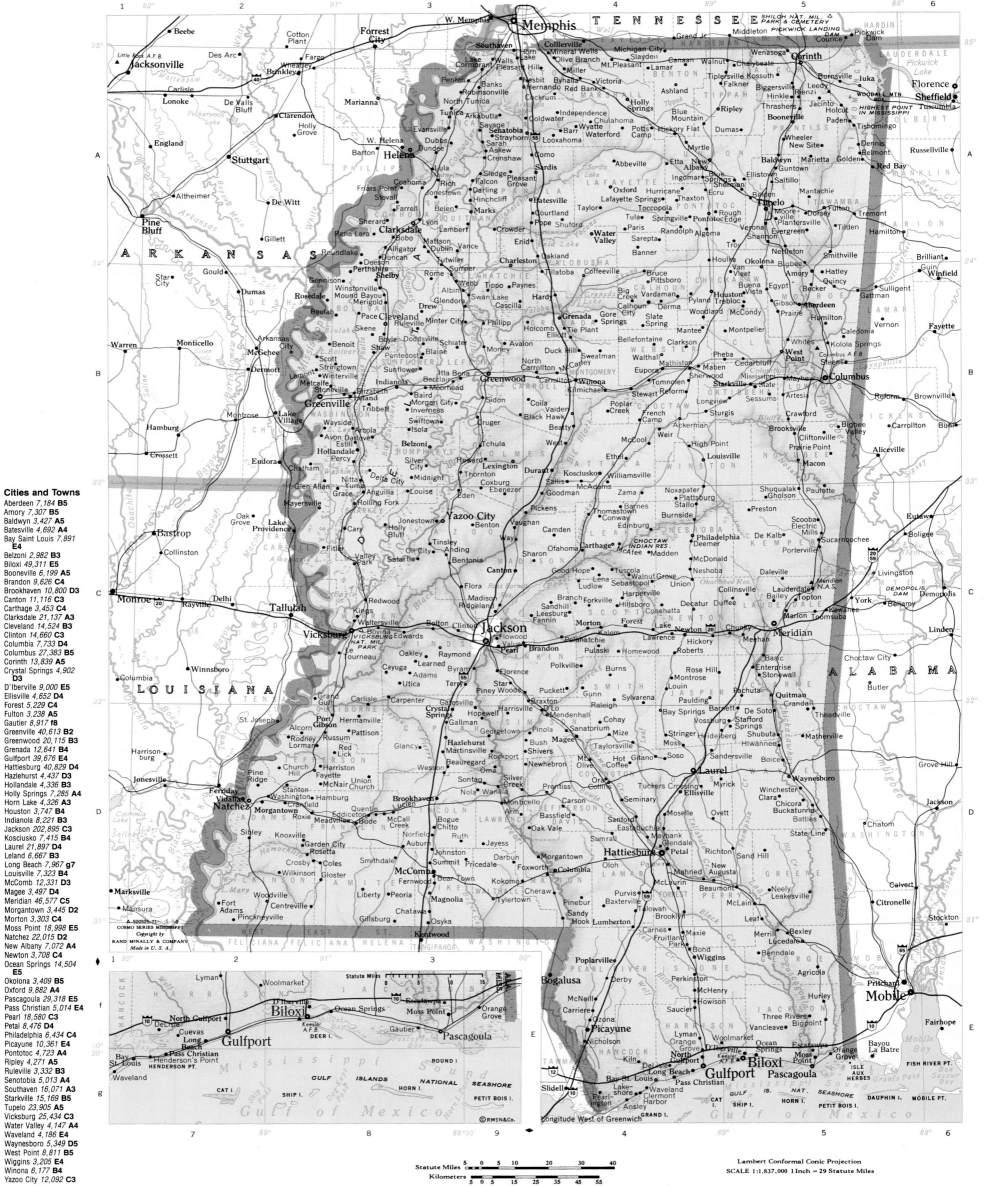

Statute Miles
Kilometers

Lambert Conformal Conic Projection
SCALE 1:1,837,000 1 Inch = 29 Statute Miles

South Carolina

POPULATION 3,121,833.
Rank: 24. *Density:* 103 people/mi² (40 people/km²). *Urban:* 54.1%. *Rural:* 45.9%.
AGE <20: 34%. 20–40: 33%. 40–65: 24%. >65: 9%.
ETHNIC GROUPS *White:* 68.8%. *Black:* 30.4%. *Spanish origin:* 1.1%. *Native American:* 0.2%. *Other:* 0.6%.

INCOME/CAPITA $7,266. *Rank:* 49.
POLITICS 1948–1980 elections: *President:* 4 Dem., 4 Rep., 1 States' Rights Dem. *Governor:* 7 Dem., 1 Rep.
ENTERED UNION May 23, 1788, 8th state.
CAPITAL Columbia, 100,385.
LARGEST CITY Columbia.

AREA 31,112 mi² (80,580 km²). *Rank:* 40. *Water area:* 909 mi² (2,355 km²).
ELEVATIONS *Highest:* Sassafras Mtn., 3,560 ft (1,085 m). *Lowest:* Atlantic Ocean shoreline, sea level.
CLIMATE Humid with long, hot summers; short, mild winters.

More than some southeastern states, South Carolina reflects the tradition of the Old South. This is expressed in the particularly southern atmosphere found in the countryside and towns, with their beautiful flower gardens and graceful architecture, and in the customs, manners, and everyday life of South Carolina's people. Yet at the same time, the state is one of the best developed and most economically varied southern states, similar to many industrialized regions in the North. Perhaps its economic success has enabled South Carolina to retain the finer points of its cultural traditions.

Mention South Carolina and most people are likely to imagine cotton fields and a slow, leisurely pace of life. But time has brought many changes, and that image is no longer representative of the state as a whole. Tobacco, soybeans, cotton, and peaches remain strong products in South Carolina, but today there are fewer farms and less land under cultivation than a few decades ago. In fact, the state has expanded into nearly every class of manufactured goods from paper to chemicals to primary metals, with the textile industry the dominant business. In addition, since World War II, naval, marine, army, and air-force installations have aided the state's development.

South Carolina has also made progress in creating a more racially and regionally balanced culture. The state is fortunate that its division into distinct regions—defined by the Atlantic Coastal Plain, Piedmont Plateau, and Blue Ridge Mountains—has not created the factionalism experienced in some neighboring states. However, South Carolina's traditional conservatism is dictating a slow, careful pace toward greater social integration and welfare.

Unlike states that have broken with the past to move rapidly into present trends, South Carolina today continues to blend the old and the new. It has always been proud of its traditions and maintains a sense of history that is likely to influence the state's development in the coming decades.

Founded in 1670, Charleston is South Carolina's oldest and one of the country's most historic cities. Its unique blend of Old and New South reflects the state's pride in the past and its success in the present. Many carefully preserved buildings date to pre-Civil War days, and Charleston's architecture, streets, and parks tell of the state's southern heritage. But at the same time, it is a major Atlantic seaport and transportation center, with diversified manufacturing activities and important air-force and navy installations.

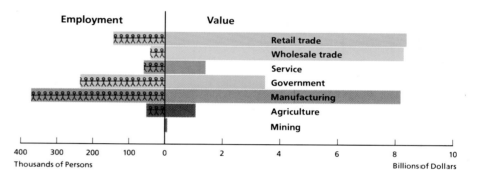

Employment	Value
Retail trade	
Wholesale trade	
Service	
Government	
Manufacturing	
Agriculture	
Mining	

400 300 200 100 0   0 2 4 6 8 10
Thousands of Persons   Billions of Dollars

Economic Activities Recent years have seen an upswing in South Carolina's fortunes. While its strong manufacturing sector is dominated largely by textiles, many new industries have found their way to the state, and existing industries, including textiles, have expanded their production. Promotional activity and job-training programs account for some of this increase.

Land Use To state residents, South Carolina is divided into two regions. The "up country" to the north and west includes a small portion of the Blue Ridge Mountains and the hilly to rugged Piedmont Plateau. The "low country" to the south and east runs across the Atlantic Coastal Plain, gradually turning to flat, swampy tidewater and fine sand beach as it meets the Atlantic Ocean.

Fall Line This "line" marks the zone where the resistant rock of the Piedmont Plateau meets the softer rock of the Coastal Plain. Rivers flowing from the plateau cut deeply into the soft rock, and as erosion lowers the surface of the plain below that of the Piedmont, waterfalls and rapids are formed. At these places, rough water necessitated a break in the boat transportation of colonial America, and settlement took place, usually on the gentler Coastal Plain. Today, cities located near the line remain as evidence of the strong influence the natural environment has upon human settlement patterns.

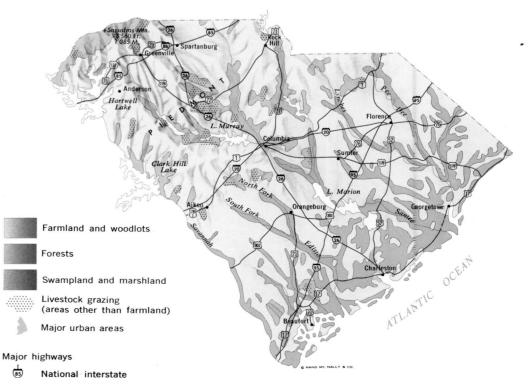

Farmland and woodlots

Forests

Swampland and marshland

Livestock grazing (areas other than farmland)

Major urban areas

Major highways

(85) National interstate

(21) U.S.

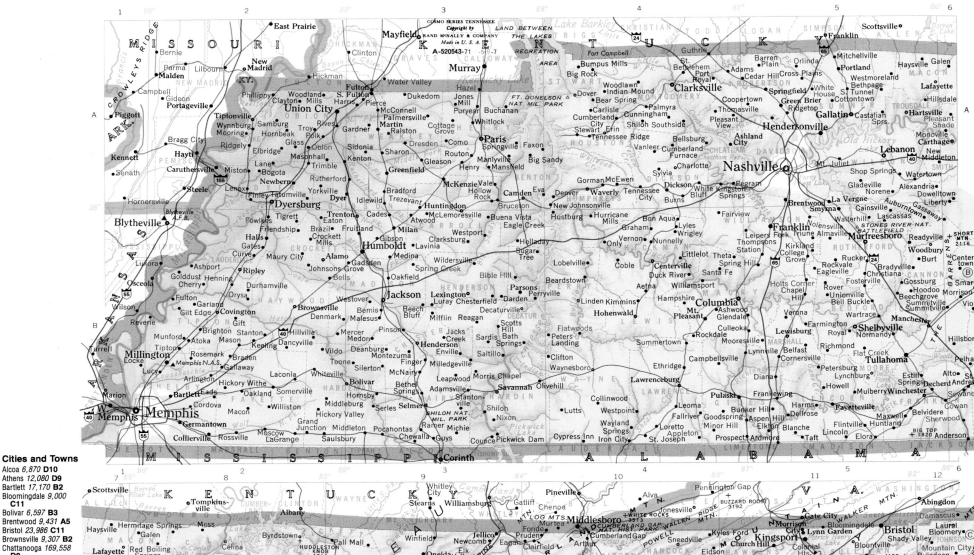

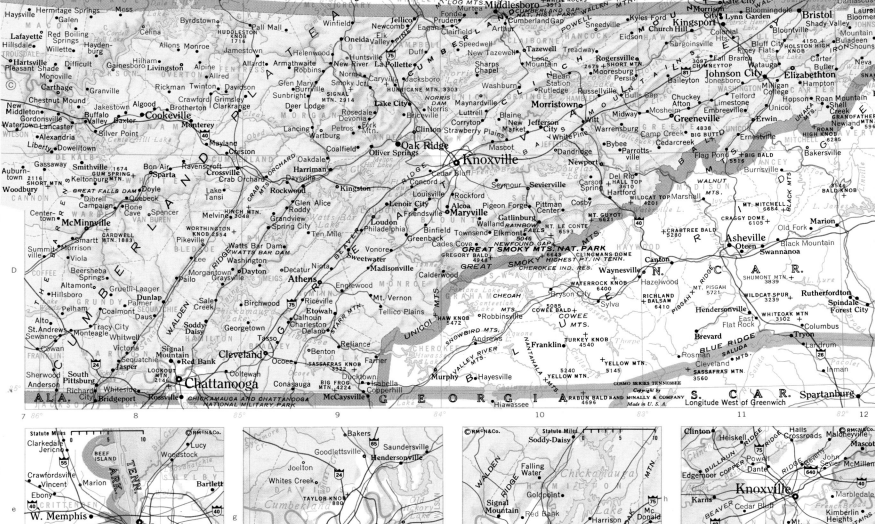

Cities and Towns

Alcoa 6,870 **D10**
Athens 12,080 **D9**
Bartlett 17,170 **B2**
Bloomingdale 9,000 **C11**
Bolivar 6,597 **B3**
Brentwood 9,431 **A5**
Bristol 23,986 **C11**
Brownsville 9,307 **B2**
Chattanooga 169,558 **D8**
Clarksville 54,777 **A4**
Cleveland 26,415 **D9**
Clinton 5,245 **C9**
Collierville 7,839 **B2**
Columbia 26,571 **B4**
Cookeville 20,535 **C8**
Covington 6,065 **B2**
Crossville 6,394 **D8**
Dayton 5,913 **D9**
Dickson 7,040 **A4**
Dyersburg 15,856 **A2**
East Ridge 21,236 **D8**
Elizabethton 12,431 **C11**
Erwin 4,739 **C11**
Fayetteville 7,559 **B5**
Franklin 12,407 **B5**
Gallatin 17,191 **A5**
Gatlinburg 3,210 **D10**
Germantown 21,482 **B2**
Greeneville 14,097 **C11**
Harriman 8,303 **D9**
Henderson 4,449 **B3**
Hendersonville 26,561 **A5**
Humboldt 10,209 **B3**
Jackson 49,131 **B3**
Jefferson City 5,612 **C10**
Johnson City 39,753 **C11**
Kingsport 32,027 **C11**
Kingston 4,441 **D9**
Knoxville 175,045 **D10**
La Follette 8,198 **C9**
Lawrenceburg 10,184 **B4**
Lebanon 11,872 **A5**
Lenoir City 5,446 **D9**
Lewisburg 8,760 **B5**
Lexington 5,934 **B3**
McKenzie 5,405 **A3**
McMinnville 10,683 **D8**
Martin 8,898 **A3**
Maryville 17,480 **D10**
Memphis 646,174 **B1**
Milan 8,083 **B3**
Millington 20,236 **B2**
Morristown 19,683 **C10**
Murfreesboro 32,845 **B5**
Nashville 455,651 **A5**
Newport 7,580 **D10**
Oak Ridge 27,662 **C9**
Paris 10,728 **A3**
Pulaski 7,184 **B4**
Red Bank 13,299 **D8**
Ripley 6,366 **B2**
Rockwood 5,767 **D9**
Savannah 6,992 **B3**
Sevierville 4,556 **D10**
Shelbyville 13,530 **B5**
Smyrna 8,839 **B5**
Soddy-Daisy 8,388 **D8**
Sparta 4,864 **D8**
Springfield 10,814 **A5**
Sweetwater 4,725 **D9**
Trenton 4,601 **B3**
Tullahoma 15,800 **B5**
Union City 10,436 **A2**
Winchester 5,821 **B5**

Statute Miles
Kilometers

Lambert Conformal Conic Projection
SCALE 1:1,713,000 1 Inch = 27 Statute Miles

Tennessee

POPULATION 4,591,120.
  Rank: 17. *Density:* 112 people/
  mi² (43 people/km²). *Urban:*
  60.4%. *Rural:* 39.6%.
AGE <*20:* 32%. *20–40:* 32%.
  40–65: 26%. >*65:* 11%.
ETHNIC GROUPS *White:* 83.5%.
  Black: 15.8%. *Spanish origin:*
  0.7%. *Native American:* 0.1%.
  Other: 0.6%.

INCOME/CAPITA $7,720. *Rank:* 44.
POLITICS 1948–1980 elections:
  President: 3 Dem., 6 Rep.
  Governor: 8 Dem., 2 Rep.
ENTERED UNION June 1, 1796,
  16th state.
CAPITAL Nashville, 455,651.
LARGEST CITY Memphis, 646,174.

AREA 42,144 mi² (109,152 km²).
  Rank: 34. *Water area:* 989 mi²
  (2,561 km²).
ELEVATIONS *Highest:* Clingmans
  Dome, 6,643 ft (2,025 m).
  Lowest: Along Mississippi River,
  182 ft (55 m).
CLIMATE Hot summers; short,
  generally mild winters. Moderate
  rainfall, some mountain snow.

Tennessee is a pivotal region among states east of the Mississippi. It is linked culturally with the South, yet a thriving industry and one of the most extensive navigable river systems in the world tie it closely to the North.

In the 1930's, the federal government recognized the economic potential of Tennessee and decided to harness its abundant water resources to spur regional development in the area. The Tennessee Valley Authority, originally established to improve navigation, came to serve several other purposes: flood control, generation of electric power for industrial and rural needs, and conservation of land and forest resources, particularly soil ravaged by years of uncontrolled erosion. The TVA proved to be a milestone experiment that gained worldwide fame and touched off a controversy regarding federal intervention in state affairs that has yet to be resolved.

Because of the TVA and other government projects, Tennessee has developed a varied economy, producing chemicals, food products, machinery, textiles, metals, and minerals, as well as crops such as soybeans and tobacco. One of the state's primary exports, however, is electrical energy, which it supplies to some of its neighbors. Additional generators, fueled by strip-mined coal and by nuclear reactors, are adding to the state's capacity but may also be adding to its future environmental problems. The state will need to weigh carefully the benefits and liabilities of such a power network.

Tennessee's regional North-South divisions, originated in Civil War times, are still evident in the state's political and cultural life. Its eastern uplands follow northern trends, while central Tennessee allies itself with the Deep South. A region to the west shares ties with both North and South. In recent years, the Memphis metropolitan area has begun to emerge as a fourth distinct region.

Just as Tennessee's riverways have been merged into a unified network of power and navigation systems, so the state may need to find ways to unify its cultural and political regions. Whether or not this happens in the near future, Tennessee will continue to play a strong pivotal role for both its southern and northern neighbors.

Suitable rainfall and latitude account for the more than one hundred species of trees covering the Great Smoky Mountains. The range's name comes from the overhanging bluish haze, the result of hydrocarbons released by the conifer trees

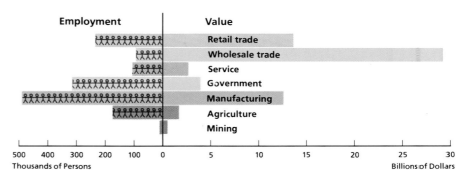

Employment		Value
		Retail trade
		Wholesale trade
		Service
		Government
		Manufacturing
		Agriculture
		Mining

500 400 300 200 100 0   5   10   15   20   25   30
Thousands of Persons   Billions of Dollars

Economic Activities   Tennessee's manufacturing sector, its largest employer, has grown substantially in the last forty years, essentially doubling the number of industrial jobs since World War II. Although it frequently takes time for such a change to affect a state's economy, in this case the income derived from these industries has already raised Tennessee's standard of living.

Political Affiliation   Tennessee's cultural and political sectionalism between the east and the west is due partially to the state's varied landscape, which ranges from eastern mountains and central plateaus to western plains. Western terrain enabled early development of large plantations with a Southern orientation. Rugged eastern slopes dictated smaller farms and a more austere life, allied with states to the north and east. The Civil War accentuated the differences, and many easterners remained loyal to the Union even after Tennessee entered the Confederacy. Today, Northern affiliation still persists in eastern Tennessee, as reflected in its predominantly Republican voting record. The center of the state and most of the west have clung to their Democratic politics, characteristic of the Southern states.

Presidential-election results, by county

Political party
  Democratic
  Republican

Election year
  1964 1968
  1972 • •
  1976 1980

  ● Democratic
  ● Republican
  ● American Independent

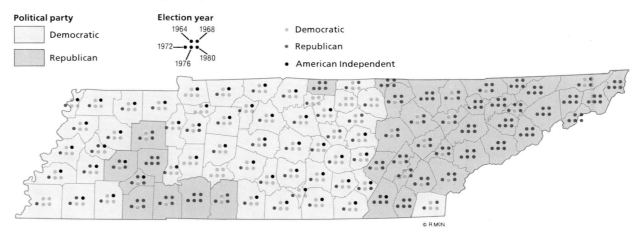

© R.McN.

Land Use   The damming of Tennessee's rivers at so many points has created a great chain of reservoirs. These long, narrow lakes along with others in neighboring states are sometimes called the Great Lakes of the South. Tennessee's reservoirs serve to control flooding and provide hydroelectric power, but they have also added another tourist attraction to the state's long list of beautiful landscapes and recreational resources.

Farmland and woodlots

Forests

Swampland and marshland

Livestock grazing
  (areas other than farmland)

Major urban areas

Major highways
  National interstate
  U.S.

© RAND McNALLY & CO.

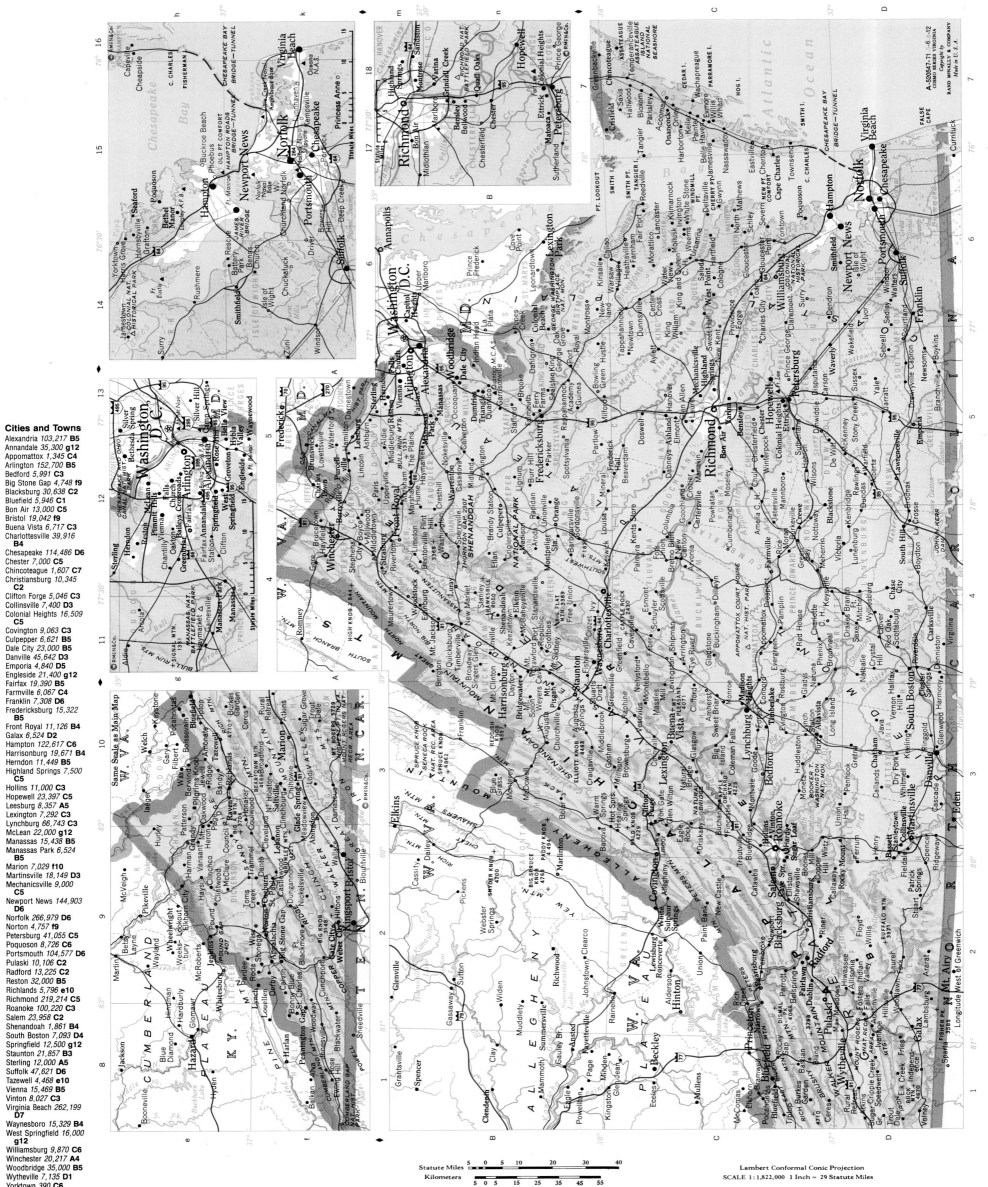

Cities and Towns

Alexandria 103,217 **B5**
Annandale 35,300 **g12**
Appomattox 1,345 **C4**
Arlington 152,700 **B5**
Bedford 5,991 **C3**
Big Stone Gap 4,748 **f9**
Blacksburg 30,638 **C2**
Bluefield 5,946 **C1**
Bon Air 13,000 **C5**
Bristol 19,042 **f9**
Buena Vista 6,717 **C3**
Charlottesville 39,916 **B4**
Chesapeake 114,486 **D6**
Chester 7,000 **C5**
Chincoteague 1,607 **C7**
Christiansburg 10,345 **C2**
Clifton Forge 5,046 **C3**
Collinsville 7,400 **D3**
Colonial Heights 16,509 **C5**
Covington 9,063 **C3**
Culpepper 6,621 **B5**
Dale City 23,000 **B5**
Danville 45,642 **D3**
Emporia 4,840 **D5**
Engleside 21,400 **g12**
Fairfax 19,390 **B5**
Farmville 6,067 **C4**
Franklin 7,308 **D6**
Fredericksburg 15,322 **B5**
Front Royal 11,126 **B4**
Galax 6,524 **D2**
Hampton 122,617 **C6**
Harrisonburg 19,671 **B4**
Herndon 11,449 **B5**
Highland Springs 7,500 **C5**
Hollins 11,000 **C3**
Hopewell 23,397 **C5**
Leesburg 8,357 **A5**
Lexington 7,292 **C3**
Lynchburg 66,743 **C3**
McLean 22,000 **g12**
Manassas 15,438 **B5**
Manassas Park 6,524 **B5**
Marion 7,029 **f10**
Martinsville 18,149 **D3**
Mechanicsville 9,000 **C5**
Newport News 144,903 **D6**
Norfolk 266,979 **D6**
Norton 4,757 **f9**
Petersburg 41,055 **C5**
Poquoson 8,726 **C6**
Portsmouth 104,577 **D6**
Pulaski 10,106 **C2**
Radford 13,225 **C2**
Reston 32,000 **B5**
Richlands 5,796 **e10**
Richmond 219,214 **C5**
Roanoke 100,220 **C3**
Salem 23,958 **C2**
Shenandoah 1,861 **B4**
South Boston 7,093 **D4**
Springfield 12,500 **g12**
Staunton 21,857 **B3**
Sterling 12,000 **A5**
Suffolk 47,621 **D6**
Tazewell 4,468 **e10**
Vienna 15,469 **B5**
Vinton 8,027 **C3**
Virginia Beach 262,199 **D7**
Waynesboro 15,329 **B4**
West Springfield 16,000 **g12**
Williamsburg 9,870 **C6**
Winchester 20,217 **A4**
Woodbridge 35,000 **B5**
Wytheville 7,135 **D1**
Yorktown 390 **C6**

Statute Miles
Kilometers

Lambert Conformal Conic Projection
SCALE 1:1,822,000   1 Inch = 29 Statute Miles

Virginia

POPULATION 5,346,818. *Rank:* 14. *Density:* 135 people/mi² (52 people/km²). *Urban:* 66%. *Rural:* 34%.
AGE *<20:* 32%. *20–40:* 34%. *40–65:* 25%. *>65:* 9%.
ETHNIC GROUPS *White:* 79.1%. *Black:* 18.9%. *Spanish origin:* 1.5%. *Native American:* 0.2%. *Other:* 1.8%.

INCOME/CAPITA $9,392. *Rank:* 22.
POLITICS 1948–1980 elections: *President:* 2 Dem., 7 Rep. *Governor:* 6 Dem., 3 Rep.
ENTERED UNION June 25, 1788, 10th state.
CAPITAL Richmond, 219,214.
LARGEST CITY Norfolk, 266,979.

AREA 40,766 mi² (105,583 km²). *Rank:* 36. *Water area:* 1,063 mi² (2,753 km²).
ELEVATIONS *Highest:* Mt. Rogers, 5,729 ft (1,746 m). *Lowest:* Atlantic Ocean shoreline, sea level.
CLIMATE Hot summers, short winters with some snow. Moderate rainfall.

In leadership, Virginia has no equal. Time and again, the forces of American history have called upon the state's citizens to face extraordinary challenges in peace and war. No other state has been the birthplace of so many presidents—eight in all. During the Revolutionary and Civil wars, Virginia was often torn by battle, its countryside scarred by the action of opposing armies. Yet it also served as the site of peace. The Revolutionary War ended at Yorktown, and Lee surrendered to Grant at Appomattox, not far from the Confederate capital in Richmond.

Virginia today still plays an important role in America's political leadership. The nation's capital lies just beyond the border to the northeast, and Virginia is one of Washington, D.C.'s, main support areas, supplying much of its work force and housing numerous government agencies. Government is a major industry in the state.

Virginia has also shown its leadership in meeting the challenges of a changing modern economy. Although no longer the great domain it was in colonial times, when its borders included West Virginia, the state is still rich in resources. Agriculture remains an important part of the state's economy, and since World War II, manufacturing has increased. Additional revenues come from a tourist industry attracted by the state's historical sites and picturesque landscapes.

Virginia continues to face new and demanding challenges that will once again tap its traditional leadership capacities. At one time a largely rural state, Virginia is now the southern anchor of the great urban-industrial corridor stretching north to Boston. Not only does this place the state in a strategic position with respect to the North, but because Virginia still identifies strongly with the South, it makes Virginia a pivot between northern and southern industrial states. And the state's proximity to the nation's capital will continue to cast it in a position of national leadership. Virginia will need to manage these and future roles carefully to maintain the high quality of natural and social environments for which it has always been known.

Virginia is rich in natural beauty as well as history. The heavily forested Blue Ridge Mountains that cross the state are part of the Appalachians and separate the Piedmont region from Virginia's Great Valley. In addition to being a major tourist attraction, the mountains contain traces of another side of America's past, different from that recalled by the colonial and Civil War landmarks found elsewhere in the state. Many of the homes and small subsistence farms of the mountain people display the country's pioneer heritage, employing farming and building techniques passed down from generation to generation.

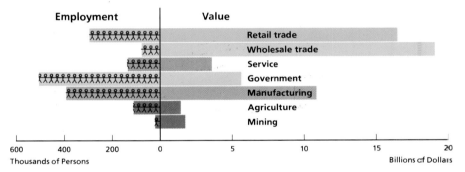

Employment	Value
Retail trade
Wholesale trade
Service
Government
Manufacturing
Agriculture
Mining

600 400 200 0   5   10   15   20
Thousands of Persons   Billions of Dollars

Economic Activities   Virginia benefits from its proximity to Washington, D.C., with federal facilities providing a large and stable government payroll for civilian and military personnel. Government activity is balanced by manufacturing—especially chemical production—trade, and other activities.

Historic Virginia   From the first permanent English settlement at Jamestown to the battlefields of the Revolutionary and Civil wars, the history of the United States can be traced within the boundaries of Virginia. The state is the site of many of the most important events in the country's development, and the presidents' homes, restored buildings, and other landmarks reflect the leadership role Virginia has often played.

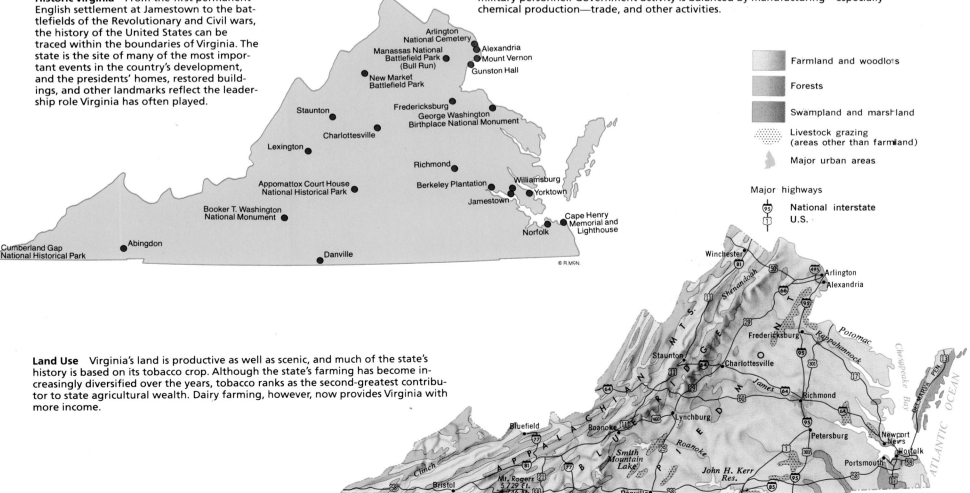

Arlington National Cemetery
Manassas National Battlefield Park (Bull Run)
Alexandria
Mount Vernon
Gunston Hall
New Market Battlefield Park
Staunton
Fredericksburg
George Washington Birthplace National Monument
Charlottesville
Lexington
Richmond
Appomattox Court House National Historical Park
Berkeley Plantation
Williamsburg
Yorktown
Jamestown
Booker T. Washington National Monument
Cape Henry Memorial and Lighthouse
Cumberland Gap National Historical Park
Abingdon
Norfolk
Danville
© R.MCN.

Farmland and woodlots
Forests
Swampland and marshland
Livestock grazing (areas other than farmland)
Major urban areas

Major highways
95 National interstate
U.S.

Winchester
Shenandoah
Arlington
Alexandria
Potomac
Fredericksburg
Rappahannock
Staunton
Charlottesville
James
Richmond
Chesapeake Bay
DELMARVA PENINSULA
ATLANTIC OCEAN

Land Use   Virginia's land is productive as well as scenic, and much of the state's history is based on its tobacco crop. Although the state's farming has become increasingly diversified over the years, tobacco ranks as the second-greatest contributor to state agricultural wealth. Dairy farming, however, now provides Virginia with more income.

Bluefield
Roanoke
Lynchburg
Petersburg
Newport News
Bristol
Mt. Rogers 5,729 ft. 1,746 m.
Smith Mountain Lake
Roanoke
John H. Kerr Res.
Portsmouth
Norfolk
Danville
© RAND MCNALLY & CO.

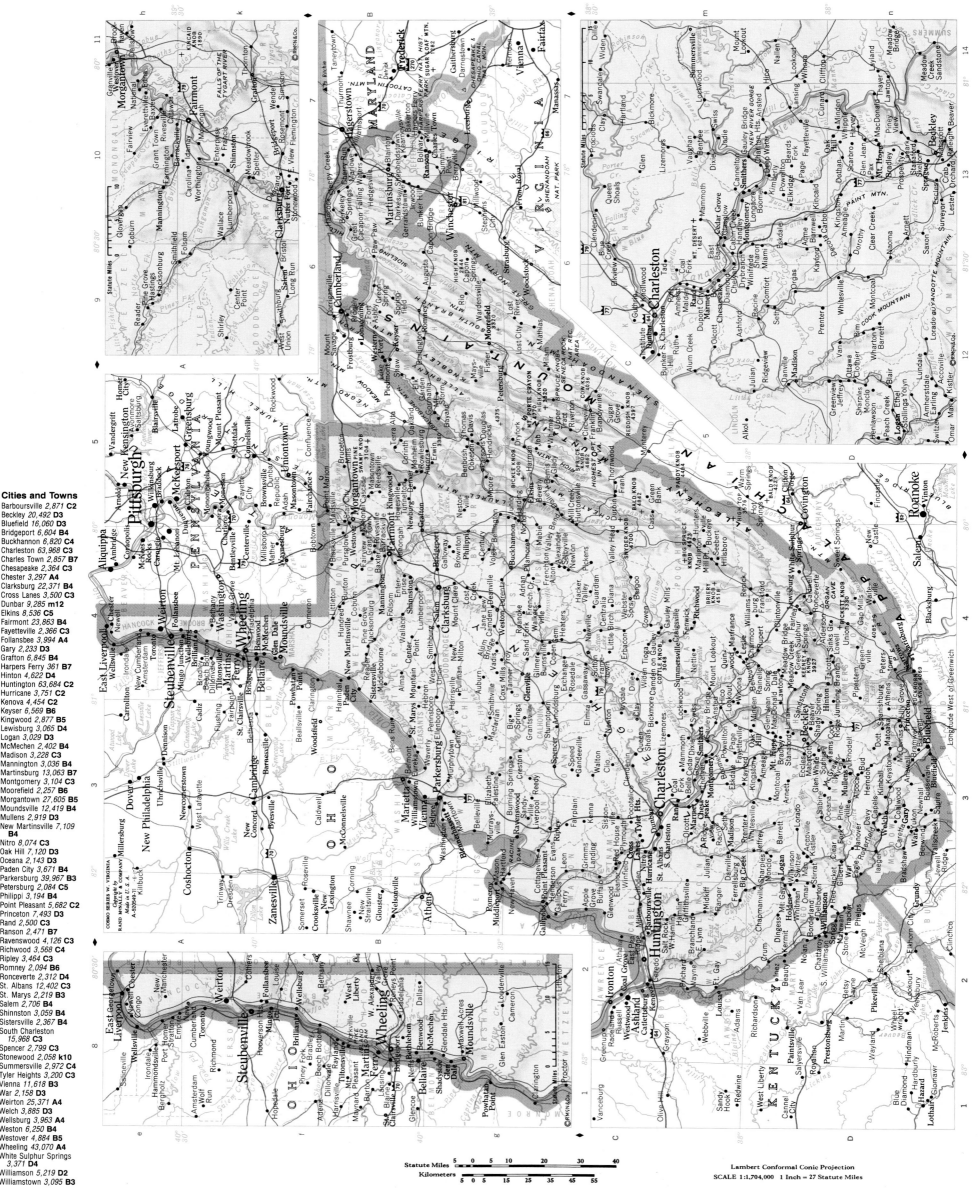

Cities and Towns

Barboursville 2,871 **C2**
Beckley 20,492 **D3**
Bluefield 16,060 **D3**
Bridgeport 6,604 **B4**
Buckhannon 6,820 **C4**
Charleston 63,968 **C3**
Charles Town 2,857 **B7**
Chesapeake 2,364 **C3**
Chester 3,297 **A4**
Clarksburg 22,371 **B4**
Cross Lanes 3,500 **C3**
Dunbar 9,285 **m12**
Elkins 8,536 **C5**
Fairmont 23,863 **B4**
Fayetteville 2,366 **C3**
Follansbee 3,994 **A4**
Gary 2,233 **D3**
Grafton 6,845 **B4**
Harpers Ferry 361 **B7**
Hinton 4,622 **D4**
Huntington 63,684 **C2**
Hurricane 3,751 **C2**
Kenova 4,454 **C2**
Keyser 6,569 **B6**
Kingwood 3,029 **B5**
Lewisburg 3,065 **D4**
Logan 3,029 **D3**
McMechen 2,402 **B4**
Madison 3,228 **C3**
Mannington 3,036 **B4**
Martinsburg 13,063 **B7**
Montgomery 3,104 **C3**
Moorefield 2,257 **B6**
Morgantown 27,605 **B5**
Moundsville 12,419 **B4**
Mullens 2,919 **D3**
New Martinsville 7,109 **B4**
Nitro 8,074 **C3**
Oak Hill 7,120 **D3**
Oceana 2,143 **D3**
Paden City 3,671 **B4**
Parkersburg 39,967 **B3**
Petersburg 2,084 **C5**
Philippi 3,194 **B4**
Point Pleasant 5,682 **C2**
Princeton 7,493 **D3**
Rand 2,500 **C3**
Ranson 2,471 **B7**
Ravenswood 4,126 **C3**
Richwood 3,568 **C4**
Ripley 3,464 **C3**
Romney 2,094 **B6**
Ronceverte 2,312 **D4**
St. Albans 12,402 **C3**
St. Marys 2,219 **B3**
Salem 2,706 **B4**
Shinnston 3,059 **B4**
Sistersville 2,367 **B4**
South Charleston 15,968 **C3**
Spencer 2,799 **C3**
Stonewood 2,058 **k10**
Summersville 2,972 **C4**
Tyler Heights 3,200 **C3**
Vienna 11,618 **B3**
War 2,158 **D3**
Weirton 25,371 **A4**
Welch 3,885 **D3**
Wellsburg 3,963 **A4**
Weston 6,250 **B4**
Westover 4,884 **B5**
Wheeling 43,070 **A4**
White Sulphur Springs 3,371 **D4**
Williamson 5,219 **D2**
Williamstown 3,095 **B3**

Statute Miles 5 0 5 10 20 30 40

Kilometers 5 0 5 15 25 35 45 55

Lambert Conformal Conic Projection

SCALE 1:1,704,000   1 Inch = 27 Statute Miles

West Virginia

POPULATION 1,950,279.
Rank: 34. *Density:* 81 people/mi² (31 people/km²). *Urban:* 36.2%. *Rural:* 63.8%.
AGE <20: 32%. 20–40: 31%. 40–65: 25%. >65: 12%.
ETHNIC GROUPS *White:* 96.2%. *Black:* 3.3%. *Spanish origin:* 0.7%. *Native American:* 0.1%. *Other:* 0.4%.

INCOME/CAPITA $7,800. *Rank:* 43.
POLITICS 1948–1980 elections: *President:* 7 Dem., 2 Rep. *Governor:* 6 Dem., 3 Rep.
ENTERED UNION June 20, 1863, 35th state.
CAPITAL Charleston, 63,968.
LARGEST CITY Charleston.

AREA 24,231 mi² (62,758 km²). *Rank:* 41. *Water area:* 112 mi² (290 km²).
ELEVATIONS *Highest:* Spruce Knob, 4,862 ft (1,482 m). *Lowest:* Along Potomac River, 240 ft (73 m).
CLIMATE Hot summers in valleys, mild in mountains; cool winters. Ample rainfall.

After more than one hundred years of statehood, West Virginia seems to be on the verge of coming into its own. For years, despite a wide variety of natural resources, its mountainous terrain has contributed to problems of a poor economy and high unemployment. Yet just as the events of history and the state's topography have sometimes worked against West Virginia, the determined efforts of its people coupled with current economic trends and modern transportation systems promise a brighter future.

West Virginia's terrain has long played a major role in determining the economy and culture of the state. It was once part of Virginia, a vast state stretching from the Atlantic Ocean to the Ohio River. But the mountainous terrain of western Virginia led to the development of an economy based on small-scale farming and industry, differing markedly from the wealthy plantation culture of the eastern part of the state. Western Virginia's growing demand for statehood was reinforced by the area's North-tending sympathies at the outset of the Civil War, and in 1863, the region gained statehood as West Virginia.

But the state found itself outside many of the economic trends that followed. West Virginia is one of the most mountainous states in the country, fragmented into small, isolated valleys that make communication and trade among villages and towns difficult. With few areas flat enough for extensive agriculture, regions available for cultivation could support only subsistence farming, an activity of little importance in the national economy. Although coal, natural gas, oil, and high-grade sand used in glassmaking were available for development, rugged terrain made transportation difficult, and growth in these industries was therefore limited. With the advent of mechanized coal mining and strip-mining, many workers found themselves out of a job.

But much of this is in the past. Today, state boundaries are less important in defining growth and decline, and transportation systems connect West Virginia with surrounding states and the nation. In addition, years of outmigration by the unemployed mean that industrial growth can more readily raise the standard of living. After years of living in the shadow of its more prosperous neighbors, West Virginia is at last emerging as a strong, developing region on its own.

Site of abolitionist John Brown's armory raid and a frequent battleground during the Civil War, Harpers Ferry reflects one side of the many conflicts between eastern and western Virginia that eventually led to West Virginia's independent statehood.

Economic Activities West Virginia's wealth of mineral resources is shown in the value of its mining and manufacturing, which makes use of these reserves. The state's principal industries produce chemicals, primary metals, and stone, clay, and glass products.

Settlement Patterns West Virginia's mountain-and-valley landscape exhibits the limitations the land imposes, with settlement concentrated in the more-level Kanawha Valley. And whereas growth usually means widespread population distribution, West Virginia's terrain continues to inhibit the urban sprawl found in many other states.

Extent of urbanization

≣ 1935 ||||| Additional as of 1976

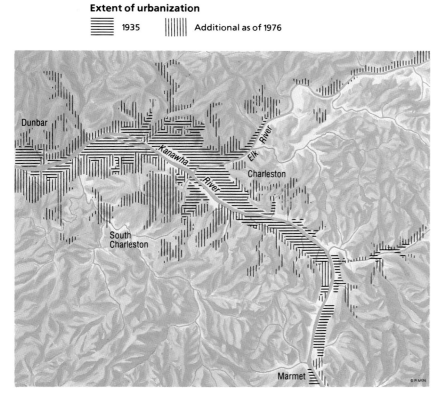

Land Use West Virginia's irregular shape is matched by those patches of land suitable for agriculture, industry, and urban growth. Valley bottom and is usually of greatest value to farmers, who profit from the rich soils deposited by rivers, and to industrialists who take advantage of river transportation.

Farmland and woodlots

Forests

Livestock grazing (areas other than farmland)

Major urban areas

Major highways

🛡77 National interstate
🛡19 U.S.

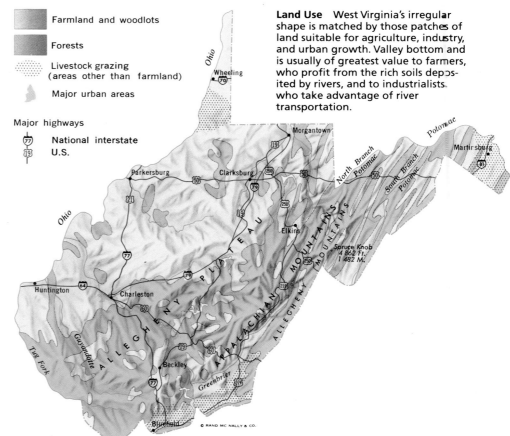

© RAND McNALLY & CO.

CORNFIELD EDGE / IOWA

The Heartland

Power from the Earth Abundant

BY HARVEY C. JACOBS

IN THE 1920s THE INDIANAPOLIS *NEWS* EMPLOYED A resident poet named William Herschell. Herschell wrote mostly regional verse, and he was assured everlasting fame in Indiana by a poem he called "Ain't God Good to Indiana?" He could have written it for the whole Heartland. In this fertile, mineral-rich land live 59 million people, whose ancestors are drawn from every quadrant of the globe. In spite of periodic wars, depressions, floods, and dust storms, the people here have lived well.

Historian Walter Havighurst said the Heartland was "massed with power and purpose." Much of the power came from the land. The purpose came from the people, many of whom broke out of the older eastern and southern colonies in the early 1800s to start new lives. They were responding to the lure of new land, which they hoped would be more fertile than the stony shelves of New England from which many of them came. They also came on horseback and in creaky wagons from the South, following the Wilderness Road through the Cumberland Gap.

When my great-great-grandfather Sam Jacobs was mus-

tered out of the Revolutionary Army, he joined the motley caravan of Virginians heading for what was to become the Northwest Territory. He paused in Ohio, where family legend has it he met a relative named John Chapman, better known as Johnny Appleseed. Chapman, an itinerant peddler-missionary of the early 1800s, traveled much of the Heartland planting appleseeds. Grandfather Sam moved on into Indiana. It was the kind of westward movement that was typical of the time.

My mother's parents, Vandiviers and Ragsdales, came to Indiana by another route, through Kentucky. I once asked Grandfather Ragsdale why his family chose central Indiana as the best place to stake their claims.

"Because they found so many sugar maple trees," he explained. "They knew that the land was fertile wherever the sugar trees grow."

In a reminiscent mood, he said, "I was just a tiny kid, but I remember that the forests were so dense here that you couldn't drive a wagon through. You could make it on horseback, but the men cut the trees out there"—he pointed toward

Illinois
Indiana
Iowa
Kansas
Michigan
Minnesota
Missouri
Nebraska
North Dakota
Ohio
South Dakota
Wisconsin

the fields of green corn rustling in the July breeze—"so they could get the wagons through."

Today, I still have 19 acres of the land from the original claims, and it's almost as well-forested with maple trees as it was when Grandfather's parents settled here. Perhaps I should say it has been "reforested," because through the years much of the timber has been harvested since the original settlement in the 1840s.

These wooded centerpieces still exist across the Heartland. Around them are fields of corn and wheat, ordered rows of soybeans, and peaceful pastures where cattle graze. Many farmers are glad they have saved their woodlots; wood stoves and fireplaces have made a comeback as alternative energy sources.

The face of the Heartland is mostly open and green. An Ohio or Illinois farmer set down in New England would say, "I'm too hemmed in." In the Southwest he might say: "Yes, I can see forever here, but the land's no good unless it can grow corn." A Texan seeing Iowa for the first time, however, might respond: "Those cornfields don't offer much variety."

The Heartland does not flaunt an imperious countenance. The land rolls along on flats and knolls. Small streams and rivers curl like commas around the fertile bottoms. The once-dense forests are preserved mostly in state and national forests—of which there are many—and by a few conservationist owners who value maple, oak, ash, and poplar more than they value annual cash crops.

The woodlands—public and private—are symbols of historical change. In the 1830s and 1840s the axe preceded the plow. Settlers helped each other "roll" the logs and build their houses. Then, woodcutters turned themselves into farmers. The farmers planted corn and clover, fenced the fields for hogs and cattle, and sent their produce into the towns and cities. A new class of workers in the small towns processed the produce and provided services to the countryside. By the mid-1920s, when my 85-year-old grandfather was reminiscing about the changes he had seen, the Heartland had become a prospering region serviced by thousands of small towns.

Small-town America found its voice and image in Sinclair

Lewis's *Main Street.* "This is America," he wrote. "Main Street is the continuation of Main Streets everywhere." His hometown was in the Heartland—Sauk Centre, Minnesota. In spite of the parochialism dramatized in his famous novel, the small town became the model setting for achieving the Good Life in America. The towns were small enough and the farm communities intimate enough that the "Howdies" and the "Hellos" were spontaneous. Friendliness and neighborliness carried over from the log-rollings.

The pioneer tradition of equality of sacrifice between husband and wife was carried forward, too. In the late 1920s the *Ladies Home Journal* published a lengthy article by an anonymous farm wife who summed up her "modern" role: "Partnership from the ground up means the farm is *ours.* Our land is ours, the home is ours, and all the work we put into improvements is ours. When you step outside your door, you have your own good brown earth and green grass under your feet. Nothing can take it away from us as long as we pay the taxes."

The American family flourished in such an environment. Reflecting upon his Kansas roots, President Dwight D. Eisenhower summed up: "All in all, we were a cheerful and vital family. Our pleasures were simple, but we had plenty of fresh air, exercise, and companionship. We would have

been insulted had anyone offered us charity."

Into this pastoral framework, the twentieth century gradually unfolded its panorama of grain elevators, steel mills, automobile factories, breweries, and coalfields. A way of life was transformed by mechanization into an integrated system for filling the nation's food basket. Yet, traced to their roots, the industrial intrusions grew mostly out of the needs of a burgeoning agriculture and a dispersed rural population. The inventors and innovators even came from the small towns and farms. Henry Ford, Harvey Firestone, Wilbur and Orville Wright, Thomas Edison, George Washington Carver— the list could go on—are only a few who came from the Heartland states.

The base on which this half rural, half industrial society rests has its origins millions of years ago. Geologists say that at least four Arctic glaciers, formed by accumulated winter snows that survived the summer sun for thousands of years, pushed southward to cover almost half of North America. The last, the Wisconsin glacier, retreated about 11,000 years ago. It had a special affinity for the Heartland states.

It rasped away the craggy mountains, dug new valleys, stripped the soil to bedrock in some places, and leveled fertile soil in others. It shifted and, in some cases, exposed rich veins of ore and minerals. Myriad lakes were scooped out,

Overleaf–MITCHELL PASS, OREGON TRAIL, SCOTTS BLUFF NATIONAL MONUMENT / NEBRASKA

is a fortune to be made.''

The Heartland has been growing things ever since, and the superficial observer may not sense the inner grandeur of the predominantly placid landscape. The New England poet Robert Frost once said the soil of Iowa looked ''good enough to eat.''

The Heartland is half agricultural and half industrial, but the cities grew out of the agriculture surrounding them. Today the huge crops of soybeans, corn, wheat, hogs, poultry, sheep, and cattle funnel into the city markets in awesome abundance. The process is industrialized of course, but the poetry remains in the green seas of corn and wheat and in the lush pastures. At night during the growing season those of us attuned to the cycle of the seasons can actually hear the corn growing to the accompaniment of a chorus of insects and night creatures.

Ohio, Michigan, Wisconsin, Illinois, and Indiana, all lying in the curving industrial corridor around the Great Lakes, are generally considered industrial. But they are also agricultural. Illinois, for example, produces more grain and legumes than Iowa, although Iowa leads all Heartland states in livestock production. The northern tier—Michigan, Wisconsin, and Minnesota—also produces food in abundance, in spite of a shorter growing season. Minnesota is third among the Heartland states in livestock production.

These three states are also ruggedly attractive, with their lakes, hills, and tall timber. Minnesota, the ''Land of 10,000 Lakes,'' lures visitors and sportsmen. The state actually has more than 15,000 lakes. Not far behind are Michigan with 11,000 and Wisconsin with 8,500. These states have soil that produces hay, orchards, and vineyards. The clover and alfalfa feed the dairy cattle, making the best milk and cheese in the land. Beneath much of the soil lie stone, gravel, granite, iron ore, and minerals.

This is timber country, too, providing the setting for the mythical lumberjack, Paul Bunyan. Paul was born across the border in Canada, but emigrated soon to Heartland lumber camps. His helper was Babe, the Blue Ox, who helped Paul build the Mississippi. She used the Great Lakes as her drinking trough. Kansas is flat, according to this folklore hero, because Paul hitched Babe to it and turned it over to make good corn and wheat land.

Kansas lore has it that in 1874 a farmer newly arrived from the Russian steppes reached down to grasp a handful of the

Left– ROCK FORMS, WISCONSIN DELLS / WISCONSIN

Above– BIG SPRING, CURRENT RIVER, OZARK NATIONAL SCENIC RIVERWAYS / MISSOURI

rich, black earth. Gazing across the flat prairie, he said, "In three years that ocean of grass will be transformed into an ocean of waving fields of grain."

The prophecy was fulfilled mostly because Mennonites from the Crimea brought seed wheat called Turkey Red. It was the beginning of making Kansas the nation's wheat capital. The state produces a fifth of the total crop in the United States.

Today, as in the beginning, the summer wind brings the wheat harvests, for the wind seems to blow the gold into the ripening wheat. The waves ripple toward infinity, swaying and twisting in a slow dance. When the wind rests and the heat settles, the wheat stands shimmering like a calm ocean in a summer sun. It's ready for the combines that gulp in the stalks and disgorge the straw in one place and the grains in another.

South Dakota produces grain, too, but mostly in the "east river" area set off by the Missouri River. Oats, flax, and hay also grow well. "West river" is cowboy and shepherd country, where flat ranches tilt up to the setting sun. Farther west the low mountains called the Black Hills nudge Wyoming. They are "black" because, viewed from the distant plain, their domed forests appear invitingly dark. Wild game thrives here.

The land was once the bottom of an inland sea, where subsequent glaciers ironed out plains and prairies, gouged tranquil lakes and rivers, and heaved up the Badlands, which were left rugged and raw, emulating a moonscape full of grandeur and mystery. The fossils they have given up document the world of dinosaurs and other prehistoric animals. This area is also the nation's largest supplier of gold.

Coming from the tree-covered Midwest, North Dakota's first settlers must have confronted the treeless tabletop west of the Red River with disappointment. From what would they build their houses?

Looking downward from the limitless sky, they saw the lush grasses—sod! The new settlers learned to slice and fit it into walls and roofs—from which the folk songs about "sod shanties" were born.

The settlers who moved on west and south, across the Missouri plateau, found trees: cottonwood, willow, elm, ash, birch, and more. Wherever they turned, the soil was fertile. Game was abundant. It still is. North Dakota has more wildlife refuges than any other state.

There is a near mystical quality to much of the Dakota landscape. Theodore Roosevelt discovered that quality in 1883 when he went there on a hunting trip. He became a Dakota cattleman and made North Dakota his second home. His description captures some of the appeal: "The grassy, scantily wooded bottoms through which the river flows are bounded by bare, jagged buttes; their fantastic shapes and sharp, steep edges throw the most curious shadows, under the cloudless glaring sky; and at evening I love to sit out in front of the hut and see their hard gray outlines gradually growing soft and purple as the flaming sunset by degrees softens and dies away."

Roosevelt was a rugged outdoorsman. He loved the challenge of weather, but the prairie winds often drove him to shelter. "Sometimes furious gales blow down from the north," he wrote, "driving before them the clouds of blinding snow-dust, wrapping the mantle of death around every unsheltered being that faces this unshackled anger."

The unshackled anger of winter can be dangerous to both man and beast in much of the Heartland. The raw winds sweep ruthlessly across Kansas, for example, where even the Indians were impressed by those who could survive the wind. The Indian name for Kansas territory was Kansa, meaning "wind people." Snow sometimes clogs the highways of all the Heartland states. It isolates communities, causes power failures, and maroons thousands of persons who can't leave their homes until the snowplows get through.

Extreme and rapid weather changes test the adaptability of every inhabitant. "You don't like our weather?" we in Indiana say to out-of-state visitors. "Stay a couple of hours and it'll be different."

To persons depending upon favorable climate for harvests, this is high risk territory. But there are compensating assets. Water in the rivers and lakes makes the landscape beautiful; water from heaven makes it green and productive. Without its annual 40-inch rainfall, the Heartland could not have become the breadbasket of America.

There is also the challenge of making weather a partner. From the beginning, the settlers learned that the anger of the elements could be channeled. Like the sod, the weather could be used. Windmills were erected to harness the wind to drive the pumps to lift drinking water from the innards of the earth. When the growing season was too short for one strain of wheat, the farmers found another. When the floods flushed away the topsoil, dams and levees were put in place. When winds, along with drought, lifted the loose soil into blankets of dust during the Depression of the 1930s, it took some time to reclaim the farms. But the people returned to build dams to retain the runoff, to farm more in harmony with the cycles of nature, and to plant more trees to anchor the soil.

In at least one Heartland state the pioneers brought their trees with them. When the westward wagons crossed the eastern boundary of Nebraska at the Missouri River, in the early 1860s, the settlers, like the ones in the Dakota caravans, searched the horizon for trees. Very few were to be found. But 10 years later J. Sterling Morton, a Nebraska journalist who later served as U.S. Secretary of Agriculture, suggested that one day of the year be designated for planting trees. And so Arbor Day, now a national observance, began. In Nebraska alone, a million trees were subsequently planted, presaging the formation of the Nebraska National Forest. It was the first completely "man-made" forest in the nation.

Whether the forests are man-made or man-managed, they exist in every Heartland state. In southern Ohio, Indiana, Illinois, and Missouri, where the Wisconsin glacier did not reach, are timbered hills and clear lakes. For 400 miles along Ohio's southern border the Ohio River has attracted steel mills, power plants, and factories—most of them powered by coal. But clusters of willow, sycamore, and ash fall away from the river. There may even be an orchard now and then frequented by the ghost of Johnny Appleseed.

Indiana is flatly agricultural except at the extreme north

PRAIRIE'S EDGE, BADLANDS NATIONAL PARK / SOUTH DAKOTA

and south. Steel is produced in the north, but alongside the grimy mills are the Indiana Dunes, a wild panorama of shifting sands rising above the shores of Lake Michigan. Some of these dunes are desertlike, while others are covered with small trees and binder grass. In the south is scenic Brown County, where the autumn foliage of the hardwood forests attracts visitors from across the nation.

Illinois has its limestone bluffs, the Mississippi palisades, in the north and the Ozarks in the south. Missouri boasts the more famous Ozarks, and there Lake of the Ozarks and hundreds of other spring-fed lakes break up the rugged landscape.

In Minnesota, Wisconsin, and Michigan there are millions of acres of wilderness, plus thousands of lakes, to tempt vacationers and sportsmen. These states have some prairie vistas, too. Minnesota's pipestone country—red stone from which Indians made peace pipes—in the southwestern part of the state has prairie grass that looks as wild and unfettered as it did the first time white men saw it.

Forests cover about half of Wisconsin, and in the north central part there are higher elevations that look as rugged as they did before the glaciers came.

Michigan has such a natural, unspoiled countenance that more of it is used for recreation than for any other purpose. Iowa, the "biggest cornfield on earth," has an area in the northeast so rugged it is called Little Switzerland—a panoply of high buttes and cliffs jutting out along the rivers. The Indians also left their mark here in animal-shaped burial grounds.

Western Nebraska is more than corn country. Toadstool Park has huge rocks carved by erosion. Agate Fossil Beds National Monument is a place where fossils of extinct plains mammals are found. They are thought to go back about 20 million years.

What, then, is the Heartland? It is tractors growling across the broad fields. It is a robot welding an automobile frame. It is also children gathering Indian arrowheads in dozens of places where native Americans once ruled the territory. It is unearthing prehistoric skeletons, hiking in the wilderness, poking among the ashes of ancient volcanic formations, or stalking wild game with camera or gun. Reclaimed and preserved, much of the Heartland is as it was 150 or more years ago.

Grandfather cleared his homestead farm so that the corn and clover could grow, but he did not clear all of it. He left hundreds of trees standing, including 200 maple trees, to provide sap for his spring "run." Many farmers followed the same pattern. They preserved the woods, and thousands of those woods break the sameness of a landscape now engaged in growing food and fiber on a mass scale.

Today, one can still go from the prevailing openness of the tilled acres into the coolness and mystery of the woods. The woods are now, and have always been, a place for renewal. All things grow here in haphazard beauty instead of in the neat and ordered rows of the tilled land. There is a harmonizing of the tame and the wild in these woods and pastures: smooth and rounded slopes, jagged gullies, short mowed meadows, and scruffy wild grass. The sunlight, so harsh on the cultivated rows, falls softened and gracious in the open spaces in the woods. The white oak and elm, the hickory and walnut trees cast their shadows in variegated patterns. There is likely to be clover humming with bees, wild gooseberry bushes, sassafras bushes, catnip, and elderberry blooming its creamy green-white tufts of lace.

Deeper in the woods, the wild flowers have given no ground for 150 years. I search them out every spring—the blue-purple windflowers, the Dutchman's breeches, the cowslips, the violets, and the saucy jacks-in-the-pulpit. The little stream turns east and leaves a northern bank shaded for the ferns breaking out of their leafy nests. Some of these flowers we shall transplant, duplicating the ritual of scores of grandparents who brought their house flowers from the woods.

This natural oasis is not much different from the time Grandfather saw it first. The tempo of living has quickened, but the cycle of seedtime and harvest continues with increasingly abundant yields from the "clearings" he made, confirming the judgment of those who chose this place over all the other places they could have gone.

Left– MUNISING FALLS, PICTURED ROCKS NATIONAL LAKESHORE / MICHIGAN

Above– ST. CROIX RIVER DALLES, INTERSTATE STATE PARK / MINNESOTA-WISCONSIN

Left– MAPLE AND BIRCH, VOYAGEURS NATIONAL PARK / MINNESOTA

Right– MINER'S CASTLE, LAKE SUPERIOR, PICTURED ROCKS NATIONAL LAKESHORE / MICHIGAN

Above– DUNE GRASS, INDIANA DUNES NATIONAL LAKESHORE / INDIANA

Right– SLUMP BLOCKS, OLD MAN'S CAVE AREA, HOCKING HILLS STATE PARK / OHIO

Overleaf– MISSOURI RIVER AT BISMARCK / NORTH DAKOTA

Above– CLAY FORMS ALONG MISSOURI RIVER NEAR HUFF / NORTH DAKOTA

Right– LITTLE MISSOURI RIVER COUNTRY, THEODORE ROOSEVELT NATIONAL PARK / NORTH DAKOTA

Left– MOONRISE, CHIMNEY ROCK NATIONAL HISTORIC SITE / NEBRASKA

Below– MOONRISE, MONUMENT ROCKS / KANSAS

Maps of the Heartland...The Midwest

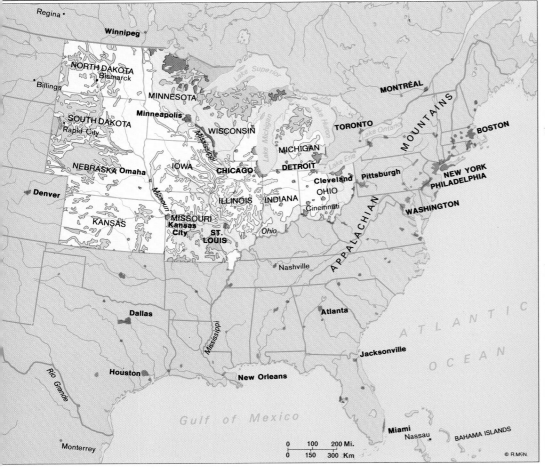

Land Use The Midwest embodies the agricultural-industrial nature of the American economy, and this dual role is reflected in the region's land use. Dominating the area is an almost continuous expanse of some of the most productive farmland in the world. And this agricultural landscape is dotted with many of the country's most important urban-industrial centers—among them Chicago, Detroit, St. Louis, and Cleveland. Northern areas contribute to the lumber industry, and forests are the principal land feature.

While nature divides the land in asymmetrical patterns, Americans rarely do; this geometric patchwork of cropland in southern Minnesota exemplifies human division of the midwestern landscape. However, regularly spaced farmsteads, cities, and roads did not develop at random. They are, instead, the result of the rectangular survey system, which was ideally suited for the relatively flat land of the Midwest. In this way, the government divided the area into right-angled parcels for settlement.

The Mississippi River played a major role in the development of the Midwest. This easily navigated transportation route was first a catalyst to settlement of the region and now continues to provide a low-cost shipping route to national and international markets. As the river flows to the Gulf of Mexico, St. Louis, shown here, is the last of the major midwestern cities through which it passes.

The Midwest leads a double life as one of the richest agricultural regions in the world and a diversified industrial center of almost unsurpassed capacity. The Midwest could easily comprise two separate, enviably productive nations, one agricultural and the other industrial, if the two activities could be separated territorially. But they overlap spatially, and their interests are inextricably entwined. Concentrations of agriculture or heavy-manufacturing activities do exist, but highly productive farmland often abuts a city, and skilled machinists and manufacturing plants are dispersed among small agriculturally based towns.

Nineteenth-century Americans recognized the Midwest's potential, and states such as Ohio, Indiana, and Illinois were quickly formed as people moved west over the Appalachian Mountains. More ingenuity was required as migrants approached the Midwest's western margin, a semiarid zone with a fragile environment, once known as the Great American Desert. That this description proved inappropriate testifies to the resourcefulness of the settlers and to the Midwest's advantageous natural situation.

The Midwest's natural assets include its climate, waterways, mineral resources, and soils. The penetration of the Gulf of Mexico into the North American continent and the lack of mountain ranges in the Southeast allow moist air masses from the Gulf to flow north, supplying the Midwest with precipitation. The waterways of the Great Lakes and St. Lawrence Seaway and the Mississippi, Missouri, and Ohio rivers endow the area with one of the best natural transportation systems in the world, allowing access to the Atlantic Ocean and the Gulf of Mexico. Thousands of years of glacial attrition and deposition have also left the region with accessible deposits of metal ores and rich soils.

Because of these excellent soils, agribusiness is of major importance to all Midwest states. However, no state escapes the conflict resulting

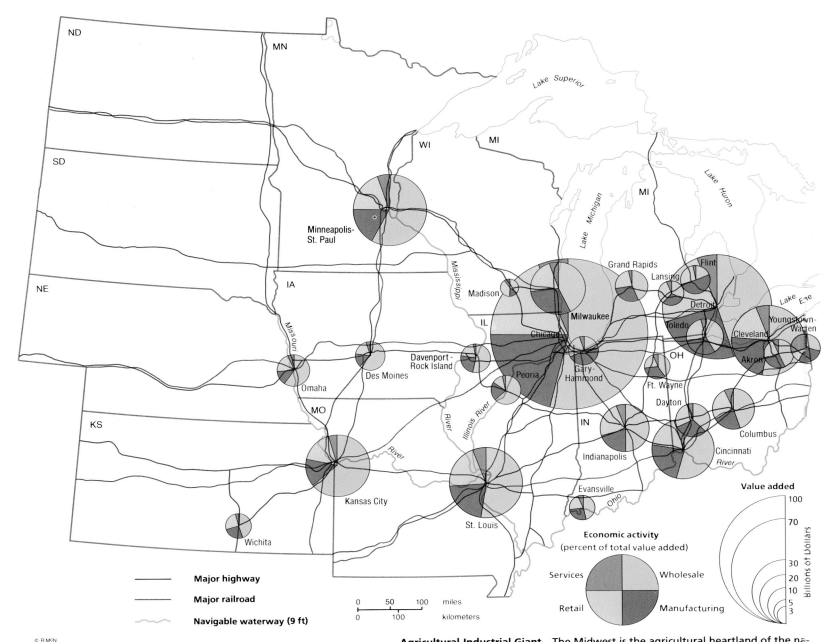

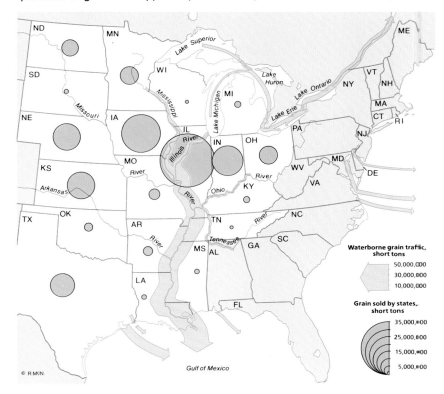

© R.McN.

Major highway
Major railroad
Navigable waterway (9 ft)

0   50   100   miles
0   100   kilometers

Value added
100
70
30
20
10
5
3
Billions of Dollars

Economic activity
(percent of total value added)

Services   Wholesale
Retail   Manufacturing

Agricultural-Industrial Giant The Midwest is the agricultural heartland of the nation, containing over forty percent of its farms and producing much of its income from agriculture. Although more than half of the land is considered cropland, the majority of the Midwest's population lives in urban centers. These cities contribute one-third of the nation's manufacturing and over twenty-five percent of its wholesale, its retail, and its shopping trade. Centrally located with access to transportation routes, the region plays a major role in national and international trade.

from competition between rural-agricultural and urban-industrial interests. This conflict is especially pronounced in Illinois, where the "Downstate" area and Chicago vie unceasingly.

The Midwest is sometimes viewed as the region where national political opinions and marketing trends can be most readily fathomed, but this is a role the region plays with hesitancy. Inasmuch as the Midwest best represents agriculture and diversified industry, the two activities that have long defined the nation's strength, it could be considered a microcosm of the country's economy. However, it would be a mistake to accept this as a sign of regional homogeneity in social outlook and political belief. On the contrary, the Midwest is a region where varying opinions are expressed and defended. Wide differences of opinion might, in fact, be seen as a hallmark of midwestern government, and this region has a history of launching both progressive and conservative movements and politicians into the political arena.

A hundred years ago, the Midwest was one of the most glamourous and rapidly growing regions in the nation. Today, it is occasionally maligned as an area with problems stemming from its changing agricultural techniques and its long industrial history. The Midwest's rural population has been moving to the cities, and many people have been leaving the region altogether for western and southern states.

Despite its problems, the Midwest still has great potential. Its transportation systems provide easy access to vast resources and markets, and the region has retained a large, skilled labor force. Today, the midwestern states continue to diversify industrially as they seek to attract more high-technology and service industries. In adapting to current situations and keeping up with national trends, the Midwest is carrying on its tradition of resourcefulness. Against the background of excellent human and natural resources, this resilience will most likely ensure the region's success in the coming decades.

Grain Shipment The Midwest acts as a grain supplier to the world, and shipments indicate the response of this extraordinary granary to international needs. Rich soils, level-to-rolling terrain, an adequate growing season, and plentiful water supplies characterize the Midwest's agricultural endowment. For maximum production, farmers employ highly mechanized systems of commercial agriculture. And even government programs to curtail production to cut surpluses do not succeed; vast quantities of grain are shipped to ports annually.

Waterborne grain traffic,
short tons
50,000,000
30,000,000
10,000,000

Grain sold by states,
short tons
35,000,000
25,000,000
15,000,000
5,000,000

© R.McN.

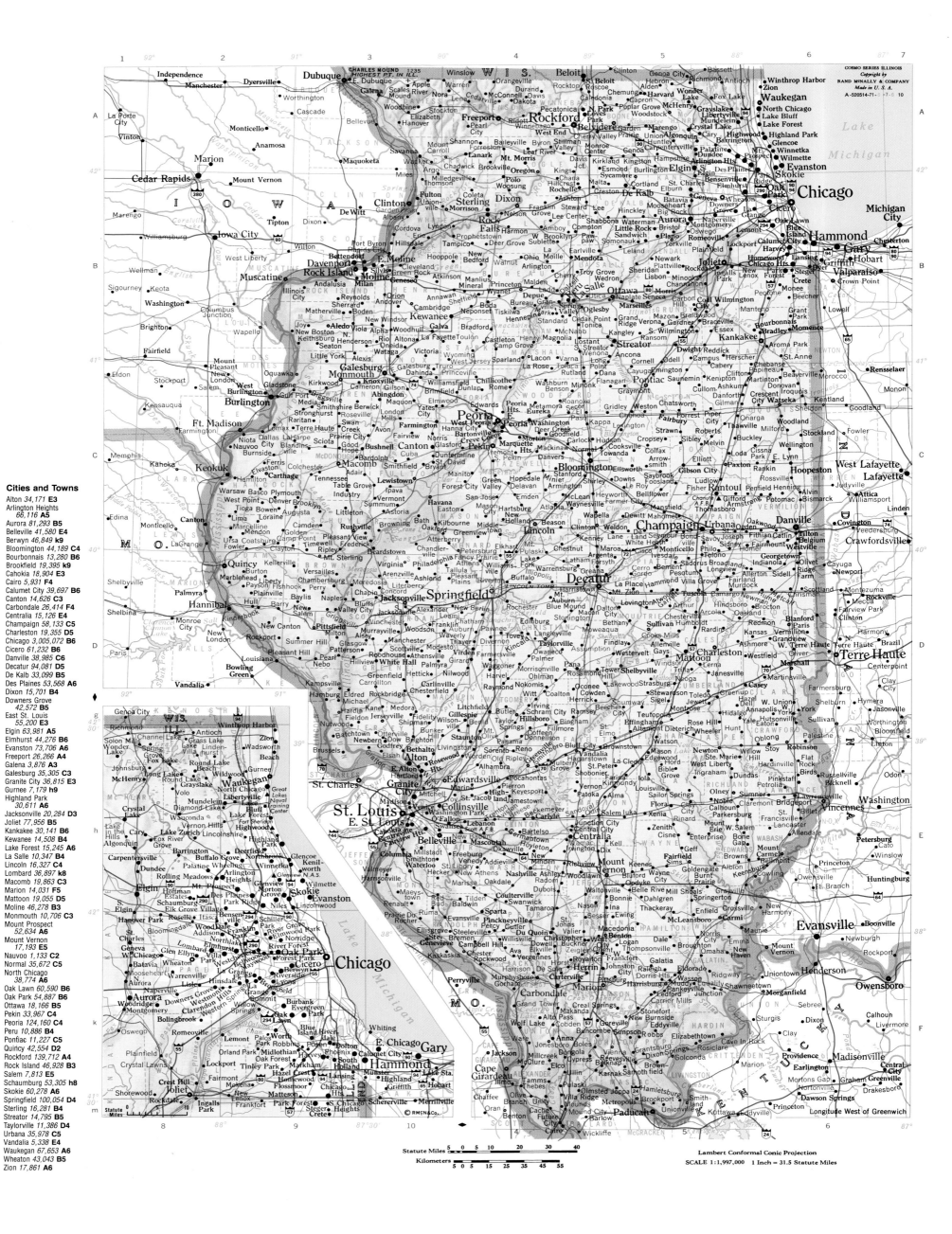

Statute Miles

Kilometers

Lambert Conformal Conic Projection
SCALE 1:1,997,000   1 Inch = 31.5 Statute Miles

Illinois

POPULATION 11,426,596.
Rank: 5. *Density:* 205 people/mi²
(79 people/km²). *Urban:* 83.3%.
Rural: 16.7%.
AGE *<20:* 32%. *20–40:* 32%.
40–65: 25%. *>65:* 11%.
ETHNIC GROUPS *White:* 80.8%.
Black: 14.7%. *Spanish origin:*
5.6%. *Native American:* 0.1%.
Other: 4.4%.

INCOME/CAPITA $10,521. *Rank:* 7.
POLITICS 1948–1980 elections:
President: 3 Dem., 6 Rep.
Governor: 4 Dem., 5 Rep.
ENTERED UNION December 3,
1818, 21st state.
CAPITAL Springfield, 100,054.
LARGEST CITY Chicago, 3,005,072.

AREA 57,871 mi² (149,885 km²).
Rank: 23. *Water area:* 2,226 mi²
(5,765 km²).
ELEVATIONS *Highest:* Charles
Mound, 1,235 ft (376 m). *Lowest:*
Along Mississippi River, 279 ft
(85 m).
CLIMATE Cold winters, hot
summers; moderate rainfall.

Illinois, one of the nation's wealthiest states, is also one of the most clearly divided, reflecting more than any of its neighbors the great division between industry and agriculture in the midwestern economy. In fact, Illinois may be regarded almost as two states. The first, based on manufacturing, is centered on the Chicago metropolitan area and other northern cities. Here, communities are often split between urban and suburban areas, among racial and ethnic groups, and between rich and poor—divisions deeply rooted in the state's history and difficult to overcome. The second "state," founded on agriculture and known as downstate, is made up of a central agricultural area and a southern region rich in coal.

Despite these regional differences, Illinois has played a vital role in the Midwest and in the nation. It leads almost all other states in many sectors of manufacturing, agriculture, and mining. Chicago has served as the transportation hub of the nation since the nineteenth century. Its railroads, water traffic, and highways have adapted easily to twentieth-century technology; and O'Hare Airport, outside of Chicago, is widely acknowledged as the busiest air terminal in the world. With access to both the Great Lakes and the Mississippi waterways, and with nationwide rail and road connections, Illinois is ideally suited to gather resources, process them, and distribute finished products throughout the country.

Yet now, in the face of a changing economy, the deep divisions in Illinois are exacting a toll that may affect the future welfare of the state. Traditionally, regional and local interests have been set above the concerns of the state as a whole, and such partisanship has led to political fragmentation. As a result, Illinois is split into more units of government and elects more officials than any other state. In addition, the conflict between Chicago and downstate is marked by a continual tug-of-war over revenues and political influence. Such divisions make integration of statewide policies particularly difficult, and the refusal to compromise could have serious, long-term consequences. In response, officials and other citizens in the two "states" are working to unify Illinois into one commonwealth that will be able to meet the needs of its people and face the challenges of the future.

The success of Illinois is largely dependent upon Chicago. A manufacturing center, the city contributes greatly to the state's income, and its location provides access to the transportation routes necessary for profitable industry and agriculture. But just as Illinois depends upon Chicago, so does Chicago depend upon the rest of the state. Resources found in other areas provide much of the input that keeps the city's factories productive. And the state's agriculture helps make Chicago an agribusiness and finance center: many crops and much of the livestock raised in other parts of the state are bought and sold through the Chicago Board of Trade.

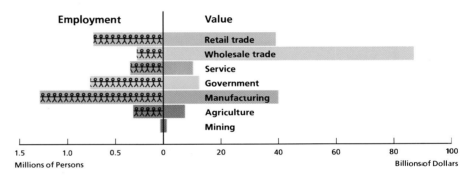

Economic Activities Illinois's economy is one of the strongest in the Midwest, and the state's productivity in virtually every sector of activity allows it to vie for national leadership.

Land Use Illinois's rich, level soils have always guaranteed a productive agriculture. This is true with respect to all the feed and grain crops and meat, dairy, and poultry products for which the Midwest is famous. But besides its environmental resources, Illinois's location between the Great Lakes and the Mississippi River system has made the state a center of transportation for the nation, assuring the rapid growth of state cities and industry. In turn, urban and industrial areas are concentrated where water, rail, road, and air connections meet.

Farmland (cropland and pastureland)

Farmland and woodlots

Swampland and marshland

Livestock grazing (areas other than farmland)

Major urban areas

Major highways

National interstate

U.S.

Energy The industry-agriculture, north-south split that is so typical of Illinois is especially reflected in reference to energy. Southern Illinois provides nearly sixty percent of the state's fuel through processing the vast southern coal deposits, but the agricultural nature of the region accounts for its relatively low fuel use. And although northern Illinois produces nearly thirty percent of the state's energy, its high level of industrialization and consequent high energy use create an overall energy deficit for the region. This deficit is taken care of by oil, gas, and coal imports.

Fuel consumption and production

Fuel consumption greatly exceeds production

Fuel consumption exceeds production

Fuel production exceeds consumption

Fuel production greatly exceeds consumption

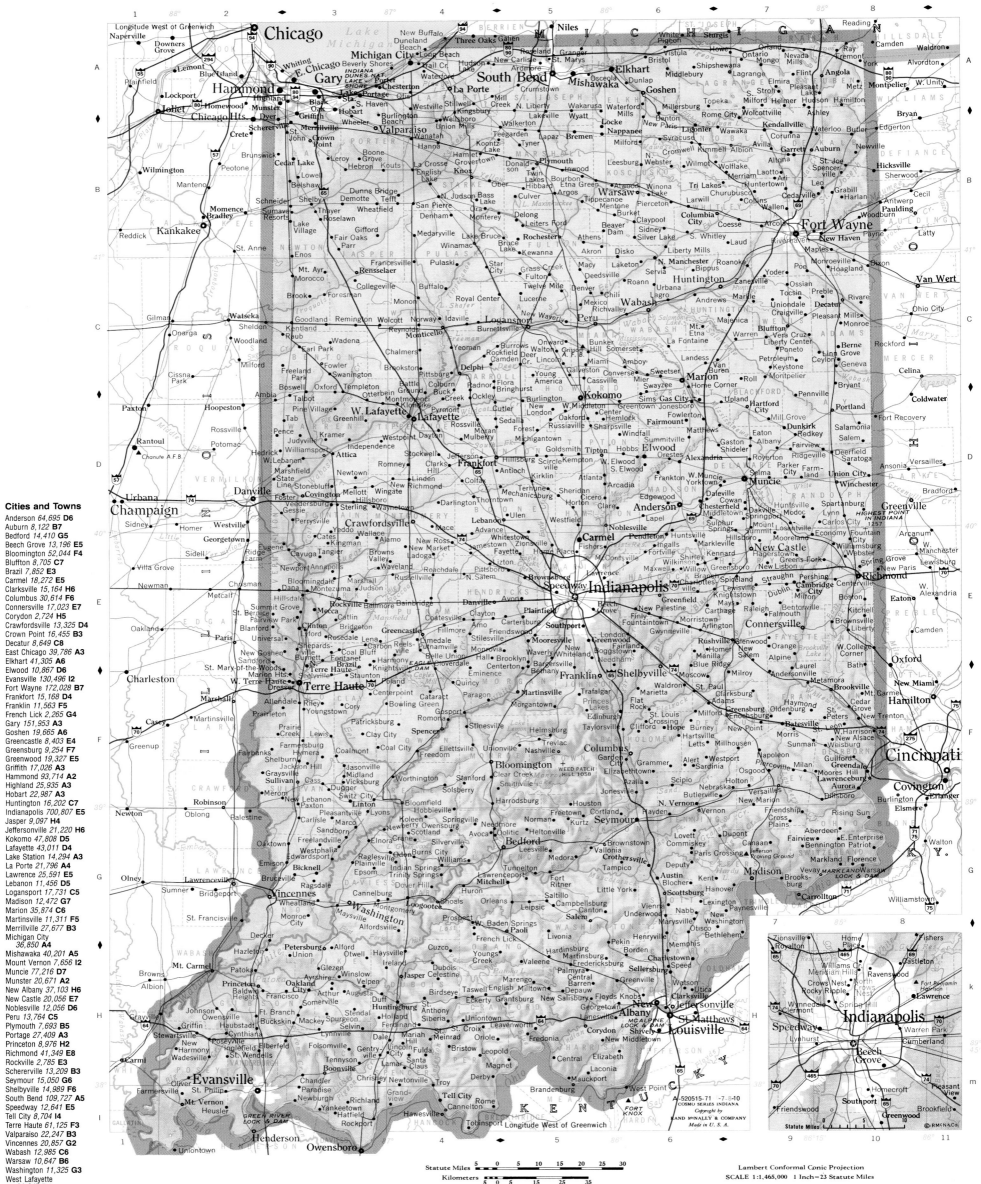

A-520515-71   -7-8-10
COSMO SERIES INDIANA
Copyright by
RAND McNALLY & COMPANY
Made in U.S.A.

Lambert Conformal Conic Projection
SCALE 1:1,465,000   1 Inch=23 Statute Miles

Statute Miles
Kilometers

Indiana

POPULATION 5,490,260.
 Rank: 12. *Density:* 153 people/
 mi² (59 people/km²). *Urban:*
 64.2%. *Rural:* 35.8%.
AGE *<20:* 33%. *20–40:* 31%.
 40–65: 25%. *>65:* 11%.
ETHNIC GROUPS *White:* 91.2%.
 Black: 7.6%. *Spanish origin:*
 1.6%. *Native American:* 0.1%.
 Other 1.1%.

INCOME/CAPITA $8,936. *Rank:* 31.
POLITICS 1948–1980 elections:
 President: 1 Dem., 8 Rep.
 Governor: 3 Dem., 6 Rep.
ENTERED UNION December 11,
 1816, 19th state.
CAPITAL Indianapolis, 700,807.
LARGEST CITY Indianapolis.

AREA 36,413 mi² (94,309 km²).
 Rank: 38. *Water area:* 481 mi²
 (1,246 km²).
ELEVATIONS *Highest:* In Wayne
 County, 1,257 ft (383 m). *Lowest:*
 Along Ohio River, 320 ft (98 m).
CLIMATE Hot, humid summers;
 cold winters; moderate rainfall.

Indiana Dunes National Lakeshore preserves nearly fifteen thousand acres of beautiful and unusual terrain along Lake Michigan. There are a number of environments here, including sandy beaches, sand dunes of varying shapes and sizes, verdant valleys, and low, flat marshlands. The lakeshore is all the more unusual because of its location within the almost solidly urban and industrial area near Gary, Indiana. At least two hundred species of birds use the lakeshore as a resting, nesting, or wintering area. The formation of the dunes is a gradual, lengthy process. After sand is carried ashore by lake water and swept inland by wind, it can be blocked by hardy vegetation. Grasses, shrubs, and small trees provide cores around which small sand cones form, and as more windswept sand enlarges the cones, they become sand dunes.

From the air, the Indiana landscape takes on the appearance of a quilt, a colorful patchwork of rectangular fields bordered by country roads and highways. This geometric design is a result of the rectangular survey system, established in 1785 to divide the land into regular townships, ranges, and sections for its orderly settlement. The pattern is typical of the Midwest, where generations have followed the basic rectangular grid to scribe property with neat, straight boundaries and well-organized counties. The pattern holds true right down to the state's county seats. Platted around courthouses set in town squares, these local-government sites are connected to one another by an intricate, systematic network of state roads.

The state's agriculture, industry, and cultural life also reflect a quilt-like design, although the pattern is more often one of striking contrasts. Indiana is an industrial state that sustains a productive agricultural economy; an urban state with deep rural roots; and a tolerant state that has its share of racial divisions and tensions. Few states can point to an awesome battery of blast furnaces in one region and a collection of rustic covered bridges in another. The geographic and cultural patterns in Indiana reflect the great variety of American life that is concentrated in this state. It can claim some identity with all four regions of the country: the South, by proximity to the Ohio River; the North, in its industrial production; the East, by path of settlement; and the West, in its outlook on resources and values.

In the past decade, however, the pattern of Indiana's life has been subjected to considerable strain. Economic development has led to increased air and water pollution, and the recent economic recession has resulted in a decline in heavy industry. Overall, however, Indiana continues to weave together the essential strands of American life in all its diversity and contrasts. Despite the strains, the fabric still holds strong.

Town Settlement The pattern of Indiana's settlement dates back to the horse-and-buggy days, when much of daily life revolved around a centralized county seat. The limited county size enabled taxpayers and other citizens to make the round trip to the courthouse, and its surrounding facilities, within one day.

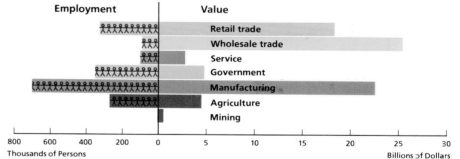

Employment   **Value**

Retail trade
Wholesale trade
Service
Government
Manufacturing
Agriculture
Mining

800 600 400 200 0   5   10   15   20   25   30
Thousands of Persons   Billions of Dollars

Economic Activities   Many of Indiana's industries are concentrated in particular cities: the steel industry in Gary, recreational-vehicle manufacture in Elkhart, and diesel-engine production in Columbus. And although mining is but a small contributor to the state's economy, one product—limestone for building construction—has found its way to most states in the nation.

Land Use   Indiana's pattern of land use is typical of much of the upper Midwest, where productive farmland and beautiful landscapes are spotted liberally with cities of substantial size and industrial potential. On Indiana's Lake Michigan shore, parks enclosing fragile sand dunes lie adjacent to areas of heavy industry, which can be damaging to the parklands if precautions are not taken.

Farmland (cropland and pastureland)

Farmland and woodlots

Forests

Livestock grazing (areas other than farmland)

Major urban areas

Major highways

National interstate

U.S.

© RAND McNALLY & CO.

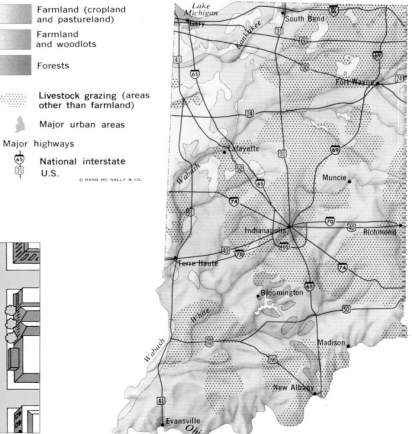

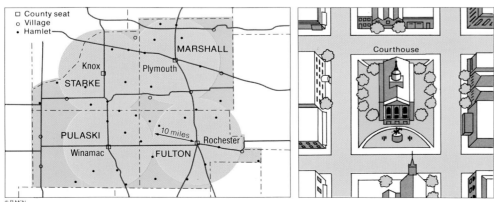

County seat
Village
Hamlet

MARSHALL
Knox   Plymouth
STARKE
PULASKI   10 miles   Rochester
Winamac   FULTON

Courthouse

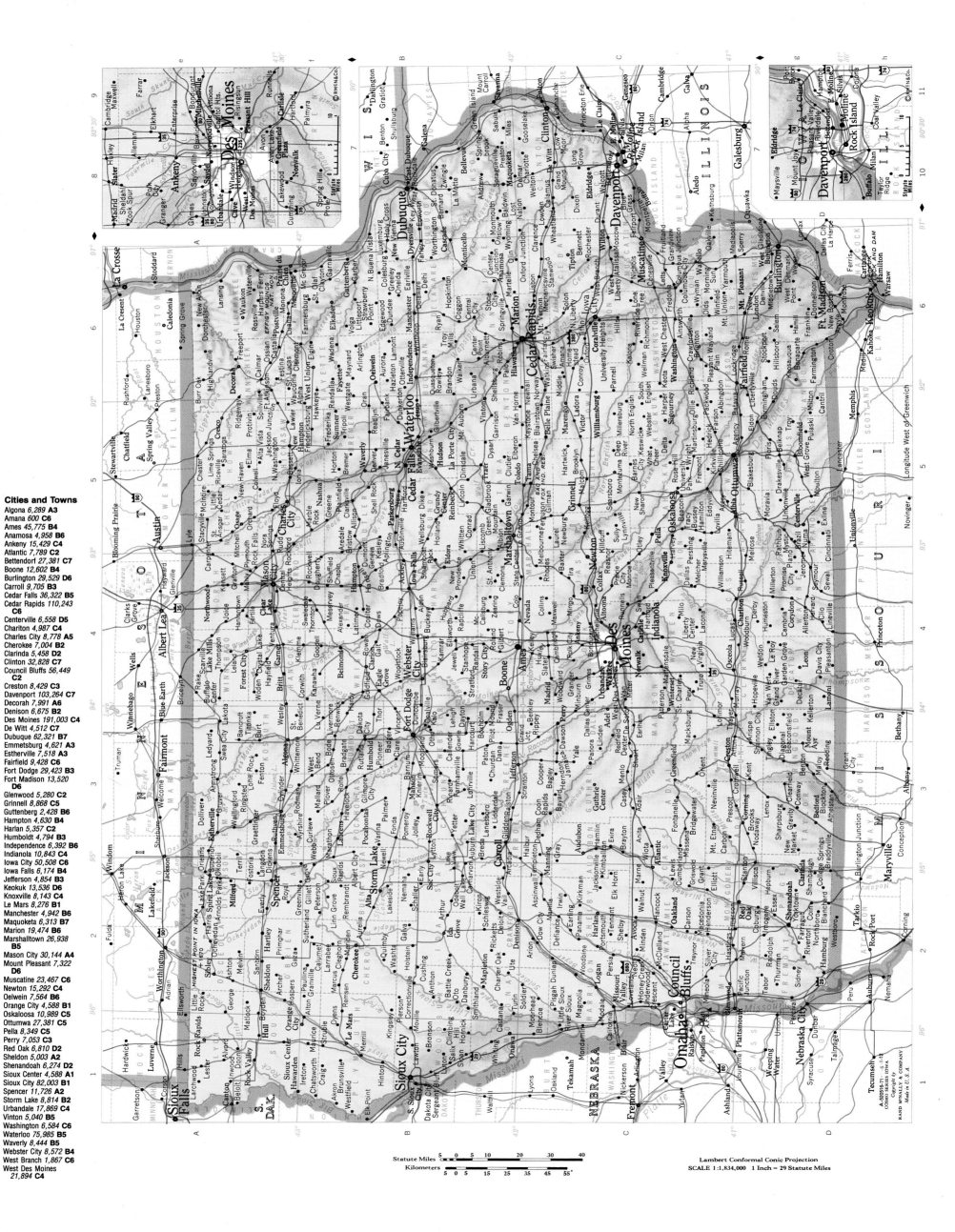

Cities and Towns

Algona 6,289 A3
Amana 600 C6
Ames 45,775 B4
Anamosa 4,958 B6
Ankeny 15,429 C4
Atlantic 7,789 C2
Bettendorf 27,381 C7
Boone 12,602 B4
Burlington 29,529 D6
Carroll 9,705 B3
Cedar Falls 36,322 B5
Cedar Rapids 110,243
  C6
Centerville 6,558 D5
Chariton 4,987 C4
Charles City 8,778 A5
Cherokee 7,004 B2
Clarinda 5,458 D2
Clinton 32,828 C7
Council Bluffs 56,449
  C2
Creston 8,429 C3
Davenport 103,264 C7
Decorah 7,991 A6
Denison 6,675 B2
Des Moines 191,003 C4
De Witt 4,512 C7
Dubuque 62,321 B7
Emmetsburg 4,621 A3
Estherville 7,518 A3
Fairfield 9,428 C6
Fort Dodge 29,423 B3
Fort Madison 13,520
  D6
Glenwood 5,280 C2
Grinnell 8,868 C5
Guttenberg 2,428 B6
Hampton 4,630 B4
Harlan 5,357 C2
Humboldt 4,794 B3
Independence 6,392 B6
Indianola 10,843 C4
Iowa City 50,508 C6
Iowa Falls 6,174 B4
Jefferson 4,854 B3
Keokuk 13,536 D6
Knoxville 8,143 C4
Le Mars 8,276 B1
Manchester 4,942 B6
Maquoketa 6,313 B7
Marion 19,474 B6
Marshalltown 26,938
  B5
Mason City 30,144 A4
Mount Pleasant 7,322
  D6
· Muscatine 23,467 C6
Newton 15,292 C4
Oelwein 7,564 B6
Orange City 4,588 B1
Oskaloosa 10,989 C5
Ottumwa 27,381 C5
Pella 8,349 C5
Perry 7,053 C3
Red Oak 6,810 D2
Sheldon 5,003 A2
Shenandoah 6,274 D2
Sioux Center 4,588 A1
Sioux City 82,003 B1
Spencer 11,726 A2
Storm Lake 8,814 B2
Urbandale 17,869 C4
Vinton 5,040 B5
Washington 6,584 C6
Waterloo 75,985 B5
Waverly 8,444 B5
Webster City 8,572 B4
West Branch 1,867 C6
West Des Moines
  21,894 C4

Iowa

POPULATION 2,913,808.
Rank: 27. *Density:* 52 people/mi²
(20 people/km²). *Urban:* 58.6%.
Rural: 41.4%.
AGE <20: 33%. 20–40: 30%.
40–65: 24%. >65: 13%.
ETHNIC GROUPS *White:* 97.4%.
Black: 1.4%. *Spanish origin:*
8.8%. *Native American:* 0.2%.
Other: 1%.

INCOME/CAPITA $9,358. *Rank:* 24.
POLITICS 1948–1980 elections:
President: 2 Dem., 7 Rep.
Governor: 5 Dem., 10 Rep.
ENTERED UNION December 28,
1846, 29th state.
CAPITAL Des Moines, 191,003.
LARGEST CITY Des Moines.

AREA 56,275 mi² (145,752 km²).
Rank: 24. *Water area:* 310 mi²
(803 km²).
ELEVATIONS *Highest:* In Osceola
County, 1,670 ft (509 m). *Lowest:*
Along Mississippi River, 480 ft
(146 m).
CLIMATE Hot summers with ample
rainfall; cold winters with some
heavy snows.

Iowa lies in the heart of the American Midwest, the most productive agricultural region in the world. This location has made the state an agricultural leader, producing the grains and livestock needed by the United States and world markets. But the state is also positioned on the fringe of Midwest industrialization, and its future may depend on its ability to balance farming with a diversified and changing industrial sector.

Even in the fertile Midwest, few states are blessed with as much prime tillable acreage or quite so abundant an agriculture. Nearly all of Iowa's soil is cultivable, and the state is a leader in soybean, corn, and livestock production. Ironically, this landlocked state makes a major contribution to America's foreign trade, selling grain to many other nations. However, this trade also makes Iowa vulnerable to foreign-policy decisions, including grain embargoes and taxes levied by governments at home and abroad.

Given Iowa's reputation as an agricultural producer, many people would be surprised that much of the state's income is derived from manufacturing. More Iowans live in cities than on farms, a situation common in other modern agricultural states. Iowa's total manufacturing output, however, is much below that of more heavily industrialized states, despite the industrial enclaves found in many of its cities. In addition, its mineral resources are negligible. But the remarkable homogeneity of Iowa's people may facilitate achievement of a unified consensus regarding the state's development and direction.

Iowa will need to diversify its economy even more in the future. Its agriculture is often caught between low market prices and the expense of machinery, fuel, fertilizers, and other supplies needed to maintain high agricultural production. As a result, Iowans are attempting to develop new industries and a better climate for business and at the same time trying to expand and stabilize markets for their agricultural products. They are hopeful that industry will provide as rich a yield as the land has given them.

Iowa's population is more urban than rural, its economy is diversifying into areas other than agriculture, and large, mechanized farms are eliminating the small family farms of the past. Yet even with all these changes, much of Iowa's strength still lies in the small towns that dot the countryside. Eldorado, in the northeastern section of the state, has a population just over one hundred and symbolizes the picturesque American small town that is partly responsible for Iowa's reputation as the typical midwestern state.

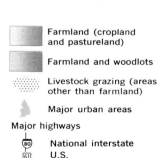

Economic Activities Much of Iowa's manufacturing and wholesaling are tied to agriculture. Several cities have meat-packing plants; some cities are home to facilities for producing corn products, milling grains, refining beet sugar, and preparing dairy products for market. Other state industries produce machinery, household appliances, and a variety of products.

Employment		Value
	Retail trade	
	Wholesale trade	
	Service	
	Government	
	Manufacturing	
	Agriculture	
	Mining	

400 300 200 100 0 5 10 15 20 25
Thousands of Persons   Billions of Dollars

Land Use Iowa is the model of an ideal farm state. Layers of fertile topsoil cover virtually the entire state; low relief—mostly flat prairies and rolling hills—makes the land easily tillable by humans and machines; water is available in just the right quantities; and the growing season is perfect for a variety of grain and feed crops. A system of cities evenly placed across the landscape connects farmers to sources of farm supplies and out-of-state markets.

Farmland (cropland and pastureland)

Farmland and woodlots

Livestock grazing (areas other than farmland)

Major urban areas

Major highways

National interstate

U.S.

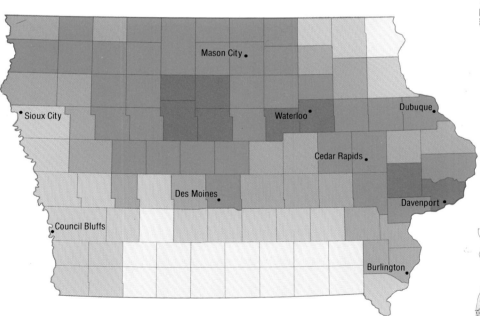

Average farmland value per acre, by county, 1982

$2,400 or more

$2,000–$2,400

$1,600–$2,000

$1,200–$1,600

$800–$1,200

Land Value Some of the best farmland in the world is found in Iowa; and soybeans and corn mean well-being for the farmers of the state. The amount of soybeans and corn that an area can produce determines the value of the land, and natural and human factors combine to influence productivity. Nature provides level terrain, good soils, and adequate heat and moisture, and by tiling for drainage and terracing to prevent erosion, farmers increase the amount of land on which these cash crops can be grown.

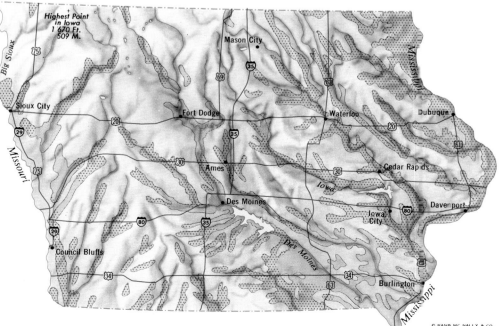

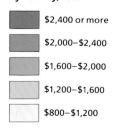

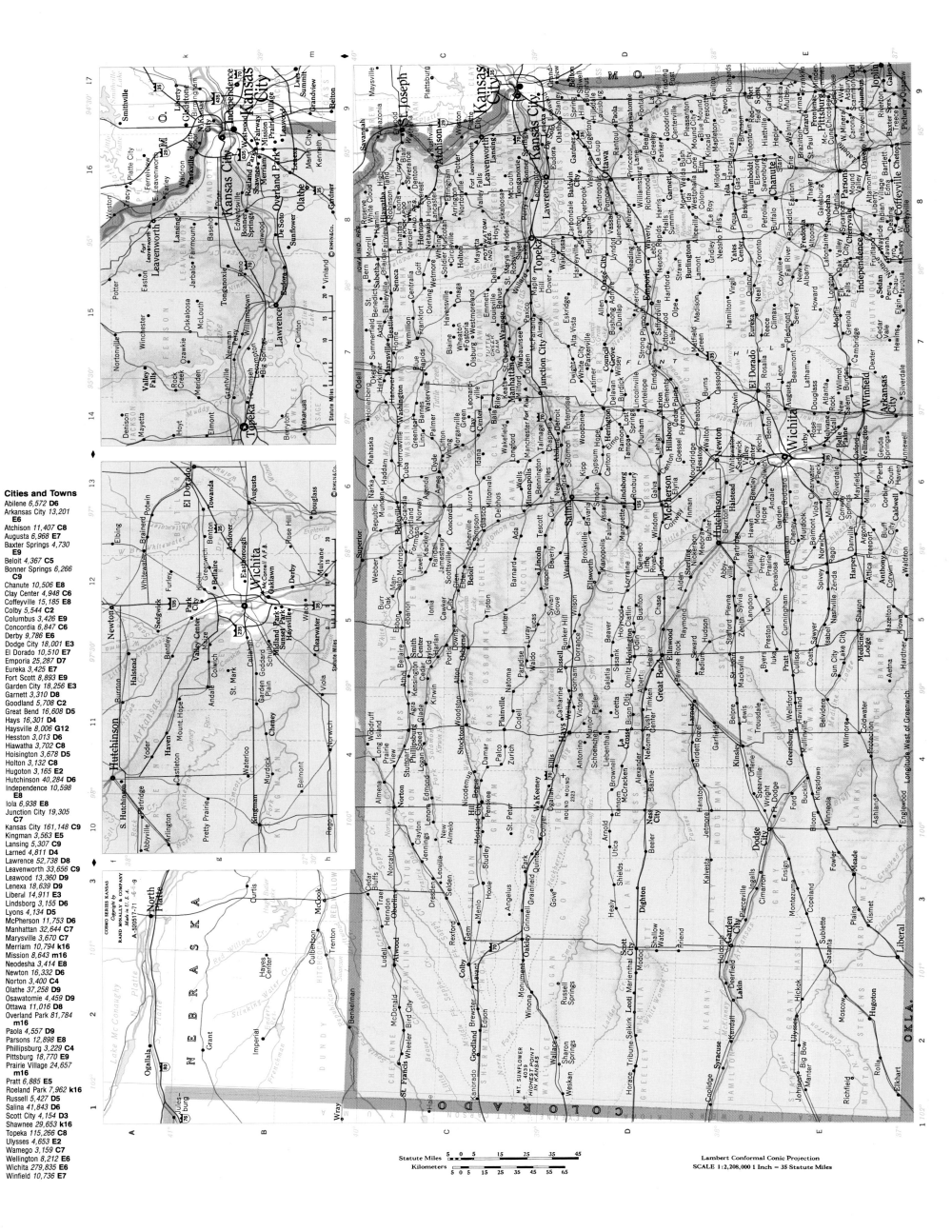

Cities and Towns

Abilene 6,572 **D6**
Arkansas City 13,201
E6
Atchison 11,407 **C8**
Augusta 6,968 **E7**
Baxter Springs 4,730
E9
Beloit 4,367 **C5**
Bonner Springs 6,266
C9
Chanute 10,506 **E8**
Clay Center 4,948 **C6**
Coffeyville 15,185 **E8**
Colby 5,544 **C2**
Columbus 3,426 **E9**
Concordia 6,847 **C6**
Derby 9,786 **E6**
Dodge City 18,001 **E3**
El Dorado 10,510 **E7**
Emporia 25,287 **D7**
Eureka 3,425 **E7**
Fort Scott 8,893 **E9**
Garden City 18,256 **E3**
Garnett 3,310 **D8**
Goodland 5,708 **C2**
Great Bend 16,608 **D5**
Hays 16,301 **D4**
Haysville 8,006 **G12**
Hesston 3,013 **D6**
Hiawatha 3,702 **C8**
Hoisington 3,678 **D5**
Holton 3,132 **C8**
Hugoton 3,165 **E2**
Hutchinson 40,284 **D6**
Independence 10,598
E8
Iola 6,938 **E8**
Junction City 19,305
C7
Kansas City 161,148 **C9**
Kingman 3,563 **E5**
Lansing 5,307 **C9**
Larned 4,811 **D4**
Lawrence 52,738 **D8**
Leavenworth 33,656 **C9**
Leawood 13,360 **D9**
Lenexa 18,639 **D9**
Liberal 14,911 **E3**
Lindsborg 3,155 **D6**
Lyons 4,134 **D5**
McPherson 11,753 **D6**
Manhattan 32,644 **C7**
Marysville 3,670 **C7**
Merriam 10,794 **k16**
Mission 8,643 **m16**
Neodesha 3,414 **E8**
Newton 16,332 **D6**
Norton 3,400 **C4**
Olathe 37,258 **D9**
Osawatomie 4,459 **D9**
Ottawa 11,016 **D8**
Overland Park 81,784
m16
Paola 4,557 **D9**
Parsons 12,898 **E8**
Phillipsburg 3,229 **C4**
Pittsburg 18,770 **E9**
Prairie Village 24,657
m16
Pratt 6,885 **E5**
Roeland Park 7,962 **k16**
Russell 5,427 **D5**
Salina 41,843 **D6**
Scott City 4,154 **D3**
Shawnee 29,653 **k16**
Topeka 115,266 **C8**
Ulysses 4,653 **E2**
Wamego 3,159 **C7**
Wellington 8,212 **E6**
Wichita 279,835 **E6**
Winfield 10,736 **E7**

COSMO SERIES KANSAS
Copyright by
RAND MCNALLY & COMPANY
Made in U.S.A.
A-520517-71 -6-8-9

Statute Miles
Kilometers

Lambert Conformal Conic Projection
SCALE 1:2,208,000 1 Inch = 35 Statute Miles

Kansas

POPULATION 2,364,236.
Rank: 32. *Density:* 29 people/mi² (11 people/km²). *Urban:* 66.7%. *Rural:* 33.3%.
AGE *<20:* 31%. *20–40:* 32%. *40–65:* 24%. *>65:* 13%.
ETHNIC GROUPS *White:* 91.7%. *Black:* 5.3%. *Spanish origin:* 2.7%. *Native American:* 0.6%. *Other:* 2.4%.

INCOME/CAPITA $9,983. *Rank:* 15.
POLITICS 1948–1980 elections: *President:* 1 Dem., 8 Rep. *Governor:* 7 Dem., 8 Rep.
ENTERED UNION January 29, 1861, 34th state.
CAPITAL Topeka, 115,266.
LARGEST CITY Wichita, 279,272.

AREA 82,280 mi² (213,104 km²).
Rank: 13. *Water area:* 499 mi² (1,292 km²).
ELEVATIONS *Highest:* Mt. Sunflower, 4,039 ft (1,231 m). *Lowest:* Along Verdigris River, 680 ft (207 m).
CLIMATE Cold winters, hot summers; moderate rainfall in east, diminishing in west.

Kansas often presents an image at odds with its reality. For decades the state was simply a stopover on the trail leading to more glamorous frontiers in the Oregon Territory and California goldfields. Even the incentive for settling the state arose not from the land itself but from the nation's growing conflict over the spread of slavery. Both the North and the South wanted this strategic territory as an ally. Despite its dubious beginnings, Kansas has emerged as a productive and progressive member of the nation.

Early settlement of the region was slow because most pioneers considered it desert land. Used to the rich, dark soils of the East, they believed Kansas's endless prairies were too dry for farming. Then in the 1870's, Mennonite settlers brought a hardy variety of Eastern European wheat, which flourished in the productive soil of the plains. Today, Kansas is one of the greatest grain-producing regions in the world.

Yet even this image belies reality. The present income of Kansas is based on industry as well as agriculture, and the state manufactures a variety of goods, including aircraft, camping gear, air-conditioning equipment, and snowmobiles. Kansas benefits as well from its strong standing as a mineral producer, exporting oil, coal, cement, lead, zinc, salt, and stone.

It would also be a mistake to equate Kansas's position at the geographic center of the United States with middle-of-the-road conservatism in its cultural and political life. Actually, Kansas has a progressive and innovative history that includes the Populist Party, direct primaries, women's suffrage, and public assistance for the needy. In the 1950's, the first court case declaring segregation in public schools as unconstitutional served as a precedent for other decisions regarding civil rights in school systems.

With its productive land, prospering industries, and forward-looking population, Kansas continues to play an important role in American life. From its central location, the state not only provides material wealth but also sets an example for the rest of the nation to follow.

Kansas is a major wheat producer, primarily in its western and central sections. As is true throughout the nation, extensive mechanization of farms has changed the economic structure of farming. The increase in fixed costs for machines means more land is needed per farm to make a profit. Also, with the present use of modern self-propelled combines, harvesting can be accomplished with a comparatively small number of workers. The increase in farm size and the decrease in farm population are nationwide trends, and although relatively stabilized, they are expected to continue.

Employment / Value

Retail trade
Wholesale trade
Service
Government
Manufacturing
Agriculture
Mining

200 150 100 50 0 5 10 15 20
Thousands of Persons — Billions of Dollars

Economic Activities Airplanes, camping gear, greeting cards, crude oil, and natural gas are only a few of the many products whose sale adds to the state income from agriculture. Some of these businesses are concentrated in particular cities—such as the aircraft industry in Wichita and the railroad-car industry in Atchison, Topeka, and Wichita—but meat-packing plants and grain and feed mills are located throughout the state. Beef cattle and wheat produce three-fourths of Kansas's farm income.

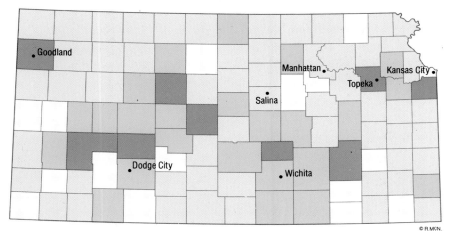

Goodland • Manhattan • Kansas City • Topeka • Salina • Dodge City • Wichita •

Number of tornadoes, by county, 1961–1981

- 15 or more
- 10–15
- 5–10
- 0–5

Tornadoes The meeting of air masses that have contrasting characteristics of temperature, moisture, density, and airflow tends to trigger many tornadoes in Kansas, Oklahoma, and Texas. Kansas records a high percentage of these disturbances, but loss of life is decreasing because of better understanding and prediction of their occurrence.

Land Use Millions of years ago, most of Kansas's land lay at the bottom of a large inland sea, and the good soil that remained after these waters drained away was supplemented through glacial activity. These processes left Kansas with many fertile prairies of low, rolling relief—ideal for agriculture. The northeastern region has the most productive land, while lack of rain and a higher sand content leaves the southwestern corner of the state with slightly lower productivity. Severe droughts in the 1930's and 1950's brought to the state's attention the importance of conserving soil and water. Today, water is held in artificial lakes and ponds, where it cannot wash away soil, and eventually it is released to nourish crops. Farmers now use contour plowing, terracing and shelterbelts of trees to conserve soil and water and to protect fields from wind erosion.

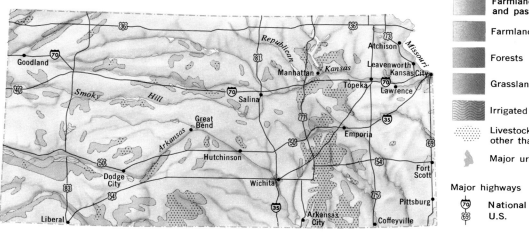

- Farmland (cropland and pastureland)
- Farmland and woodlots
- Forests
- Grassland
- Irrigated areas
- Livestock grazing (areas other than farmland)
- Major urban areas

Major highways
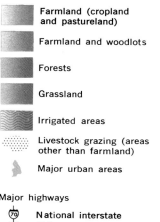
🛣 National interstate
🛣 U.S.

© RAND McNALLY & CO.

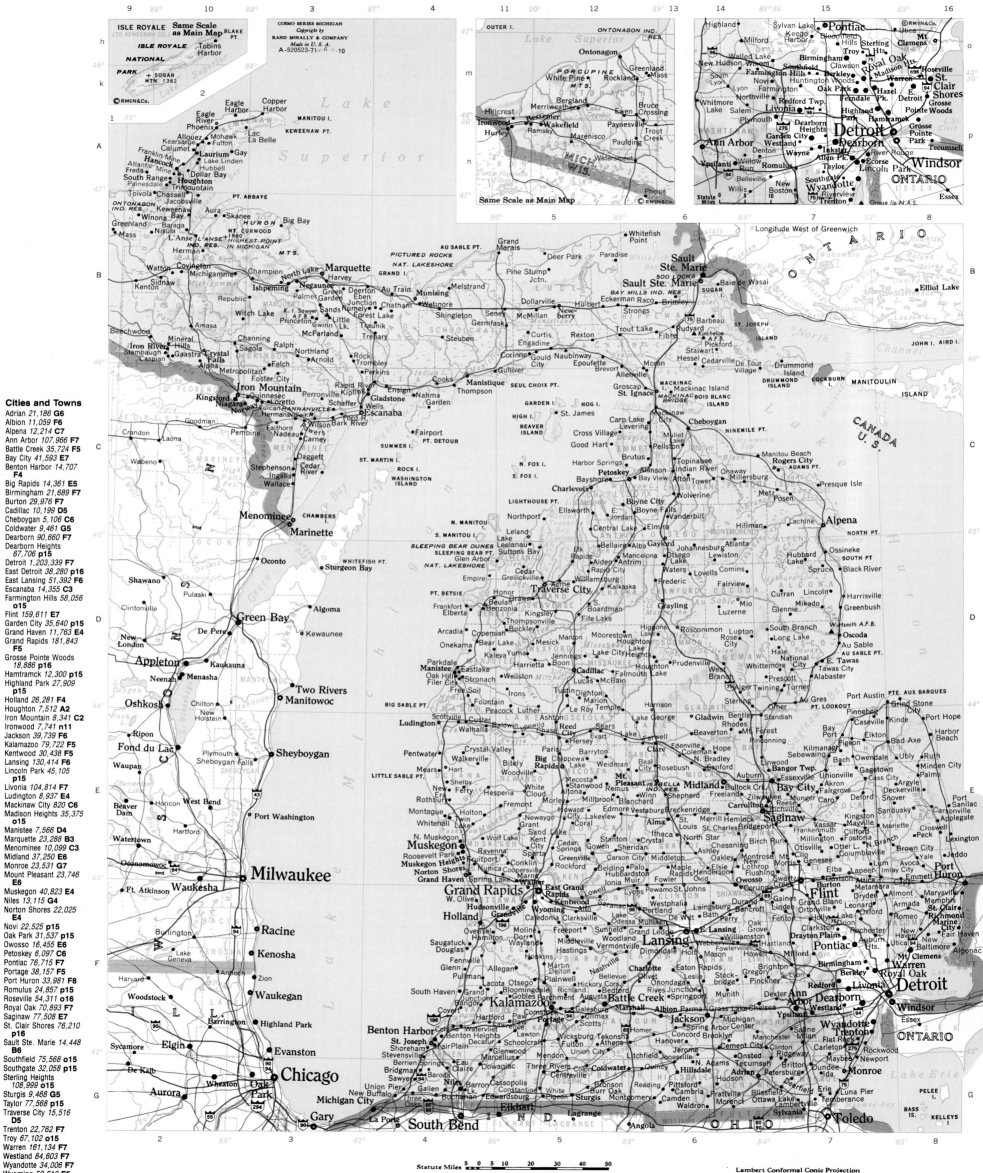

Michigan

POPULATION 9,262,078.
Rank: 8. *Density:* 163 people/mi²
(63 people/km²). *Urban:* 70.7%.
Rural: 29.3%.
AGE <20: 34%. 20–40: 32%.
40–65: 24%. >65: 10%.
ETHNIC GROUPS *White:* 85%.
Black: 12.9%. *Spanish origin:*
1.8%. *Native American:* 0.4%.
Other: 1.7%.

INCOME/CAPITA $9,950. *Rank:* 16.
POLITICS 1948–1980 elections:
President: 3 Dem., 6 Rep.
Governor: 7 Dem., 6 Rep.
ENTERED UNION January 26, 1837,
26th state.
CAPITAL Lansing, 130,414.
LARGEST CITY Detroit, 1,203,339.

AREA 97,102 mi² (251,493 km²).
Rank: 22. *Water area:* 40,148 mi²
(103,983 km²).
ELEVATIONS *Highest:* Mt.
Curwood, 1,980 ft (604 m).
Lowest: Lake Erie shoreline, 572
ft (174 m).
CLIMATE Cold, snowy winters; mild
summers; adequate rainfall.

Michigan's role in the Midwest has largely been determined by the Great Lakes, which divide the state into a lower and an upper peninsula. The Lower Peninsula, larger and more populated, is the home of heavy industry. Though Detroit has long been recognized as the automobile capital of the world, manufacturing is spread throughout the peninsula, in such cities as Flint, Lansing, Grand Rapids, and Muskegon. The Upper Peninsula is primarily wilderness, rich in copper, iron ores, and heavy stands of timber. Tourism is important to both regions, with their dense forests, glacial lakes, and great stretches of beach along Lake Michigan and Lake Huron.

Low-cost water transport on the Great Lakes was a key factor in encouraging the concentration of manufacturing in Michigan. Raw materials and finished products could be shipped easily and cheaply into and out of the state. Along the coastal zone, the lakes also affect the weather, moderating winter and summer temperatures, and thus are vital to the state's agriculture. Slight differences in temperature can mean success or failure for the state's fruit and vegetable crops.

Michigan faces the last decades of the twentieth century with a number of difficult problems. The manufacturing that made the state one of the pivotal areas in the nation's economy is now suffering under the double assault of an overall decline of heavy industry and a rise in foreign competition in the automobile and steel industries. Further, although mineral and timber resources continue to provide jobs and revenue, these resources have been seriously depleted by well over a century of industrial use. High unemployment, urban redevelopment, and technological change are issues that will occupy a prominent place on Michigan's future agenda.

There are no easy solutions, but Michigan has weathered economic storms before. And although experiencing the turmoil of change sweeping the country, at a deeper level, Michigan may harbor an enduring strength that will enable it to keep stride with national trends.

Centrally located on the Great Lakes–St. Lawrence Seaway system, Detroit is one of the nation's busiest ports. Ships deliver raw materials for use in the city's factories and pick up automobiles, automobile parts, and other products for shipment to United States and foreign markets. Supplementing Detroit's water transportation is a network of rail, air, and truck routes, all of which have contributed to the development of Detroit's industry. But because of the city's dependence on commerce and industries such as automaking, it is also dependent upon market forces outside of its control. Thus, Detroit often acts as a barometer of the national economy, being one of the first areas to register a decline or rise in employment and profits.

Land Use   Michigan has abundant plant and animal life, primarily because of its mild summer weather and moderate, evenly distributed rainfall. The Great Lakes increase humidity, lessen frosts, and prolong growing seasons in the state. Southern Michigan's rich, sandy soils are especially suited for agriculture.

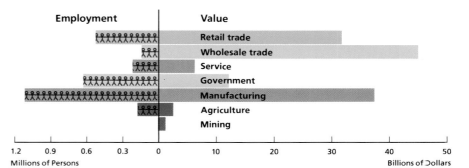

Employment		Value
	Retail trade	
	Wholesale trade	
	Service	
	Government	
	Manufacturing	
	Agriculture	
	Mining	

1.2   0.9   0.6   0.3   0   10   20   30   40   50
Millions of Persons   Billions of Dollars

Economic Activities   Michigan's famed automobile industry requires the coordination of subsidiary manufacturers who specialize in the production of automobile parts. These firms spread across much of the Lower Peninsula.

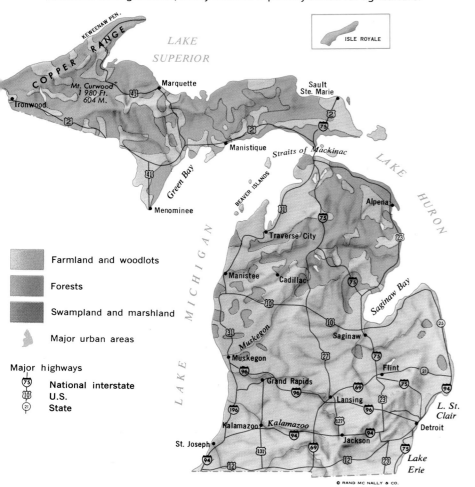

Farmland and woodlots

Forests

Swampland and marshland

Major urban areas

Major highways
  National interstate
  U.S.
  State

© RAND McNALLY & CO.

The Great Lakes   The Great Lakes and St. Lawrence River form one of the most important inland waterway systems in the world, linking the cities of the United States interior with the Atlantic Ocean. With coasts bordering all but Lake Ontario, Michigan was shaped by and profits from its key position on this international transportation artery. The lakes provide access not only to international shipping routes, but also to abundant quantities of water and an incomparable recreational resource.

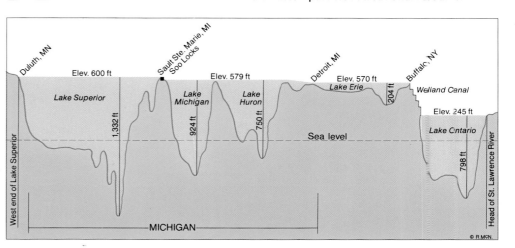

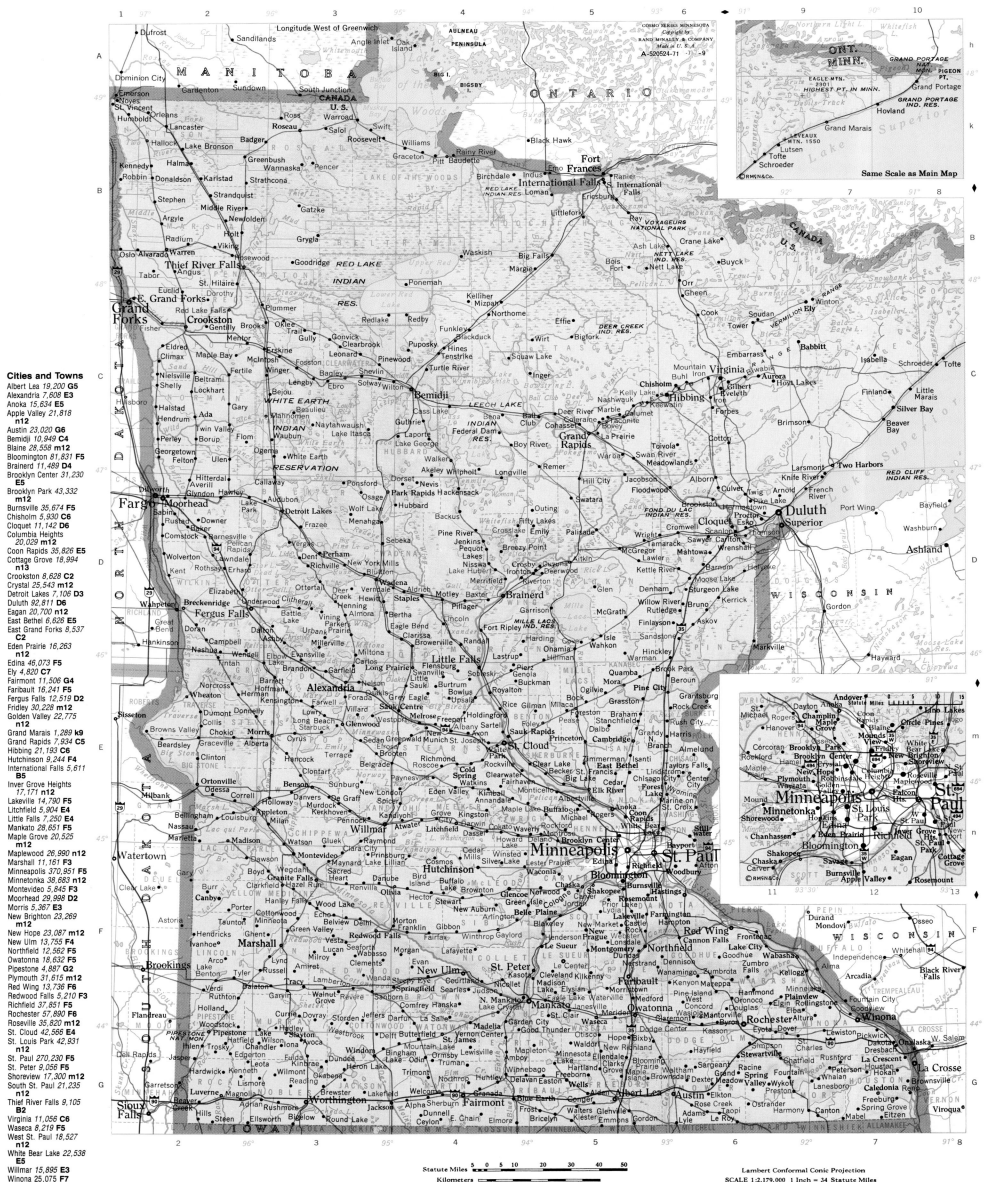

Minnesota

POPULATION 4,075,970. *Rank:* 21. *Density:* 51 people/mi² (20 people/km²). *Urban:* 66.9%. *Rural:* 33.1%.
AGE <20: 33%. *20–40:* 32%. *40–65:* 23%. *>65:* 12%.
ETHNIC GROUPS *White:* 96.6%. *Black:* 1.3%. *Spanish origin:* 0.8%. *Native American:* 0.9%. *Other:* 1.2%.

INCOME/CAPITA $9,724. *Rank:* 17.
POLITICS 1948–1980 elections: *President:* 6 Dem., 3 Rep. *Governor:* 6 Dem., 6 Rep.
ENTERED UNION May 11, 1858, 32nd state.
CAPITAL St. Paul, 270,230.
LARGEST CITY Minneapolis, 370,951.

AREA 86,614 mi² (224,329 km²). *Rank:* 14. *Water area:* 7,066 mi² (18,301 km²).
ELEVATIONS *Highest:* Eagle Mtn. 2,301 ft (701 m). *Lowest:* Lake Superior shoreline, 602 ft (183 m).
CLIMATE Long, cold winters; short summers; moderate rainfall.

While immense glaciers shaped the landscape and character of Minnesota millions of years ago, its people have created a rich, productive life in this varied and surprising land. Although many states bear marks of the Ice Age, almost all of the features for which Minnesota is best known—its iron ore, myriad blue lakes, and fertile southern farmland—reflect glacial action.

In the northern part of the state, retreating ice exposed the iron-rich bedrock of the Canadian Shield, making Minnesota a major source of high-quality ore for the American steel industry. The Mesabi iron-ore range in the northwest was once one of the world's greatest mining regions. Although producing lower-quality ore today, the range is still an important supplier.

As the great glaciers melted, they left behind new soil, rock deposits, and waterways. Streams and lakes by the thousands were created, giving Minnesota one of the greatest water areas of all the states and a reputation as a wonderland for outdoor recreation. Dairy and feed-grain farms place Minnesota in the company of its neighbors, who form the great agricultural heartland of the nation.

It is Minnesota's people, however, who put these resources to work. Settled first by New Englanders, the state quickly became the adopted home of hardworking Swedish, German, and Norwegian families. Within a few decades, Minneapolis and St. Paul were the dominant centers of the upper Midwest, extending their influence from western Wisconsin to Montana and south to Iowa. From the late nineteenth to the early twentieth centuries, Minnesota was a leading exporter of flour, lumber, and iron ore.

Today, Minnesota must adapt to an economy less dependent on these primary products. The iron ranges in the north and the agricultural lands in the south are losing population as demand for Minnesota's products declines and as farming becomes more mechanized. But overall, the state has adjusted remarkably well to change, and Minnesota continues to play an important part in the economy of the upper Midwest region. Its natural beauty and the quality of life fashioned by its population attract people and businesses each year.

Positioned at the end of the Great Lakes–St. Lawrence Seaway system, Duluth acts as the commercial center of northern Minnesota. This port provides access to markets for agricultural and industrial goods produced both inside and outside the state, including iron ore from Minnesota's ranges and grain from the fields of North and South Dakota.

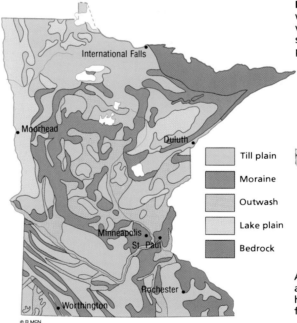

Glacial Effects The history of Minnesota can be traced in the lakes, streams, and landforms created millions of years ago by the glaciers. In the north, the glaciers' scouring action exposed the iron-rich deposits of the Mesabi Range. Agricultural lands were provided by deposits left on the outwash plains. And the kettle lakes, esker troughs, and other depressions established the state's topography in its lake, stream, and forest regions, the focal points of a successful tourist industry.

- Till plain
- Moraine
- Outwash
- Lake plain
- Bedrock

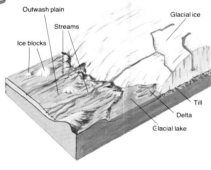

Retreating Glacier The body and meltwater of a glacier carry and deposit a variety of materials—including clay, sand, gravel, and boulders—which comprise both the till and outwash plains.

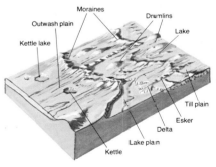

After a glacial mass has retreated from an area, the many new landforms that have been created under its surface and from its meltwater are exposed to view.

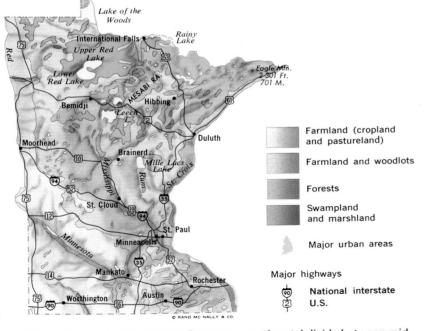

- Farmland (cropland and pastureland)
- Farmland and woodlots
- Forests
- Swampland and marshland
- Major urban areas
- Major highways
- National interstate
- U.S.

Land Use Minnesota lies across an important continental divide between midwestern prairies and northern forests, and this division is apparent in the state's land use. Farming is concentrated in the south, where prairie soils support a productive agriculture. Marking the limit of America's prairies, northern forests contribute to the state's wood-products industry.

Economic Activities Minnesota's role in trade is striking. St. Paul and Minneapolis are important Mississippi River ports, shipping Midwest grain and western coal south in exchange for the petroleum and other supplies not found in the state.

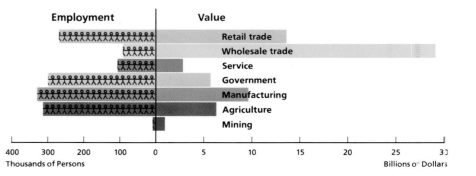

Employment	Value
	Retail trade
	Wholesale trade
	Service
	Government
	Manufacturing
	Agriculture
	Mining

400 300 200 100 0 5 10 15 20 25 30
Thousands of Persons   Billions of Dollars

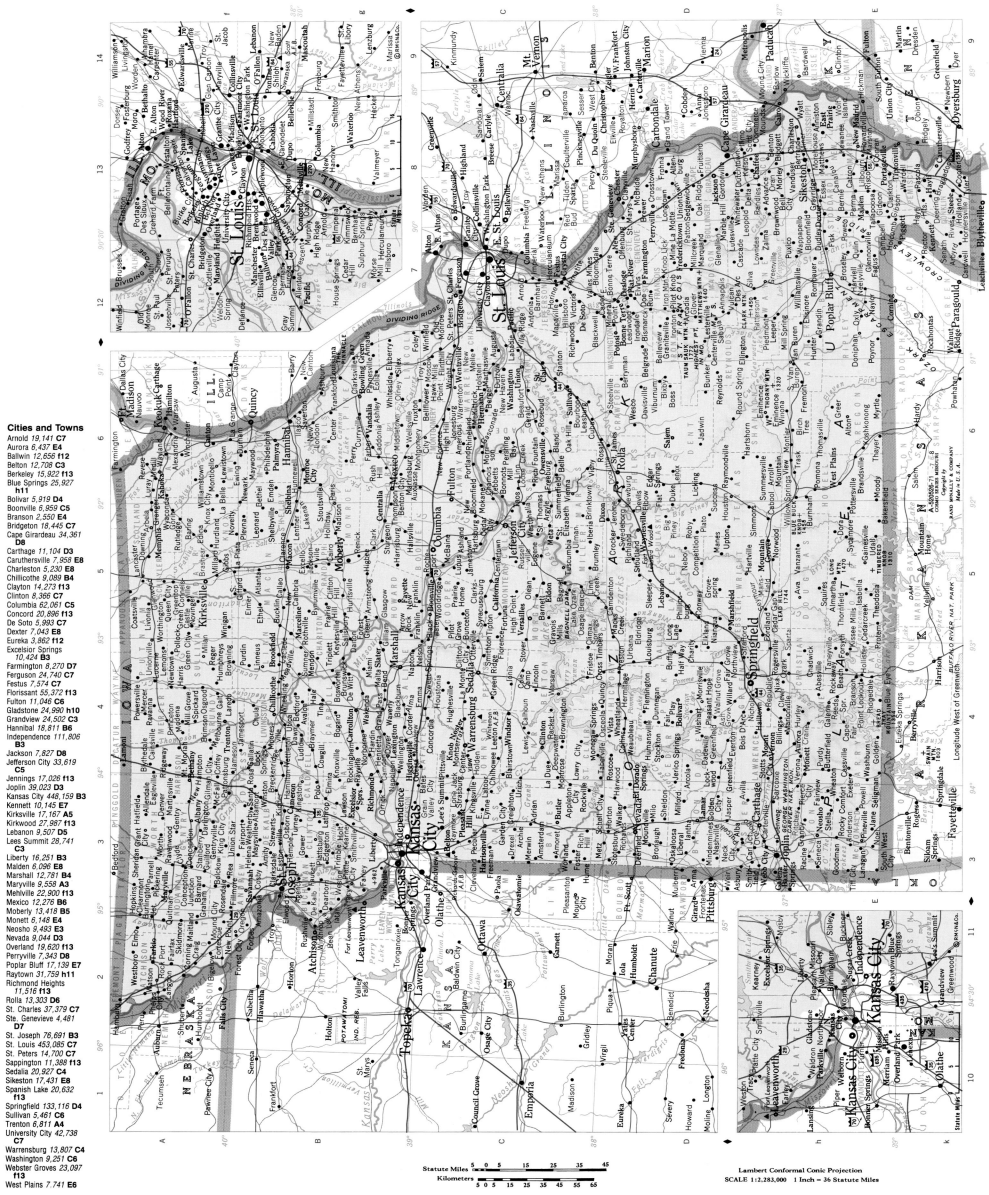

Cities and Towns

Arnold 19,141 **C7**
Aurora 6,437 **E4**
Ballwin 12,656 **f12**
Belton 12,708 **C3**
Berkeley 15,922 **f13**
Blue Springs 25,927 **h11**
Bolivar 5,919 **D4**
Boonville 6,959 **C5**
Branson 2,550 **E4**
Bridgeton 18,445 **C7**
Cape Girardeau 34,361 **D8**
Carthage 11,104 **D3**
Caruthersville 7,958 **E8**
Charleston 5,230 **E8**
Chillicothe 9,089 **B4**
Clayton 14,273 **f13**
Clinton 8,366 **C5**
Columbia 62,061 **C5**
Concord 20,896 **f13**
De Soto 5,993 **C7**
Dexter 7,043 **E8**
Eureka 3,862 **f12**
Excelsior Springs 10,424 **B3**
Farmington 8,270 **D7**
Ferguson 24,740 **C7**
Festus 7,574 **C7**
Florissant 55,372 **f13**
Fulton 11,046 **C6**
Gladstone 24,990 **h10**
Grandview 24,502 **C3**
Hannibal 18,811 **B6**
Independence 111,806 **B3**
Jackson 7,827 **D8**
Jefferson City 33,619 **C5**
Jennings 17,026 **f13**
Joplin 39,023 **D3**
Kansas City 448,159 **B3**
Kennett 10,145 **E7**
Kirksville 17,167 **A5**
Kirkwood 27,987 **f13**
Lebanon 9,507 **D5**
Lees Summit 28,741 **C3**
Liberty 16,251 **B3**
Malden 6,096 **E8**
Marshall 12,781 **B4**
Maryville 9,558 **A3**
Mehlville 22,900 **f13**
Mexico 12,276 **B6**
Moberly 13,418 **B5**
Monett 6,148 **E4**
Neosho 9,493 **E3**
Nevada 9,044 **D3**
Overland 19,620 **f13**
Perryville 7,343 **D8**
Poplar Bluff 17,139 **E7**
Raytown 31,759 **h11**
Richmond Heights 11,516 **f13**
Rolla 13,303 **D6**
St. Charles 37,379 **C7**
Ste. Genevieve 4,481 **D7**
St. Joseph 76,691 **B3**
St. Louis 453,085 **C7**
St. Peters 14,700 **C7**
Sappington 11,388 **f13**
Sedalia 20,927 **C4**
Sikeston 17,431 **E8**
Spanish Lake 20,632 **f13**
Springfield 133,116 **D4**
Sullivan 5,461 **C6**
Trenton 6,811 **A4**
University City 42,738 **C7**
Warrensburg 13,807 **C4**
Washington 9,251 **C6**
Webster Groves 23,097 **f13**
West Plains 7,741 **E6**

Statute Miles   5 0 5   15   25   35   45

Kilometers   5 0 5 15 25 35 45 55 65

Lambert Conformal Conic Projection
SCALE 1:2,283,000   1 Inch = 36 Statute Miles

Missouri

POPULATION 4,916,759.
Rank: 15. *Density:* 71 people/mi²
(28 people/km²). *Urban:* 68.1%.
Rural: 31.9%.
AGE <20: 32%. 20–40: 30%.
40–65: 25%. >65: 13%.
ETHNIC GROUPS *White:* 88.4%.
Black: 10.5%. *Spanish origin:*
1.1%. *Native American:* 0.2%.
Other: 0.9%.

INCOME/CAPITA $8,982. *Rank:* 30.
POLITICS 1948–1980 elections:
President: 5 Dem., 4 Rep.
Governor: 7 Dem., 2 Rep.
ENTERED UNION August 10, 1821,
24th state.
CAPITAL Jefferson City, 33,619.
LARGEST CITY St. Louis, 453,085.

AREA 69,697 mi² (180,515 km²).
Rank: 18. *Water area:* 752 mi²
(1,948 km²).
ELEVATIONS *Highest:* Taum Sauk
Mtn., 1,772 ft (540 m). *Lowest:*
Along St. Francis River, 230 ft
(70 m).
CLIMATE Generally hot summers,
cold winters; moderate rainfall.

Missouri stands at a crossroads among the states. Here the forested areas of the East meet the plains of the West, and the cornfields of the North border the cotton fields of the South. The state is also a transportation center, linking the East, West, North, and South with air, rail, water, and truck routes.

Missouri has a long history as the Gateway to America's West, a reputation commemorated in the monumental Gateway Arch in St. Louis. Both the Santa Fe and Oregon trails originated in the state, and so many pioneers traveled through Missouri on their way West that it wasn't long before the state itself was settled. Its rich prairies and grasslands supported a variety of grain and seed crops, and the state quickly found its niche as an important grain and cattle market.

Missouri's key position at the head of supply routes to the western regions encouraged the development of manufacturing as well. The Missouri and Mississippi rivers converge near St. Louis, and the city once marked the northernmost limit of navigation for oceangoing vessels traveling up the Mississippi. In addition, decades of competition between the commercial centers of St. Louis and Chicago spurred the growth of commerce and industry in the state.

Today, Missouri is a leader in the production of aerospace and transportation equipment, including cars, trucks, and trains. Furthermore, Missouri makes a contribution to the country's mineral production. And it is a mark of the state's continued importance in midwestern and western finance that it is the site of two of the country's twelve Federal Reserve banks.

But Missouri's crossroads position creates problems as well as opportunities. For decades, rural people from the South have been migrating to urban areas, and the state's urban populace is now suffering from the industrial decline affecting many of the country's cities. Recent developments in service and professional industries and urban-renewal projects may be essential first steps in solving current problems and preparing for the future. Missouri today may stand at the crossroads of a movement toward a new economy and a new way of life.

The Ozark National Scenic Riverways contain miles of free-flowing streams. Natural underground water reservoirs feed the area's many springs, which in turn feed the rivers. Shown here is the Alley Springs flow on the Jacks Fork River.

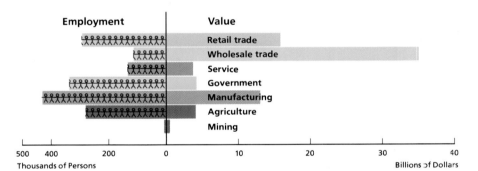

Economic Activities Missouri has established one of the strongest and most diversified economies in the Midwest, a region rich in competitive agricultural and industrial state economies. With an important financial and industrial city at either side of the state, Missouri is able to take advantage of economic currents flowing from both the East and the West.

Population Change Missouri's North-South crossroads position is reflected in its population change of the past decade. In the northern United States, many rural areas have been faced with decreasing population, and northern Missouri seems to ally with this region in its pattern of population loss. In the southern part of the country, population growth is often the rule, and southern Missouri displays this general trend.

Land Use In Missouri, pioneers found prime land for farming and industry. To the north and west are plains that are capable of supporting a productive agriculture and that are similar to land found in Iowa, Nebraska, and Kansas. The southeastern corner of the state lies in the Mississippi River's alluvial basin, which the state shares with its southern neighbors. Finally, the Ozark Plateau covers much of the state south of the Missouri River and is reminiscent of the forested uplands east of the Mississippi.

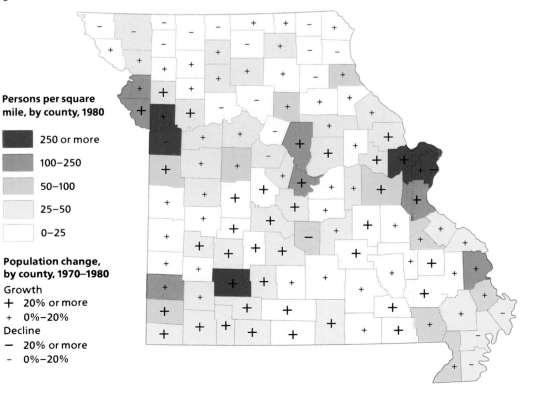

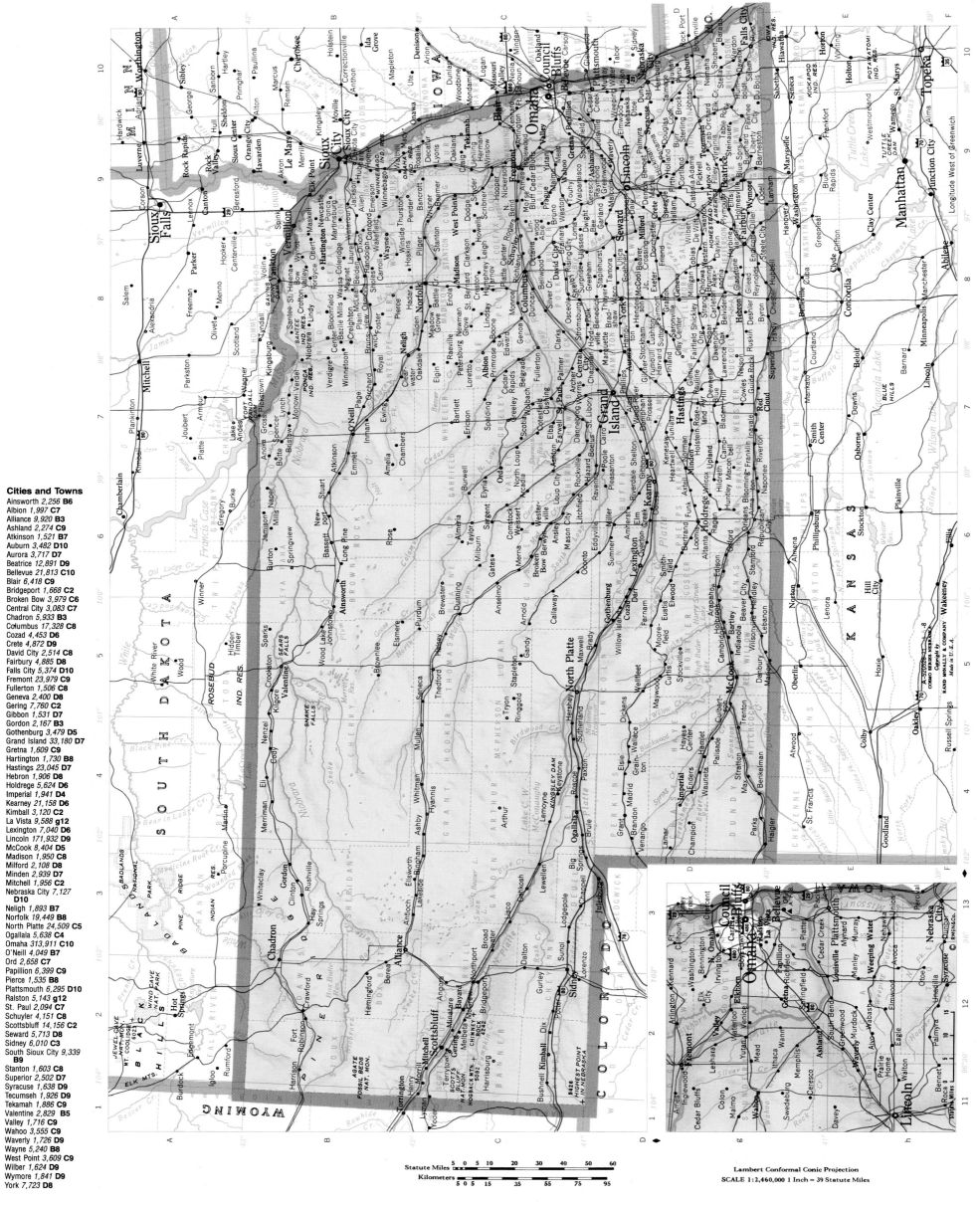

Cities and Towns

Ainsworth 2,256 **B6**
Albion 1,997 **C7**
Alliance 9,920 **B3**
Ashland 2,274 **C9**
Atkinson 1,521 **B7**
Auburn 3,482 **D10**
Aurora 3,717 **D7**
Beatrice 12,891 **D9**
Bellevue 21,813 **C10**
Blair 6,418 **C9**
Bridgeport 1,668 **C2**
Broken Bow 3,979 **C6**
Central City 3,083 **C7**
Chadron 5,933 **B3**
Columbus 17,328 **C8**
Cozad 4,453 **D6**
Crete 4,872 **D9**
David City 2,514 **C8**
Fairbury 4,885 **D8**
Falls City 5,374 **D10**
Fremont 23,979 **C9**
Fullerton 1,506 **C8**
Geneva 2,400 **D8**
Gering 7,760 **C2**
Gibbon 1,531 **D7**
Gordon 2,167 **B3**
Gothenburg 3,479 **D5**
Grand Island 33,180 **D7**
Gretna 1,609 **C9**
Hartington 1,730 **B8**
Hastings 23,045 **D7**
Hebron 1,906 **D8**
Holdrege 5,624 **D6**
Imperial 1,941 **D4**
Kearney 21,158 **D6**
Kimball 3,120 **C2**
La Vista 9,588 **g12**
Lexington 7,040 **D6**
Lincoln 171,932 **D9**
McCook 8,404 **D5**
Madison 1,950 **C8**
Milford 2,108 **D8**
Minden 2,939 **D7**
Mitchell 1,956 **C2**
Nebraska City 7,127 **D10**
Neligh 1,893 **B7**
Norfolk 19,449 **B8**
North Platte 24,509 **C5**
Ogallala 5,638 **C4**
Omaha 313,911 **C10**
O'Neill 4,049 **B7**
Ord 2,658 **C7**
Papillion 6,399 **C9**
Pierce 1,535 **B8**
Plattsmouth 6,295 **D10**
Ralston 5,143 **g12**
St. Paul 2,094 **C7**
Schuyler 4,151 **C8**
Scottsbluff 14,156 **C2**
Seward 5,713 **D8**
Sidney 6,010 **C3**
South Sioux City 9,339 **B9**
Stanton 1,603 **C8**
Superior 2,502 **D7**
Syracuse 1,638 **D9**
Tecumseh 1,926 **D9**
Tekamah 1,886 **C9**
Valentine 2,829 **B5**
Valley 1,716 **C9**
Wahoo 3,555 **C9**
Waverly 1,726 **D9**
Wayne 5,240 **B8**
West Point 3,609 **C9**
Wilber 1,624 **D9**
Wymore 1,841 **D9**
York 7,723 **D8**

Statute Miles
Kilometers

Lambert Conformal Conic Projection
SCALE 1:2,460,000 1 Inch = 39 Statute Miles

Nebraska

POPULATION 1,569,825.
Rank: 35. *Density:* 20 people/mi²
(7.9 people/km²). *Urban:* 62.9%.
Rural: 37.1%.
AGE *<20:* 32%. *20–40:* 31%.
40–65: 24%. *>65:* 13%.
ETHNIC GROUPS *White:* 94.9%.
Black: 3.1%. *Spanish origin:*
1.8%. *Native American:* 0.6%.
Other: 1.4%.

INCOME/CAPITA $9,365. *Rank:* 23.
POLITICS 1948–1980 elections:
President: 1 Dem., 8 Rep.
Governor: 6 Dem., 7 Rep.
ENTERED UNION March 1, 1867,
37th state.
CAPITAL Lincoln, 171,932.
LARGEST CITY Omaha, 313,911.

AREA 77,355 mi² (200,348 km²).
Rank: 15. *Water area:* 711 mi²
(1,841 km²).
ELEVATIONS *Highest:* In Kimball
County, 5,426 ft (1,654 m).
Lowest: In Richardson County,
840 ft (256 m).
CLIMATE Hot summers, cold
winters; semiarid in west, more
rain in east.

N ebraska owes its reputation as part of America's great agricultural heartland to the resourcefulness of its settlers, who recognized the prairie as a fertile region. Without their industriousness, Nebraska's abundant potential might have remained undiscovered under miles of tough prairie grass and sagebrush.

The first explorers passing through the Nebraska area looked beyond it to the tempting land and mineral wealth farther west. This section of the so-called Great American Desert appeared to have little to recommend it—no forests, few minerals, and a virtually unbroken expanse of grassland stretching from horizon to horizon. For many decades, Nebraska was merely one section of the transcontinental railroad, linking the East and the West.

But the railroads brought European settlers who recognized the land's possibilities and decided to travel no farther. Soon they had a steel plow strong enough to break through the thick prairie sod, and the settlement of Nebraska was under way. Although semiarid, the state is far from being a desert. In summer, humid tropical air masses from the Gulf of Mexico move far enough north to bring thunderstorms and sudden rain showers. Not long after the first settlers began farming, Nebraska became one of the fastest growing states of its time.

Nebraska's tradition of pioneer resourcefulness continues today. Farmers have quickly adopted mechanized, highly efficient agricultural methods, reducing the number of people needed to till the land. The resulting migration of rural people to the cities has increased Nebraska's urban population and fueled the expanding manufacturing, food-processing, and service industries. Although Nebraska remains a major agricultural state, its people have developed a more diversified economy and will continue to explore new possibilities in the coming decades, meeting the challenges presented by modern economic trends.

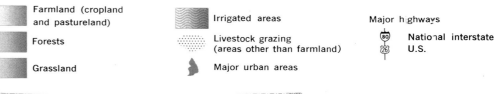

In north-central Nebraska, the Sand Hills and the surrounding farmland reflect Nebraskans' successful adaptation to the land. Formed of loose sand, the hills are covered with grass and offer abundant grazing land. The grass holds the soil in place, and because plowing or overgrazing can turn the area into a windblown dust bowl, agriculture is practiced according to conservation guidelines. Nebraskans make the most of the region by using rainfall absorbed by the sand to irrigate areas nearby.

Economic Activities Omaha and Lincoln are Nebraska's dominant cities partly because of the former's meat-packing and insurance industries and the latter's role in education and government. But many other production facilities are located away from these centers, close to the farms that provide raw input for mills and food-processing plants.

Employment	Value
	Retail trade
	Wholesale trade
	Service
	Government
	Manufacturing
	Agriculture
	Mining

200 150 100 50 0   2   4   6   8   10   12
Thousands of Persons   Billions of Dollars

Center-Pivot Irrigation Beneath Nebraska at a shallow depth lie the water-bearing rock strata called the High Plains Aquifer. Development of the center-pivot irrigation system has enabled farmers far from river-irrigated areas to pump water from the aquifer. Extensive use of the systems in recent decades has dramatically increased Nebraska's cropland.

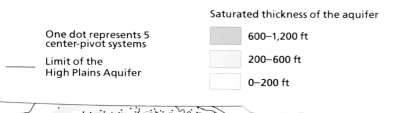

Saturated thickness of the aquifer

One dot represents 5
center-pivot systems

Limit of the
High Plains Aquifer

600–1,200 ft

200–600 ft

0–200 ft

Land Use Almost all Nebraska's soil has high agricultural potential. In the wetter, eastern part of the state, the land can be employed to maximum capacity more easily. Western Nebraska is semiarid, and intensive farming is practiced mostly on irrigated land. Here, cattle grazing is a productive alternative to grain farming, since it requires much less water.

Farmland (cropland
and pastureland)

Forests

Grassland

Irrigated areas

Livestock grazing
(areas other than farmland)

Major urban areas

Major highways

National interstate

U.S.

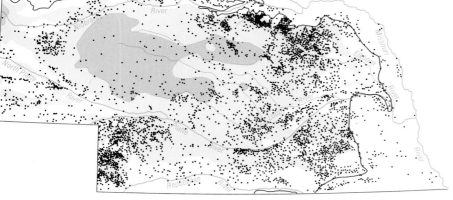

Circular patterns result in fields irrigated by center-pivot systems.

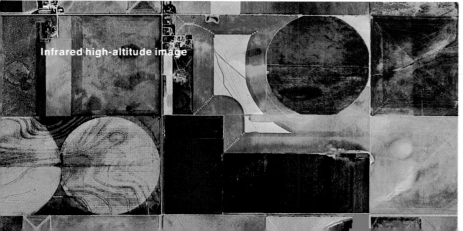

Infrared high-altitude image

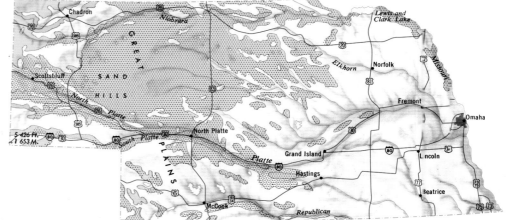

© RAND MC NALLY & CO.

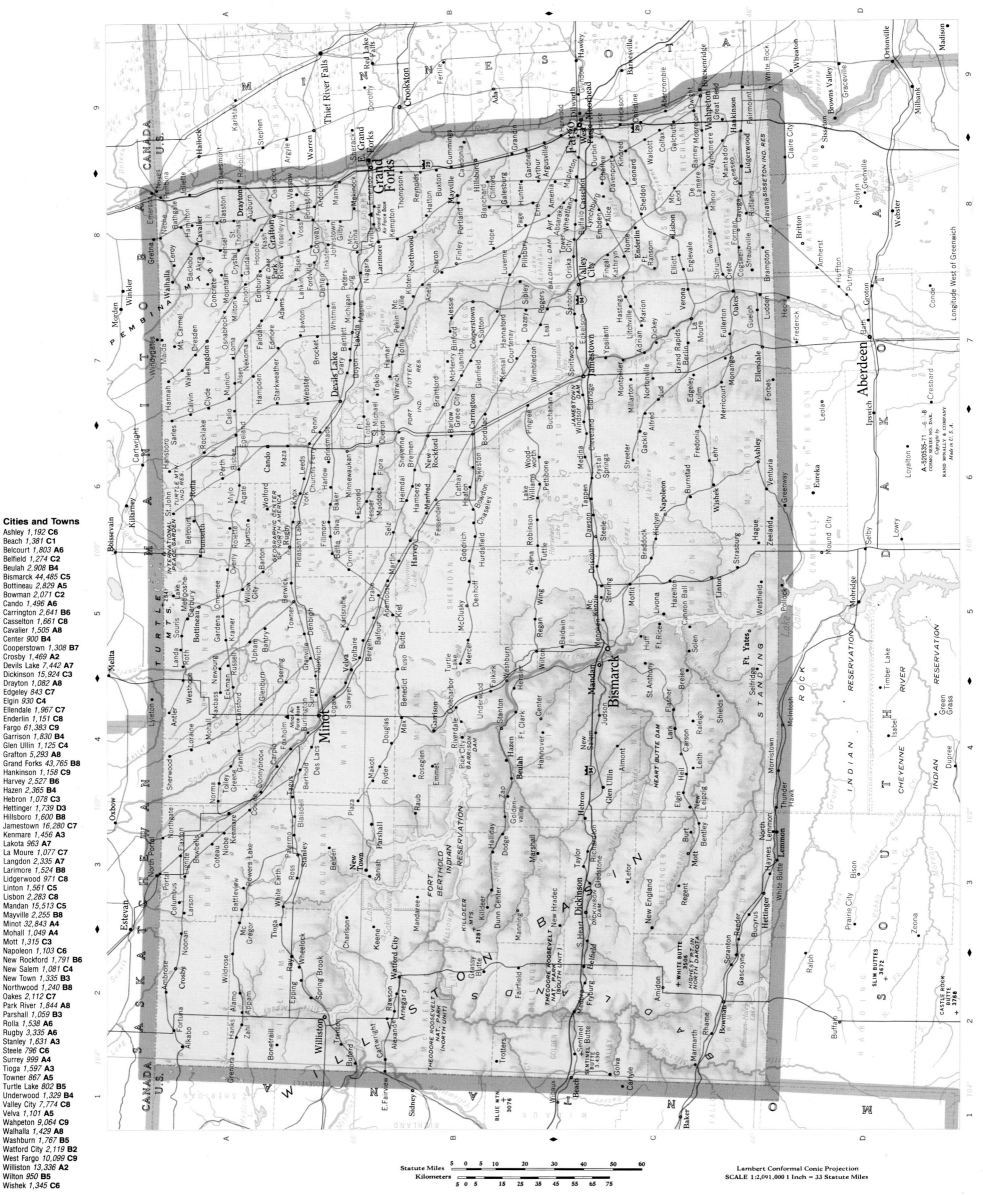

Cities and Towns

Ashley 1,192 C6
Beach 1,381 C1
Belcourt 1,803 A6
Belfield 1,274 C2
Beulah 2,908 B4
Bismarck 44,485 C5
Bottineau 2,829 A5
Bowman 2,071 C2
Cando 1,496 A6
Carrington 2,641 B6
Casselton 1,661 C8
Cavalier 1,505 A8
Center 900 B4
Cooperstown 1,308 B7
Crosby 1,469 A2
Devils Lake 7,442 A7
Dickinson 15,924 C3
Drayton 1,082 A8
Edgeley 843 C7
Elgin 930 C4
Ellendale 1,967 C7
Enderlin 1,151 C8
Fargo 61,383 C9
Garrison 1,830 B4
Glen Ullin 1,125 C4
Grafton 5,293 A8
Grand Forks 43,765 B8
Hankinson 1,158 C9
Harvey 2,527 B6
Hazen 2,365 B4
Hebron 1,078 C3
Hettinger 1,739 D3
Hillsboro 1,600 B8
Jamestown 16,280 C7
Kenmare 1,456 A3
Lakota 963 A7
La Moure 1,077 C7
Langdon 2,335 A7
Larimore 1,524 B8
Lidgerwood 971 C8
Linton 1,561 C5
Lisbon 2,283 C8
Mandan 15,513 C5
Mayville 2,255 B8
Minot 32,843 A4
Mohall 1,049 A4
Mott 1,315 C3
Napoleon 1,103 C6
New Rockford 1,791 B6
New Salem 1,081 C4
New Town 1,335 B3
Northwood 1,240 B8
Oakes 2,112 C7
Park River 1,844 A8
Parshall 1,059 B3
Rolla 1,538 A6
Rugby 3,335 A6
Stanley 1,631 A3
Steele 796 C6
Surrey 999 A4
Tioga 1,597 A3
Towner 867 A5
Turtle Lake 802 B5
Underwood 1,329 B5
Valley City 7,774 C8
Velva 1,101 A5
Wahpeton 9,064 C9
Walhalla 1,429 A8
Washburn 1,767 B5
Watford City 2,119 B2
West Fargo 10,099 C9
Williston 13,336 A2
Wilton 950 B5
Wishek 1,345 C6

Statute Miles

Kilometers

Lambert Conformal Conic Projection
SCALE 1:2,091,000 1 Inch = 33 Statute Miles

North Dakota

POPULATION 652,717.
Rank: 46. *Density:* 9.4 people/mi² (3.6 people/km²). *Urban:* 48.8%. *Rural:* 51.2%.
AGE *<20:* 34%. *20–40:* 32%. *40–65:* 22%. *>65:* 12%.
ETHNIC GROUPS *White:* 95.8%. *Black:* 0.4%. *Spanish origin:* 0.6%. *Native American:* 3.1%. *Other:* 0.7%.

INCOME/CAPITA $8,747. *Rank:* 33.
POLITICS 1948–1980 elections: *President:* 1 Dem., 8 Rep. *Governor:* 6 Dem., 7 Rep.
ENTERED UNION November 2, 1889, 39th state.
CAPITAL Bismarck, 44,485.
LARGEST CITY Fargo, 61,383.

AREA 70,703 mi² (183,120 km²). *Rank:* 17. *Water area:* 1,403 mi² (3,634 km²).
ELEVATIONS *Highest:* White Butte, 3,506 ft (1,069 m). *Lowest:* Along Red River, 750 ft (229 m).
CLIMATE Severe winters; short, hot summers. Semiarid areas subject to droughts, moderate rainfall in southeast.

In the southwest corner of North Dakota lie the Badlands, following the Missouri River through Theodore Roosevelt National Park. So named because early travelers found the region difficult to cross, these landforms owe their unique formations to the area's sandstone, shale, and clay as well as to its semiarid climate. The lack of heavy vegetation has caused sudden torrential rains to sculpt these soft, colorful rocks into strangely shaped buttes, mesas, valleys, and gullies. Because of the special character of this land, prehistoric fossils abound, preserved under stone that eventually eroded.

North Dakota, far from the nation's major population centers, has always been a hinterland of the United States. Yet its story is one of a strong, industrious people adapting to a harsh environment and eventually winning economic independence.

North Dakota possesses an unforgiving climate with long, cold winters and short, hot summers that bring little moisture to support crops. But with the coming of the railroads, settlers rushed into the territory, eager to farm the open prairie despite the severe weather and lack of forests. Huge wheat farms were established, and these attracted still more people to the area, many inexperienced in agriculture and many with farming methods geared to the water-rich East. Through trial and error, the people adjusted to the special character of the land, while population and cultivated areas grew. But the fragile environment had been disturbed, and the prairie became a dust bowl during the drought of the 1930's, with winds carrying off topsoil that had taken centuries to form. Farmers prospered again when projects preventing erosion and providing irrigation were instituted. Today, adaptation continues and is evidenced by the increasing mechanization of agriculture.

The state's economic independence proved equally hard to win. For many years North Dakota was virtually a colony of Minneapolis and St. Paul. The Twin Cities served as the major markets for North Dakota's produce, the headquarters of its railroads and banks, and the main source of its farming supplies. Populist agrarian movements of the late nineteenth and early twentieth centuries wrested control from centers outside North Dakota, and through state and private cooperatives, the state overcame its "colonial" status.

Since the 1950's, North Dakota's economy has become more varied. The state serves as a strategic site for air-force bomber and missile squadrons. Vast deposits of lignite have been discovered, and oil production has given the state a new importance in the energy field. North Dakota's future may be largely determined by how well these resources are managed. The state's population may have learned from its past to balance environmental and economic factors carefully in planning for the coming decades.

Agricultural Trends Over the years, scientific and technological advances have changed the character of agriculture all over the world. North Dakota displays the results of these changes. The state's level terrain allows farmers to utilize almost every type of machinery, and today farming in North Dakota is almost completely mechanized. As a result, farmers are able to decrease their labor force while increasing their acreage and productivity, and farms have decreased in number while growing larger. This trend has its drawbacks as well as assets. Because of the high cost of modern equipment, the day of the small farm is past. But at the same time, agriculture is more productive than ever before and better able to meet the world's growing demand for food.

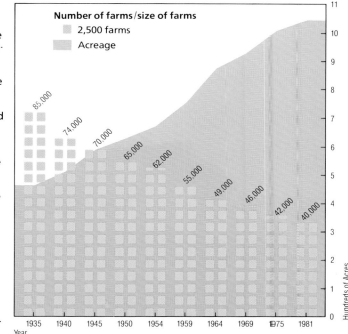

Number of farms/size of farms
- 2,500 farms
- Acreage

85,000 74,000 70,000 65,000 62,000 55,000 49,000 46,000 42,000 40,000

1935 1940 1945 1950 1954 1959 1964 1969 1975 1981
Year

Hundreds of Acres

Land Use Influenced by its climate, North Dakota's agriculture is restricted to only a few crops, but these can be grown in great quantities. Vulnerable to careless management, the state's land requires soil and water conservation to maintain its productivity. Development of underground coal beds threatens some of this land with potentially damaging strip-mining.

- Farmland (cropland and pastureland)
- Farmland and woodlots
- Forest
- Grassland
- Irrigated areas
- Livestock grazing (areas other than famland)
- Major highways
  - (94) National interstate
  - (2) U.S.

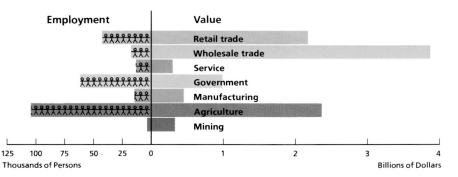

Employment | **Value**
- Retail trade
- Wholesale trade
- Service
- Government
- Manufacturing
- Agriculture
- Mining

125 100 75 50 25 0   1   2   3   4
Thousands of Persons   Billions of Dollars

Economic Activities Compared with the economies of many states, North Dakota's economy is relatively undiversified and supports few manufacturing and service industries. Most state industry involves processing agricultural products for market. Further development of lignite deposits may dramatically increase the contribution of mining to state income.

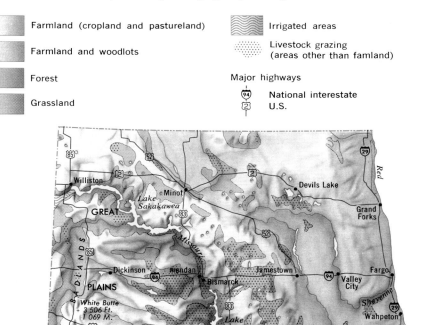

Williston · Minot · Devils Lake · Grand Forks · Lake Sakakawea · GREAT PLAINS · Dickinson · Mandan · Jamestown · Valley City · Fargo · Bismarck · BADLANDS · White Butte 3,506 Ft. 1,069 M. · Lake Oahe · Missouri · Red · Sheyenne · Wahpeton

© RAND MCNALLY & CO.

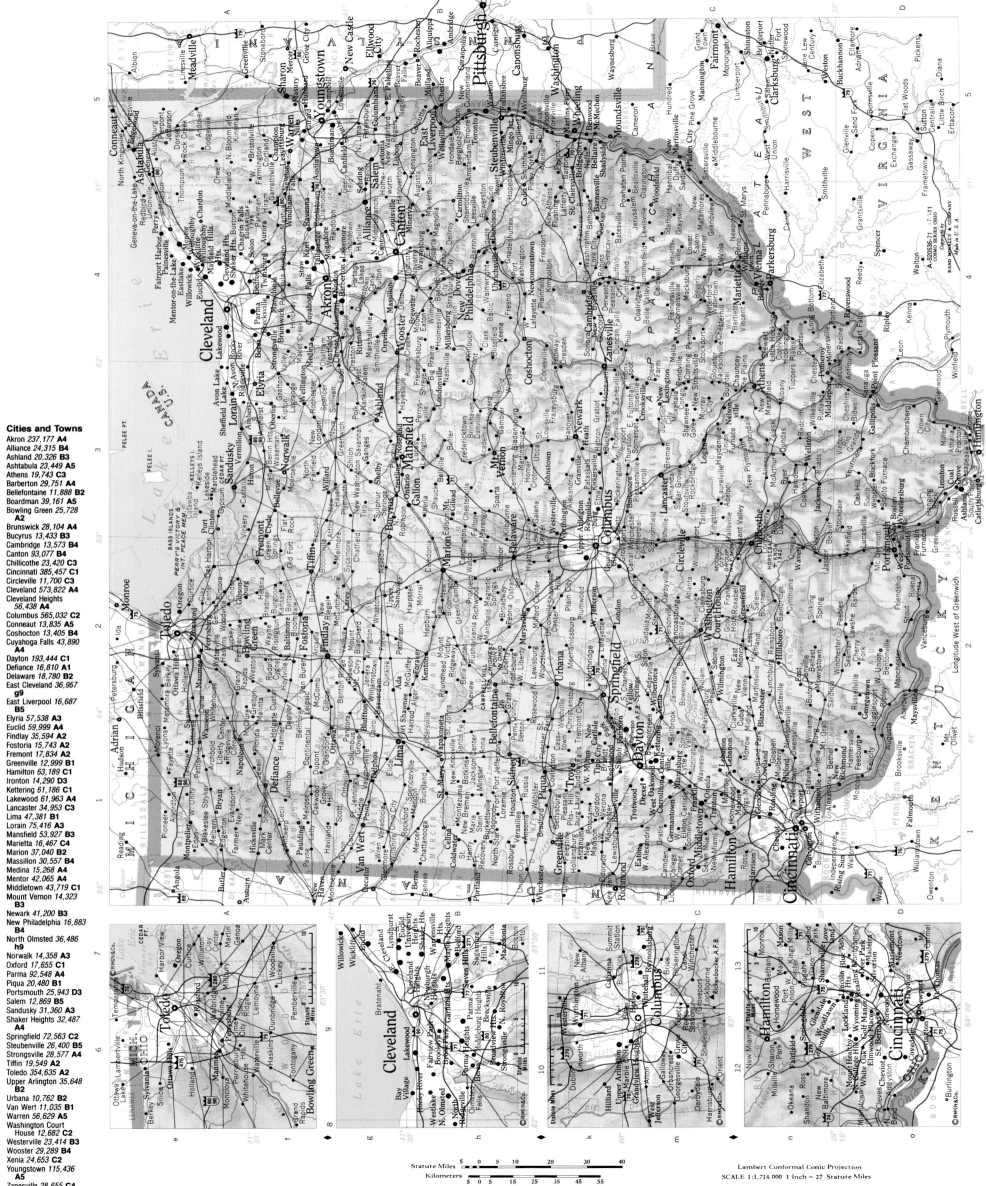

Cities and Towns

Akron 237,177 **A4**
Alliance 24,315 **B4**
Ashland 20,326 **B3**
Ashtabula 23,449 **A5**
Athens 19,743 **C3**
Barberton 29,751 **A4**
Bellefontaine 11,888 **B2**
Boardman 39,161 **A5**
Bowling Green 25,728
   A2
Brunswick 28,104 **A4**
Bucyrus 13,433 **B3**
Cambridge 13,573 **B4**
Canton 93,077 **B4**
Chillicothe 23,420 **C3**
Cincinnati 385,457 **C1**
Circleville 11,700 **C3**
Cleveland 573,822 **A4**
Cleveland Heights
   56,438 **A4**
Columbus 565,032 **C2**
Conneaut 13,835 **A5**
Coshocton 13,405 **B4**
Cuyahoga Falls 43,890
   A4
Dayton 193,444 **C1**
Defiance 16,810 **A1**
Delaware 18,780 **B2**
East Cleveland 36,957
   g9
East Liverpool 16,687
   B5
Elyria 57,538 **A3**
Euclid 59,999 **A4**
Findlay 35,594 **A2**
Fostoria 15,743 **A2**
Fremont 17,834 **A2**
Greenville 12,999 **B1**
Hamilton 63,189 **C1**
Ironton 14,290 **D3**
Kettering 61,186 **C1**
Lakewood 61,963 **A4**
Lancaster 34,953 **C3**
Lima 47,381 **B1**
Lorain 75,416 **A3**
Mansfield 53,927 **B3**
Marietta 16,467 **C4**
Marion 37,040 **B2**
Massillon 30,557 **B4**
Medina 15,268 **A4**
Mentor 42,065 **A4**
Middletown 43,719 **C1**
Mount Vernon 14,323
   B3
Newark 41,200 **B3**
New Philadelphia 16,883
   B4
North Olmsted 36,486
   h9
Norwalk 14,358 **A3**
Oxford 17,655 **C1**
Parma 92,548 **A4**
Piqua 20,480 **B1**
Portsmouth 25,943 **D3**
Salem 12,869 **B5**
Sandusky 31,360 **A3**
Shaker Heights 32,487
   A4
Springfield 72,563 **C2**
Steubenville 26,400 **B5**
Strongsville 28,577 **A4**
Tiffin 19,549 **A2**
Toledo 354,635 **A2**
Upper Arlington 35,648
   B2
Urbana 10,762 **B2**
Van Wert 11,035 **B1**
Warren 56,629 **A5**
Washington Court
   House 12,682 **C2**
Westerville 23,414 **B3**
Wooster 29,289 **B4**
Xenia 24,653 **C2**
Youngstown 115,436
   A5
Zanesville 28,655 **C4**

Statute Miles
Kilometers

Lambert Conformal Conic Projection
SCALE 1:1,714,000 1 Inch = 27 Statute Miles

Ohio

POPULATION 10,797,624.
Rank: 6. *Density:* 263 people/mi²
(102 people/km²). *Urban:* 73.3%.
Rural: 26.7%.
AGE <20: 32%. 20–40: 31%.
40–65: 26%. >65: 11%.
ETHNIC GROUPS *White:* 88.9%.
Black: 10%. *Spanish origin:*
1.1%. *Native American:* 0.1%.
Other: 1%.

INCOME/CAPITA $9,462. *Rank:* 19.
POLITICS 1948–1980 elections:
President: 3 Dem., 6 Rep.
Governor: 6 Dem., 5 Rep.
ENTERED UNION March 1, 1803,
17th state.
CAPITAL Columbus, 565,032.
LARGEST CITY Cleveland, 573,822.

AREA 44,786 mi² (115,995 km²).
Rank: 35. *Water area:* 3,782 m²
(9,795 km²).
ELEVATIONS *Highest:* Campbell
Hill, 1,550 ft (472 m). *Lowest:*
Along Ohio River, 433 ft (132 m).
CLIMATE Abundant rainfall. High
but not oppressive summer
temperatures; cool to cold
winters.

A s the first state hewn from the old Northwest Territory, Ohio
quickly became a leader of states and a state of leaders. Ohio's
combined manufacturing and agricultural production is among
the highest in the nation, and with the exception of Virginia, no state
can claim to be the birthplace of so many presidents. The ethnic mix
and urban concentration of its people reflect the ethnic and urban
character of the United States as a whole. This fact is not lost on poll-
sters seeking to fathom public opinion, politicians implementing new
government programs, and retailers interested in test marketing products. Ohio serves as the sounding board for them all.

Ohio's leadership has always been expressed in terms of its powerful industry and agriculture. The state is a major contributor to the
nation's manufacturing, and large deposits of high-quality coal, oil,
natural gas, stone, clay, and salt help support Ohio's commerce. As
part of America's great midwestern farmland, Ohio also makes a substantial contribution to the country's agriculture.

Ohio owes much of its success to its location and impressive transport systems. Set between Lake Erie and the Ohio River and overlaid
with a dense web of roads, railways, and canals, Ohio is able to take
in raw materials from all over the country and the world, then ship
finished products to domestic and overseas markets. The state also
lies within the heavily traveled corridor stretching from the midwestern to eastern states, a corridor that represents one of the greatest
concentrations of industry in the world.

Modern-day Ohio has suffered its share of problems—pollution
and urban decay associated with the decline of heavy industry and an
economy fighting to adapt to radical changes. But Ohio is still a beautiful state of rolling hills, upland plateaus, and plains—all within easy
reach of urban dwellers. Also, few states have invested as heavily as
has Ohio in public and private education and social services. These
investments are sure to yield dividends both in furthering economic
growth and in solving the state's environmental problems. If so, then
Ohio's leadership status will be ensured for some time to come.

Ohio owes much of its success to the Ohio River, which makes the state an important transportation link. Located on the banks of the Ohio, Cincinnati displays the
effect that access to transportation routes has upon industrial development.

Employment / Value

Retail trade
Wholesale trade
Service
Government
Manufacturing
Agriculture
Mining

1.5   1.0   0.5   0   20   40   60   80
Millions of Persons   Billions of Dollars

Economic Activities Ohio's manufacturing and wholesale distribution of its products clearly dominate the state's economy. Although many industries involve metals
in one way or another—forming them into anything from steel beams to parts for
airplanes—other Ohio industries are based on materials such as clay, chemicals,
paper, and plastics.

Manufacturing Unlike many other states in which manufacturing is concentrated
in specific areas, Ohio has relatively well-dispersed industrial centers. Each of the 11
counties shown on the map is one of the country's top 150 counties in total value
added by manufacturing.

Land Use With Ohio's mineral resources, fertile soils, and good location, settlers
found virtually all parts of the state ripe for development. This accounts for the
relatively even spread of cities, industry, and agriculture across the state. Besides
crops such as soybeans and corn, dairy farming makes an important contribution
to agricultural income.

Industry group

Primary-metal industries	Petroleum refining	Paper products
Fabricated-metal products	Chemicals	Printing and publishing
Machinery	Rubber and plastic products	Food processing
Transportation equipment	Stone, clay, and glass products	Other
Electric and electronic equipment		

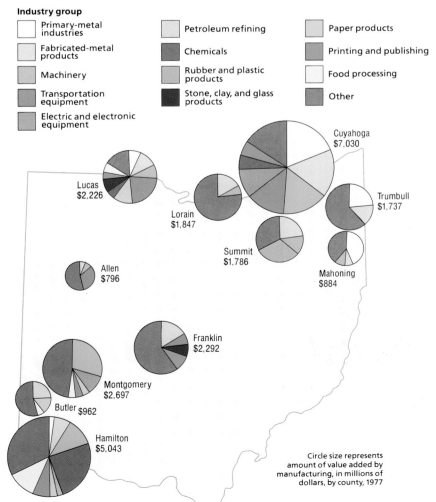

Cuyahoga
$7,030

Lucas
$2,226

Lorain
$1,847

Trumbull
$1,737

Summit
$1,786

Mahoning
$884

Allen
$796

Franklin
$2,292

Montgomery
$2,697

Butler $962

Hamilton
$5,043

Circle size represents
amount of value added by
manufacturing, in millions of
dollars, by county, 1977

© R. McN

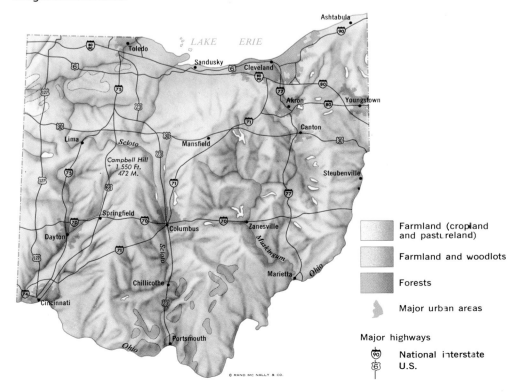

Farmland (cropland
and pastureland)

Farmland and woodlots

Forests

Major urban areas

Major highways

National interstate

U.S.

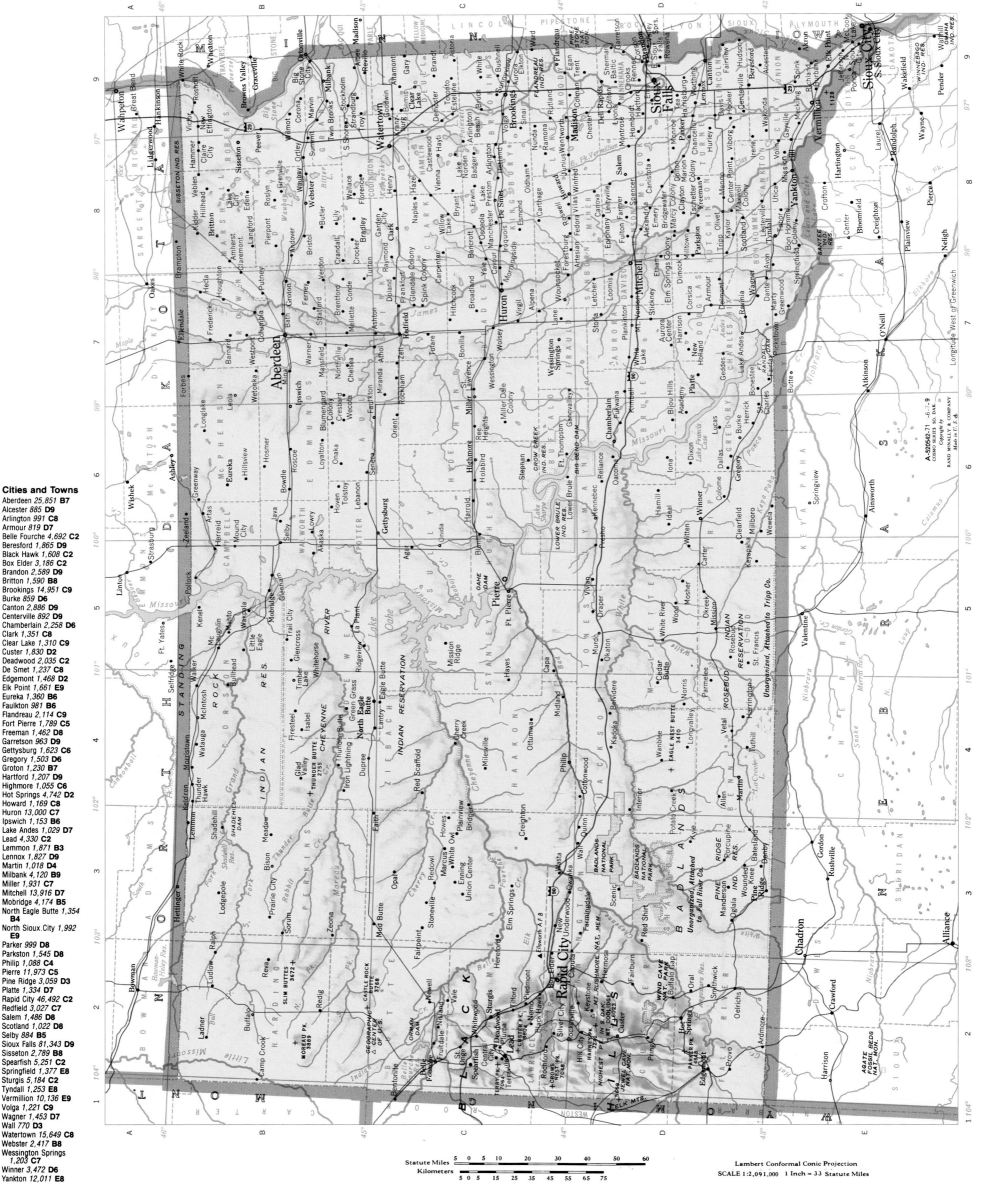

Cities and Towns

Aberdeen 25,851 **B7**
Alcester 885 **D9**
Arlington 991 **C8**
Armour 819 **D7**
Belle Fourche 4,692 **C2**
Beresford 1,865 **D9**
Black Hawk 1,608 **C2**
Box Elder 3,186 **C2**
Brandon 2,589 **D9**
Britton 1,590 **B8**
Brookings 14,951 **C9**
Burke 859 **D6**
Canton 2,886 **D9**
Centerville 892 **D9**
Chamberlain 2,258 **D6**
Clark 1,351 **C8**
Clear Lake 1,310 **C9**
Custer 1,830 **D2**
Deadwood 2,035 **C2**
De Smet 1,237 **C8**
Edgemont 1,468 **D2**
Elk Point 1,661 **E9**
Eureka 1,360 **B6**
Faulkton 981 **B6**
Flandreau 2,114 **C9**
Fort Pierre 1,789 **C5**
Freeman 1,462 **D8**
Garretson 963 **D9**
Gettysburg 1,623 **C6**
Gregory 1,503 **D6**
Groton 1,230 **B7**
Hartford 1,207 **D9**
Highmore 1,055 **C6**
Hot Springs 4,742 **D2**
Howard 1,169 **C8**
Huron 13,000 **C7**
Ipswich 1,153 **B6**
Lake Andes 1,029 **D7**
Lead 4,330 **C2**
Lemmon 1,871 **B3**
Lennox 1,827 **D9**
Martin 1,018 **D4**
Milbank 4,120 **B9**
Miller 1,931 **C7**
Mitchell 13,916 **D7**
Mobridge 4,174 **B5**
North Eagle Butte 1,354
  B4
North Sioux City 1,992
  E9
Parker 999 **D8**
Parkston 1,545 **D8**
Philip 1,088 **C4**
Pierre 11,973 **C5**
Pine Ridge 3,059 **D3**
Platte 1,334 **D7**
Rapid City 46,492 **C2**
Redfield 3,027 **C7**
Salem 1,486 **D8**
Scotland 1,022 **D8**
Selby 884 **B5**
Sioux Falls 81,343 **D9**
Sisseton 2,789 **B8**
Spearfish 5,251 **C2**
Springfield 1,377 **E8**
Sturgis 5,184 **C2**
Tyndall 1,253 **E8**
Vermillion 10,136 **E9**
Volga 1,221 **C9**
Wagner 1,453 **D7**
Wall 770 **D3**
Watertown 15,649 **C8**
Webster 2,417 **B8**
Wessington Springs
  1,203 **C7**
Winner 3,472 **D6**
Yankton 12,011 **E8**

Statute Miles
Kilometers

Lambert Conformal Conic Projection
SCALE 1:2,091,000   1 Inch = 33 Statute Miles

South Dakota

POPULATION 690,768. *Rank:* 45. *Density:* 9.1 people/mi² (3.5 people/km²). *Urban:* 46.4%. *Rural:* 53.6%.
AGE *< 20:* 34%. *20–40:* 30%. *40–65:* 23%. *>65:* 13%.
ETHNIC GROUPS *White:* 92.6%. *Black:* 0.3%. *Spanish origin:* 0.6%. *Native American:* 6.5%. *Other:* 0.6%.

INCOME/CAPITA $7,806. *Rank:* 42.
POLITICS 1948–1980 elections: *President:* 1 Dem., 8 Rep. *Governor:* 4 Dem., 11 Rep.
ENTERED UNION November 2, 1889, 40th state.
CAPITAL Pierre, 11,973.
LARGEST CITY Sioux Falls, 81,343.

AREA 77,116 mi² (199,730 km²). *Rank:* 16. *Water area:* 1,164 mi² (3,015 km²).
ELEVATIONS *Highest:* Harney Peak, 7,242 ft (2,207 m). *Lowest:* Along Big Stone Lake, 962 ft (293 m).
CLIMATE Hot summers, cold winters. Adequate rainfall during growing season, winter blizzards.

The Missouri River cuts through South Dakota as if marking a regional boundary between the Midwest and the West. The eastern part of the state contains the same fertile prairie grasslands as its midwestern neighbors, supporting wheat and small-grain crops in the north and feed grain and livestock in the south. Western South Dakota, however, resembles the West, with its sparse population and open-range cattle ranching. Yet despite the distinct boundary established by the Missouri, the land changes gradually from east to west. Only the Black Hills in the southwest corner of the state mark a dramatic contrast to South Dakota's rolling plains.

The state's dependence on grain farming and grazing makes it one of the few states in which agriculture outweighs manufacturing. And South Dakota's industry remains tied to agriculture, mainly processing raw farm products for market. In addition, forested areas in the western region provide valuable timber and wood products.

South Dakota is also one of the few states in which rural population outnumbers urban. However, this situation may change if more farms become mechanized, forcing farm workers off the land and encouraging migration to the cities. For the most part, South Dakota has managed to balance demand for its products with the resources and people available within the state.

Despite South Dakota's basically rural focus, its potential for future growth is sizable. Damming major rivers has made the state a producer of hydroelectric power. In a region that suffers from periodic drought, the dams have made more water available for irrigation and livestock. Continued development of the Missouri Basin could give South Dakota more power and water in the future, along with greater flood control of the Missouri.

In South Dakota, the Midwest and the West meet in a balance of natural and developed environments. Economic diversification, when and if it comes, in all likelihood will only strengthen the stable base of South Dakota's life.

South Dakota's dams and reservoirs alter the natural environment for the benefit of the state. Not only do they serve as sources of hydroelectric power, flood control, and irrigation, but they also create lakes that are important to tourism. Oahe Dam, shown here, is part of the Missouri River development program.

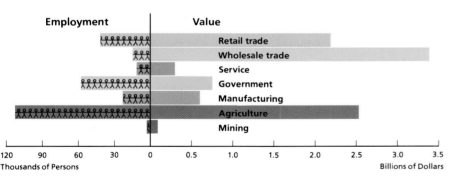

Economic Activities Agriculture still dominates South Dakota's economy, and even manufacturing revolves primarily around the processing of farm products for wholesale trade. Because of the value of their agriculture, South Dakota's farmers have implemented conservation techniques designed to conserve rainfall, prevent erosion, and maintain soil fertility.

Employment	Value
Retail trade	
Wholesale trade	
Service	
Government	
Manufacturing	
Agriculture	
Mining	

120 90 60 30 0   0 0.5 1.0 1.5 2.0 2.5 3.0 3.5
Thousands of Persons   Billions of Dollars

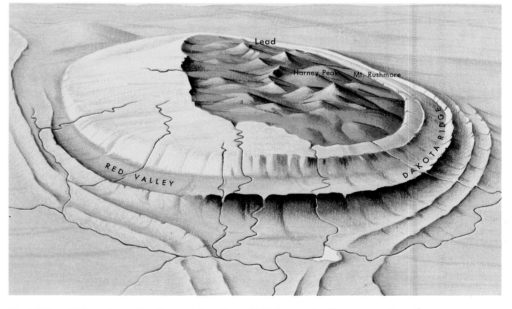

Black Hills Rising above the Great Plains, these "hills" are actually an extension of the Rocky Mountains. Their higher elevation results in greater precipitation, and the mountains are covered with a thick forest of pines that appears to be black from a distance. In addition to being a major tourist attraction, the area contains Homestake Mine, the nation's largest gold mine.

Land Use South Dakota is a land of wide, open spaces; yet the state's broad vistas reveal interesting detail. Except for the Black Hills, South Dakota west of the Missouri River is an unglaciated part of the Missouri Plateau, the northernmost portion of the Great Plains in the United States. And lying for the most part east of the Missouri River is a section of North America's Central Lowland. Covered by thick sheets of ice during the last Ice Age, this region has been buried under a relatively even coat of ice-transported soil. The environmental transition from glaciated prairie to unglaciated plain appears in the state's pattern of land use. Wheat and feed-grain farming prevail in the east, cattle grazing in the west.

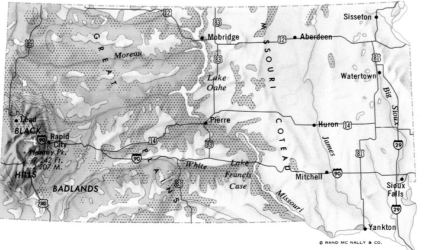

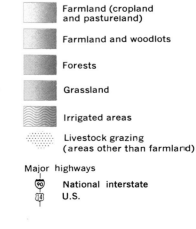

Farmland (cropland and pastureland)

Farmland and woodlots

Forests

Grassland

Irrigated areas

Livestock grazing (areas other than farmland)

Major highways

National interstate

U.S.

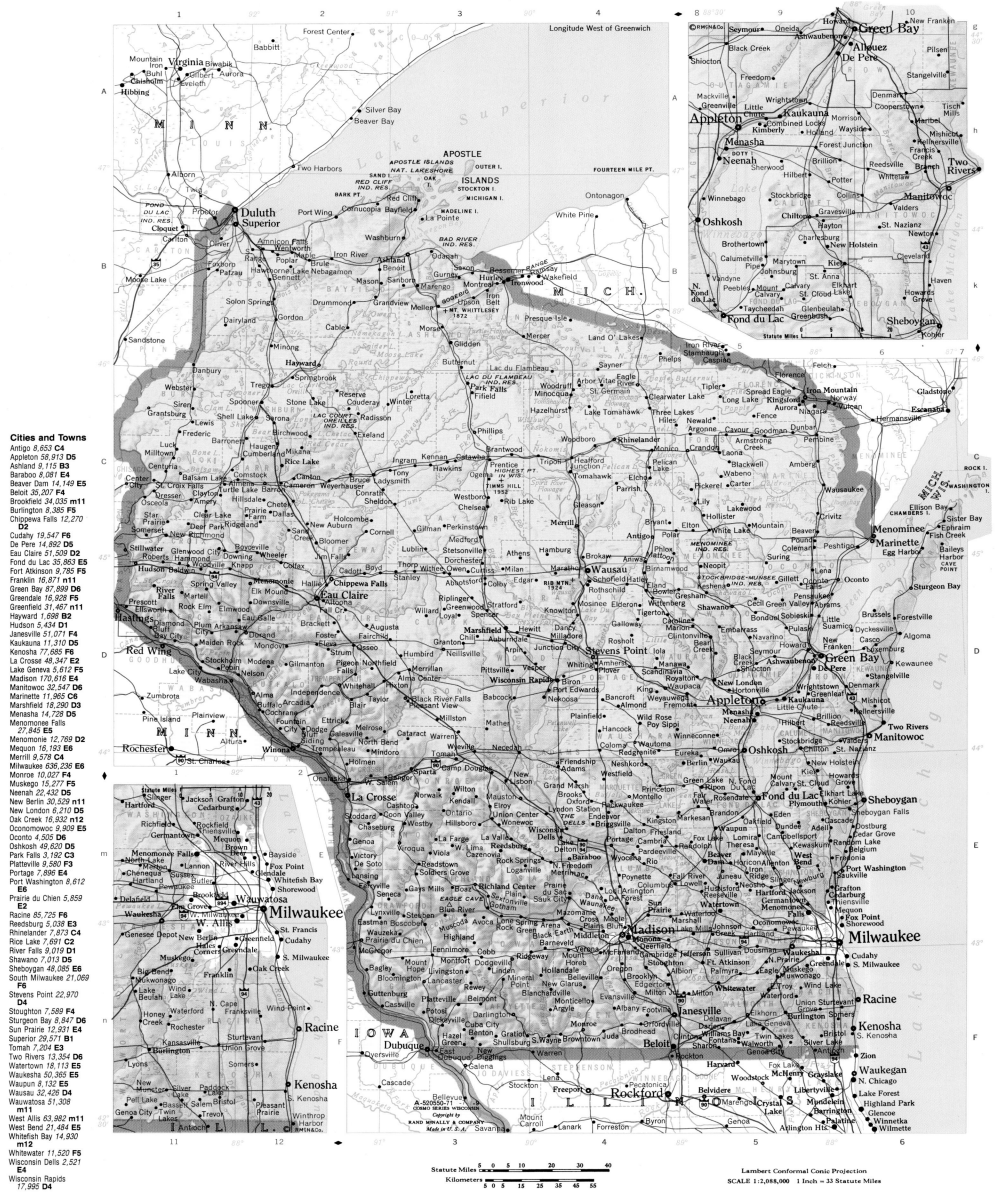

Wisconsin

POPULATION 4,705,521.
  Rank: 16. *Density:* 86 people/mi²
  (33 people/km²). *Urban:* 64.2%.
  Rural: 35.8%.
AGE <20: 33%. 20–40: 31%.
  40–65: 24%. >65: 12%.
ETHNIC GROUPS *White:* 94.4%.
  Black: 3.9%. *Spanish origin:*
  1.3%. *Native American:* 0.6%.
  Other: 1.1%.

INCOME/CAPITA $9,348. *Rank:* 25.
POLITICS 1948–1980 elections:
  President: 3 Dem., 6 Rep.
  Governor: 5 Dem., 9 Rep.
ENTERED UNION May 29, 1848,
  30th state.
CAPITAL Madison, 170,616.
LARGEST CITY Milwaukee, 636,236.

AREA 66,215 mi² (171,496 km²).
  Rank: 25. *Water area:* 11,789 mi²
  (30,533 km²).
ELEVATIONS *Highest:* Timms Hill,
  1,952 ft (595 m). *Lowest:* Along
  Lake Michigan, 581 ft (177 m).
CLIMATE Warm summers, cold
  winters, both marked by
  extremes of temperature.
  Moderate rainfall.

Wisconsin is a model of balance. Its economy is a well-managed combination of agriculture, industry, and tourism; its population, a mix of many ethnic groups; and its political and educational systems are a blend of practical and progressive outlooks.

No single factor stands out as the basis for Wisconsin's success. With ample precipitation, its climate and growing season support a variety of staple and cash crops, and the state is located near major Midwest markets. In addition, the many lakes, rivers, and landforms carved out and molded by glaciers make Wisconsin an inviting recreational area for visitors and tourists.

However, Wisconsin was not always the model of balance it is today. The state experienced a spectacular rise and equally rapid decline of wheat farming before growers turned to dairy and cheese products to make better use of their agricultural resources. Excessive lumbering in the nineteenth century drew attention to the need for conservation programs. And in addition, industries had to compete for markets and raw materials with nearby Chicago and Minnesota's Twin Cities of Minneapolis and St. Paul. But with the aid of a large influx of immigrants in the nineteenth century, the state's agriculture and industry were successfully developed.

Making the most of its resources and opportunities, Wisconsin has become a major processor of primary products. Even though energy supplies and many raw materials for manufacturing must be imported, the state has established itself as an important producer of a wide variety of industrial goods.

Wisconsin will most likely continue to be a model of balance for other states, many of which share the problems Wisconsin faces, such as a lack of the high-technology industries that play an important role in today's economy. The state's long-term investment in education, as evidenced by the University of Wisconsin, may provide solutions to this and the issues often generated by economic development. Wisconsin's heritage is one of skillfully balancing economic growth and environmental quality within a flexible and forward-looking political system.

Wisconsin has a long history of conservation activities, and the Horicon Marsh Wildlife Refuge in southeastern Wisconsin reflects this tradition. Each year, the refuge serves as a nesting and feeding ground for thousands of migrating waterfowl.

Economic Activities   In both agriculture and manufacturing, Wisconsin has created national markets for products that were once largely of local significance, such as cheese, beer, agricultural equipment, and small motor-driven tools. Mining and lumbering, important earlier in the state's history, have declined in significance, although some production is locally important.

Employment	Value	
		Retail trade
		Wholesale trade
		Service
		Government
		Manufacturing
		Agriculture
		Mining

600   400   200   0   5   10   15   20
Thousands of Persons   Billions of Dollars

Land Use   Southeastern Wisconsin is the most urban and industrialized section of the state, although cities are interspersed with excellent farmland. This productive land is shared with the southwest, which is more exclusively rural in character. The north is covered with forests, lakes, and streams, offering scenic attractions for tourists.

Ethnic Diversity   Established by 1900, the settlement patterns of various nationality groups were still present in 1940, as this map reflects. As society grew more mobile and rural population migrated to urban areas, ethnic groups became more dispersed. Still, the descendants and the culture of various groups predominate in many areas of Wisconsin, imparting variety and stability to the state.

Farmland (cropland and pastureland)

Farmland and woodlots

Forest

Swampland and marshland

Livestock grazing
(areas other than farmland)

Major urban areas

Major highways

🛡 U.S.
🛡 National interstate

Origin of predominating groups

American Indian

Germany

British Isles

Eastern Europe

Scandinavia

Belgium or Netherlands

Switzerland or France or Italy

Mixture

Largely unsettled

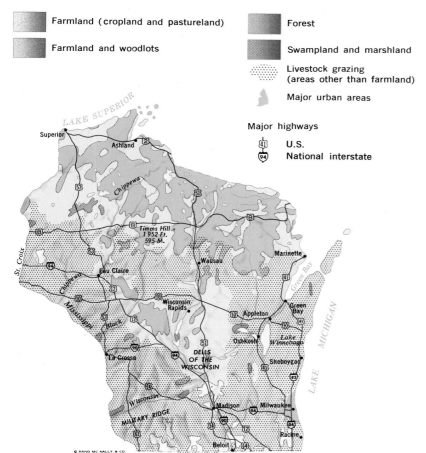

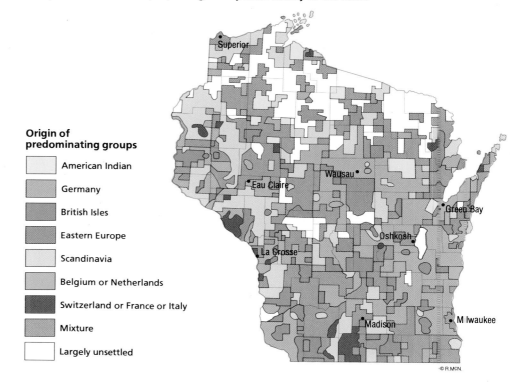

GRANITES ALONG NORTH SHORE OF LAKE TAHOE / NEVADA

The High Country

The High Country

Rooftop of the Continent

BY DAVID SUMNER

AMERICA'S HIGH COUNTRY IS AN ASTONISH-ingly vast and varied province. From Devils Tower in northeast Wyoming it reaches westward to the multiple, isolated, riblike ranges of Nevada. From the gracefully sculpted peaks of Montana's Glacier National Park, tight against the Canadian border, it plunges south to the desert tablelands of Monument Valley in southern Utah. From the depths of Idaho's rugged western edge in Hells Canyon it flows eastward in peak and plain to the waving wheat fields of Colorado's eastern third.

Backbone of this region is the great Rocky Mountain chain dropping south from Montana to southern Colorado and beyond, sprawling laterally from the Front Range to the height of mountains surrounding Lake Tahoe, a complexity of innumerable systems collectively known as the Rockies. But much of the High Country is not mountainous. More than half of Montana, much of Idaho, a third of Colorado, a quarter of Wyoming are plains. The Great Basin comprising most of Nevada and a lot of Utah has its mountain ranges, but much of it consists of irrigated valleys and flat, dry lake beds. This

unique self-contained area has no outlet to the sea but drains into the desert sands or into depressions like the Great Salt Lake. The Colorado Plateau is heavily cut by rivers of snow-melt water from distant mountains. Much of the region is desert: Nevada and Utah are our two driest states; western Colorado is largely desert; so is much of Wyoming, most of southern Idaho, and a good bit of Montana.

The misconception that the Rockies and their associated westerly ranges are all of a piece is dispelled only as one flies over them or travels through them by car or train. The Rocky Mountains are, in fact, a massive chain of ranges that in their total context run from Alaska to the southern tip of South America. Running along this erratic weaving line, frequently veering and looping laterally, is the Continental Divide, the crest of the Rockies that separates the waters that flow east from those that run west. Climb to the rim of the Divide in any of a dozen places by car, a hundred on horseback, a thousand on foot, and you can see how fine this line is.

In southwestern Colorado's San Juan range, for example, near the tiny 1880s silver camp of Lake City, the Divide traces

Colorado
Idaho
Montana
Nevada
Utah
Wyoming

a meandering line along a vast rolling expanse of grassy alpine tundra, the land above the trees. Spines of rock and sharp ridges that often characterize the Divide elsewhere are largely absent here. Instead, viewed from above, the terrain seems more like a high, gentle, undulating plain. Almost lost is a small, unnamed lake that seems to lie exactly on the crest of the Divide.

Look closely and you'll see that the land tilts just enough southward so this three-acre scenic lake drains gently into Pole Creek, then more swiftly into the upper Rio Grande, and ultimately into the Gulf of Mexico and to the Atlantic thousands of miles to the east. Look more closely and you'll see that a slight northward slant (a minor earthquake could do the job) would change everything: The same unnamed lake would drain down Cataract Creek into the Lake Fork of the Gunnison River, then into the main Gunnison, next into the mighty Colorado, and finally into the Gulf of California, an arm of the Pacific.

When I moved to this region from the East Coast in the 1960s, I was first bemused by the number of different ranges—then agog, finally challenged: I wanted to hike and explore every one of them, but the more I studied maps, the more that became an obviously gargantuan task. Colorado, I learned, has 33 named ranges; Idaho has 81. Colorado alone has more than 50 peaks above 14,000 feet.

To date I've explored some 20 High Country ranges. The rest lure me on, their names like the folk poetry of the West: Tobacco Root and Bitterroot; Wasatch and Sawatch; White River, Wind River, and Lost River; Absaroka and Cochetopa; Elkhead, Rabbit Ears, Mosquito, and Swan. And over in Nevada is an irregular, disjunct array of ranges that few Americans have ever heard of: the Goshute and Pequop mountains; the Toana, Reveille, and Pancake ranges; the Toiyabe, and many more.

All are inviting, each has its own distinct way. One of these days I'm going to hike Montana's Crazy Mountains simply because of the name. After you have lived in and roamed America's High Country for a spell, the differences become increasingly vivid. In Colorado I go to the San Juans for an experience in sheer mass; to the Sangre de Cristos for

Overleaf– SNAKE RIVER, GRAND TETON NATIONAL PARK / WYOMING

intense, angular power; to the Elks for a finer, sculptured grace. Each range, like a favorite national park, has its distinctions.

You soon learn what areas have their special gifts: Wyoming's Wind River range has an awesome mix of high lakes, small glaciers, and granite walls; the Tarryall Mountains in Colorado have more bizarre granites, shaped like gargoyles and ghosts, but relatively little water; the Beaverhead Mountains, along the Montana-Idaho border, are unique for their history—especially Lemhi Pass, where the explorers Lewis and Clark first crossed the Continental Divide on their epic journey to the Pacific in 1805.

Travel down the twisted dirt road on the west flank of this pass and you will find a commemorative marker with a quotation from the Lewis and Clark journal: "Here we first tasted the waters of the mighty Columbia River." Shoshone Indians who lived in the area had told them that they were in the Pacific watershed, and the explorers were soon eating salmon they obtained in trade with the Indians, further proof that these waters drained to the Pacific.

All of this region was Indian country—as was all of America at one time—the land of the Shoshone and Blackfoot, the Arapaho and Cheyenne, the Ute and Paiute, the Nez Perce and Assiniboine, the Lakota and Crow. Some tribes had been pushed into the region by settlers on the plains to the east. Before long these native peoples would experience more pressure from the growing populations of the white man.

The first of these were the mountain men—John Colter, a member of the Corps of Discovery under Lewis and Clark who elected to stay in the northern Rockies; Jim Bridger, Ceran St. Vrain, Jedediah Smith. Smith, whose scholarly biography is subtitled "The Opening of the West," was with the first party to cross South Pass, which became the standard route over the Divide, the route of the Oregon Trail. He was the first to discover the Great Basin, to realize it had no outlet, to travel its length and breadth. He knew this High Country from the Missouri River to the Green, from the Great Salt Lake to the Flathead country.

Following the paths pioneered by these "white Indians"—who trapped beaver, often took Indian wives, and learned the lay of the land—the settlers came, flowing through the region like rivers along narrowly prescribed routes to the fertile, well-watered valleys farther west and to the coastal lowlands. It is a curious fact that this Rocky Mountain region was settled only after the West Coast was well populated, when the tide of immigration swept back from the Pacific into the High Country.

It was the Mormons, a tough and determined people full of religious zeal, who first subdued this region. Driven out of the East and the Midwest for their religious beliefs and practices, the Latter-day Saints settled in the valley of the Great Salt Lake, then colonized what later became Idaho, Wyoming, Montana, Colorado, Nevada, and well beyond, where their beliefs remain the single most influential religious force.

In this Mormon land lie two ranges notably isolated from their neighbors—like the Mormons in the early days. The Henry Mountains, the last major range discovered in the

YUCCA, CHOLLA, AND JOSHUA TREE IN
RED ROCK CANYON / NEVADA

United States and home to a small herd of free-ranging bison, tower over the canyonlands of southeastern Utah. In Utah's great west desert where the Pony Express route goes into Nevada, the Deep Creek Mountains rise to 12,000 feet from the dry bed of an ancient lake, a range so isolated in elevation and distance that unique species of plants, fish, and insects have evolved here. From the summit of this range you can see—on a clear day—almost the whole Great Basin. One characteristic of the region is open space, broad vistas, a sense of vastness.

The high valleys and tablelands are themselves a surprise. Of all the sights in Colorado, none is more purely breathtaking than the drive southwest from Denver on U.S. 285 over Kenosha Pass to South Park. In the High Country "park" means large, open, high-mountain valley (as "hole" signifies smaller, narrower, mountain-rimmed valley). South Park is huge—100 by 50 miles of windswept grassland erratically broken by low, rounded ridges thatched with fir, spruce, limber pine, and—less often—aspen. This is lush, green cattle country in summer, but a bitter no-man's-land in winter, especially when ground blizzards whip across the park, reducing visibility to a foot or two. Ground blizzards occur when severe low-elevation winds blast loose snow from the already-fallen pack, whipping it relentlessly across the land. Stand in one of these phenomena (you'll have to lean hard into the wind) and you may be able to see the stars overhead but not your own feet planted in the drifting snow.

Rivers carve great canyons from the mountains too, not only the famous ones like the Grand Canyon of the Yellowstone, the Black Canyon of the Gunnison, and the legendary Hells Canyon of the Snake, but also countless other mountain gorges whose names only begin to suggest their variety: Bluejay, Dark, Crystal, Canyon del Diablo, Forest, Impassable, and literally hundreds more including the popular rafting runs on the Salmon, Yampa, Green, Dolores, Arkansas, Selway, and Flathead rivers.

The truly remarkable canyon country of this region lies out of the mountains, around the edges—as if the forces of geology had found a need to match the grandeur of the peaks with another kind of majesty below. East of the southern Colorado Rockies, Purgatory Canyon (called by natives "Picket Wire" and sometimes "Piggitwa") cuts a sinuous gash into the high plains. In southwest Idaho the great Bruneau Canyon, a wild river at its bottom and more than enough rattlesnakes for a roundup, appears as a sudden, inexplicable crack in the land.

For the fullest canyon feast, explore south of the Uinta Range in Utah and west of Colorado's sprawling San Juans. Southern Utah's remarkable canyon country is the site of America's greatest concentration of national parks: Arches, Bryce, Canyonlands, Capitol Reef, and Zion. All of them are carved, one way or another, by waters that gather from mountain snowfields at higher elevations—snowfields that, each spring, send fresh water, filled with sand and silt, to carve canyon floors deeper and bends wider, more undercut and overhanging. These same spring waters, when they reach Utah's canyon country, also sharpen spires and pinnacles, widen natural arches, and begin their work of creating new

Left– LOWER FALLS OF THE YELLOWSTONE, YELLOWSTONE NATIONAL PARK / WYOMING

Below– DOUGLAS FIR, LIVINGSTONE RANGE, GLACIER NATIONAL PARK / MONTANA

AUTUMN TRANSITION, ANIMAS RIVER CANYON, NEEDLES RANGE / COLORADO

rock forms wherever the geology is suitable. Utah has one area called Goblin Valley, full of red rocks carved into strange forms. The town of Mexican Hat is named for a sombrero-like rock formation nearby. Once, hiking in an isolated patch of Canyonlands National Park, I came upon a perfect mushroom-shaped rock twice my height. Out here you learn to expect the unexpected.

Many of the canyons of this area—geologically known as the Colorado Plateau—are large, carved by great rivers. The Green River carves Desolation and Gray canyons, Labyrinth and Stillwater, and the Colorado carves rapids-strewn Cataract Canyon. One stretch of Labyrinth Canyon is so convoluted that the river flows 28 miles to gain nine miles in a direct line.

But for a canyon to explore and enjoy on a temperate spring day, my choice is a 30-square-mile infinitely tangled system in the western reach of Canyonlands National Park called the Maze. It is remote: You must hike 13 miles overland just to get your first look at it. "A labyrinth with the roof removed," it has been called, but that barely begins to describe what must be the most intensely concentrated canyon system in the world.

Standing on the rim facing the Maze, you are confronted with a 250-degree panorama of canyons—winding, twisting, sinuous—that resemble nothing so much as the infinite, intricate folds of a human brain. But descend the 1,200 feet from rim to canyon floor—using toe holds, friction, and, if you are carrying a heavy pack, a rope—and you arrive in a wholly different world. You lose your bird's-eye perspective and find yourself in that maze, faced with a lifetime of choices of high desert canyons to explore, an experience both frightening and exciting. The red and white strata of candy-striped walls offer no clue to the way out of the labyrinth, and you proceed like the first person on earth.

Rocky summit and deep valley, graceful ridge and twisted canyon floor. All this is America's High Country to explore. Major John Wesley Powell explored it in 1869, leading a small expedition through the canyons of the Green and Colorado rivers in Wyoming, Colorado, Utah, and beyond. Powell fathered both the U.S. Geologic Survey and the Bureau of Reclamation. He dreamed of turning this arid region into productive land so that it could be settled. He set in motion a century-long movement to correct nature's mistake in leaving so large a region arid.

For an overriding characteristic of this region is its lack of water, a major reason so few people settled here—along with the fact that winters are long and severe and growing seasons correspondingly short and fickle. Even today this six-state region is sparsely populated, with not quite 8 million people in its 629,000 square miles—that's an average of fewer than 13 people per square mile.

The area may not seem all that dry. Many of the nation's best-known ski resorts are here—Alta, Aspen, Big Sky, Jackson Hole, Snowbird, Sun Valley, Vail—and they measure snowfall in feet, not inches. There's a lot of moisture stored in the snowpack, but the moisture comes at the wrong time for crops. The moisture that falls here can't be utilized except for winter sports, and it all runs off somewhere else. The major cities of the region—Denver, Salt Lake City, Boise, Las Vegas, Great Falls, Casper—all anticipate water shortages in the next decade; some experience them already.

This region is rich in national parks and monuments, wildlife refuges and recreation areas, forests and national resource lands. In fact, the federal government manages more than half of this land. It has vast mineral wealth and energy resources: gold, silver, copper, molybdenum, lead, and zinc; oil, gas, uranium, coal, tar sands, oil shale, and solar energy—and all these competing uses demand water. The pinto bean, sugar beet, and alfalfa field are all grown on irrigated land, but irrigation pumping requires vast amounts of electricity: Use the water for irrigation, and there may not be enough to produce the electricity to pump that water. In this land of the fly fisherman and the logger, the elk hunter and the energy developer, the wilderness backpacker and the hard-rock miner—who may be the same individuals—there simply isn't enough water to go around.

From my home at an elevation of 8,885 feet in the Colorado Rockies, higher than any point east of the Mississippi, the first snows of the season may be visible on the high peaks as early as Labor Day. One year the summits picked up a dusting on August 4: The high strata looked like layers of frosting on a cake. Another year, on July 23, I hiked to a favorite spot not far from where I live, the scenic Oh-Be-Joyful Valley. There, at timberline and above, I found snowfields from the previous winter. In a high lake, large chunks of ice floated like pieces of an old glacier, and on the adjoining slope I could have skied.

My home is in a small mountain community, Crested Butte (pop. 1,200), which in many ways typifies this region.

Like many other towns, it was born in the 1880s, a supply center for the hurley-burley, boom-or-bust silver mines higher in the mountains. For several decades it was a coal town; for the last two, it has been an attractive out-of-the-way ski resort. I am lucky: Crested Butte is the kind of place where many Americans dream of living, a mountain Brigadoon.

As I write, it is high autumn, the first week in October. Outside my studio window brisk winds are gusting from the west: Light snow flurries churn in the bright sunlight. In the front yard, leaves of the elaborate, many-branched cottonwoods have yellowed and turned gold. Just outside the town limits on the north-facing flank of Gibson's Ridge, scattered patches of aspen are an even brighter yellow. If I drive the gravel road 10 miles west and south to Ohio Pass, I will find that the aspens have taken over completely, flowing down whole mountainsides in bright avalanches of shimmering gold. This is truly fall in the High Country.

From fall in Crested Butte, turn to midwinter in Wyoming's Yellowstone National Park, not the storied part with all the geysers and falls, but rather the remote southwest corner where the Bechler River oxbows through broad meadows. In February the landscape is leveled by many feet of snow, ideal terrain for ski touring. In the week I spend here—traveling 65 miles, camping in the snow—the winter weather has a rhythm, though in the High Country you can never count on it: three days of bright sun and luminous, starry nights with temperatures near zero, then a warmer day with snow followed by three more days of sun, and then another of snow. It could be colder, but I am lucky.

Yellowstone makes up for the seasonal chill in its offerings. When the first fur trappers probed the area in 1811, they were intrigued by the thermal phenomena. But when they

Left– WINTER SUNRISE ON CATHEDRAL GROUP, GRAND TETON NATIONAL PARK / WYOMING

Above– PIKES PEAK AND GARDEN OF THE GODS / COLORADO

returned to civilization with tales of their strange encounters, of mud volcanoes, geysers, hot springs, and grumbling fumaroles, their words were dismissed as fiction. Not until the early 1870s, when photographer William Henry Jackson—hauling a huge, cumbersome camera, wet photographic plates (glass), and all his chemicals on a mule named Hypo—made the first real images of Yellowstone's wonders, would the rest of America believe. His works, displayed in the Capitol rotunda in Washington, D.C., helped convince Congress to designate Yellowstone as the country's (and the world's) first national park.

From the rich yellows of autumn, the color of the land is reduced to black and white and drab conifer tones. But what winter takes away in color, it gives back in design: Tiny tracks crisscross and meander over the snow, telling wonderful and terrible tales; wind-sculptured snow and rimed trees, ghosts in the steamy air, stimulate the imagination; the icy edge of an open river is fine lace.

Even as the snow grows deeper with each winter storm, the days grow longer with the promise of spring in the aspen and willow buds. As the snow recedes, wild flowers edge upward from the desert and prairie to the foothills and lower slopes, returning color to the land. The warblers return and the insect hatches on the rivers herald another fishing season. Rising runoff waters mark the beginning of whitewater season. Spring may be the region's most fickle season for fair weather, but it's the best for river running.

At 7,000 feet in Idaho's Sawtooth range on my drive to the Middle Fork of the Salmon, drifts of snow still lie on the pass and a brief snowstorm flurries in mid-June. Creeks are swollen and meadows are swampy with standing water. At the launch site, the Middle Fork surges near flood, still clear but swift and loud, crashing over rocks, foaming through a narrow gorge.

The Middle Fork is one of the Rockies' most exciting rivers, by most standards too big to be called a "fork" of anything. It flows for more than 100 miles, dropping 3,000 feet through a granitic canyon, the walls of which rise—brooding and gray—4,000 feet above the frigid water. The Middle Fork, one of the original wild rivers in a national system of wild

Left– SNAKE RIVER, BIRDS OF PREY NATURAL AREA / IDAHO

Below– JUDITH RIVER, MISSOURI RIVER TRIBUTARY / MONTANA

and scenic rivers, has, by guidebook count, 341 rapids in its lower runable 96 miles, many of them mere riffles. But it is river enough to keep one on a keen edge, and during spring runoff, it adds a note of fear.

The current literally yanks my boat downriver, the surge of its water and the energy of the season becoming one. The maneuvering to avoid rocks and churning holes, icy waves and nasty snags is exhilarating, tiring. The river is fast, the water cold, but I have less trouble with the river than with the weather, which again has a pattern: rain every day. Twice it snows, but that is spring on the Middle Fork. By the time my party reaches the main Salmon—near the point at which Lewis and Clark turned away from the raging river to cross the mountains on horseback—summer is here, both by the calendar and by the weather, which improves as we float out of Impassable Canyon.

Spring weather is iffy, and autumn can bring sudden snowstorms to spoil a trip, even threaten life. Fear of winter's avalanches and extreme temperatures may keep me out of my favorite places much of the year, but summer is the time for backpacking in the mountains. On the drive home from the Middle Fork—through the desert, past the canyonlands, into the mountains—I plan my next trip into the vastness of America's High Country where summer reaches its climax: My choice this time is the Maroon Bells-Snowmass Wilderness not far from home.

The name comes from three mountains: the two Maroon Bells, which are shaped and colored as they are named, and Snowmass, so called for a perennial snowfield on its eastern flank. This wilderness lies halfway between Crested Butte and the resort town of Aspen. From either, it's a short drive and a shorter hike to the wilderness boundary.

Backpacking is a quieter, more personal activity than either river running or cross-country skiing. I hike north from Crested Butte into a large bowl called Scofield Basin, then over a ridge and a pass into another bowl, Farvert Basin, which rolls in a modified stairstep to the southern flank of South Maroon Bell. If autumn is yellow and winter is white, summer in the High Country is green, an almost iridescent rainbow green that immediately strikes the eye. Yet that green is deceiving because on closer inspection it is seen to be dotted with innumerable vivid wild flowers.

I am talking about the zone known as alpine tundra, where life is so severe the plants have adopted an array of defenses against the wind and cold, short growing season, and deep-snow pressure. They are largely perennials, requiring more than a year or two to mature in the harsh setting. Most of them are smaller, tougher, brighter in color than their lowland relatives. They may grow in dense clusters for insulation or have soft gray hairs to protect them from the ultraviolet light in this land of thin air and little atmospheric screening.

I hike here with full pack and marveling eyes, stopping to admire, photograph, and absorb. Any day now the first storm will again dust the higher peaks with snow. This gentle tundra, soft and rolling, will turn colorful with autumn as the seasons flow into one another in a recurring pattern that is as consistent as the hydrologic cycle. Water falls into this

High Country to be stored as snow and ice, to be held by shady slopes and protective vegetation, to be captured by plants, and to be carried away to distant oceans where it forms clouds again, eventually to be returned by the winds to the skies over the High Country.

Sometimes the seasons get mixed up or overlap one another: It snows in midsummer or a sunny warm spell brings an unseasonable thaw to January. Sometimes the water cycle goes haywire and floods the valleys, or a drought makes the arid region even drier for a year or two. But in the long run there is a constancy in these natural systems you can depend on, even as we have come to depend on systems we have created—political systems and social systems—to preserve our natural world in bits and pieces here and there as wilderness areas, wild and scenic rivers, parks and monuments.

The national park idea, first implemented with the creation of Yellowstone in 1872, has expanded to include a nationwide network of parks, monuments, historic sites, and recreation areas. It was the first step in a long progression of conservation measures that have left a bolder imprint on the High Country than on any other region of the United States south of Alaska. In more recent years we have created a national wilderness preservation system (1964) and a national wild and scenic rivers system (1968).

The wilderness areas are phenomena primarily of the national forests, though the National Park System and the Bureau of Land Management have also created a network of preserves embracing lands that have outstanding primeval qualities, to remind people of what this country was like before man first set foot on it.

In a sense the wilderness system is a bank where the principal is saved, earns interest, and is available to use if it is ever needed desperately enough. It is protected from short-term economic exploitation for the people of the nation to use as they see fit: for scientific study and public recreation, for genetic and species diversification and wildlife habitat, for watershed protection and livestock grazing.

Lands designated as wilderness basically cannot be destroyed or even encroached upon by mechanical devices. There are no roads. Logging is prohibited and mining carefully regulated. Access is limited. The Wilderness Act of 1964 has both historic and ecologic significance in that it attempts to preserve natural systems in a way that will provide scientists with information on their functioning without human disturbance, while it gives lay people a chance—in a remnant but very forceful form—to experience the wilderness that once covered the continent.

The experience of travel into a wilderness area today is akin to that of the country's first pioneers. A few of the dangers and uncertainties have been removed, but you can still know a sense of wonder, feel fear, find solitude, experience what self-reliance really means. You may encounter a grizzly bear, get lost, or even freeze to death if you aren't prepared—it happens every year in America's High Country. If wilderness means anything, such possibilities must exist. Yet the farther you have to travel on your own, the more rewarding the experience. In wilderness you have to earn your way, whether on foot or on horseback, on touring ski

ABOVE LOGAN PASS, CONTINENTAL DIVIDE EAST, GLACIER NATIONAL PARK / MONTANA

Left– QUEENS GARDEN, BRYCE CANYON NATIONAL PARK / UTAH

Below– ERODED TOWER IN LIGHT BLIZZARD, CATHEDRAL GORGE / NEVADA

or snowshoe—or in a muscle-powered boat on a wild river.

You can appreciate the High Country from an airplane flying over the Rockies, looking down on the vast landscape highlighted by forest and snowfield, marked by irrigated valley and manmade reservoir. You can see it by car or train, but to experience it you have to become part of it. It can be as low as the bedrock of the Snake River in Hells Canyon or as high as the windswept bristlecone pines atop Nevada's Wheeler Peak; as level as Bonneville Salt Flats or as rough and rugged as the Waterpocket Fold. It can be as dry as a black widow's web in the hollow of a juniper log or as wet as a beaver's belly; as hot as a barren blackrock desert or as cold as the chill factor at the top of the Jackson Hole Ski Area tram in an 80-mile-an-hour winter wind.

It may be winter-white, summer-green, autumn-yellow, or as multicolored as the algae in a Yellowstone hot pool or the rock formations in Utah's Kodachrome Basin. It is vast and varied, a collection of states and a state of mind that is no more bound by state lines than the rivers it nurtures. The High Country has a character all its own, a hang-loose, homespun, friendly western attitude that is part of the American character. It is a land that has shaped its people, a harsh land and a beautiful one.

Even as the land has shaped its people, so the people have shaped the land. They have dammed its rivers, gouged its mountains, and clearcut its forests. But they have also made the desert bloom in unlikely spots and preserved its special places, its unique features, and its character.

Left– COLUMBINES IN SAN JUAN MOUNTAINS / COLORADO

Right– COLUMBINES IN GRANITE, MOSQUITO RANGE / COLORADO

Above– ICEBERG LAKE AND MOUNT HENKEL,
GLACIER NATIONAL PARK / MONTANA

Left– ALPINE POOL, ISLAND LAKE TRAIL, BRIDGER WILDERNESS,
WIND RIVER RANGE / WYOMING

Above– AUTUMN STORM OVER STILLWATER FORK,
BEAR RIVER, UINTA RANGE / UTAH

Left– PAHOEHOE LAVA, CRATERS OF THE MOON NATIONAL MONUMENT / IDAHO

Above– STEAMING TERRACE, MAMMOTH HOT SPRINGS, YELLOWSTONE NATIONAL PARK / WYOMING

Left– GREAT GOOSENECKS, SAN JUAN RIVER / UTAH

Above– RAINBOW BRIDGE NATIONAL MONUMENT / UTAH

WHITE SANDS NATIONAL MONUMENT / NEW MEXICO

The Southwest

A Land of Infinite Variety

BY TONY HILLERMAN

THE THREE OF US—MARIE, THE BLUE HERON, and I—are all Southwesterners. On this balmy January day, we are in Texas, Marie and I watching birds near Washington Beach, where the Rio Grande joins the Gulf of Mexico, and the Blue Heron 30 yards away, shuffling along in the shallows stirring up a meal. A week ago we three were doing approximately the same things 800 miles upstream in New Mexico's Bosque del Apache Wildlife Refuge—my wife and I admiring the snow geese on the open water of the marshes, while the Blue Heron stalked along shin deep among the cattails, long beak poised and beady eyes alert.

Same river, same Blue Heron (Marie says no, last week's heron was older and female), same Southwest. But all else is different. Take winter. Winter at the Gulf Coast end of the Rio Grande is palm trees, shirtsleeves, and a balmy south breeze blowing up from the Yucatan tropics. But last week winter in New Mexico was a light icing of snow on the Coyote Hills, a bit of frost on the earlobes, and the dark blue sky of high country aridity. In the high country of New Mexico

and Arizona, winter can be 40 below zero and 100 inches of snow. Here on the fertile flatlands of the Texas Gulf, winter seems an implausible rumor from another world.

In Oklahoma and Texas, spring is the time that inspired the poets. It comes early, exploding northward from the Gulf with the spreading colors of bluebonnets, poppies, spring beauties, wild violets—more wild flowers than I can name. The pastures turn blue and white and the creeks smell of plum blossoms. But in New Mexico and Arizona there are two springs. Below 6,000 feet, spring is 18 days of blowing dirt followed by summer, while in the mountains, spring climbs slowly up from the foothills. In the highest country, in the meadows between the spruce forests, it doesn't arrive until July and lingers into August, with columbines, wild irises, and lupines blooming everywhere.

Summer is just as different. While Texas and Oklahoma are smothering in August humidity, the dry June forest fire season is already over farther west. August brings what the Navajo calls "time when thunder is awake"—monsoon season. Towering thunderheads build over the mountains each

Arizona
New Mexico
Oklahoma
Texas

afternoon and cool the valleys with showers.

In the desert, this late summer rainy season substitutes for spring. Yuccas send forth their towering spikes of blossoms, and sand poppies and asters flourish everywhere. Even the Sonoran and Yuma deserts, dry as they are, are ablaze with sand verbena, prickly poppy, and the rich, red blossoms of hedgehog cactus.

Autumn in Texas and Oklahoma is red and orange with the turning leaves of hardwoods. Autumn in New Mexico and Arizona has no reds. Just the gold of cottonwoods along the rivers, bright yellow aspen and chamisa in the higher country, and the silver of sage and seeding desert grasses.

That marked degree of difference is the story of the Southwest. No other region of the United States matches its wild leap across the spectrum of zones of climate, biology, and geology. Our Blue Heron, for example, has already changed his environment dramatically by flying down the Rio Grande from the desert landscape of central New Mexico to Texas's western tip. He can change it again by simply flying up the long curve of Texas coastline. As he moves

northeast along Laguna Madre, over Padre Island, and across Galveston Bay, the shoreline beneath him begins to change. The great white sweep of sand, the high dunes, the blowing grasses fade away. He flies into more humid territory, into the wetter winds and cloudier skies of bayou country at the mouth of the Sabine River. Here no sharp division of blue water and white beach draws a line between continent and ocean. This eastern margin of Texas is a drowned land of salt marshes, tidal pools, great expanses of floating hyacinth, sheets of water coated pale green with acres of blooming chickweed—a place where universes of triangle grass are being gobbled down by hundreds of thousands of voracious waterfowl spending their winter vacation. No great, sandy barrier islands here. The coastline changes with the tides.

Why this marked difference along the same coastline? Here the winds make the difference. The sky over the Sabine River is not the sky over the Rio Grande. There winter winds blow from the north—drier and cooler. Here on the Sabine the Gulf winds dominate. Average sunshine decreases. Average humidity soars. Rainfall almost doubles. In the same

Overleaf– SUNRISE, MONUMENT VALLEY NAVAJO TRIBAL PARK / ARIZONA

Above– RIO GRANDE RIVER AND SIERRA DEL CARMEN, BIG BEND NATIONAL PARK / TEXAS

year the south coast may receive less than 30 inches of rain while more than 60 inches drench the Sabine wetlands. The winds determine the landscape here. But as you move west, it becomes a matter of altitude.

The Southwest is tilted. It slopes out of the warm Gulf waters with almost incredible gradualness, rising toward the north and west. Dallas, the glitterdome of north Texas, is some 300 miles inland from the mouth of Galveston Bay, but the land has risen less than 500 feet—less than the height of a modest downtown office building. Follow the Rio Grande 200 miles upstream to Laredo and you have risen only 440 feet above the sea. Tulsa, in the northeastern corner of the Southwest, is more than 500 miles from salt water but only 600 feet above the tideline. As you move westward from the Gulf marshes, from the green rivers of eastern Oklahoma, the land rises steadily. The rolling croplands of central Texas and Oklahoma lie 1,000 feet above sea level, the wheat and cattle country of the panhandles is 2,000 feet and higher, rising faster as the New Mexico border is crossed, then soaring into the ridges of the Southern Rockies. In the 1,300 miles from Port Arthur, Texas, to Yuma, Arizona, you move from a low, flat, humid landscape into high, dry, vertical country where nothing much is flat except the table-top mesas and the bottoms of intermountain valleys.

Some years ago this "tilt" was inadvertently—and fatally—demonstrated by a private pilot with the help of a shaker of martinis. He left Hobby International Airport in Houston en route to San Diego via Albuquerque, climbed to 5,000 feet, set his autopilot for that altitude, and headed west, tapping the martinis en route. Apparently he was fast asleep later that day when a rancher saw his Cessna, still cruising faithfully at 5,000 feet above sea level but now less than three feet above the ground, fly through a barbed-wire fence and into a hayfield in eastern New Mexico's Guadalupe County.

The Southwest is like two different worlds, and the Rio Grande, which ties these two together, illustrates that point. It seems like two rivers. The Spanish explorers who found its Texas end called it River of Palms or River of May and wrote reports praising it as a gentle, hospitable stream. But the Spanish who discovered it at what is now the New Mexico border, where it drowned their horses with sudden floods and then went completely dry, called it Rio Bravo del Norte, the Wild River of the North. Today the clear, icy snowmelt stream that boils over the black basalt boulders in the Taos Gorge—drawing daredevil rapids runners from across the world and killing them often enough to keep its reputation—is a different river than the stream that meanders through the cabbage fields of south Texas.

The Southwest needs east Texas as a contrast, for it is what the rest of the territory is not. It is lush, shady, damp, fecund, bursting with life—insect, plant, bird, bacterial, reptile, and mammal. Twelve million acres of pine, cypress, walnut, oak, magnolia, dogwood and, quite literally, a hundred other tree varieties are its dominant feature. The Big Thicket— once a bona fide wilderness—is here. Where road and terrain permit, much of this great forest has been cut over by loggers. The hardwoods and magnolias are mostly gone, and

Left– CANYON DEL MUERTO, CANYON DE CHELLY NATIONAL MONUMENT / ARIZONA

Below– NAVAJO HOME, YEI BE CHEI ROCKS, AND ROOSTER ROCK, MONUMENT VALLEY NAVAJO TRIBAL PARK / ARIZONA-UTAH

the pines are harvested like hay and replanted in orderly rows. The country also bears the scars of more than 25,000 oil wells, which have pumped an ocean of petroleum from under the forests. Since the famous Spindletop boom in 1901, east Texas oil production would be worth more than $100 billion at 1982 prices. The process has left in its wake pollution and creeks ruined by salt water. Cattlemen have added their brand, draining wetlands to make way for the grass this rich, black land will grow. Still, thousands of acres are left in the Big Thicket National Preserve and in scattered places where nature defends itself with swamps too boggy for exploitation.

The eastern fringe of Oklahoma is distinctly different. Here the Ouachita Mountains (pronounced Washita) and the Ozark Plateau intrude their pine-covered slopes into the valleys of the Arkansas, Red, and Little rivers. This is Oklahoma's hillbilly territory. Rainy country still, but the Gulf winds that drench the coastal swamps curl to the east and have lost much of their moisture this far north. This is steeply rolling land shaded by a mixture of soft pine and scores of deciduous species. It is poor country for grubbing out a living, but great for white-tailed deer, raccoons, and big mouth bass.

In fact, all of eastern and much of central Oklahoma is fishing country—a land of lakes produced in an orgy of dam building by the U.S. Army Corps of Engineers. There are the Grand, Gibson, Oologah, Pine Creek, Tenkiller, and Atoka reservoirs, Lake of the Cherokees, Eufaula, Murray, Texoma, Kaw, Keystone, Arbuckle, Canton, and numerous others.

When I was a boy in Oklahoma, one rowed along the shorelines of these reservoirs amid forests of drowned trees and sometimes over the chimneys of submerged creekside cabins. Time and decay have eliminated such obstacles now, leaving these lakes sheets of blue water abuzz with the outboard motors of bass fishermen and their mortal enemies, the water-skiers.

In Texas, the pine flats of the bayou country give way to open hill croplands, which transmute into the vast central flatness called the Grand Prairie. In Oklahoma the wooded hills are replaced by gently rolling grasslands—the Osage Hills, the Cherokee and Enid plains. This is family farm country, marked off in square miles by "section line" roads with a farmhouse about every half mile. It is a country where gullies left by exploitive cotton farming of 50 years ago are

now being healed by grass, time, and modern agricultural techniques. This is the territory that produced the "Okies" of John Steinbeck's *Grapes of Wrath*. The migration caused then by drought, Dust Bowl, and Depression has continued ever since on a slower scale, caused now by the high price of tractors and the low price of corn. Economics has meant bigger farms and fewer farmers, and the countryside is dotted with artifacts of that evolution—the abandoned, weatherbeaten, windowless shacks and collapsing barns left behind by those who sold out and moved to town.

This part of Oklahoma was the Southwest of my childhood, a place where the woods filled with fireflies on summer evenings, whippoorwills called from the hills, mockingbirds sang on moonlight nights. The gullies that killed the cornfields were mines for the red clay we used to mold

BLUEBONNETS AND INDIAN PAINTBRUSH, HILL COUNTRY / TEXAS

the "bullets" for our endless game of Cowboys and Indians. (Most of my playmates were genuine Indians—Pottawatomies, Seminoles, and Blackfeet—but their people had left the old gods behind when the government moved them to the Oklahoma Territory. Their sons, having learned who wins and who loses from the movies, insisted on taking their turn at the cowboy role.) It was also a place where—in contrast to New Mexico and Arizona—the humid air carried a cornucopia of smells: clover, dogwood blossoms, dust, the rotten-egg aroma of a distant oil well, the mustiness of old hay, plowed earth, horse urine, the spoiling windfalls under the apple tree, honeysuckle. Persons raised in the mountains, where the thin, dry air is a poor conductor of such perfumes, may spend their entire lives without learning how important the nose can be in stimulating nostalgia.

Here in central Oklahoma, and southward in Texas, you have moved across that vague boundary between what climatologists call the moist subhumid and the dry subhumid. In practical terms, you are in country where—in July and August—farmers pray for rain. In Texas as you move west from Austin you climb the vast Edwards Plateau and enter the beautiful Hill Country, where clear streams run through a land of folded, faulted limestone hills—a land of small fields, fenced feedlots, and pastures. It is mild, hospitable country, shaded and rolling, undramatic, but in the minds of many, the prettiest part of Texas. North, across the Red River Valley in Oklahoma, that state, too, puts on its most handsome face. In the Arbuckle Mountains, the structures left by ancient volcanic action mix with great folds of upthrust hills to form a landscape of ridges and narrow valleys. Again

there are limestone, clear streams, gushing springs, and places where underground heat produces geysers and fills the air with the smell of sulphur. To the west, the Wichita Mountains form a larger, more open setting. The world's largest buffalo herd roams the Wichita Mountains Wildlife Refuge, in a natural environment of prairie grasses and uncut timber—the way it was when the Kiowas, who have their reservation here, were "Lords of the Plains."

From the granite ridges of the Wichitas one looks westward toward those Great Plains. If one had to draw a line indicating where the "west" of the Southwest begins, the 100th meridian would be as fair a border as any. Before the white man came and exercised his power to change ecology, east of the 100th could have been described as a world dominated by trees, while the land west of that line was a world of grass. As you approach Oklahoma's western boundary, trees are already becoming scarcer—limited mostly to shading the creeks, which themselves have become less frequent

as countryside dries and flattens. Grass is the dominant natural flora here, commonly a short bluestem giving way to needlegrass where fertility is low. The color, too, has changed. Grass here is a paler green, verging into the gray, tan, and silver of dry country species—grama, buffalo, Indian rice, and various bunch grasses. Except for irrigated fields and the cottonwood bosques of river valleys, you leave dark green behind you on the prairie.

In the Oklahoma Panhandle and north of Amarillo, Texas, this prairie country is called the High Plains. Southward, it's the Staked Plains, the Llano Estacado. Whatever the name, it is a treeless, undulating sea of grass. The Gulf winds rarely bring their moisture here—just enough in the High Plains to grow winter wheat. The landscape tends to overwhelm the eye with the single-season color of the grain: deep green in spring, gray-green with summer, merging into tan, then to harvest gold, the yellow-gray of stubblefields and, as winter looms, the rich black of the plowed and planted earth.

Farther south in Texas, diminishing rainfall makes wheat a bad gamble. These Staked Plains are watered by pumps tapping the Ogallala Aquifer, an underground lake that extends into New Mexico and as far north as Nebraska. But here the lake is running dry, the water table is falling too low for economic pumping, and the green summers of the Staked Plains are turning brown. Crops requiring less water are being developed, but it now seems likely that this part of the Southwest will eventually revert to something closer to its natural state, which was mesquite, dry country grasses, juniper, and cactus. My mother, who homesteaded in the Panhandle before pump irrigation, enriched my childhood with legends of the prairie's inhospitality to humankind. Hers were stories of sod dugout hardships, of hauling water, of dried cow chips burned for cooking fuel, of riding 20 miles just to see a tree, of blizzards blowing snow horizontally across the flatness, and of blistering summers where the only shade for miles around was under your own sunbonnet.

> Goodbye to Greer County, where the blizzards arise,
> Where the sun never rests, and the flea never dies,
> And the wind never ceases, but always remains
> Till it starves us to death on our government claim.

There were a hundred verses contained in that sodbuster ballad, each of them an ironic celebration of the Panhandle's intolerance of man.

Wherever you leave the prairie headed west, you go uphill, and uphill fast. The rise from the flatness of the Gulf has been slow for 700 miles. Now the climb is neither slow nor gradual. In eastern New Mexico you leave the Great Plains behind you. The horizon no longer fades into the distance. Now it is outlined by the blue shape of mountains.

Mountains are the dominant feature of New Mexico. Except for the eastern fringe, no part of the state is without them. The good maps name 73 ranges, from Animas to Zuni. They include seven peaks rising above 13,000 feet, 85 more than two miles high, and more than 300 notable enough to warrant names. All are part of the Southern Rockies and, with a few purely volcanic exceptions, they are arranged in irregular north-south ridges that feature an exhausted old volcano or two and that dominate the valleys their snowpacks water. They extend all the way south into the empty southwest corner of Texas, giving that state its most spectacular scenery in the Big Bend country. There the Rio Grande cuts a series of awesome canyons through the plateau between the Sierra del Consuelo and Sierra del Carmen on the Mexican side and the Chiso range in Texas. This strip of Texas is utterly uncharacteristic of the Lone Star State. The Franklin Mountains at El Paso, the Guadalupes, and the Chisos rival the most forbidding ridges of southern Arizona for rocky barrenness. It is a stony landscape of cactus, mesquite, creosote bush, and yucca.

The desert's invasion of New Mexico and Arizona is more successful. The Chihuahuan Desert flora spreads up the Rio Grande and other valleys for some 200 miles—almost as far north as Albuquerque—and the Sonoran Desert surrounds the timbered highlands of southern Arizona with its own distinctive species of cacti, grasses, shrubs, and thorn bushes. But deserts are a relatively minor feature of the Southwest's high west side. The story of both states is really the story of mountains, highland plateaus, and the sky.

The sky, the difference in the air, is partially responsible for the difference in the visual character of this high country. It's an effect that westbound air travelers can't fail to notice. Over Texas and Oklahoma the landscape below the airliner is, more often than not, at least partially obscured by clouds; even on clear days it is seen through layers of humidity, dim and hazy. As the plane crosses the prairie the haze thins and the land rises clear and distinct, like the shores of a distant continent emerging from the sea. This is partially due to diminishing moisture and partially to the effects of altitude. The earth's troposphere loses more than 3 percent of its density with each 900 feet of altitude. New Mexico and Arizona each average more than a mile above sea level, with their northern plateaus much higher. Thus when one looks from Flagstaff toward the San Francisco Peaks, or from Santa Fe

PUEBLO BONITO, CHACO CULTURE NATIONAL HISTORICAL PARK / NEW MEXICO

across the Rio Grande toward the glittering lights of Los Alamos in the Jemez Mountains, one looks through air that has lost a fourth of its weight. It is rich in hydrogen but thin in oxygen and carbon dioxide and thus offers less to refract and diffuse the light. The lights of Albuquerque, seen from Sandia Crest just above the city, lack the soft glow of the lights of Galveston and appear instead as a million glittering pinholes punched through the darkness. Eyes conditioned to the less transparent air of lower altitudes are deceived by distances—incredulous that the sharp blue outline on the horizon is a mountain range 100 miles away. And natives of this high, dry country find themselves suffering claustrophobic oppression under the heavy, hazy skies of Texas, Oklahoma, and points east.

The mountains affect the western skyscape, just as they affect everything in New Mexico and Arizona. They collect almost all of the area's scanty moisture. From early autumn through May, while the valleys are basking in sunshine, they accumulate layer after layer of snow—10 feet deep or more on the higher slopes—and become playgrounds for skiers and the source of water for irrigation. With spring runoff, it comes roaring down mountain streams into the Rio Grande, the Gila, the Salt, the Colorado, the San Juan, and the smaller streams. Once this meant devastating annual floods, but now reservoirs hold back the surplus, allowing extended irrigation seasons. In the summer, when the monsoon season brings moisture in from the Pacific, warm updrafts of air build towering cauliflower-shaped thunderheads over the mountain peaks, where they bombard the high country with lightning bolts before drifting away on the west wind. The last time I

was at Walpi on the rim of the Hopi Second Mesa in Arizona, I counted six such thunderstorms operating simultaneously. The largest had formed over Humphreys Peak and was obscuring the San Francisco Peaks with curtains of rain. Another was rumbling over the Black Mesa to the north, three smaller storms were drifting across the sky to the south, trailing narrow bands of water across the painted desert, and still another was forming far to the southwest over the Mogollon Rim. At Walpi the hot sun shone from a blue sky and, between the shadows of the thunderheads, the desert below was dappled with sunlight.

Unlike the Texas-Oklahoma end of the Southwest, where average rainfall lessens very gradually as you move west, differences in the mountain high country are abrupt and drastic, with altitude the determinant. Albuquerque, for example, receives eight inches of rain annually (enough for a rainy day in Houston). Sandia Crest, 10 miles from the city but about a mile higher, receives three times that amount. The west side of Santa Fe averages three inches less moisture per year than the northeast side— which has more than 1,000 feet greater altitude. Your street address determines whether or not you need snow tires.

This marked difference is visible no matter where you go in the two states. The short drive from the Tularosa Basin in southern New Mexico into the Sacramentos takes you from a landscape of cactus, creosote bush, and desert grasses into cool, spruce-fir forests carpeted with alpine flowers. Just north of Albuquerque the Simms ranch (not particularly large by New Mexico standards) included all but one of North America's biological life zones, from Upper Sonoran Desert to Hudsonian—a feat it accomplished by climbing from the Rio Grande to the top of Sandia Crest. In Arizona's equally vertical landscape more than 3,300 species of plants have been identified—believed to be America's broadest botanical spectrum.

As with Texas and Oklahoma, Arizona and New Mexico generally rise from south to north, but their mountain ridges and plateaus complicate the topography. In New Mexico, the Guadalupes, the Sacramentos, the San Andres, the Caballos, and the massive highlands of the Black Range extend southward almost to the Mexican border with fingers of desert landscape extending northward between them. New Mexico's most spectacular desert lies in the Tularosa Basin, the great rift between the Sacramentos and the Organ Mountain ridge. Within it are almost 200 miles of military bomb and missile ranges and an expanse of windblown ridges held in place by giant yucca, mesquite, and a great variety of prickly, almost leafless cacti. It also holds Lake Lucero, an ancient, dry lake bed that is now White Sands National Monument. It comes as near as anyplace on our continent to giving the appearance of total lifelessness. Across the flat floor of this ancient lake, 20 miles wide and 100 miles long, march mile after mile of great gypsum dunes, glittering white in the sunlight. They rise as high as 30 feet, moved inexorably northeastward by prevailing winds, their backsides firm, carved and sculptured by the moving air, their faces as soft as flour.

This high side of the Southwest is rich with such dramatic places, most of them seeming out of scale for human sight. In Arizona, there are the sculpture gardens of the Navajo National Monument, where immense fingers and thumbs of sandstone sprout from a floor of red sand; the wilderness of red, black, blue, and gray erosion of the cliffs of the Kaibab Plateau; and the endless carpet of green of the world's largest ponderosa pine forests spreading endlessly across the central highlands.

New Mexico has the aspen forests of the Sangre de Cristo Mountains—underfoot a yellow carpet of leaves, overhead a glittering blue-and-yellow ceiling of sky and leaves-not-yet-fallen, and floor and ceiling tied together with the stark black-and-white lines of ruler-straight aspen trunks. Bigger than life are the giant echo amphitheaters that seepage forms under the mass walls in northern New Mexico. There is New

PRICKLY PEAR CACTUS AND CASA GRANDE, BIG BEND NATIONAL PARK / TEXAS

LOG FRAGMENTS, BLUE MESA, PETRIFIED FOREST NATIONAL PARK / ARIZONA

Mexico's malpais, badlands of cooled lava spread below extinct volcanoes. Depending on its vintage, the malpais can resemble a lake of boiling, frothing black ink magnified to giant scale and somehow frozen mid-bubble. Or, when softened by eons of erosion, it can become a rolling, green-black plain, its basalt humps coated with multicolored lichens and its pits forming little rainwater pools lined with cattails and marshgrass. There is the saguaro cactus desert—fields of giant green exclamation marks, many sprouting thumbs, which defy simile because there is nothing else in nature like them. And there is the view from the Rio Grande Gorge bridge, where one can look down on the wings of golden eagles hunting rodents along the cliffs far below. The rapids of the river are 800 feet beneath your feet, a silver ribbon at the bottom of a great black lava slit. There is the monolith of Shiprock, the igneous core of a Pleistocene volcano, rising like a baroque cathedral with a thousand spires out of the rolling Navajo reservation grassland. There are the grotesque sandstone sculptures of the Bisti Badlands, which suggest the creations of a thousand Disneyland designers gone mad.

There are the Bosque del Apache marshes on a February morning when the sound carried on the cold dawn air is the conversation of a million birds—the odd fluting of sandhill cranes, the piping of red-winged blackbirds, the blended sounds of ducks, geese, grebes, herons, sandpipers, and scores of other species. And then, as dawn forms a hot pink glow behind the Sierra Oscura, the sudden roar of wings. Hundreds of snow geese rise from the marsh. Then thousands, rousing the Canada geese, and great flocks of greater sandhill cranes, and battalions of mallards, and pintails, and teal, until the sky is crowded. They rise above the bare cottonwoods, not like a rabble of blackbirds or crows, but in hundreds of separate, orderly formations. The air above is filled with the sound of geese. You see and hear what America was like when the Apaches used this lovely place as a camping ground.

The Apaches are gone from the Rio Grande now—the Mescaleros operating their ski resort on Sierra Blanca, the Jicarillas grazing their Herefords on New Mexico's edge of the Colorado Plateau, the Mimbrenos, the San Carlos, and the other bands keeping their culture alive in Arizona's White Mountain high country. But the Rio Grande, and the desert Southwest that lies west of it, is very much Indian country. Unlike my Indian friends in Oklahoma who had forsaken their old gods, the Navajos, Zunis, Hopis, Papagos, and the 17 little village-states where the Pueblo Indians live have kept their old religion and their old values alive and well.

Each morning when I drive to the University of New Mexico, and each evening when I go home, I see landmarks of this Native American Holy Land in which we live. Sandia Crest, looming over my rooftop at the east limits of the city, is Oko-Piu—the Turtle Mountain of Tiwa Indian mythology. This was the goal of the migration adventures of the Tiwas when they were new to this universe, the place Spider Grandmother taught them would be the center of their homeland. If you know where to look on the mountain you can visit the shrines where the kiva religious societies of the Rio Grande Pueblos leave their feathered prayer sticks as offerings, just as they were doing when the first Spanish explorers came up the river in the seventeenth century.

My favorite landmark (and my favorite mountain) is the one the white man calls Mount Taylor. As I drive west on Interstate 40 in the morning, the old volcano rises above the long, level line of Albuquerque's west mesa, snowcapped from autumn until spring, wearing a scarf of clouds on most summer days. It is 65 miles away, but it looks near enough to touch. Mount Taylor is Black Mountain for the Pueblo Indians, the place where the Twin War Gods dwell to warn their people away from the desert dangers beyond it. But for the Navajos (and for me) it is Turquoise Mountain, Tsoo'dzil, where the sky rests his left hand on Mother Earth.

West of the Rio Grande, the landscape is dotted with many such landmarks. San Antonio Mountain, the grassy old volcano cone north of Tres Piedras, New Mexico, was the place where Ute shamans communicated with God. Blue Lake, in the Sangre de Cristos above Taos, is the sacred home of the spirits that bless the people of Taos Pueblo. Black Mesa in Arizona is the home of the Navajo Black God and of the shrines of a dozen Hopi clans. Most sacred of all are the San Francisco Peaks, which rise above Flagstaff, Arizona. Humphreys Peak is the gateway between the worlds for the Hopis; for the Navajos, it is another of those mountains built by First Man, the place where the sky rests his forehead, and—like Mount Taylor—a place where the Navajo singers of curing ceremonials gather materials for their medicine bundles.

Once I climbed down into Canyon de Chelly, the deep sandstone slot cut into the Chuska Plateau northwest of Window Rock, Arizona, and spent a long summer day walking its sandy bottom, surrounded by its towering cliffs, engulfed in isolation. I found pictographs painted on the stone in sheltered places, most of them fairly modern Navajo stick-figure representations of Rainbow Man, Talking God, and other holy people. Not far from the so-called White House cliff ruins there was a faded image of the humpbacked figure of Water Sprinkler, a Pan-like deity of the Hopi Flute clan, who lived in this canyon before the Navajos came. The breeze had died and in the sudden silence I heard a whistle. It approached, a wavering, rising, falling sound like nothing I'd heard before. I found myself remembering that Water Sprinkler is usually depicted playing a flute. Then a dog trotted around the cliff, behind him a jostling column of goats, and behind the goats a Navajo boy. The goats were belled, and in this echo chamber below the cliffs their tinkling had been homogenized and merged into a single, singing sound.

I have other favorite places. The timeless stone adobe walls of Acoma Pueblo, the stone villages that perch on the Hopi Mesas, Zuni Pueblo on the night of the Shalako Ceremonial, the grandeur of Arizona's Oak Creek Canyon, the place in New Mexico's Jemez Mountains called Valle Grande, where a million years have converted a volcano caldera into a grassy bowl 14 miles long and rimmed with a collar of spruce and aspen. The list could be almost endless, but nothing on it could ever match the Grand Canyon.

It has been called the most spectacular sight on earth—this incredible, mind-boggling gap cut through the Kaibab

Plateau by the Colorado River. Erosion has been at work here for an estimated 65 million years, although geologists believe that much of the sculpturing we see today is the product of less than 10 million years. As seen from the rim, thousands of feet above its surface, the river is nothing but silver thread, implausibly small to have produced a chasm of such planet-splitting proportions, but that's only one of the optical problems the scene presents. A student of mine from Finland went to see it for a weekend and stayed more than a week. Why? "It was three days before my mind would accept it," she said. "It does not seem compatible with human reason."

The problem the mind has is variety as well as scale. At the rim, the first 100 yards of stone beneath your feet is Kaibab limestone, a tough, off-white rock, which fades into a layer of gray Toroweap formation of about the same depth.

Beneath this is Coconino sandstone, and next, a stripe of Hermit Shale about the color of dried blood. This rests atop 1,000 feet of mottled red-and-white Supai limestone. Each layer represents eons of the planet's formation. As you gaze at this stratification there is an awareness that you are looking backward through millions, perhaps billions, of years. The thick faded scarlet layer of Redwall limestone, which forms the stark cliffs below the Supai formation, was settled there when life on earth was new and limited to seawater. The pale tan stone on which it rests formed millions of years earlier, and the greenish Bright Angel shale was earlier still.

This green shale—tough and fine-grained—has resisted erosion better than most of the formations and forms the great flat table deep in the canyon known as the Tonto Rim. The lower canyon of the Colorado, the Inner Gorge, is cut

through this shale. Far below the Tonto Rim, the great river can be heard wearing away at the earth's bedrock, the Vishnu schist, which lies near the base of the earth's mantle and which formed more than a billion years before the planet knew life.

The Grand Canyon bedazzles its viewers with more than vastness, depth, or layering of colors. Each of its myriad strata seems to erode at a different rate and in a different way. Thus its walls are cut and carved into a hundred thousand forms. Each time the eye moves it focuses on something new and strange.

Among the dramatic surroundings of the Kaibab Plateau the flat world of the Panhandle hardly seems possible. And in the desert outside Yuma (where an old-timer once told me that "average annual rainfall is three inches, but it never

actually rains that much") the humid swamps of the Sabine seem memories of another planet.

Marie and I, who have spent our lives in both worlds of the Southwest, have learned to see these differences everywhere—from the way rainstorms form in the summer to the way such things as soda crackers and the human complexion become hard and dry in Arizona air and soft and moist in Texas. The seasons are different, and so are attitudes.

Why are attitudes different? Here's my theory: Most of Texas and Oklahoma seem designed for human comfort—fertile, well-watered, built to human scale, a land where living is easy. We see beauty here in fat cattle, lush cornfields, all those things that demonstrate that man has conquered the earth and made it flow with milk and honey.

In contrast, New Mexico and Arizona offer landscapes

Left– HAVASU FALLS, GRAND CANYON NATIONAL PARK / ARIZONA

Above– LOOKING WEST FROM TOROWEAP OVERLOOK, GRAND CANYON NATIONAL PARK / ARIZONA

that overpower man. He lives in oases where water supplies allow him to live. Thus much of the countryside is empty of human inhabitants. (I could walk 50 miles northwest from Albuquerque's west mesa with little risk of meeting anyone.) Mountains and deserts tend to keep man in perspective—aware that he is something small and impermanent on a very large planet. That affects attitude, and here's an illustration of what I mean:

A Navajo friend named Alex Atcitty was taking me to find a shaman who would tell me some things I needed to know about the Enemy Way ceremonial. Taking a shortcut across Rock Mesa on the way to Chinle, Arizona, Atcitty stopped his truck and pointed to the view. From the mesa rim we saw a 50-mile panorama of badlands drained by Bis E Ah Wash, a wilderness of stony erosion; flats of cracking white alkali deposits, gigantic humps of blue shale, cliffs of red clay, sandstone outcroppings carved by the wind and, here and there, great black intrusions of igneous rock. It is a landscape without water, poisoned by leached chemicals, without a blade of grass, without even the durable creosote bush or flatleaf cactus. It's as lifeless and inhospitable a place as you'll find this side of the moon. If Oklahoma had offered such a view we'd have named it the Pit of Desolation.

But Atcitty, a member of the Many Goats clan, was raised in the Chuska Mountains just east of here, and he was looking down at this desolation fondly.

"This is Hozhoni Teeh," Atcitty said.

That's Navajo for "Beautiful Valley."

I have now been away from the east end of the Southwest, and into the west end, long enough to adopt the Navajo attitude.

Left– SAGUARO CACTUS, PICACHO PEAK STATE PARK / ARIZONA

Above– AUTUMN, CANYON DE CHELLY NATIONAL MONUMENT / ARIZONA

Left– THUNDERSTORM, PANHANDLE COUNTRY / OKLAHOMA

Center– WICHITA MOUNTAINS NATIONAL WILDLIFE REFUGE / OKLAHOMA

Right– SHEEP'S HEAD, TRUCHAS PEAK, SANGRE DE CRISTO MOUNTAINS / NEW MEXICO

Left– YEI BE CHEI ROCKS, MONUMENT VALLEY NAVAJO TRIBAL PARK / ARIZONA-UTAH

Above– DUNES ABOVE SURF, PADRE ISLAND NATIONAL SEASHORE / TEXAS

Maps of the High Country and Southwest

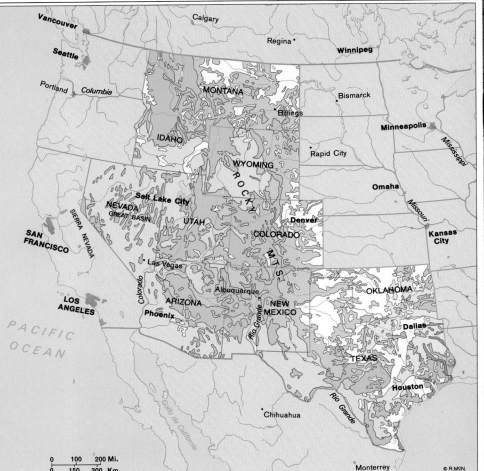

Land Use The Rocky Mountains mark a division in the land use of the Mountain and Southwest region. West of the Rockies lies a vast semiarid-to-arid area, containing diverse landscapes that include alpine forests, sparse grasslands, and extensive sections of brush and bush vegetation. East of the Rockies begin the grasslands, grazing lands, and farmland of the Great Plains. Moisture increases farther east on the Great Plains, and the landscape changes, with grasslands giving way to more farmland.

Preserved in the arid climate of the Southwest are reminders of the native heritage of America. These monuments to ancient Indian cultures display the sophistication, skills, and communal life-style of the country's earliest settlers. Keet Seel, shown here, is a community of cliff dwellings built around one thousand years ago by the Anasazi, the ancestors of modern Pueblo tribes, such as the Hopi and Zuni.

It is not supernatural that so many of America's ghost towns lie within the Mountain and Southwest region. The boomtown, abandoned mine, and battered cattle pen beside a dusty rail spur tell stories that ring true even in modern times. Although these stories might evoke visions of frontier life in the Old West, their significance is less romantic. None of these states can any longer be considered part of a vast frontier. They are crisscrossed with highway, rail, and air routes; and urban areas such as Denver, Dallas, Houston, Phoenix, Salt Lake City, and Las Vegas are true twentieth-century cities in outlook and appearance. The ghost town today is a symbol of the risky boom-to-bust cycle of growth and decline that each of these states faces year after year.

The Mountain and Southwest region is, for the most part, an arid and desolate land of extreme daily and seasonal temperatures; mountain ranges, plains, and wide basins make up the terrain. Within the area lies a great concentration of mineral wealth. An inventory of resources would run from gold and silver, which attracted early fortune seekers; to coal, oil, and gas, which help to fuel the nation; to exotic metals, such as uranium, vanadium, and molybdenum, which are essential to modern manufacturing. However, a state's economic dependence on any one of these resources is risky business. Their markets are distant and volatile, changing with swings in the national economy and the availability of other domestic and foreign supplies. Resource development is frequently intense and brief; towns can grow and die in a short lifetime.

Following the lead of Native Americans, the region's residents have been ingenious in balancing the development of these and other resources to assure survival. Not only do the cities act as bases from which mineral-extraction projects are carried out, but they also form a network for the coordination of development of other resources. The eastern margin of this region is really an outlier of the Midwest's Great Plains, and it shares the plains' agricultural potential for ranching and grain farming. The area's rivers have been dammed and tapped for irrigation water and hydroelectric power. And the warm, dry climate of Arizona, New Mexico, and Nevada is employed to advantage to attract tourists, retirees, high-technology industry, and military installations. Although any of these activities alone may sometimes falter, the Mountain and Southwest states are diversifying economically to counterbalance the economic fluctuation of their individual industries.

Even without the region's material rewards, its beauty would be enough to draw people to it. The sight of the Rockies rising abruptly from Montana's plains at Glacier National Park or the Front Range looming above Colorado's foothills ranks in drama with the Grand Canyon, Monument Valley, and Yellowstone National Park. A growing number of visitors, impressed by the quality of the environment, return to take up permanent residence. Tourism has become a major industry for many of these states.

The Mountain and Southwest region still faces some of the problems that have shaped its development, and the image of the ghost town persists. The states are experiencing rapid growth, and concern for environmental quality is sometimes the first value to wither away. Present knowledge and technological skills can counter the damaging effects of some activities; however, the future development of the region's coal and oil-shale deposits could dwarf almost all previous projects. The potential costs and benefits of such development and the effect on the environment may be among the main concerns of the region in the coming decades. Meanwhile, the states are continuing to work toward economic diversification, countering the uncertainty of their traditional boom-to-bust economies.

Energy Riches of an Arid Land In this region lie about one-half of the nation's oil, gas, and coal reserves; nearly all the uranium needed to fuel nuclear power plants; and roughly half the country's geothermal-resource areas. Besides providing resources to meet current needs, the region also contains nonconventional sources of energy for the future, exemplified by the abundant tar sands of Utah and the oil shale of Colorado and Wyoming.

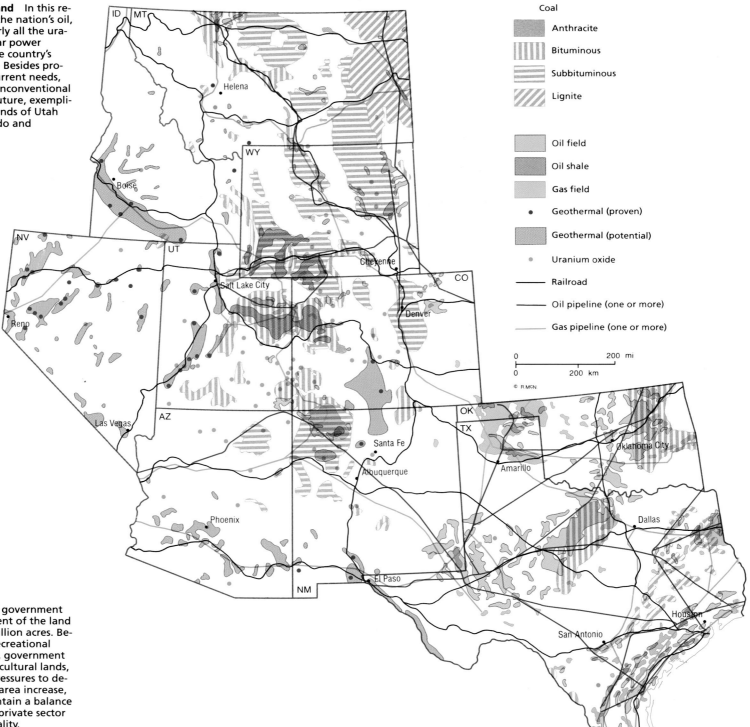

Coal

- Anthracite
- Bituminous
- Subbituminous
- Lignite

- Oil field
- Oil shale
- Gas field
- • Geothermal (proven)
- Geothermal (potential)
- Uranium oxide
- Railroad
- Oil pipeline (one or more)
- Gas pipeline (one or more)

0   200 mi
0   200 km
© R.MGN

Federal Presence and the Environment The federal government administers nearly 40 percent of the land in this region—over 250 million acres. Besides parks, monuments, recreational areas, and wildlife refuges, government jurisdiction extends to agricultural lands, forests, and minerals. As pressures to develop the resources of the area increase, the government must maintain a balance between the needs of the private sector and the environmental quality.

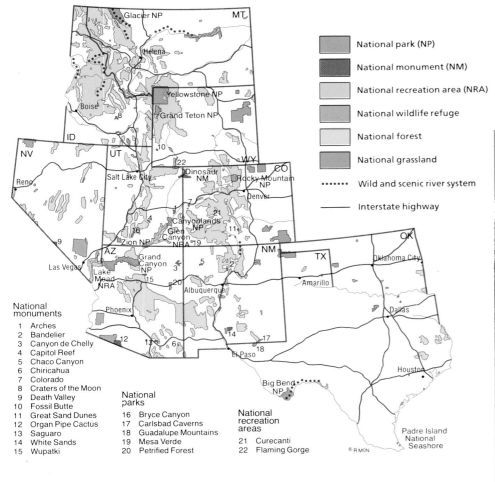

- National park (NP)
- National monument (NM)
- National recreation area (NRA)
- National wildlife refuge
- National forest
- National grassland
- ••••• Wild and scenic river system
- ——— Interstate highway

National monuments

1 Arches
2 Bandelier
3 Canyon de Chelly
4 Capitol Reef
5 Chaco Canyon
6 Chiricahua
7 Colorado
8 Craters of the Moon
9 Death Valley
10 Fossil Butte
11 Great Sand Dunes
12 Organ Pipe Cactus
13 Saguaro
14 White Sands
15 Wupatki

National parks

16 Bryce Canyon
17 Carlsbad Caverns
18 Guadalupe Mountains
19 Mesa Verde
20 Petrified Forest

National recreation areas

21 Curecanti
22 Flaming Gorge

© R.MGN

Covering a large portion of the Mountain and Southwest region, the Rocky Mountains have greatly influenced the character of the states they cross. Because of the mountains' rugged terrain and the region's arid nature, settlement and growth have occurred mainly in the river valleys, where land is level and water more plentiful. The Rockies also contribute to the area's economy, providing a vast store of mineral wealth, abundant forest resources, and one of the country's most spectacular recreational areas.

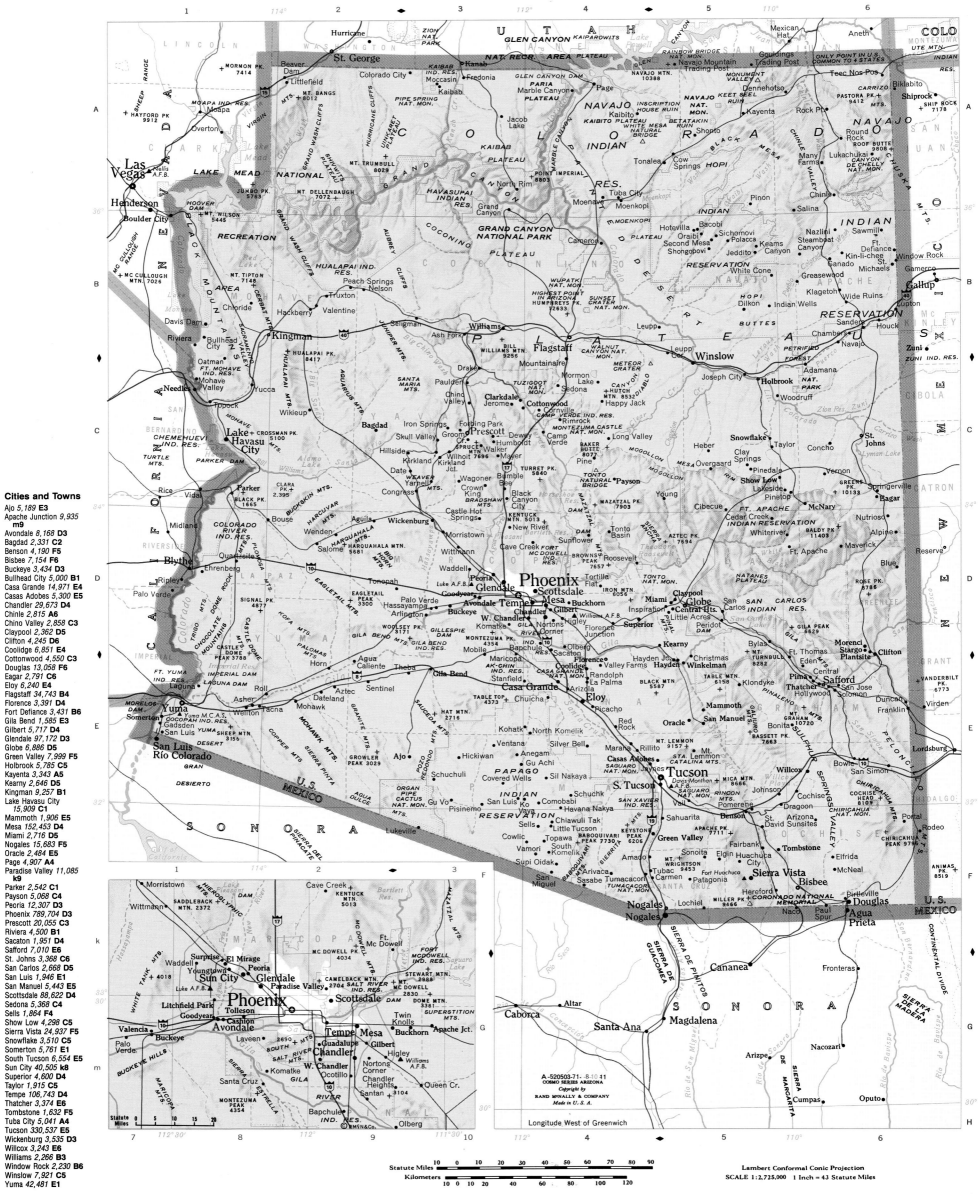

Cities and Towns

Ajo 5,189 **E3**
Apache Junction 9,935 **m9**
Avondale 8,168 **D3**
Bagdad 2,331 **C2**
Benson 4,190 **F5**
Bisbee 7,154 **F6**
Buckeye 3,434 **D3**
Bullhead City 5,000 **B1**
Casa Grande 14,971 **E4**
Casas Adobes 5,300 **E5**
Chandler 29,673 **D4**
Chinle 2,815 **A6**
Chino Valley 2,858 **C3**
Claypool 2,362 **D5**
Clifton 4,245 **D6**
Coolidge 6,851 **E4**
Cottonwood 4,550 **C3**
Douglas 13,058 **F6**
Eagar 2,791 **C6**
Eloy 6,240 **E4**
Flagstaff 34,743 **B4**
Florence 3,391 **D4**
Fort Defiance 3,431 **B6**
Gila Bend 1,585 **E3**
Gilbert 5,717 **D4**
Glendale 97,172 **D3**
Globe 6,886 **D5**
Green Valley 7,999 **F5**
Holbrook 5,785 **C5**
Kayenta 3,343 **A5**
Kearny 2,646 **D5**
Kingman 9,257 **B1**
Lake Havasu City 15,909 **C1**
Mammoth 1,906 **E5**
Mesa 152,453 **D4**
Miami 2,716 **D5**
Nogales 15,683 **F5**
Oracle 2,484 **E5**
Page 4,907 **A4**
Paradise Valley 11,085 **k9**
Parker 2,542 **C1**
Payson 5,068 **C4**
Peoria 12,307 **D3**
Phoenix 789,704 **D3**
Prescott 20,055 **C3**
Riviera 4,500 **B1**
Sacaton 1,951 **D4**
Safford 7,010 **E6**
St. Johns 3,368 **C6**
San Carlos 2,668 **D5**
San Luis 1,946 **E1**
San Manuel 5,443 **E5**
Scottsdale 88,622 **D4**
Sedona 5,368 **C4**
Sells 1,864 **F4**
Show Low 4,298 **C5**
Sierra Vista 24,937 **F5**
Snowflake 3,510 **C5**
Somerton 5,761 **E1**
South Tucson 6,554 **E5**
Sun City 40,505 **k8**
Superior 4,600 **D4**
Taylor 1,915 **C5**
Tempe 106,743 **D4**
Thatcher 3,374 **E6**
Tombstone 1,632 **F5**
Tuba City 5,041 **A4**
Tucson 330,537 **E5**
Wickenburg 3,535 **D3**
Willcox 3,243 **E6**
Williams 2,266 **B3**
Window Rock 2,230 **B6**
Winslow 7,921 **C5**
Yuma 42,481 **E1**

A-520503-71- -8-10-11
COSMO SERIES ARIZONA
Copyright by
RAND McNALLY & COMPANY
Made in U.S.A.

Longitude West of Greenwich

Statute Miles
Kilometers

Lambert Conformal Conic Projection
SCALE 1:2,725,000   1 Inch = 43 Statute Miles

Arizona

POPULATION 2,718,425.
Rank: 29. *Density:* 24 people/mi²
(9.2 people/km²). *Urban:* 83.8%.
Rural: 16.2%.
AGE *<20:* 33%. *20–40:* 32%.
40–65: 24%. *>65:* 11%.
ETHNIC GROUPS *White:* 82.4%.
Black: 2.8%. *Spanish origin:*
16.2%. *Native American:* 5.6%.
Other: 9.2%.

INCOME/CAPITA $8,791. *Rank:* 32.
POLITICS 1948–1980 elections:
President: 1 Dem., 8 Rep.
Governor: 6 Dem., 8 Rep.
ENTERED UNION February 14,
1912, 48th state.
CAPITAL Phoenix, 789,704.
LARGEST CITY Phoenix.

AREA 114,000 mi² (295,258 km²).
Rank: 6. *Water area:* 492 mi²
(1,274 km²).
ELEVATIONS *Highest:* Humphreys
Peak, 12,633 ft (3,851 m).
Lowest: Along Colorado River,
70 ft (21 m).
CLIMATE Nearly constant sunshine,
low humidity, low rainfall. Hot
summers, mild winters.

Arizona blends a colorful past with a present shaped by modern technology. Legends and rodeos recall the state's rugged Wild West days, the frontier prospector has been replaced by large copper-mining companies, and air conditioning and sophisticated water systems buffer residents and tourists from the hot, dry climate.

Arizona has always harbored mineral riches. In the 1800's, gold and silver lured prospectors and miners to the state in search of fabulous wealth. The ghost towns that dot the landscape stand as mute testimony to countless bonanzas that soon died out. Today, Arizona's mineral wealth is founded on less exotic materials, such as copper, coal, and oil.

One of the greatest contributors to Arizona's growing economy is a continuous influx of retirees and tourists. Excellent transportation routes and a year-round warm climate make the state an inviting destination, with the added attraction of recreation areas built specifically for new residents and vacationers. The populations of Phoenix and Tucson are booming, and many new communities are being created in one-time barren terrain.

But this mountain-desert state's most precious commodity is water; and although beneficial to the state's economy, rapid population growth places an additional strain on an already overburdened water supply. The limits of this supply will affect urban growth for some time to come, but most of Arizona's water is currently used for agricultural irrigation, which demands huge quantities of water. Even with the aid of rivers and dams, the state's underground water is being pumped away faster than nature can replenish it. State control over these reserves is somewhat restricted, since much of the land is owned by the federal government.

As technology works to ensure Arizona's future, the state serves as an example of an oasis community solving the problems a desert environment presents. The landscaped yards of palms and cacti and the irrigated cropland of cotton and wheat stand against a background of ghost towns and Indian ruins, reflecting Arizona's successful blend of past and present, and its positive approach to the future.

Native American Culture   Arizona has the largest American Indian population of any other state, and reservations occupy a large proportion of the state's land area. Archaeological evidence indicates that Indians were present in the area more than 25,000 years ago. Today, numerous prehistoric ruins, as well as current expressions of Indian life, are important to Arizona's culture.

Once a center of mining activity, the town of Bisbee contains vivid illustrations of how humans can leave permanent imprints upon their environment; one such example is this open-pit mine. Characteristic of the geometric patterns usually left by humans, an open-pit mine consists of a series of terraces, caused by succeeding blasts within the land's surface. This method allows for very large production rates at low unit costs. Most of Arizona's mines have been converted to these highly efficient operations, resulting in the state's high income from copper production.

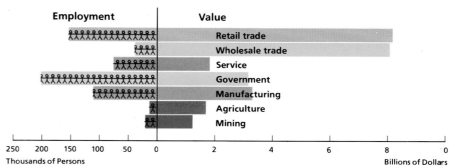

Employment	Value
Retail trade	
Wholesale trade	
Service	
Government	
Manufacturing	
Agriculture	
Mining	

250 200 150 100 50 0   0 2 4 6 8 0
Thousands of Persons   Billions of Dollars

Economic Activities   Prior to World War II, Arizona was best known for its mild climate, copper ore, cattle, and cotton. Since then, Arizona's labor supply, electric power, and low construction and land costs have helped to make the state's manufacturing income surpass that of mining and farming. Today, Arizona's economy is thoroughly modern, with well-developed retail, wholesale, and service trades.

Land Use   Contrary to popular stereotypes and although much of Arizona is semi-arid, actual desert land complete with drifting sand constitutes a small proportion of state land. In fact, with the exception of a few closed basins, all of Arizona lies within the watershed of the Colorado River. Proper utilization of the river water for irrigation and power is of major importance.

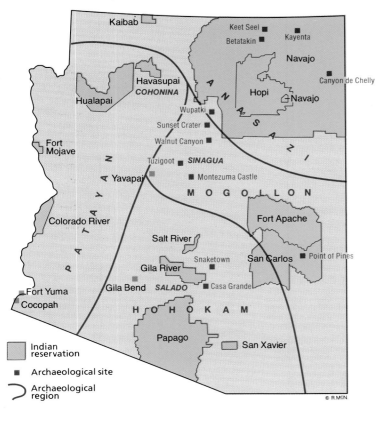

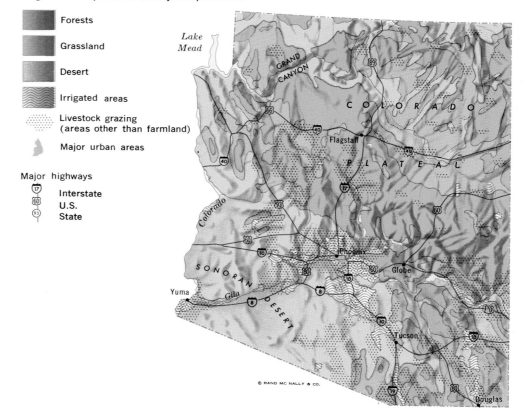

- Forests
- Grassland
- Desert
- Irrigated areas
- Livestock grazing (areas other than farmland)
- Major urban areas

Major highways
- Interstate
- U.S.
- State

Indian reservation
■ Archaeological site
Archaeological region

Cities and Towns

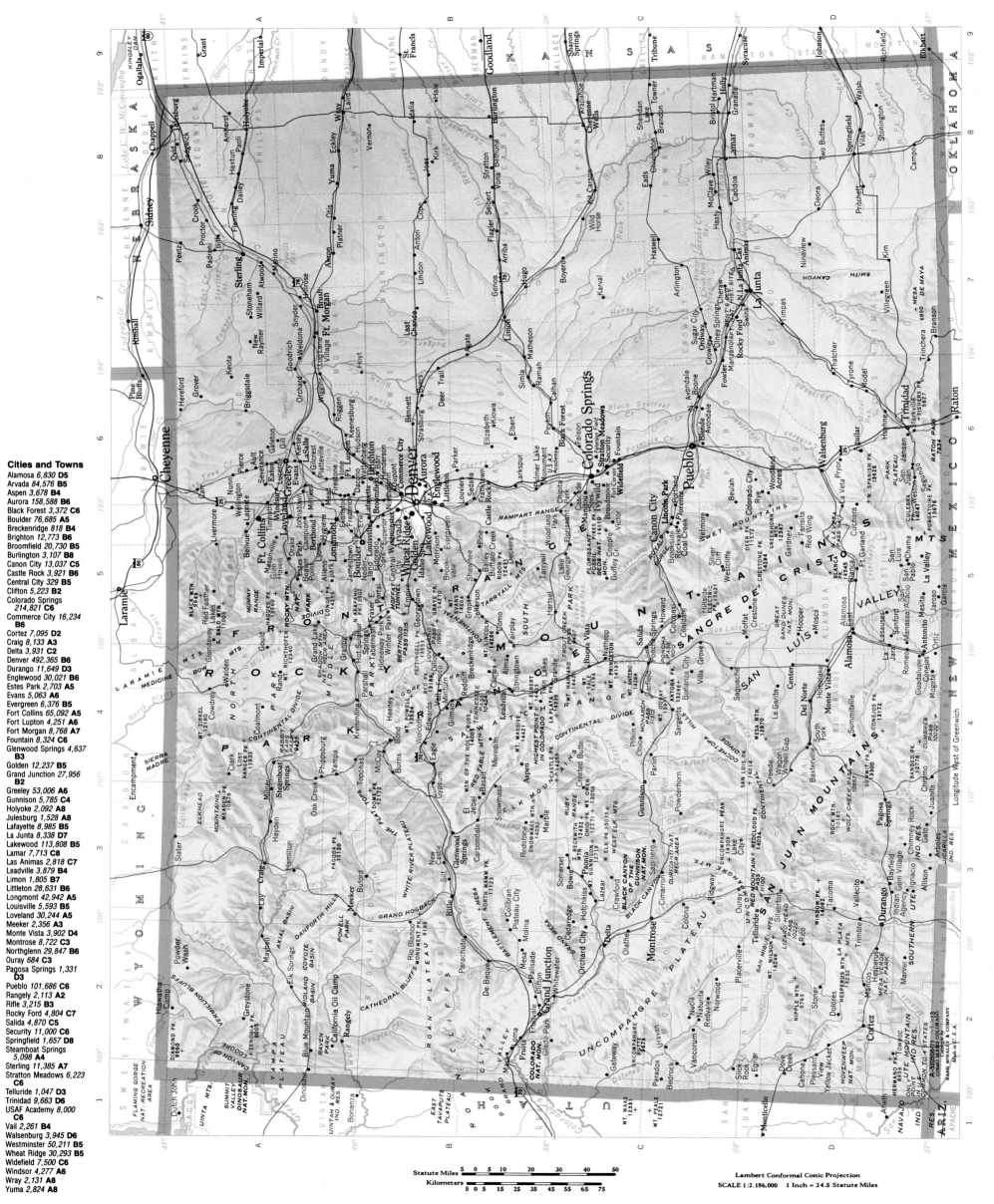

Statute Miles 5 0 5 10 20 30 40 50
Kilometers 5 0 5 15 25 35 45 55 65 75

Lambert Conformal Conic Projection
SCALE 1:2,186,000   1 Inch = 34.5 Statute Miles

Colorado

POPULATION 2,889,735.
  Rank: 28. *Density:* 28 people/mi²
  (11 people/km²). *Urban:* 80.6%.
  Rural: 19.4%.
AGE <*20:* 32%. *20–40:* 37%.
  40–65: 23%. >*65:* 8%.
ETHNIC GROUPS *White:* 89%.
  Black: 3.5%. *Spanish origin:*
  11.7%. *Native American:* 0.6%.
  Other: 6.9%.

INCOME/CAPITA $10,025. *Rank:* 14.
POLITICS 1948–1980 elections:
  President: 2 Dem., 7 Rep.
  Governor: 6 Dem., 5 Rep.
ENTERED UNION August 1, 1876,
  38th state.
CAPITAL Denver, 492,365.
LARGEST CITY Denver.

AREA 104,091 mi² (269,595 km²).
  Rank: 8. *Water area:* 496 mi²
  (1,285 km²).
ELEVATIONS *Highest:* Mt. Elbert,
  14,433 ft (4,399 m). *Lowest:*
  Along Arkansas River, 3,350 ft
  (1,021 m).
CLIMATE Hot, sunny summers; cold
  winters. Varying rainfall, heavy
  mountain snows.

Colorado's natural beauty alone would set it apart from other states. Graceful, rolling plains in the east gradually give way to the spectacular Front Range of the Rockies and farther west to the jagged, snow-lined peaks of the mountains themselves. But beyond having beauty, Colorado stands at the divide between the Great Plains and the Rocky Mountains, where it is influenced by the changing currents of American life from both West and East. With its mineral wealth, rich soil, and water resources, Colorado is well suited to its role as a leader among western states. In fact, Denver could easily claim the title "Capital of the Mountain West."

Early in its history, Colorado attracted explorers and miners with its flourishing fur trade, abundant veins of precious metals, and deposits of lead. The settlers who followed were quick to recognize the value of the land itself, particularly when water from the Rockies was diverted to the fertile, but dry, regions to the east. Today, few states have more acres of cropland under irrigation, and the legal innovations that made large-scale irrigation possible in Colorado have become the foundation of water law in other western states. Colorado has capitalized on industrial growth as well, and manufacturing now surpasses mining and agriculture as a major source of revenue. A large share of this industry is composed of light- and high-technology and research-oriented businesses, key components in the new American economy. In addition, tourists flock to the state's mountain valleys and camping grounds in the summer and to its ski slopes in the winter.

Colorado's population, largely concentrated along the Front Range, benefits from a state made strong and stable by its diversity and investment in the latest technology. Yet some Coloradans worry that their state is too inviting and that its natural beauty will succumb to urban and industrial growth. Careful management of that growth will remain a major concern in the coming years. Colorado is aware that one of its greatest assets is the grandeur of its unspoiled wilderness and the wild, remote beauty of the Rockies.

Trapped at the foot of the Sangre de Cristo Mountains are the Great Sand Dunes, which rise to heights of more than six hundred feet. The dunes, with their occasionally forming quicksands, were both a risk and a barrier to settlers of the surrounding area.

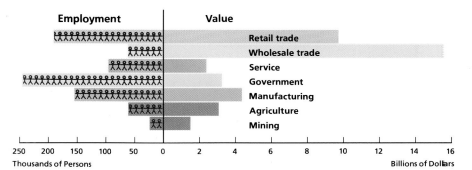

Economic Activities   With so many distinct regions to draw upon, Colorado has one of the most balanced economies of the Mountain West. Agriculture, commerce, manufacturing, mining, and tourism all contribute to the state's vitality.

Land Use   An east-west transect of Colorado cuts across the major environmental regimes of the West—from grassland prairies, through the spectacular Rocky Mountains, to the deserts beyond.

- Farmland (cropland and pastureland)
- Farmland and woodlots
- Forests
- Grassland
- Desert
- Irrigated areas
- Barren and ice covered areas
- Livestock grazing (areas other than farmland)
- Major urban areas

Major highways
- ㉕ National interstate
- ⑤⓪ U.S.
- ⑦⑧⑨ State

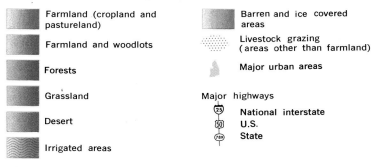

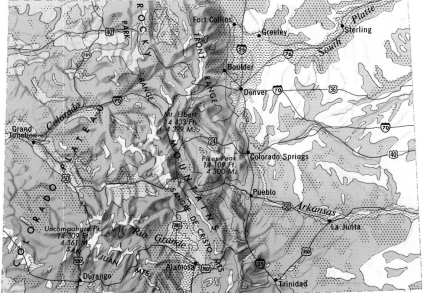

© RAND MC NALLY & CO.

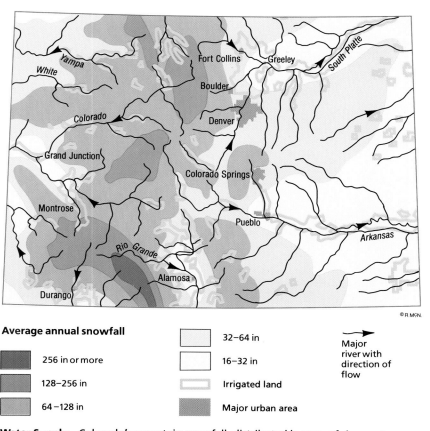

© R.MGN.

Average annual snowfall

- 256 in or more
- 128–256 in
- 64–128 in
- 32–64 in
- 16–32 in
- Irrigated land
- Major urban area

→ Major river with direction of flow

Water Supply   Colorado's mountain snowfall, distributed by way of river systems, furnishes much of the water for irrigation of crops in the valleys and High Plains. It also supplies water for industrial and residential use in cities throughout the state.

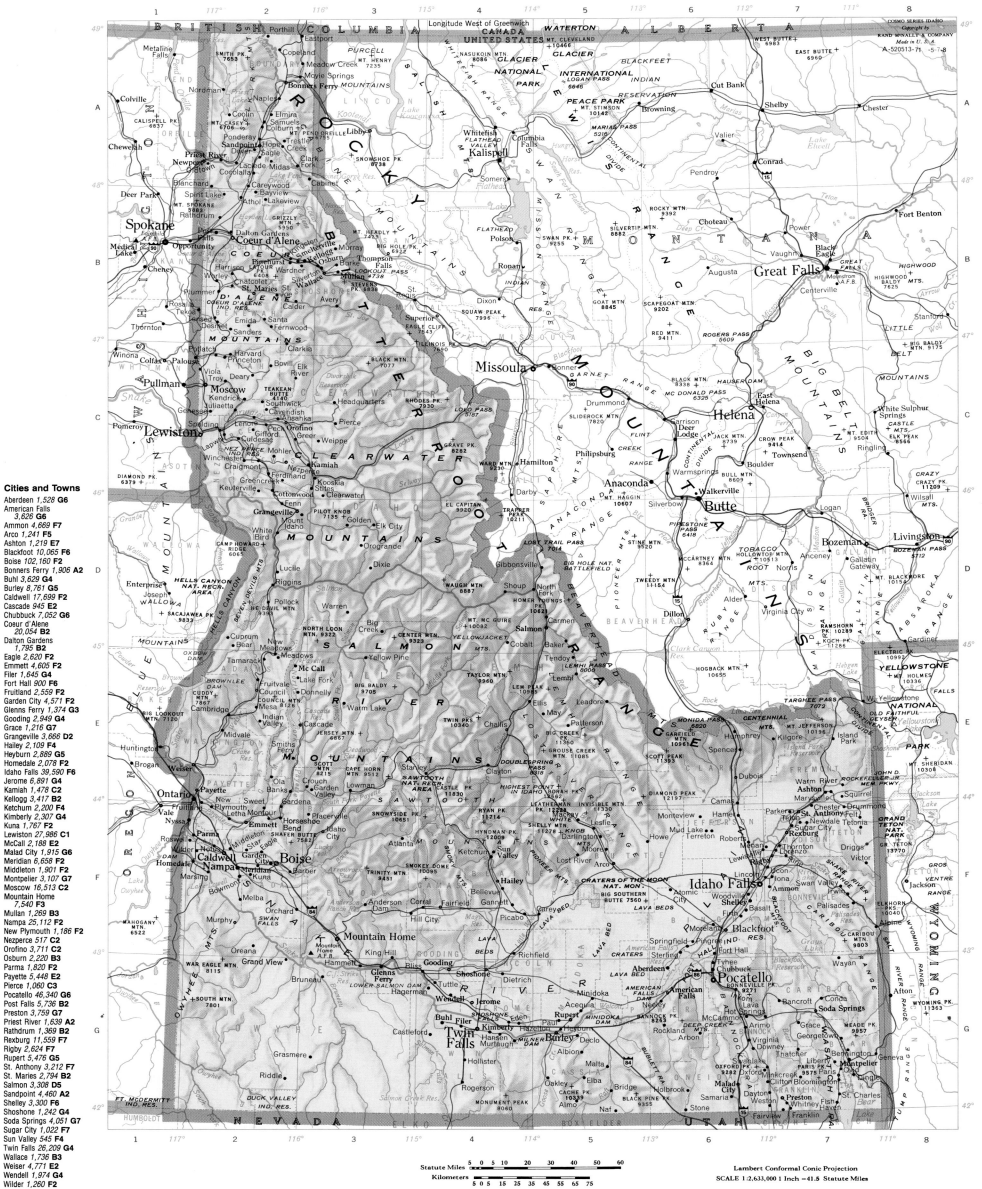

Cities and Towns

Aberdeen 1,528 **G6**
American Falls
  3,626 **G6**
Ammon 4,669 **F7**
Arco 1,241 **F5**
Ashton 1,219 **E7**
Blackfoot 10,065 **F6**
Boise 102,160 **F2**
Bonners Ferry 1,906 **A2**
Buhl 3,629 **G4**
Burley 8,761 **G5**
Caldwell 17,699 **F2**
Cascade 945 **E2**
Chubbuck 7,052 **G6**
Coeur d'Alene
  20,054 **B2**
Dalton Gardens
  1,795 **B2**
Eagle 2,620 **F2**
Emmett 4,605 **F2**
Filer 1,645 **G4**
Fort Hall 900 **F6**
Fruitland 2,559 **F2**
Garden City 4,571 **F2**
Glenns Ferry 1,374 **G3**
Gooding 2,949 **G4**
Grace 1,216 **G7**
Grangeville 3,666 **D2**
Hailey 2,109 **F4**
Heyburn 2,889 **G5**
Homedale 2,078 **F2**
Idaho Falls 39,590 **F6**
Jerome 6,891 **G4**
Kamiah 1,478 **C2**
Kellogg 3,417 **B2**
Ketchum 2,200 **F4**
Kimberly 2,307 **G4**
Kuna 1,767 **F2**
Lewiston 27,986 **C1**
McCall 2,188 **E2**
Malad City 1,915 **G6**
Meridian 6,658 **F2**
Middleton 1,901 **F2**
Montpelier 3,107 **G7**
Moscow 16,513 **C2**
Mountain Home
  7,540 **F3**
Mullan 1,269 **B3**
Nampa 25,112 **F2**
New Plymouth 1,186 **F2**
Nezperce 517 **C2**
Orofino 3,711 **C2**
Osburn 2,220 **B3**
Parma 1,820 **F2**
Payette 5,448 **E2**
Pierce 1,060 **C3**
Pocatello 46,340 **G6**
Post Falls 5,736 **B2**
Preston 3,759 **G7**
Priest River 1,639 **A2**
Rathdrum 1,369 **B2**
Rexburg 11,559 **F7**
Rigby 2,624 **F7**
Rupert 5,476 **G5**
St. Anthony 3,212 **F7**
St. Maries 2,794 **B2**
Salmon 3,308 **D5**
Sandpoint 4,460 **A2**
Shelley 3,300 **F6**
Shoshone 1,242 **G4**
Soda Springs 4,051 **G7**
Sugar City 1,022 **F7**
Sun Valley 545 **F4**
Twin Falls 26,209 **G4**
Wallace 1,736 **B3**
Weiser 4,771 **E2**
Wendell 1,974 **G4**
Wilder 1,260 **F2**

Idaho

POPULATION 944,038.
Rank: 41. *Density:* 11 people/mi²
(4.4 people/km²). *Urban:* 54%.
Rural: 46%.
AGE < 20: 36%. 20–40: 32%.
40–65: 22%. >65: 10%.
ETHNIC GROUPS *White:* 95.5%.
Black: 0.3%. *Spanish origin:*
3.9%. *Native American:* 1.1%.
Other: 3.1%.

INCOME/CAPITA $8,056. *Rank:* 37.
POLITICS 1948–1980 elections:
President: 2 Dem., 7 Rep.
Governor: 3 Dem., 5 Rep.
ENTERED UNION July 3, 1890,
43rd state.
CAPITAL Boise, 102,160.
LARGEST CITY Boise.

AREA 83,566 mi² (216,435 km²).
Rank: 11. *Water area:* 1,153 mi²
(2,986 km²).
ELEVATIONS *Highest:* Borah Peak,
12,662 ft (3,859 m). *Lowest:*
Along Snake River, 710 ft
(216 m).
CLIMATE Cold winters, fairly cool
summers. Light rainfall, heavy
winter snows in mountains.

Over millions of years, the Snake River has sculpted a dramatic trench into the rock along the Idaho-Oregon border. This is Hells Canyon—the deepest gorge in North America. In places, the canyon walls plunge to depths of over one mile, while the river alternates between white-water rapids and calm pools. Uninhabitable and beautiful, the canyon characterizes much of Idaho's land area. Yet just to the south, the river, topography, and human influence have created the Snake River Plain—the state's most productive and populated area.

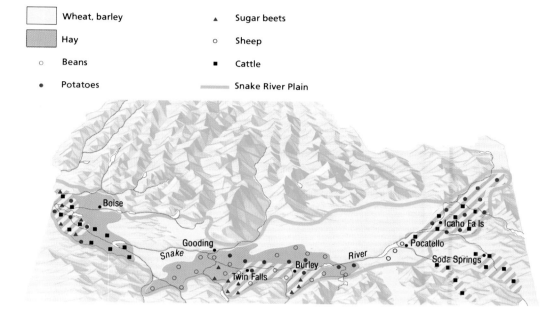

Snake River Plain Beginning around 1900, the fertile but arid earth of southern Idaho was excavated with hundreds of canals and ditches, and the waters of the Snake River were diverted to feed them. Irrigation now permits extensive cultivation, and this is Idaho's major agricultural region, with numerous hydroelectric plants providing power for the area's farms and cities.

In a country where state boundaries reflect political expediency more often than common sense, Idaho seems to have been drawn with a particularly whimsical hand. Its borders encompass the bits and pieces of mountain, valley, and desert left unclaimed by the adjoining six states and one Canadian province. As a result, Idaho is fragmented geographically and in its sense of statehood.

Idaho is roughly divided into three regions. The first lies north of the Salmon River Mountains, where the state looks to western Washington as a trading partner. The area south of these mountains is divided between the Snake River Plain—an arc touching Boise, Twin Falls, and Pocatello—and a third region south of the plain, whose predominantly Mormon settlements turn to Salt Lake City for economic and political leadership.

One measure of the state's fragmented identity is the unpredictable nature of its electorate. The state has a large number of independent voters, and their weight can shift the outcome of local and state contests and even sway the state from one national party to the other in a federal election. Idaho voters are strongly issue oriented, and their crossover voting can make any election decidedly difficult to call.

However, Idaho is fortunate in that its bits and pieces of territory are rich in natural resources. Agriculture, sheep and cattle ranching, lumbering, and mining make up the traditional base of the state's economy. Manufacturing flourishes where abundant hydroelectric power and raw materials are available, while the state's spectacular scenery and popular Sun Valley area have created a strong tourist trade.

Over the years, Idaho has developed a relatively stable and growing, if small, economy. The recent arrival of light- and high-technology industries may facilitate inventive solutions to the problems of Idaho's regional divisions. It may be that Idaho's sense of statehood will not come from its past but will emerge from its future.

Land Use The potential of Idaho's land has been difficult to realize. Much of its most fertile land requires irrigation, and the rugged terrain of the Salmon River Mountains makes lumbering difficult. Rough terrain and fast-flowing mountain streams, complete with waterfalls and rapids, make transportation difficult and expensive.

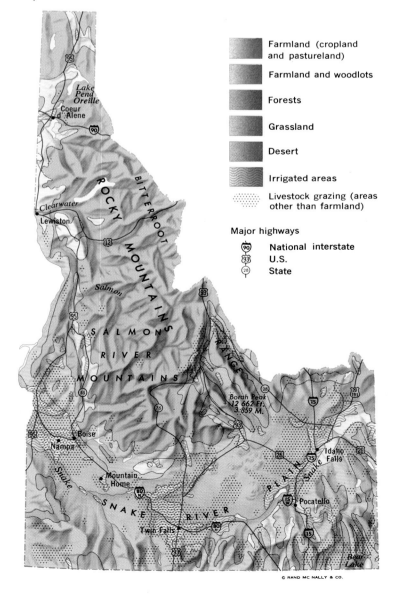

Farmland (cropland and pastureland)

Farmland and woodlots

Forests

Grassland

Desert

Irrigated areas

Livestock grazing (areas other than farmland)

Major highways

National interstate

U.S.

State

Economic Activities Divided into regions by terrain, Idaho's economy represents the sum of several distinct parts that contribute to Idaho's wealth and are closely allied with the adjoining states of Washington and Utah. Also, its economy is similar to that of other western states in its overall mix of agriculture, mining, and manufacturing.

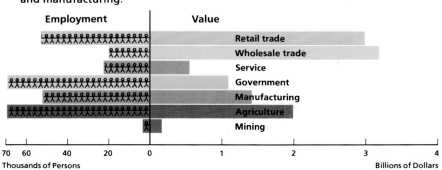

Employment	Value	
	Retail trade	
	Wholesale trade	
	Service	
	Government	
	Manufacturing	
	Agriculture	
	Mining	

70 60 40 20 0
Thousands of Persons

0 1 2 3 4
Billions of Dollars

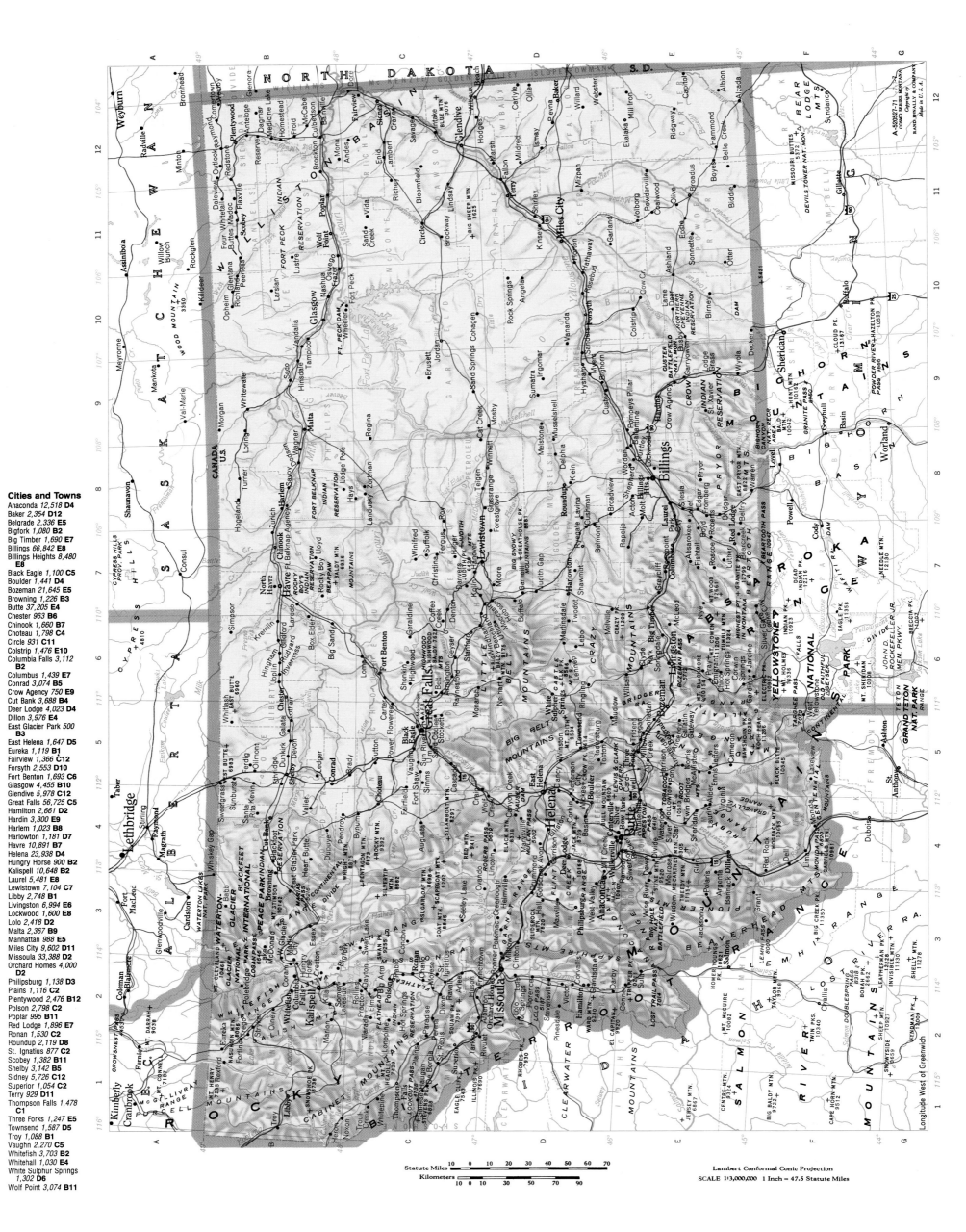

Montana

POPULATION 786,690.
Rank: 44. *Density:* 5.4 people/mi²
(2.1 people/km²). *Urban:* 52.9%.
Rural: 47.1%.
AGE *<20:* 33%. *20–40:* 32%.
40–65: 24%. *>65:* 11%.
ETHNIC GROUPS *White:* 94.1%.
Black: 0.2%. *Spanish origin:*
1.3%. *Native American:* 4.7%.
Other: 1%.

INCOME/CAPITA $8,536. *Rank:* 34.
POLITICS 1948–1980 elections:
President: 2 Dem., 7 Rep.
Governor: 5 Dem., 4 Rep.
ENTERED UNION November 8,
1889, 41st state.
CAPITAL Helena, 23,938.
LARGEST CITY Billings, 66,824.

AREA 147,049 mi² (380,856 km²).
Rank: 4. *Water area:* 1,657 mi²
(4,292 km²).
ELEVATIONS *Highest:* Granite Peak,
12,799 ft (3,901 m). *Lowest:*
Along Kootenai River, 1,800 ft
(549 m).
CLIMATE Hot summers, cold winters in east. Cool summers, mild
winters in west. Rainfall varies.

Compared with other western and southwestern states, Montana stands alone. Some states have similar natural-resource-based economies; some may be larger; and some, more sparsely populated. But in no other state in the region are these characteristics combined to the same degree that they are in Montana. While this creates certain problems, it also gives Montana a unique appeal for its people and the many visitors who enjoy this wilderness state.

Montana is an agricultural state and a primary producer in the midst of a nation of urban centers and an economy shifting toward a marriage of manufacturing and high technology. It specializes in products sold outside its borders and must depend on imports to meet many of its needs. This situation is likely to continue, even though vast areas of Montana remain untouched. Livestock production, along with crops such as wheat, sugar beets, hay, and barley, combine with Montana's income from oil, coal, and copper to account for most of the state's revenues.

Because of its large size and low population density, Montana faces some of the same problems that rural areas in other states experience. Long-distance driving, for example, is a part of everyday life for Montanans, and as a result, transportation costs can be high, both at the private and public level.

But the people of Montana are proud of its wide-open spaces and lack of sprawling urban centers. Outdoor recreational areas make the state a haven for hunters, campers, fishers, skiiers, and those just interested in the history and atmosphere of the Old West. Wonders like Glacier National Park continue to draw more tourists and nature lovers each year. Future strip-mining of Montana's extensive coal reserves could affect this rich natural beauty, but current environmental laws provide a measure of protection for the wilderness.

Thus, in spite of the changes development may bring, Montana is likely to remain unaffected by the modest growth in industry and mining. With an economy based upon the land, a vast unspoiled wilderness, and an environmentally aware population, Montana should be able to maintain its unique character, offering residents and the nation a life-style duplicated in no other state.

In northern Montana, Glacier National Park contains a rugged, snowcapped section of the Rocky Mountains. Many of the snowfields on the peaks are glaciers—huge, mobile ice masses—and meltwater feeds the park's lakes, rivers, and waterfalls.

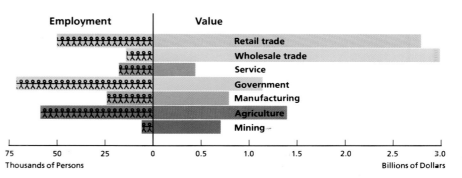

Land Use Montana is a vast state, spanning the transition from mountain to plain on a scale befitting its size. It includes part of the Rocky Mountains and a large portion of the Missouri Plateau region of the Great Plains. Agriculture is an important activity, and ranches and farms are large and mechanized, averaging around 2,500 acres.

- Farmland (cropland and pastureland)
- Farmland and woodlots
- Forests
- Grassland
- Desert
- Irrigated areas
- Livestock grazing (areas other than farmland)

Major highways
- ⑮ National interstate
- ⑫ U.S.

Economic Activities In large part, Montana's economy is based on the land itself. Rich in natural resources, the state receives much of its income through the primary activity of wresting products from the earth through agriculture, mining, and lumbering. The state's tourist industry is also dependent upon the land, with visitors drawn to Montana because of its natural beauty.

Medical Facilities The effect of Montana's size and low population density can be measured in the residents' access to amenities easily available in highly urbanized states. Sparsely populated areas cannot support a large number of hospitals, and many people are without ready access to health care. But to most state residents, the benefits of a life free from urban problems are worth the inconvenience.

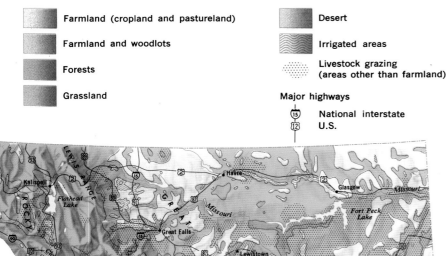

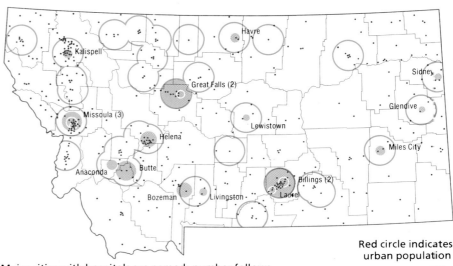

Major cities with hospitals are named; number follows if city has more than one hospital
- ◯ Area served by accredited hospital (20-mile radius)

Red circle indicates urban population

5,000 10,000 20,000 40,000 65,000

· One red dot represents 1,000 nonurban persons

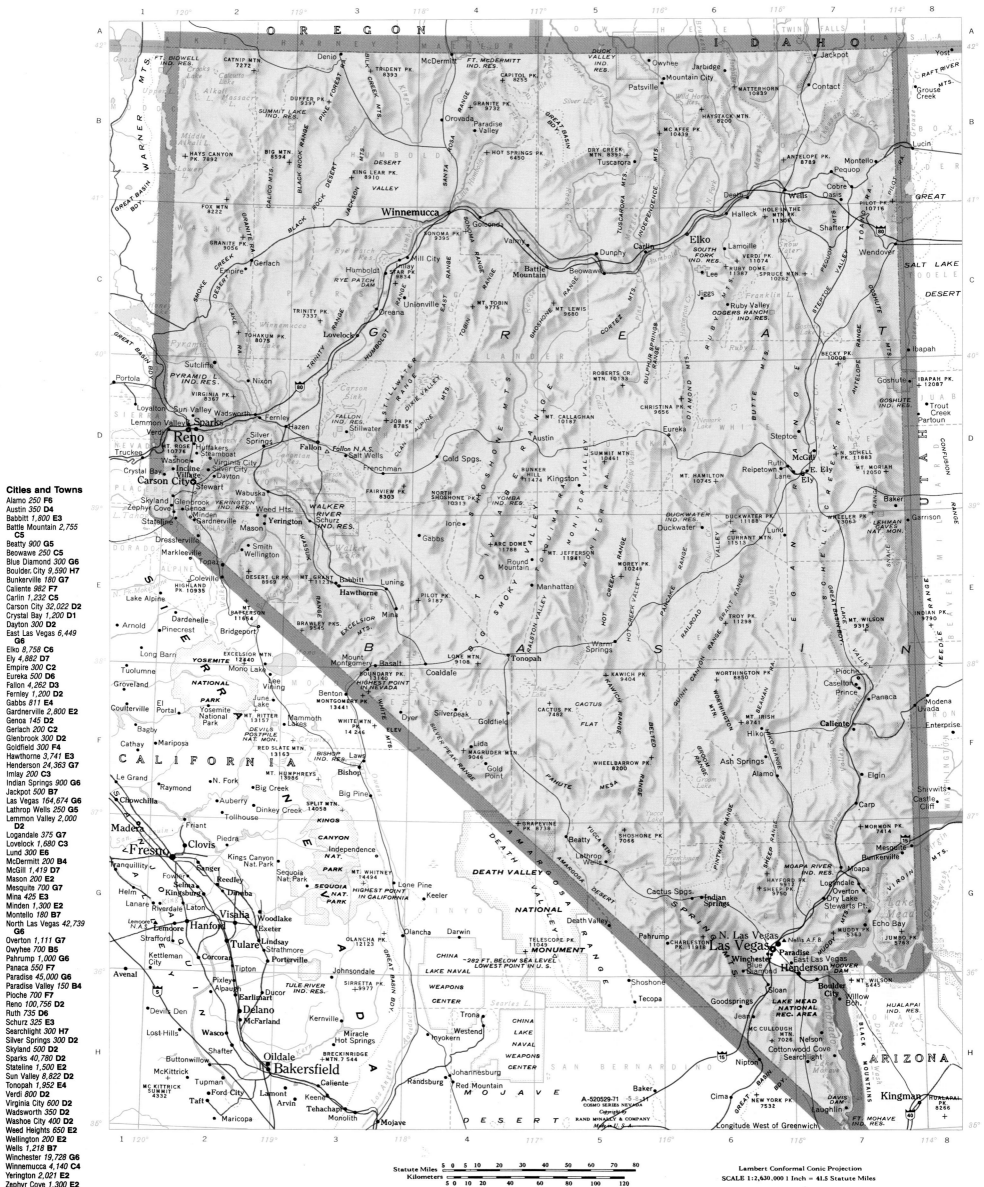

Nevada

POPULATION 800,493.
Rank: 43. *Density:* 7.3 people/mi²
(2.8 people/km²). *Urban:* 85.3%.
Rural: 14.7%.
AGE <*20:* 30%. *20–40:* 35%.
40–65: 27%. *>65:* 8%.
ETHNIC GROUPS *White:* 87.5%.
Black: 6.4%. *Spanish origin:*
6.7%. *Native American:* 1.7%.
Other: 4.4%.

INCOME/CAPITA $10,727. *Rank:* 6.
POLITICS 1948–1980 elections:
President: 3 Dem., 6 Rep.
Governor: 4 Dem., 4 Rep.
ENTERED UNION October 31, 1864,
36th state.
CAPITAL Carson City, 32,022.
LARGEST CITY Las Vegas, 164,674.

AREA 110,560 mi² (286,350 km²).
Rank: 7. *Water area:* 667 mi²
(1,728 km²).
ELEVATIONS *Highest:* Boundary
Peak, 13,140 ft (4,005 m).
Lowest: Along Colorado River,
470 ft (143 m).
CLIMATE Dry and sunny. Hot
summers, cool winters. Light
rainfall, deep mountain snow.

L ife in Nevada has always been a calculated risk. Its population and what little agriculture the state supports exist under the constant threat of drought, and its mineral wealth depends on markets that fluctuate wildly from boom to bust. Regardless of such risks, the people of Nevada have created a unique and prosperous state.

Nevada is one of the most arid states in the Union, lying east of the great Sierra Nevada range, which blocks moisture-laden clouds coming from the West Coast. Irrigation is costly and can be used only in limited areas. Even ranching, the other agricultural possibility for the state, is successful in only a few small regions.

Nature, as if to compensate for the lack of water, has endowed Nevada with rich deposits of copper, tungsten, gold, and other minerals. However, since the markets for these are volatile, much of the state's revenue from such resources is unpredictable—high one year, low the next.

In view of these realities, it is not surprising that the mainstay of Nevada's economy is legalized gambling. The state has tapped a national demand for gaming, entertainment, recreation, and convention facilities; and income from these businesses now surpasses the combined outputs of Nevada's mines and ranches. The federal government has also played a role in Nevada's development. After World War II, it began testing nuclear weapons in the bleak desert areas and built an array of high-technology installations in the state.

Agriculture, mining, gambling, tourism, the atom—all have helped Nevada thrive, even though the state remains vulnerable to outside economic and governmental forces. Gradual expansion into high-growth industries as well as a continued military and federal presence will help stabilize the state's economy. Nevertheless, risk will continue to play a major part in Nevada's future.

Las Vegas serves as an example of the effect humans can have upon the land. Nothing more than a quiet meadow in a desert valley around 150 years ago, Las Vegas today is a city of neon, air-conditioned hotels, and palm trees. Growth was minimal, however, until the 1930's, when Nevada legalized gambling. Around the same time, construction began on nearby Hoover Dam, and incoming workers swelled the city's population. Today the Strip of Las Vegas is famous worldwide, and income from the city's tourism industry is a major contributor to the state's economy.

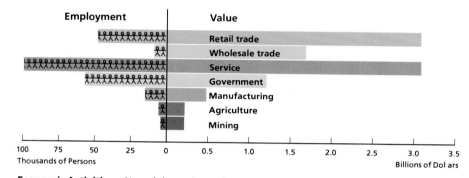

Economic Activities   Nevada's tourist and convention industry results in the strength of the state in retail trade and service industries, where tourist dollars are spent.

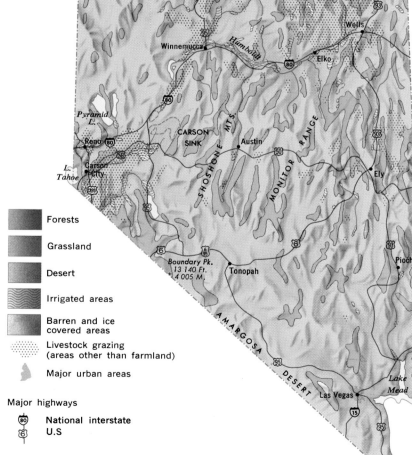

Forests
Grassland
Desert
Irrigated areas
Barren and ice covered areas
Livestock grazing (areas other than farmland)
Major urban areas

Major highways
National interstate
U.S

Land Use   Agricultural development of Nevada is tempered by lack of water. Huge tracts of federal land are left open for military-weapons test grounds, gunnery ranges, and depots that cannot be located on more productive land in other states.

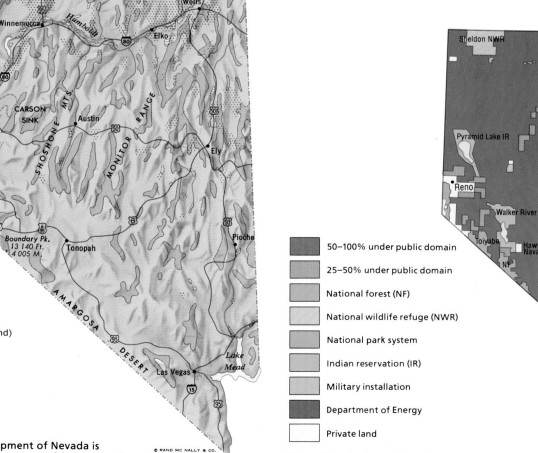

50–100% under public domain
25–50% under public domain
National forest (NF)
National wildlife refuge (NWR)
National park system
Indian reservation (IR)
Military installation
Department of Energy
Private land

Federal Land   Over eighty-five percent of Nevada's land area is owned by the United States government. Public-domain areas—land not earmarked for development—is rented by ranchers for sheep and cattle grazing.

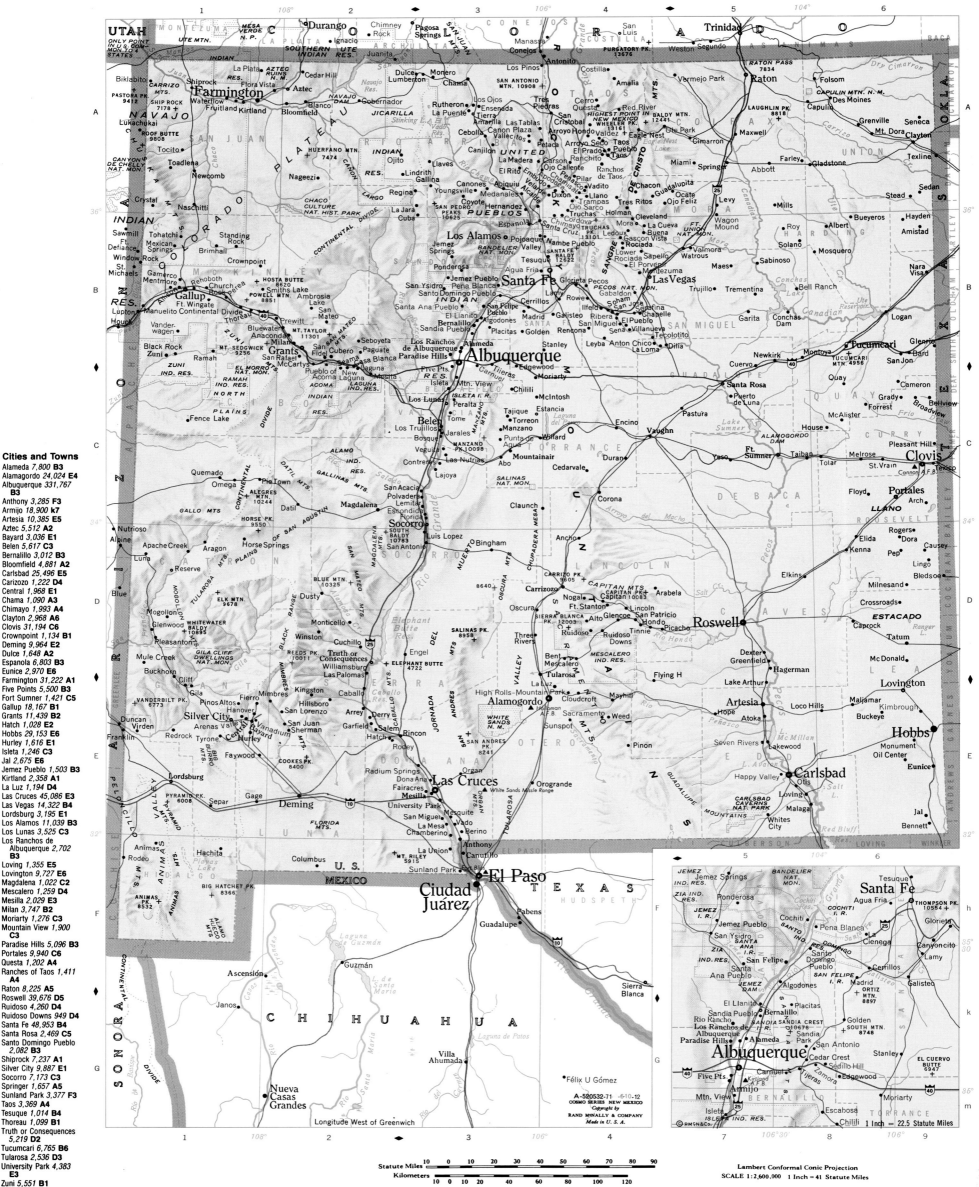

Statute Miles

Kilometers

A-520532-71 -6·10-12
COSMO SERIES NEW MEXICO
Copyright by
RAND MCNALLY & COMPANY
Made in U.S.A.

Lambert Conformal Conic Projection
SCALE 1:2,600,000   1 Inch = 41 Statute Miles

1 Inch = 22.5 Statute Miles

New Mexico

POPULATION 1,302,981.
Rank: 37. *Density:* 11 people/mi²
(4.1 people/km²). *Urban:* 72.1%.
Rural: 27.9%.
AGE *<20:* 36%. *20–40:* 32%.
40–65: 23%. *>65:* 9%.
ETHNIC GROUPS *White:* 75.1%.
Black: 1.8%. *Spanish origin:*
36.6%. *Native American:* 8%.
Other: 15.1%.

INCOME/CAPITA $7,841. *Rank:* 39.
POLITICS 1948–1980 elections:
President: 3 Dem., 6 Rep.
Governor: 8 Dem., 6 Rep.
ENTERED UNION January 6, 1912,
47th state.
CAPITAL Santa Fe, 48,953.
LARGEST CITY Albuquerque,
331,767.

AREA 121,593 mi² (314,924 km²).
Rank: 5. *Water area:* 258 mi²
(668 km²).
ELEVATIONS *Highest:* Wheeler
Peak, 13,161 ft (4,011 m).
Lowest: Along Red Bluff
Reservoir, 2,817 ft (859 m).
CLIMATE Nearly constant sunshine,
low humidity, little rainfall. Hot
summers, mild winters.

The Very Large Array, or VLA, telescope makes New Mexico a major contributor to scientific discovery. In seeking a site on which to erect the twenty-seven antennas of the VLA, the National Radio Astronomy Observatory found the state's unique terrain near Socorro the perfect location. From the flat, arid Plains of San Agustin, scientists from all over the world observe galactic objects ranging from the sun to far-distant planets. Each eighty-two-foot antenna is a delicate instrument but sturdy enough to withstand the harsh climate of the seven-thousand-foot elevation.

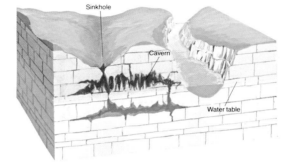

Cave Formation   Caves such as the Carlsbad Caverns in southeast New Mexico are formed when groundwater seeps through limestone, reaching the water table. A chemical reaction begins, and the limestone is eaten away by the water, which contains carbon dioxide from the soil and air above.

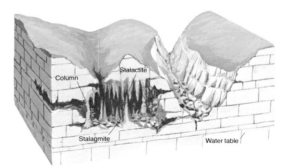

As the water table drops, more cavities are formed, and air fills the upper caves. Water carrying dissolved minerals creates stalagmites, stalactites, and columns as it drips down to the water table. When the rock above collapses, a natural entrance called a sinkhole is formed.

New Mexico is a complex tapestry of cultural traditions. Spanish and Indian place-names grace the cities and countryside; cattle ranches and irrigated cropland reflect the melding of Hispanic and Anglo-American agriculture; Indian reservations include ruins of some of the oldest settlements in North America; and the Los Alamos laboratories represent the impact of the latest high-technology advances. This interweaving of cultural legacies has created a unique combination of assets and problems defined by the state's geography and people.

New Mexico is rich in natural beauty but has only modest natural resources. Its rugged mountains and deserts attract thousands of tourists, artists, and new residents to the state each year. But tillable land is limited primarily to the narrow Rio Grande Valley, cutting through the middle of the state, and much of that land must be irrigated. Mineral resources account for New Mexico's mining industry, and potash, uranium, oil, and gas are important products. Lack of water, however, is a major constraint on the growth of industry and agriculture.

The recent migration to the Sun Belt has added to the cultural and economic diversity of the state, but it has also created new tensions among the people. As more Anglo-Americans travel to New Mexico to live or visit, they threaten to overwhelm the Hispanic and Native American populations. The situation is aggravated by economic inequalities. Many Hispanics and Native Americans are poor, while much of the Anglo-American population is relatively prosperous. Job opportunities resulting from more federal military and research installations and light industries coming into the state may ease this problem somewhat. But heavy job competition will make it difficult to eliminate cultural tensions and economic imbalance. The state faces great challenges now and in the future.

Nevertheless, the nation's enchantment with New Mexico continues and is evidenced by the steady migration of new residents and industry to the mountain-desert state. As New Mexico adjusts to its changing population and the impact of a more sophisticated technology, it will need to find imaginative ways to blend modern and ancient traditions into its historical tapestry.

With miles of caves and passageways, the Carlsbad Caverns contain some of the world's largest and most beautiful stalagmites and stalactites. But the caverns contribute to the state's economy as well as its beauty. Each year, thousands of tourists flock to this great natural wonder.

Land Use   Since prehistoric times, settlement of New Mexico has largely been restricted to the Rio Grande Valley and the valleys of its tributaries where water is available. This valley is the backbone of the state and the home of most of New Mexico's farms. Grazing and dry farming are possible elsewhere, however, and are of importance on New Mexico's eastern plains.

Economic Activities   Mining in New Mexico ranges from coal and copper production to the excavation of molybdenum and uranium ores. New Mexico's economy also owes much to tourism, which contributes to retail trade and services, while government investment also supports the state's economy.

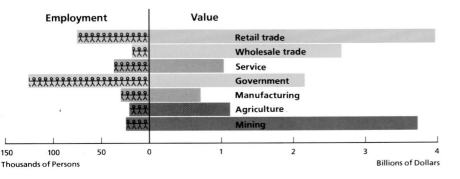

Farmland (cropland and pastureland)

Forests

Grassland

Desert

Irrigated areas

Barren and ice covered areas

Livestock grazing (areas other than farmland)

Major urban areas

Major highways
National interstate
U.S.

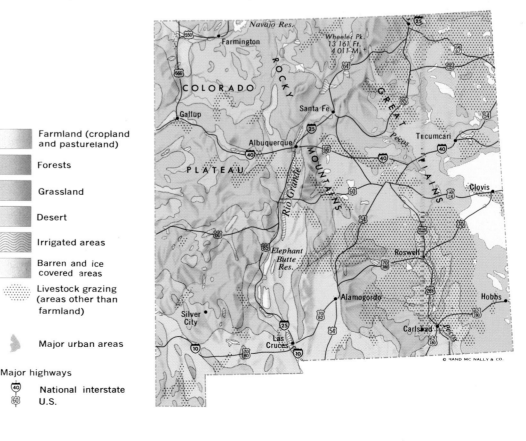

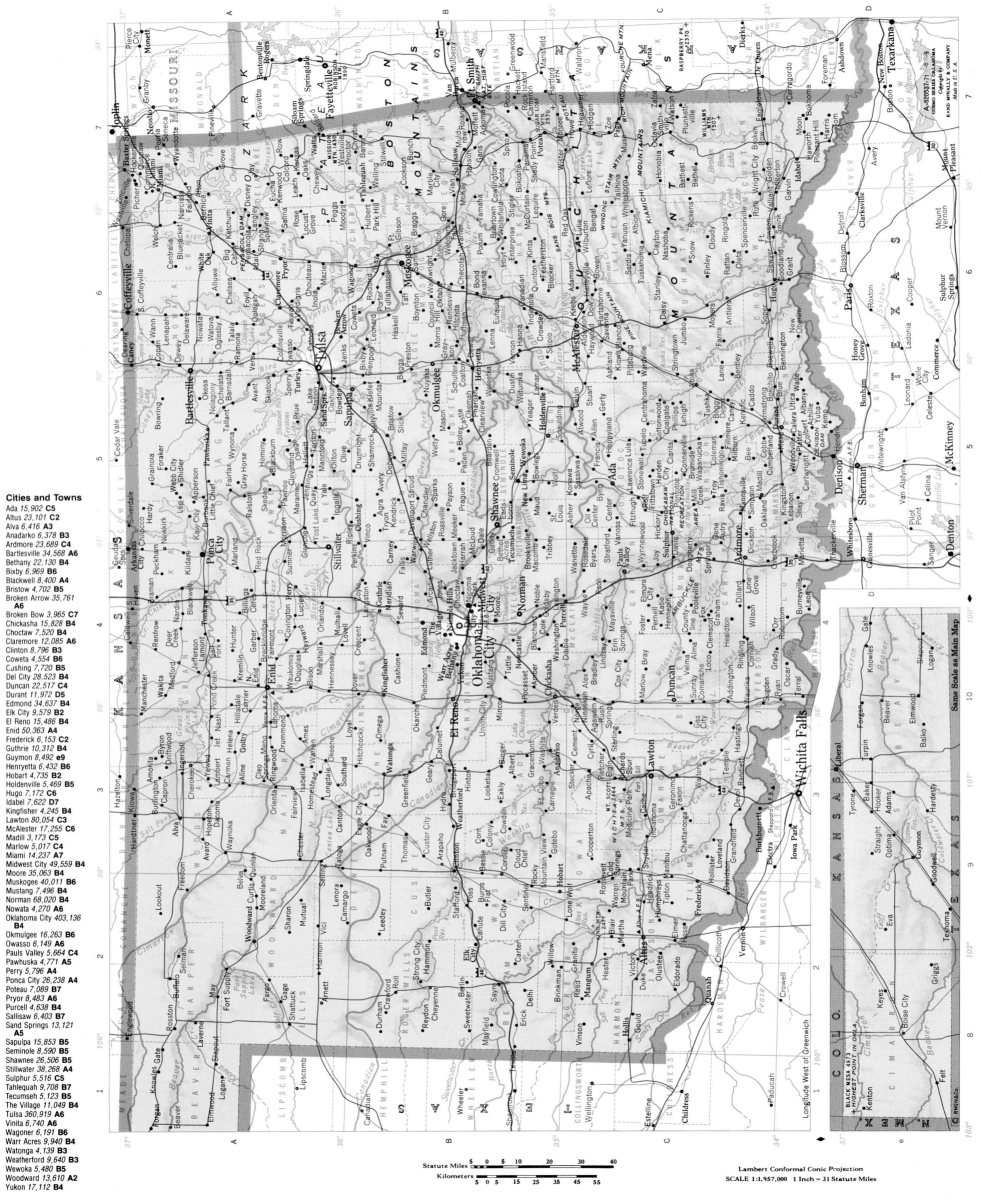

Cities and Towns

Ada 15,902 **C5**
Altus 23,101 **C2**
Alva 6,416 **A3**
Anadarko 6,378 **B3**
Ardmore 23,689 **C4**
Bartlesville 34,568 **A6**
Bethany 22,130 **B4**
Bixby 6,969 **B6**
Blackwell 8,400 **A4**
Bristow 4,702 **B5**
Broken Arrow 35,761
  A6
Broken Bow 3,965 **C7**
Chickasha 15,828 **B4**
Choctaw 7,520 **B4**
Claremore 12,085 **A6**
Clinton 8,796 **B3**
Coweta 4,554 **B6**
Cushing 7,720 **B5**
Del City 28,523 **B4**
Duncan 22,517 **C4**
Durant 11,972 **D5**
Edmond 34,637 **B4**
Elk City 9,579 **B2**
El Reno 15,486 **B4**
Enid 50,363 **A4**
Frederick 6,153 **C2**
Guthrie 10,312 **B4**
Guymon 8,492 **e9**
Henryetta 6,432 **B6**
Hobart 4,735 **B2**
Holdenville 5,469 **B5**
Hugo 7,172 **C6**
Idabel 7,622 **D7**
Kingfisher 4,245 **B4**
Lawton 80,054 **C3**
McAlester 17,255 **C6**
Madill 3,173 **C5**
Marlow 5,017 **C4**
Miami 14,237 **A7**
Midwest City 49,559 **B4**
Moore 35,063 **B4**
Muskogee 40,011 **B6**
Mustang 7,496 **B4**
Norman 68,020 **B4**
Nowata 4,270 **A6**
Oklahoma City 403,136
  B4
Okmulgee 16,263 **B6**
Owasso 6,149 **A6**
Pauls Valley 5,664 **C4**
Pawhuska 4,771 **A5**
Perry 5,796 **A4**
Ponca City 26,238 **A4**
Poteau 7,089 **B7**
Pryor 8,483 **A6**
Purcell 4,638 **B4**
Sallisaw 6,403 **B7**
Sand Springs 13,121
  A5
Sapulpa 15,853 **B5**
Seminole 8,590 **B5**
Shawnee 26,506 **B5**
Stillwater 38,268 **A4**
Sulphur 5,516 **C5**
Tahlequah 9,708 **B7**
Tecumseh 5,123 **B5**
The Village 11,049 **B4**
Tulsa 360,919 **A6**
Vinita 6,740 **A6**
Wagoner 6,191 **B6**
Warr Acres 9,940 **B4**
Watonga 4,139 **B3**
Weatherford 9,640 **B3**
Wewoka 5,480 **B5**
Woodward 13,610 **A2**
Yukon 17,112 **B4**

Statute Miles
Kilometers

Lambert Conformal Conic Projection
SCALE 1:1,957,000 1 Inch = 31 Statute Miles

Oklahoma

POPULATION 3,025,290.
Rank: 26. *Density:* 44 people/mi²
(17 people/km²). *Urban:* 67.3%.
Rural: 32.7%.
AGE *<20:* 32%. *20–40:* 31%.
40–65: 24%. *>65:* 13%.
ETHNIC GROUPS *White:* 85.9%.
Black: 6.8%. *Spanish origin:*
1.9%. *Native American:* 5.6%.
Other: 1.7%.

INCOME/CAPITA $9,116. *Rank:* 28.
POLITICS 1948–1980 elections:
President: 2 Dem., 7 Rep.
Governor: 6 Dem., 2 Rep.
ENTERED UNION November 16,
1907, 46th state.
CAPITAL Oklahoma City, 403,136.
LARGEST CITY Oklahoma City.

AREA 69,956 mi² (181,186 km²).
Rank: 19. *Water area:* 1,301 mi²
(3,370 km²).
ELEVATIONS *Highest:* Black Mesa,
4,973 ft (1,516 m). *Lowest:* Along
Little River, 287 ft (87 m).
CLIMATE Generally mild winters,
hot summers with great
temperature fluctuations.

The development of the Dust Bowl in the 1930's united Oklahoma and surrounding states in the common goal of reviving their land. The Great Plains Agricultural Council that was formed introduced such conservation practices as contour farming, tree planting, and crop rotation. These methods continue today to make Oklahoma and its neighbors successful agriculturally. The area shown here, from Oklahoma's Panhandle in the heart of the Dust Bowl, shows that the once-denuded land can be revitalized. Deep wells in the Panhandle, as well as in southwestern Oklahoma, also serve as sources of irrigation for the state.

Oklahoma, once set aside as Indian Territory, was not opened for settlement until about twenty-five years after the Civil War. Land rushes, oil booms, and the devastating Dust Bowl drought have all left their indelible marks on the state's natural and human landscapes. It is a state of contrasts, where forested mountains and rolling grassy plains, Indians and whites, oil and agriculture, and poverty and plenty exist side by side.

The land rush of the late 1800's brought thousands of settlers to the state to establish homesteads and begin farming the prairie soil. Within two generations, poor agricultural methods and prolonged drought had changed the once-fertile region into the Dust Bowl of the 1930's. Thousands of "Okies" migrated to California and to the North in search of work. Today, improved conservation and soil-management programs have restored a great deal of the land's productivity, but periodic droughts still threaten this fragile environment.

Reconciling Oklahoma's many contrasts has been a more difficult task, complicated by its isolation from the main cultural and economic centers of the nation. The state lies on the fringe of the agriculturally rich Midwest, just beyond the southern and western edges of the Midwest-to-East industrial area, and slightly north of the vital Gulf Coast economies of Texas and Louisiana. However, the nation's demand for Oklahoma oil and gas has helped somewhat to reduce the state's isolation. As an energy producer and an exporter of raw materials and foodstuffs, Oklahoma has been able to establish itself as a center of finance and commerce for the sparsely settled regions of the lower Great Plains. The state has made similar progress culturally, gradually reducing some of the barriers that divide whites, blacks, and Native Americans.

Few states have progressed as rapidly as has Oklahoma in overcoming the isolation that shaped its history and identity. Oklahoma's ability to reconcile its many contrasts may well prove to be the source of its future strength.

Gas Deposits Drilling in the Deep Anadarko Basin, directed by seismic mapping and computer analysis, has uncovered new gas deposits approximately five miles beneath the land's surface. This new field, together with many others, has helped to make Oklahoma one of the largest mineral-producing states in the nation.

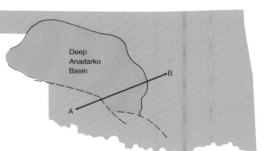

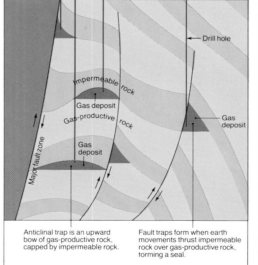

Anticlinal trap is an upward bow of gas-productive rock, capped by impermeable rock.

Fault traps form when earth movements thrust impermeable rock over gas-productive rock, forming a seal.

Cross section through the basin

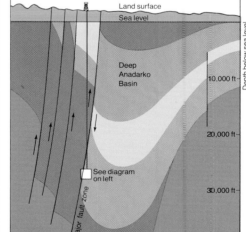

Land Use Although Oklahoma's land supports a wide variety of uses, large areas are exposed to the drama of high winds, thunderstorms, blizzards, and tornadoes, which not only make life hazardous but can damage valuable land.

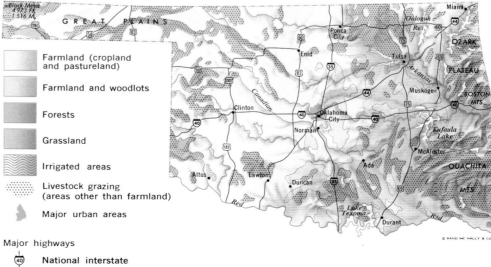

Farmland (cropland and pastureland)

Farmland and woodlots

Forests

Grassland

Irrigated areas

Livestock grazing (areas other than farmland)

Major urban areas

Major highways

National interstate

U.S.

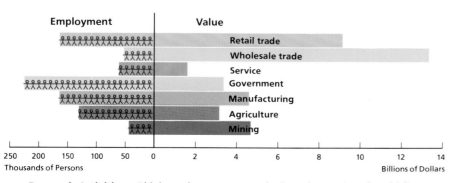

Economic Activities Oklahoma's economy was built up in a series of rapid-fire waves, or "runs." First there was agriculture, then the development of petroleum and natural-gas wealth, and finally the realization of potential in manufacturing and commerce. Rather than overwhelming the state, the runs have served to stimulate economic diversification.

Employment | Value

Retail trade
Wholesale trade
Service
Government
Manufacturing
Agriculture
Mining

250 200 150 100 50 0
Thousands of Persons

0 2 4 6 8 10 12 14
Billions of Dollars

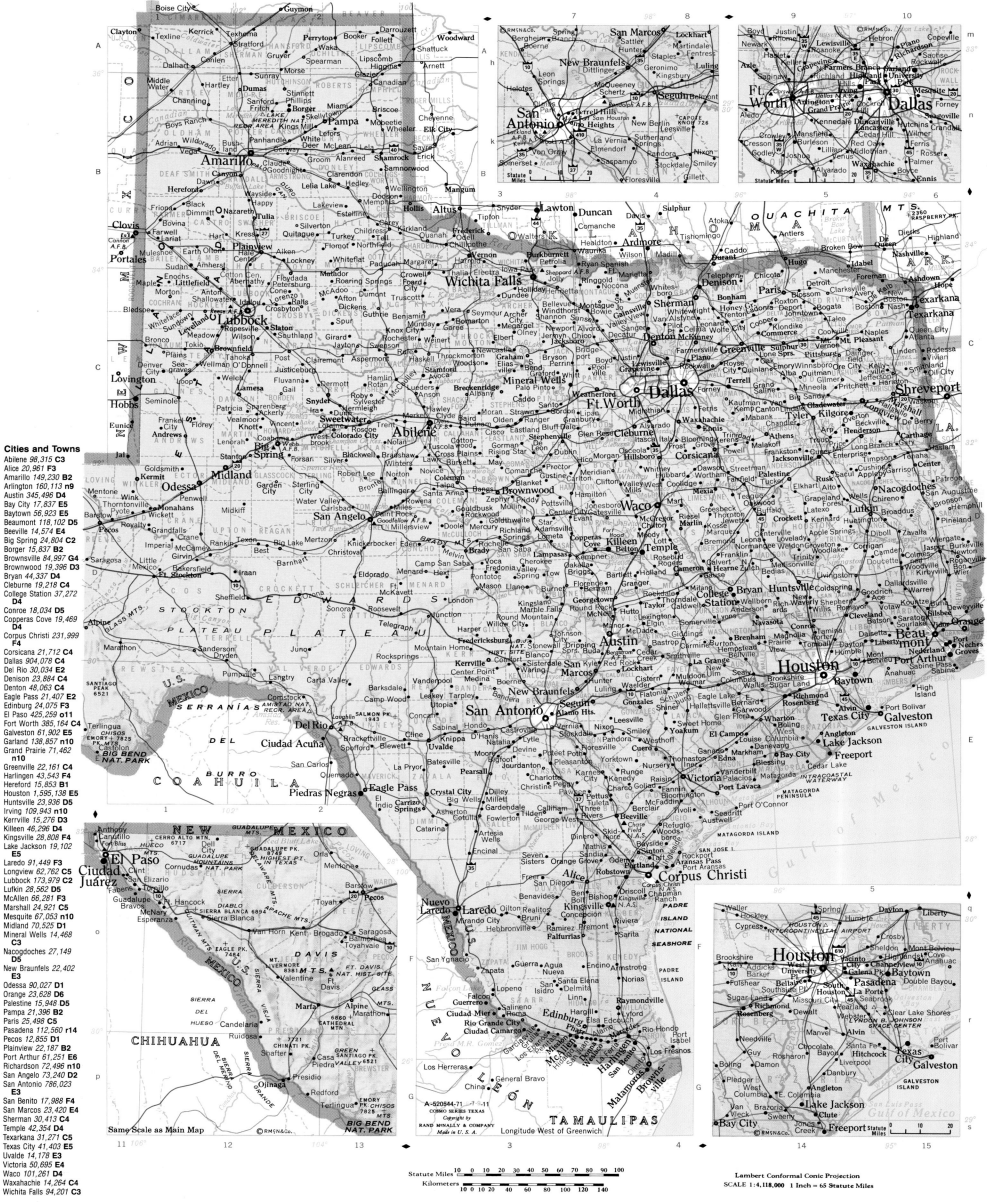

Statute Miles 10 0 10 20 30 40 50 60 70 80 90 100
Kilometers 10 0 10 20 40 60 80 100 120 140

Lambert Conformal Conic Projection
SCALE 1:4,118,000 1 Inch = 65 Statute Miles

Texas

POPULATION 14,229,288.
Rank: 3. *Density:* 54 people/mi²
(21 people/km²). *Urban:* 79.6%.
Rural: 20.4%.
AGE *<20:* 34%. *20–40:* 33%.
40–65: 23%. *>65:* 10%.
ETHNIC GROUPS *White:* 78.7%.
Black: 12%. *Spanish origin:* 21%.
Native American: 0.3%.
Other: 9%.

INCOME/CAPITA $9,545. *Rank:* 18.
POLITICS 1948–1980 elections:
President: 5 Dem., 4 Rep.
Governor: 14 Dem., 1 Rep.
ENTERED UNION December 29,
1845, 28th state.
CAPITAL Austin, 345,496.
LARGEST CITY Houston, 1,595,138.

AREA 266,807 mi² (691,027 km²).
Rank: 2. *Water area:* 4,790 mi²
(12,406 km²).
ELEVATIONS *Highest:* Guadalupe
Peak, 8,749 ft (2,667 m). *Lowest:*
Gulf of Mexico shoreline, sea
level.
CLIMATE Coastal areas and eastern
interior humid with mild winters,
hot summers. West very dry.

The vast resources of Texas befit a region, even a nation, more than
a state; and it is appropriate that Texas was once an independent
republic. It is a leader in oil and natural-gas production, total
reserves, refining capacity, and petrochemical output. Cattle ranching
and cotton, which together with oil have fashioned the state's history,
remain major sources of wealth. Texas is also blessed by its vast size
and its location between the Gulf Coastal Plain and the high peaks of
the Rockies. Its land routes command access to the North and West,
while its ports open the state to seagoing trade from all over the world.

Texas has used its wealth to enter every sector of the economy,
turning out producers' and consumers' goods ranging from high technology to high fashion. Oil and gas can be shipped in their unrefined
state or converted into petrochemicals and plastics, then made into
consumer products for national markets.

Despite its assets, however, Texas's social development has not
always kept pace with its spectacular economic and urban boom. The
Hispanic minority remains below the rest of the state in educational
attainment, income, and political power. Blacks have achieved some
gains in political and educational fronts, but still lag behind the majority.
These two groups are becoming more aware of their common problems
and are learning to cooperate in their efforts to gain a greater voice in
the affairs of their state.

But these problems may be no more than growing pains in this
nation-sized state. Economic development and diversification in the
past decade have been unusually rapid. This is partly due to the changing
American economy, with its new emphasis on high technology, and
the state's participation in this trend. In addition, the country is looking
to resource-rich Texas for solutions to its energy problems. The potential
for growth in this one-time frontier of cattle and cowboys is great, and
progress is already being made in matching social improvements with
economic expansion, as evidenced by the state's growing per capita
income. In the coming years, Texas's political and social ideals may
very well equal the state's vast size and abundant wealth of resources.

Traditional scenes of Texas complement the development occurring elsewhere in
the state. Agriculture is still a major industry, and the High Plains region in the
Texas Panhandle contains some of the state's most productive farmland.

Employment		Value	
		Retail trade	
		Wholesale trade	
		Service	
		Government	
		Manufacturing	
		Agriculture	
		Mining	

1000   750   500   250   0   0   20   40   60   80   100
Thousands of Persons   Billions of Dollars

Economic Activities   Industries in Texas are developing at an extremely rapid
rate, reflected in substantial growth in population and state income. Despite
Texas's extraordinary petroleum and natural-gas production and thriving agriculture, even more income is derived from other sectors of the economy.

Land Use   Stretching from the Gulf Coast to the Rockies and from Mexico nearly
halfway to Canada, Texas lies within so many environmental regimes that no one
region can be called typical. Often pictured as a state of uninterrupted flat plains
dotted with cattle and oil rigs, Texas has large areas that are hilly and rugged, and
about half of Texas's area is forest and brushland.

Metropolitan Areas   The rapid changes that continue to affect Texas and much of
the Sun Belt are reflected in metropolitan population growth. Texas has more metropolitan areas than any other state and a higher percentage of metropolitan residents than the nation as a whole. In addition, twenty-three Texas metropolitan
areas have growth rates above the national average of 10.2 percent.

Metropolitan growth rate, 1970 – 1980

- 30% or more
- 10.2% – 30%
- 0% – 10.2%

Legend (Land Use map):
- Farmland (cropland and pastureland)
- Farmland and woodlots
- Forests
- Grassland
- Desert
- Swampland and marshland
- Irrigated areas
- Livestock grazing (areas other than farmland)
- Major urban areas
- Major highways
  - National interstate
  - U.S.

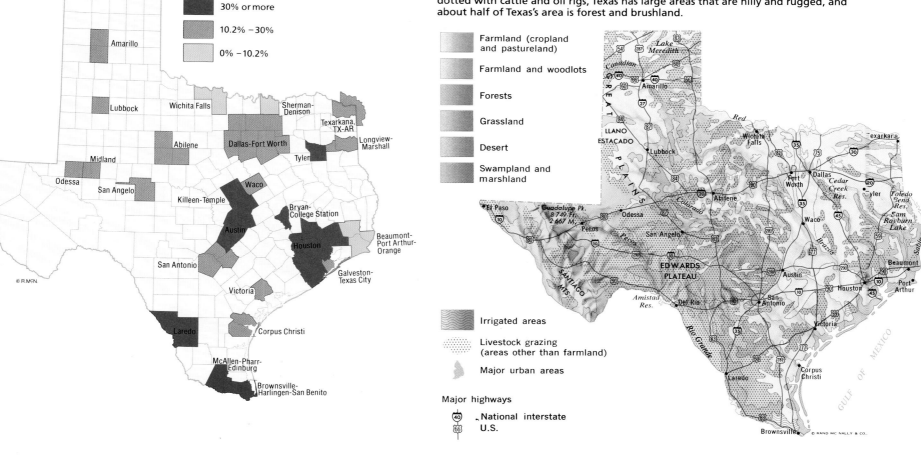

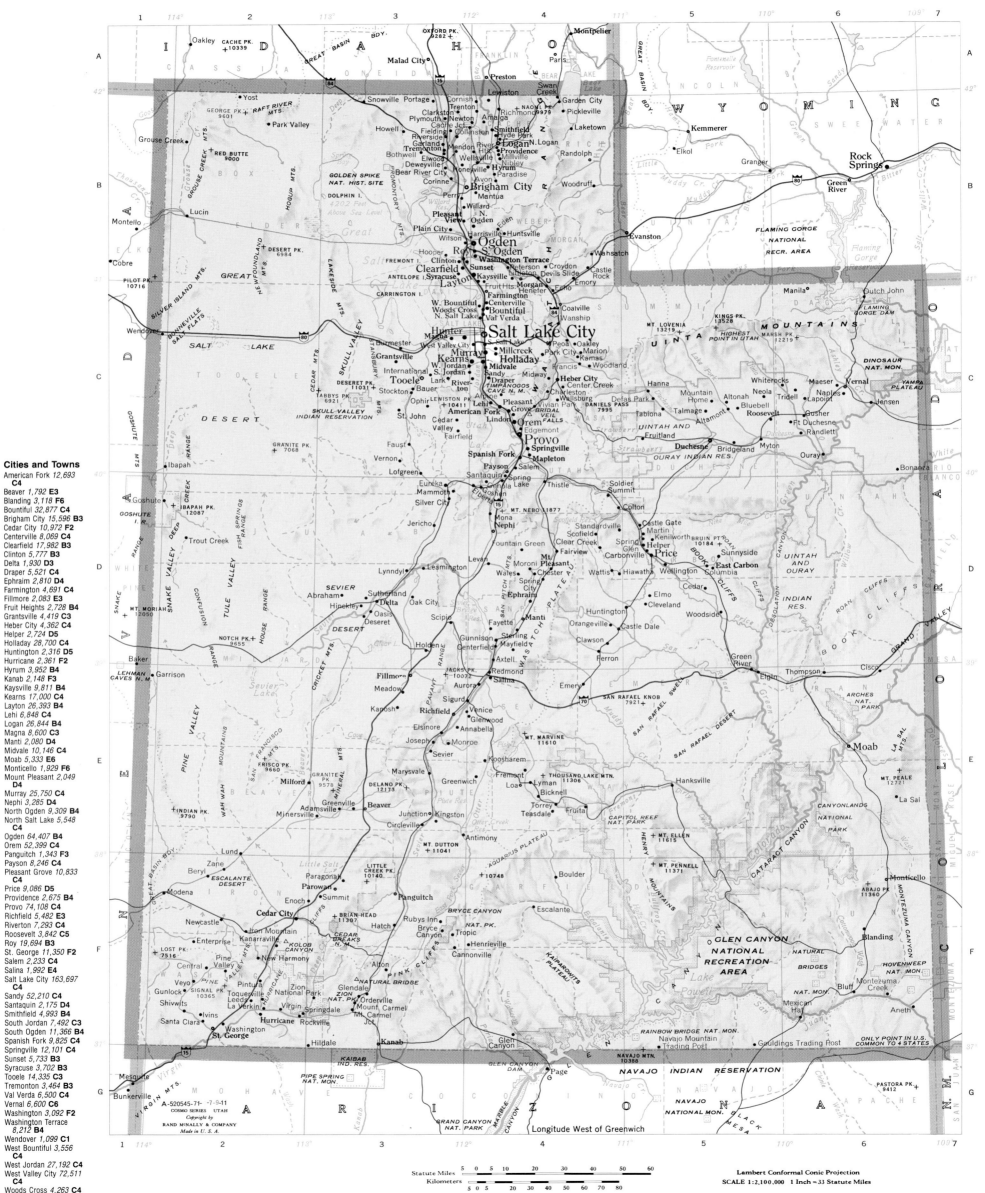

Cities and Towns

American Fork 12,693 **C4**
Beaver 1,792 **E3**
Blanding 3,118 **F6**
Bountiful 32,877 **C4**
Brigham City 15,596 **B3**
Cedar City 10,972 **F2**
Centerville 8,069 **C4**
Clearfield 17,982 **B3**
Clinton 5,777 **B3**
Delta 1,930 **D3**
Draper 5,521 **C4**
Ephraim 2,810 **D4**
Farmington 4,691 **C4**
Fillmore 2,083 **E3**
Fruit Heights 2,728 **B4**
Grantsville 4,419 **C3**
Heber City 4,362 **C4**
Helper 2,724 **D5**
Holladay 28,700 **C4**
Huntington 2,316 **D5**
Hurricane 2,361 **F2**
Hyrum 3,952 **B4**
Kanab 2,148 **F3**
Kaysville 9,811 **B4**
Kearns 17,000 **C4**
Layton 26,393 **B4**
Lehi 6,848 **C4**
Logan 26,844 **B4**
Magna 8,600 **C3**
Manti 2,080 **D4**
Midvale 10,146 **C4**
Moab 5,333 **E6**
Monticello 1,929 **F6**
Mount Pleasant 2,049 **D4**
Murray 25,750 **C4**
Nephi 3,285 **D4**
North Ogden 9,309 **B4**
North Salt Lake 5,548 **C4**
Ogden 64,407 **B4**
Orem 52,399 **C4**
Panguitch 1,343 **F3**
Payson 8,246 **C4**
Pleasant Grove 10,833 **C4**
Price 9,086 **D5**
Providence 2,675 **B4**
Provo 74,108 **C4**
Richfield 5,482 **E3**
Riverton 7,293 **C4**
Roosevelt 3,842 **C5**
Roy 19,694 **B3**
St. George 11,350 **F2**
Salem 2,233 **C4**
Salina 1,992 **E4**
Salt Lake City 163,697 **C4**
Sandy 52,210 **C4**
Santaquin 2,175 **D4**
Smithfield 4,993 **B4**
South Jordan 7,492 **C3**
South Ogden 11,366 **B4**
Spanish Fork 9,825 **C4**
Springville 12,101 **C4**
Sunset 5,733 **B3**
Syracuse 3,702 **B3**
Tooele 14,335 **C3**
Tremonton 3,464 **B3**
Val Verda 6,500 **C4**
Vernal 6,600 **C6**
Washington 3,092 **F2**
Washington Terrace 8,212 **B4**
Wendover 1,099 **C1**
West Bountiful 3,556 **C4**
West Jordan 27,192 **C4**
West Valley City 72,511 **C4**
Woods Cross 4,263 **C4**

Utah

POPULATION 1,461,037.
Rank: 36. *Density:* 18 people/mi²
(6.9 people/km²). *Urban:* 84.4%.
Rural: 15.6%.
AGE *< 20:* 41%. *20 – 40:* 33%.
40 – 65: 19%. *>65:* 7%.
ETHNIC GROUPS *White:* 94.6%.
Black: 0.6%. *Spanish origin:*
4.1%. *Native American:* 1.3%.
Other: 3.5%.

INCOME/CAPITA $7,649. *Rank:* 45.
POLITICS 1948 – 1980 elections:
President: 2 Dem., 7 Rep.
Governor: 5 Dem., 4 Rep.
ENTERED UNION January 4, 1896,
45th state.
CAPITAL Salt Lake City, 163,697.
LARGEST CITY Salt Lake City.

AREA 84,899 mi² (219,887 km²).
Rank: 12. *Water area:* 2,826 mi²
(7,319 km²).
ELEVATIONS *Highest:* Kings Peak,
13,528 ft (4,123 m). *Lowest:* In
Washington County, 2,000 ft
(610 m).
CLIMATE Generally very dry. Warm
summers, cold winters. Heaviest
rain in mountains, winter snow.

The dry climate and the unique geologic nature of southeastern Utah largely account for the formation of the region's many fascinating landforms, such as the natural arches shown above. The arches, spires, pinnacles, and alcoves of the area combine to form scenery that is considered to be among the most spectacular in North America.

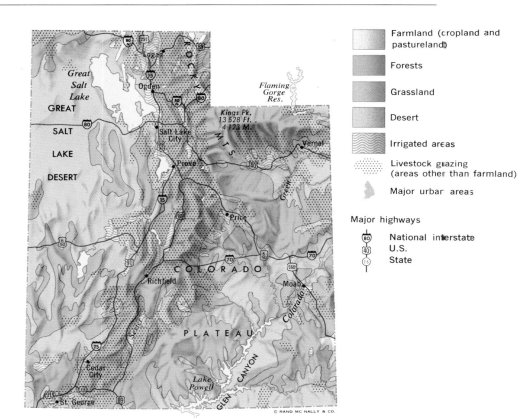

Land Use   Human settlement and agriculture have followed the baselines of Utah's mountains. Here lie deltas of fertile soils watered by springs from the high mountains. The generally dry climate throughout the state necessitates wise management of moisture provided by precipitation.

Since pioneer times, Utah has acted as both a pathway and a destination. While thousands crossed the state, headed for adventure and opportunity in the West, many travelers remained to build a home in Utah's beautiful, if somewhat harsh, landscape.

Utah lies along the main route leading from the Great Plains to the Pacific Coast. Modern cross-country travelers using Utah's main highways are actually following paths blazed long ago by pioneers and wagon trains coming from the Mississippi Valley. In the late 1800's, builders of the transcontinental railway laid their tracks along these same early trails. Today, Salt Lake City and its neighbors form the hub of a vast intermontane transportation system stretching from the Rockies to the Sierra Nevada range.

For members of the Church of Jesus Christ of Latter-day Saints—or Mormons—Utah represented a land of religious freedom. The church, founded in New York State in 1830, was persecuted by local religious and legal authorities from Ohio to Illinois and Missouri. Finally driven farther west, the Mormons found biblical parallels between Utah's deserts and salt flats and the land promised to God's Chosen People. They settled in the Great Salt Lake Valley, building a city in the desert. Salt Lake City, in turn, became the center from which Mormons set out to settle other areas in the Southwest. The Mormons are still Utah's largest religious group, and their presence is expressed in the state's social life, including its high marriage and birth rates, and in the spaciously platted towns throughout the region.

Though semiarid, Utah has been blessed with valuable natural resources. It is a leading producer of copper and petroleum, and gold, silver, lead, molybdenum, magnesium, uranium, coal, and salt contribute to the state's economy as well. Utah's natural scenic beauty, its unusual landforms, and its magnificent resort areas draw tourists in increasing numbers, many lured by the challenge of downhill skiing on Utah's steep slopes.

Today, far from being simply a pathway to the West, Utah is a regional center for trade, industry, and commerce. As both a westward route and a destination promising freedom and opportunity, Utah has always played an important role in American life.

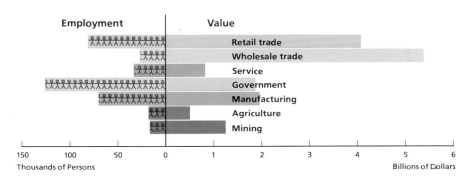

Economic Activities   Utah's resources have been forged into a stable, mixed economy. The interdependence of economic sectors was particularly evident during World War II, when an increased need for products caused the development of many new industries in the state. Today, Utah's products range from steel to advanced electronic systems.

Demographics   A large percentage of Utah's population consists of members of the Church of Jesus Christ of Latter-day Saints, and the importance of children and family in Mormon life is reflected in the state's demographics. Utah is characterized by a higher-than-average birth rate, which in turn contributes to a high population growth rate and a lower-than-average median age. These characteristics affect the state's economy as well as its demographics. Because of a relatively large, young labor force, the state is attractive to businesses, and the growing population creates a market for consumer goods.

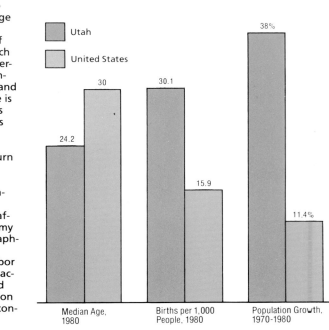

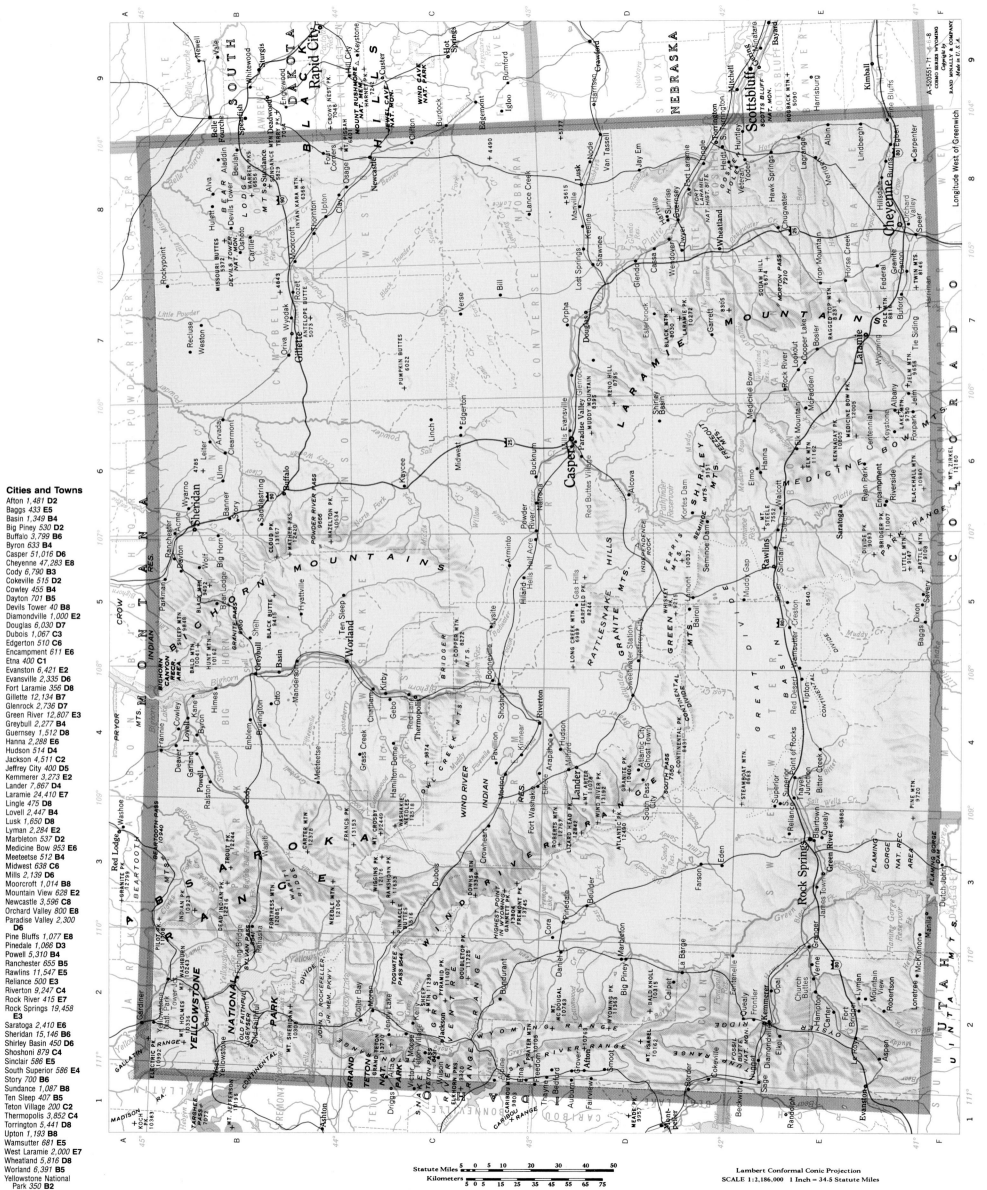

Cities and Towns

Afton 1,481 D2
Baggs 433 E5
Basin 1,349 B4
Big Piney 530 D2
Buffalo 3,799 B6
Byron 633 B4
Casper 51,016 D6
Cheyenne 47,283 E8
Cody 6,790 B3
Cokeville 515 D2
Cowley 455 B4
Dayton 701 B5
Devils Tower 40 B8
Diamondville 1,000 E2
Douglas 6,030 D7
Dubois 1,067 C3
Edgerton 510 C6
Encampment 611 E6
Etna 400 C1
Evanston 6,421 E2
Evansville 2,335 D6
Fort Laramie 356 D8
Gillette 12,134 B7
Glenrock 2,736 D7
Green River 12,807 E3
Greybull 2,277 B4
Guernsey 1,512 D8
Hanna 2,288 E6
Hudson 514 D4
Jackson 4,511 C2
Jeffrey City 400 D5
Kemmerer 3,273 E2
Lander 7,867 D4
Laramie 24,410 E7
Lingle 475 D8
Lovell 2,447 B4
Lusk 1,650 D8
Lyman 2,284 E2
Marbleton 537 D2
Medicine Bow 953 E6
Meeteetse 512 B4
Midwest 638 C6
Mills 2,139 D6
Moorcroft 1,014 B8
Mountain View 628 E2
Newcastle 3,596 C8
Orchard Valley 800 E8
Paradise Valley 2,300
  D6
Pine Bluffs 1,077 E8
Pinedale 1,066 D3
Powell 5,310 B4
Ranchester 655 B5
Rawlins 11,547 E5
Reliance 500 E3
Riverton 9,247 C4
Rock River 415 E7
Rock Springs 19,458
  E3
Saratoga 2,410 E6
Sheridan 15,146 B6
Shirley Basin 500 D6
Shoshoni 879 C4
Sinclair 586 E5
South Superior 586 E4
Story 700 B6
Sundance 1,087 B8
Ten Sleep 407 B5
Teton Village 200 C2
Thermopolis 3,852 C4
Torrington 5,441 D8
Upton 1,193 B8
Wamsutter 681 E5
West Laramie 2,000 E7
Wheatland 5,816 D8
Worland 6,391 B5
Yellowstone National
  Park 350 B2

Statute Miles 5 0 5 10   20   30   40   50
Kilometers 5 0 5 15   25   35   45   65   75

Lambert Conformal Conic Projection
SCALE 1:2,186,000   1 Inch = 34.5 Statute Miles

Wyoming

POPULATION 469,557.
Rank: 49. *Density:* 4.8 people/mi²
(1.9 people/km²). *Urban:* 62.7%.
Rural: 37.3%.
AGE *<20:* 35%. *20–40:* 36%.
40–65: 21%. *>65:* 8%.
ETHNIC GROUPS *White:* 95.1%.
Black: 0.7%. *Spanish origin:*
5.2%. *Native American:* 1.5%.
Other: 2.7%.

INCOME/CAPITA $10,898. *Rank:* 5.
POLITICS 1948–1980 elections:
President: 2 Dem., 7 Rep.
Governor: 3 Dem., 5 Rep.
ENTERED UNION July 10, 1890,
44th state.
CAPITAL Cheyenne, 47,283.
LARGEST CITY Casper, 51,016.

AREA 97,809 mi² (253,324 km²).
Rank: 9. *Water area:* 820 mi²
(2,124 km²).
ELEVATIONS *Highest:* Gannett
Peak, 13,804 ft (4,207 m).
Lowest: Along Belle Fourche
River, 3,100 ft (945 m).
CLIMATE Mostly dry with severe
winters and fairly cool summers.
Light summer rain.

Wyoming is one of the last refuges of the fabled American cowboy. Its dude ranches, rodeos, and ranchers on horseback all recreate the atmosphere of the Old West. In preserving this aspect of Wyoming's culture, the state's topography has played a major role. Wide-open spaces and rugged terrain slowed settlement and development, resulting in a sparsely populated state with few of the problems found in heavily urbanized areas.

Because of its harsh terrain, Wyoming was long a thoroughfare rather than a destination. During the gold rush, thousands of prospectors passed through the state on the Oregon Trail, bound for California. The construction of the Union Pacific Railroad across the state led to permanent settlements along the rail route; and in 1868, the Territory of Wyoming was created. Wyoming quickly acquired its reputation for equality by being first to grant women the right to vote, a reputation reinforced in the 1920's when the state elected the first woman governor.

The land shaped not only Wyoming's settlement patterns but its economy as well. The state is a leading mineral producer, with extensive natural resources, including large deposits of oil, coal, natural gas, iron ore, and uranium. In agriculture, sheep and cattle ranching are major industries. And finally, the unsurpassed beauty of Wyoming's natural landscape supports a large-scale tourist business, with people drawn to the Tetons, Jackson Hole, and Yellowstone National Park, among other attractions.

Energy problems in the United States have recently created a new interest in this resource-rich state, and its abundant mineral deposits foretell the great potential of Wyoming's economy. But profits in the energy business fluctuate widely, dependent upon forces outside the state's control, and an energy-based economy is not always a stable one. In addition, many state residents who take pride in the natural beauty of their land are concerned about the effects of development of these resources. For now, however, Wyoming is likely to remain a preserve of mountains, minerals, cattle, and cowboys.

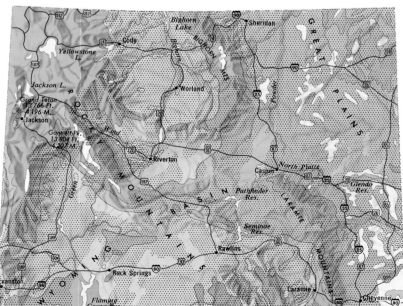

Wyoming's natural environment supports a large variety of animal life, both domesticated and wild. In addition to cattle, grazing horses are a common sight, such as those shown here in Grand Teton National Park. Wild areas provide refuge for large animals such as elk, grizzly and black bears, antelopes, mountain lions, and lynxes plus a wide range of small animals and birds, including bald and golden eagles.

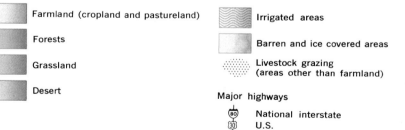

Employment	Value
	Retail trade
	Wholesale trade
	Service
	Government
	Manufacturing
	Agriculture
	Mining

50 40 30 20 10 0   0.5   1.0   1.5   2.0   2.5   3.0
Thousands of Persons   Billions of Dollars

Economic Activities   The importance of Wyoming's abundant mineral resources is reflected in mining's contribution to the state's economy. Manufacturing remains of lesser importance, partially because of distance to markets and sparse population.

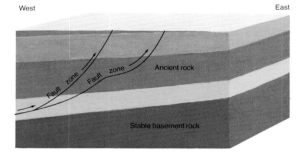

West   East

Thrust Zone Minerals
Wyoming's heritage of mineral riches is the result of millions of years of geologic activity. About 550 to 325 million years ago, massive and gradual earth movements caused rock layers containing the basic elements for oil and gas to move over stable basement rock.

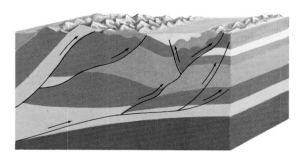

Around 325 to 225 million years ago, pressures inside the earth pushed these rocks together, causing faulting and folding, with rocks thrust over one another to form mountain ranges. As these mountains eroded, more sediments were deposited, containing elements with potential for oil and gas formation.

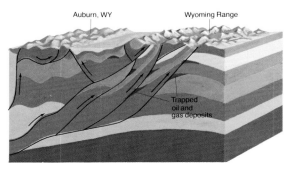

From about 225 million years ago to the present, continued pressure has been converting these basic elements into oil and gas deposits. Today, the nation looks to southwest Wyoming's Thrust Zone to ensure energy supplies for the coming years.

Land Use   Much of Wyoming's land is used for agriculture, mainly sheep and cattle ranching. Modern conservation practices are widely employed, including regulation of irrigation with computers.

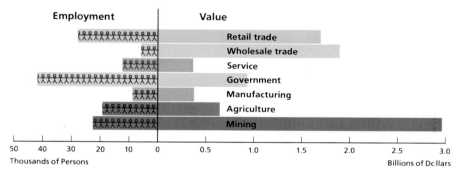

Farmland (cropland and pastureland)

Forests

Grassland

Desert

Irrigated areas

Barren and ice covered areas

Livestock grazing
(areas other than farmland)

Major highways

National interstate
U.S.

SUNSET, TRINIDAD BAY / CALIFORNIA

Pacific America

Living Along the Ring of Fire

BY NEIL MORGAN

I LIVE ALONG THE RING OF FIRE. THIS IS THE folk name for that sensuous and unstable Pacific oval that follows the west coasts of both Americas, then loops across Alaska to Asia and meanders in a southerly direction about the western Pacific. In past eons, its turmoils thrust Hawaii up out of the Pacific. And today its earth faults set off tremors that titillate and terrify. Its volcanoes erupt and propel ash into the skies for thousands of miles, insuring extravagantly hued sunrises and sunsets for months.

All of this I know to be true, for I have seen and felt the furies of the Ring of Fire. But all I see of it from my study window is Devil's Slide, a benign ravine that leads from a residential street in California down to a Pacific surf where round boulders tumble over each other, their clatter reverberating across La Jolla Bay. The bay's surface is a calm and bewitching blue, a tranquil coverlet for a submarine canyon that no man has yet fathomed. We swim and sail over this canyon throughout our temperate seasons in Southern California, and seldom recall that if the Pacific Ocean were drained away, the gash in the earth's surface below us would appear

almost as sheer and deep as that of the Grand Canyon. Yet this is our swimming hole, and the Devil's Slide is an eroded coastal gully. Both are part of one of the most diverse shorelines in the world. Most Americans refer to it casually as the West Coast.

There are close to 5,000 miles of shoreline along our Pacific Coast from San Diego to the Strait of Georgia, where an invisible line in the water separates the United States from Canada. If one counts the shore of every inlet and bay and real and artificial island on this coast, California land meets water along a span of 3,427 miles. From north to south, if you glance across a map of America, you see that California stretches between latitudes comparable to those of Boston and Savannah along the Atlantic Coast.

Above California is the Northwest: Oregon and Washington, with shorelines so storm-battered and often gray that habitation moves inland for shelter, and only small towns of hardy fisherpeople and lumberers inhabit the coasts. Northwesterners' pride in their coastline approaches religious fervor. The people of Oregon exhibited this early: In 1913 they

Alaska
California
Hawaii
Oregon
Washington

reserved the state's shoreline for themselves, and even now they have unrestricted access to all but 23 miles of the bellicose sea along a 341-mile coastline. By contrast, almost two-thirds of the California coast is privately owned.

The Northwest coastline is a bonanza to the casual motorist. Driving between the Golden Gate at San Francisco and the Columbia River, which separates Oregon and Washington, you can see the shoreline in most areas without ever leaving your car. Since most of the Oregon coast is public land, it is a haven for those who hunt driftwood and the glass floats swept up by Pacific currents from the Orient, torn from fishing nets thousands of miles away.

The theme that pervades American history is westering. For many pioneers, the plains of the Heartland held dreams of land and freedom. Fur trappers pushed the frontier farther west, into the Rocky Mountains. But it was finally the land beyond the High Country that stirred passions and set off a massive, ongoing migration of Americans to the West Coast. First gold, then rich farmland, and soon more diverse visions

lured them. The name of California became magic, and within a century after gold was discovered at Sutter's Mill in 1848, the name had come to mean strange and marvelous things to the migrants, and to hundreds of millions who knew this distant coast only from rotogravures or from movie screens.

From the beginning and to each surprising new day, the allure of the Pacific Coast has been closely related to land, sea, and climate.

The wealth yielded in gold by California's Mother Lode was dwarfed by the fortunes of those whose farms fed the gold hunters. Vast valleys and hillsides of tall grass brought smart cattlemen west. With intricate irrigation on a scale unmatched since the Roman aqueduct, desert became farmland. Rivers were diverted. The indomitable Colorado River, drained and dammed and pumped over desert mountains, became the lifeline that transformed arid Southern California into tomorrowland.

Offshore fisheries from San Diego to Puget Sound lured migrants from the Old World: Portugal, Italy, Scandinavia. Verdant forests were cut to build cities and corporate em-

Overleaf– LA JOLLA COASTLINE / CALIFORNIA

pires, and yet enough trees still remain sheltered in state and national parks to provide wilderness sanctuary and an eternal magnet for tourists. The massive sequoia of the Sierra Nevada and the towering redwood of the foggy coastline are as exotic to most visitors as the palm trees of Hollywood. Striking, too, are those unlikely Southern California neighbors Mount Whitney, 14,495 feet high, and Death Valley, 282 feet below sea level, the highest and lowest points of the contiguous United States.

Even Hollywood owes it presence to sunshine and climate and the exotic locales that lured early moviemakers from studios in New York and Chicago to form the basis of an entertainment industry that shapes social mores and tastes around the world. It was the benign climate that brought the aircraft industry to the Pacific Coast. No single more specific example can be found than the move in 1934, by special trains, of a Buffalo, New York, company that was testing a new navy seaplane, and escaped Buffalo's ice for the open waters of San Diego Harbor to become the Convair division of General Dynamics.

While California grew to become the nation's most populous state, and Oregon and Washington swelled at a more sedate pace, enough wide-open spaces remained to hold appeal for the pioneers of the space age. It was to the dry lake beds of the high California desert that America's first space shuttle, *Columbia*, made its dramatic homecomings. There are still parts of California and the Northwest where you may drive for an hour or two without seeing a sign of human presence.

It is water, more than history or ethnology, that divides and causes friction between the people of Southern California and those in the north. In desert Southern California, about four of every five residents live within 40 miles of the sea; rainfall averages about 10 inches a year, almost all in winter. The north is rich in rainfall and free-flowing rivers. But the diversion of water by aqueduct and pipeline to the politically stronger south has polarized California. Range wars of bygone years pall beside the water wars of the more recent past, now most often fought out at election polls, in legislative halls, and in the courts. There are attorneys who have specialized solely in water rights along the Colorado River. Some judges have spent much of their careers hearing such lawyers invoke statutes unknown in other parts of the country.

Yet it is toward the shoreline and horizon that the people of the Pacific Coast face. This coast is the western climax of America; inland farming valleys and cattle ranges provide substance. Tall mountains and their parks—Yosemite is a star among them—provide sanctuary. Along the sea, currents that begin off Japan and New Zealand gnaw away at the jagged, outthrust arc of the Pacific Coast, throwing sand beachward in summer and eroding it with winter tides.

Probing the seas along this coast, early European mariners made their way warily northward; the first settlement was established above San Diego Harbor in 1769 after an overland trek by Spaniards from Mexico. More northerly seas forced back many explorers. Captains of Spanish galleons loaded with Philippine booty learned to follow trade winds across the Pacific to Cape Mendocino, at the apogee of Cali-

SEASTACKS, CANNON BEACH / OREGON

fornia's littoral, and then to coast south to Acapulco. Others' logs tell repeatedly of turning back southward in the face of heavy seas, fogs, and winds. But in 1792 Capt. Robert Gray, out of Boston, brought his brig *Columbia* in over a foaming bar and entered the glorious river he named the Columbia.

For decades thereafter, the land surrounding the river Gray discovered was known as the Oregon Country, and it was not annexed by the United States until 1846. Opposite the site that is now Portland, the Hudson's Bay Company set up its Oregon Country headquarters in 1824. Soon came Yankee fur traders, fish packers, farmers, and missionaries, moving northward into today's Washington. The transcontinental migrations of 1843 and 1845 were climactic for their era: They brought about 4,000 land-hungry settlers across the Oregon Trail.

From Devil's Slide outside my window I stare across the bay at sandstone cliffs which, in late light, take on the profiles of presidents. It is a foretaste of the long Pacific Coast shoreline: a high coastal littoral interrupted by wide beaches and valleys where dammed rivers once flowed. From San Diego northward to Los Angeles, the shoreline is built up almost solidly except for a 17-mile strip, part of Camp Pendleton Marine Corps Base. Newport Harbor, close by Disneyland in Orange County, is one of the great boating meccas of the southland, and then come the clutters of the industrial harbors of Long Beach and Los Angeles. Freeways and cities overwhelm this coast, and jets take off from Los Angeles International Airport over a denuded shoreline. Yet one evening not long ago a friend spoke wistfully of her childhood on a family ranch, part of an old Mexican land grant beside the sea. It took only a little probing to learn that it was Rancho Sausal Redondo, which became the city of Inglewood and Los Angeles Airport, itself a daytime community of more than 30,000. As the history of the land goes, such change in Southern California seems instantaneous.

Beside the urban sea of Los Angeles the dry and mostly barren Channel Islands begin to loom offshore. North of Santa Barbara the coast grows more pastoral. A long and lonely seafront has been sold in 100-acre parcels for gentleman farmers, with the seashore held in common. Nearby, one Sunday, in a century-old adobe house on another old ranch grant from the Mexican era, I visited Vicente Ortega, his white hair slicked back and his blue bandana knotted at his throat. He was lean and taut, but almost as old as the house. He had been a cowboy all his life here at the ranch called Arroyo Hondo.

"I used to come to this house to see my grandmother," he said. "I remember the Indian who helped my grandfather make this house. My aunt lived up the canyon near the pepper tree. That old olive tree up there, I had to water that when I was a kid. In those days there was land enough for everybody."

A few miles north, at Gaviota Pass, the coastal highway tunnels beneath cliffs that rise from the sea and eventually become the Tehachapi Range, transverse mountains that cross most of the state and mark the northern boundary of South-

Left– PROXY FALLS, CASCADE RANGE / OREGON

Right– SURGE AND FLOW, CARMEL COAST / CALIFORNIA

Below– SHROUDED GIANTS, SEQUOIA NATIONAL PARK / CALIFORNIA

Right– FAN PALM, NEAR SANTA BARBARA / CALIFORNIA

ern California. As one nears Point Conception, a central California landmark for sailors and seamen, the coast turns to run nearly due east and west. It becomes rolling range country, studded with live oaks, paralleling the inland Great Central Valley that is the agricultural heartland of California. Much of the destiny of this coast has been shaped in the valley, which extends more than 400 miles up and down the length of California, from 30 to 60 miles wide between coastal mountains and Sierra Nevada foothills. From Red Bluff at the north, the horizon southward is broken only once, by the Sutter Buttes, volcanic remains that rise 650 feet above flat, monotonous fields criss-crossed by irrigation canals.

About $14 billion in annual agricultural production comes from California, typically from 6,000-acre ranches hiring seasonal labor and using mechanical pickers. About one-third of America's canned and frozen vegetables and fruits come from this valley, including almost all of the commercial supply of pears, plums, prunes, grapes, and apricots. Most of the asparagus, broccoli, carrots, lettuce, and celery consumed in America is grown here. The bulk of the nation's figs, nectarines, olives, almonds, artichokes, dates, lemons, and walnuts come from here. The state ranks first in production of tomatoes, strawberries, beet sugar, beef cattle, turkeys, and second in cotton. Its wine industry is America's largest.

West of the coastal mountains, the monotony of the valley is contrasted by converging ocean tides that make central California waters nightmarish for small-craft sailors. At Big Sur, where the Santa Lucia range soars from the sea with ethereal abruptness, two-lane California Highway 1 winds 800 feet above the surf. The desert of Southern California is forgotten, and the coast becomes windblown and chilly. Cypress and pine cling in rocky crevices against the shear of wind along the Monterey Peninsula. It is 22 miles across

Monterey Bay, the setting of some of John Steinbeck's best writing. Past flat acres of artichoke fields, thriving in fog, one pushes northward toward Half Moon Bay. Soon the arches of the Golden Gate Bridge come into view.

To me there is no more stunning cleavage in nature than the Golden Gate of San Francisco Bay. Its visual drama is classic. Beyond that, it is the point of separation, geographically, botanically, and socially, between the California of legend, both past and present, and a pastoral northern coast that bears more kinship to the highland shores of Scotland and Wales. North from the Golden Gate the coast presents a thousand miles of rugged beauty along which one finds no cities. For almost 400 miles the largest town is Eureka, with about 30,000 people. The Pacific reaches full frenzy. At Duncan's Point, behind a barbed wire fence, a sign warns that 21 persons have been swept off the rocks to their deaths, each underestimating the reach of the waves breaking far below. (One learns to believe. To the north at Trinidad Head Light, Coast Guard annals report a wave in 1913 that "struck the bluff and shot over the level of the lantern." The light, then as now, is 196 feet above the sea.) But along Highway 1, the driver braves the headlands of the coast, crossing countless small streams and rivers jammed with splintered logs. After each, the highway climbs to a high meadow within sight of the sea. Weathered rail fences run beside the road, and firs and redwoods begin to appear. Lumber mills mix the scent of burning chips with smells of the sea. Among the ferns in spring the calla lily and iris thrive.

The San Andreas Fault, which slashes across California and which caused the San Francisco earthquake of 1906, can be traced easily by its seams and scarps as it moves over coastal mountains and then along the coast past Drake's Bay, where the British explorer Sir Francis Drake careened his *Golden Hind* in 1579, to brace it to carry on its load of silver booty from the Philippines. The San Andreas is a chilling reminder of the Ring of Fire. It passes hard by Fort Ross, where between 1812 and 1841 Russian sea otter hunters established the only Russian intrusion along this Pacific Coast. At Alder Creek, north of Point Arena, the fissure leaves the land and disappears in the floor of the Pacific. The seismic energy of the Ring of Fire, which geologists call the circum-Pacific seismic belt, is at its most visible in this vicinity. Point Reyes National Seashore moves northward about two inches a year while the mainland three miles across Tomales Bay is stationary. Some plant and animal species cannot endure even so slight a shift and are unable to survive on opposite sides of the bay. Lands on the west side of the San Andreas Fault strain to the northwest. In the past 15 million years, they have journeyed about 200 miles, in sudden and usually short, harmless wrenches.

The relatively gloomy countenance of much of the northern California and Northwest coastline carries with it the tensions of excitement and the enticement of danger. Some of the darkness comes from the lofty umbrellas of redwood trees. Majestic groves of them once graced slopes in a 20-mile-wide belt for more than 400 miles along the coasts of California and Oregon, reaching as far south as the Monterey Peninsula and Big Sur. Relatively few remain except in parklands, most of them concentrated in California's far northwest. Outside the parks one comes across lumber mills, fishing harbors, and steep coastal mountains. Wild rivers named Elk and Eel and Mad tumble down to the sea, leaving records of flood-level violence in their plains.

The world's tallest known tree is a 367-foot redwood near the harbor town of Eureka. Redwood National Park, of which it is a part, is a narrow preserve that is sometimes less than a mile wide and never more than seven miles from east to west. It straddles the coastal highway between Orick and Crescent City, halfway between San Francisco and Portland. The coastal redwood, *Sequoia sempervirens,* often grows from 200 feet to 300 feet in height. Its tapering trunk is bare of branches far above the ground; then its foliage explodes, feathery and delicate. It thrives in the coastal fogs so common to this region, in about 50,000 acres of state and national parks that span more than a 100-mile length of this coast.

Off to the west of the Humboldt redwood groves is a rugged promontory where, for more than 50 miles, there is no coastal highway; for decades it was referred to as California's Unknown Coast. In its midst the King Range rises a sheer 4,000 feet from the sea, a crossroads called Honeydew nestled in its lee. Nothing much is there but a country store and a tiny post office—and a rain gauge that has given Honeydew its sole distinction in the record books. One day Leonard Meland sat on the post office bench and told me of Honeydew's fame:

"For 29 years my wife Marie and I ran the store and post office. Part of my job was to measure the rainfall for the state of California. We had 178 inches one year. It never quit raining for 32 straight days. In one month alone in 1973 we had 46 inches. It can rain up to six inches a night."

Spreading his rain charts on his knee, he pointed up toward the wall of the King Range.

"Clouds come in off the Pacific and ride up and over the King like a roller coaster, and dump on Honeydew. That's how come we set rain records."

His little lesson is one that applies to much of Pacific America, where the weather comes from the ocean, borne inland by prevailing winds. Coastal mountains that extend along most of western America trap the moisture of the winds and dump it as rain at Honeydew, or as snow in the Sierra Nevada, or as the stuff of rain forests in the lee of the Olympic Mountain range in Washington's national parkland. This pattern also holds in Alaska, where high, steep snows are impacted to ice and begin their slow downward journey as glaciers. The same law prevails in the mountainous islands of Hawaii, where every visitor sees the contrasts of the lush windward sides of islands and the drier lee sides.

In the northwest corner of California, Crescent City is a town with an unlikely harbor. Its jetty is topped with 25-ton concrete tetrapods, like tumbled jacks. They were placed there soon after seismic sea waves, triggered by an earthquake at Anchorage, Alaska, a day earlier, flooded the town on March 28, 1964. (One of the heaviest of modern times, the earthquake destroyed parts of Anchorage; tsunami waves that followed it wiped out Valdez; the waves that struck little Crescent City moved with deadly aim, like rifle shots across

LIVE OAKS, SANTA YNEZ VALLEY / CALIFORNIA

the Pacific.) The fourth and worst of the waves that battered Crescent City during that night rolled over the town at a height of 21 feet and left 11 persons dead. The people of Crescent City can be forgiven for feeling put upon by nature: The waves traveled more than 1,700 miles from the Alaskan shore, and damage on the West Coast was confined to Crescent City.

Aboard a Coast Guard cutter one stormy December day I rode out of this harbor to the site of the worst maritime disaster in California history, the wreck of the side-wheel steamer *Brother Jonathan* in 1865. More than 200 people drowned when it grounded on St. George Reef, nine miles off Crescent City. Through dense fog around the reef I saw the looming bulk of a lighthouse like a gray castle. It was built in 1891; now, after claiming the lives of several of the Coast Guardsmen who manned it, it is automated.

Once the Oregon coastland was carpeted with forest almost 50 miles inland from the surfline. Douglas firs still persevere in awesome stands, their dark green fingering down into farmland and orchard. Oregon's Klamath Mountains follow an irregular angle to close off the top of the long parallel of California's coastal mountain ranges and the 450-mile Sierra Nevada, separated by the great trough of the agricultural Central Valley. As in California, quiet riches lie inland in the Northwest. Oregon breaks away from California along the 42nd parallel, where Spanish rule once gave way to British influence. Over the Oregon Trail came farmers and merchants who stood aloof from the California gold rush, and their towns and farms perpetuate the contrast. Many who settled Oregon came from New England, built church spires and trim white farmhouses, and gave settlements transplanted names like Portland, Salem, and Albany. Portland in Oregon and Seattle in Washington are the two large cities of the Northwest. Eastward across the wooded mountains from the sea rainfall diminishes, ranches swell in size, and sparseness rules. Eastern Oregon is one of the most rural sectors remaining in Pacific Coast states. Cattle graze in eastern Oregon and Washington, and wheat fields roll off to the horizon in postscript to the Midwest.

For a time the state of Washington seemed almost colonial, ruled from Seattle near the coast. Spokane has emerged as a strong farm center in the east, but rain is sparse at Spokane, and rain at Seattle is legend. Between Spokane and Seattle lies the Grand Coulee Dam, which gave birth to the aluminum industry of the Northwest in World War II and later facilitated the construction of the Atomic Energy Commission plutonium plant at Hanford.

Left– SAN JACINTO PEAK FROM SANTA ROSA MOUNTAINS / CALIFORNIA

Below– DUMONT DUNES, MOJAVE DESERT / CALIFORNIA

RAIN FOREST, ECOLA STATE PARK / OREGON

Up the center of Oregon and Washington marches the Cascade Range; rich valleys lie between it and the wind-blown coast. The best known of them is the broad Willamette Valley, the historic center of Oregon settlement and the site of Portland. Down to the coast through the Klamath Mountains flows the Rogue River, known and loved wherever steelhead and salmon fishermen are found. Coos Bay interrupts the sparseness of the southern Oregon coast to provide the world's largest lumber shipping port. Dunes soar to 200 feet halfway up the Oregon coast; state parks dot the shore, and sea lions lounge on offshore rocks. North of Tillamook, a coastal town famed for its cheese, is Seaside, where a monument marks the end of the trail for the Lewis and Clark Expedition of 1805, which had followed the mighty Columbia River to its mouth and opened it as a trade artery for the Pacific Northwest. The meandering delta of the Columbia is best seen from Astoria, where the 125-foot-tall Astor Column on Coxcomb Hill memorializes John Jacob Astor, who set up a fur trading station here in 1811.

Nowhere else along the Pacific Coast is there the insistent botanical lushness that is found along much of the Washington coast. From it one looks up to the distant Cascades, which separate the coastal area from the arid east. The tallest of the Cascades is Mount Rainier, 14,410 feet high. But the peak that most quickly reminds us of the Ring of Fire is Mount St. Helens, whose spectacular volcanic eruption on the morning of May 18, 1980, blew away almost a cubic mile of its summit and lowered its elevation from 9,677 feet to 8,364 feet. Continuing eruptions have left a familiar conundrum in this seismic ring: Will it continue to blow itself apart, or rebuild and surpass its former majesty?

Tucked cozily into the protected reaches of Puget Sound, Seattle is the center of Pacific America's forest and fishing industries. The Sound itself is a coastal marvel, part of a 200-mile extension of the Pacific that begins as the Strait of Juan de Fuca, along the Canadian border. This sea arm turns southward and becomes Puget Sound. Like Portland, Seattle is a seaport far from the sea. To its west, oceanward, rise the jagged peaks of one of the densest wildernesses on the American continent: the Olympic Peninsula, where rainfall reaches 135 inches a year. At the northern tip of the Olympic Peninsula one discovers a network of ferries that ply this island wonderland, some of them serving on Alaskan runs.

For many, the San Juan Islands are sacred in their beauty. There are 172 of them, lying between the United States and Canada's British Columbia in the southern end of Georgia Strait and the northern end of Puget Sound. Many of the islands are wooded and hilly. Their sandspits and glacial fjords are preserved by deed restrictions of private owners. Seaplane service is the only link with the outside for many of them. On some islands live families who find no reason to visit the mainland more than once every year or two. Others love these islands so much that they commute to their jobs in more urban areas, and their children use ferries to reach islands with schools.

When Alaska achieved statehood in 1959, the people of Seattle envisioned closer ties and economic boom; the Alaskan gold rush, after all, had been a major factor in building Seattle as a city in the years after 1897. Alaska is more than eight times larger in area than the state of Washington. When it became the 49th state it increased the nation's area by nearly 20 percent. But much of Alaska remains unexplored—and unexploited—because of its difficult climate and terrain and its great distance from the rest of the States. Fewer than half a million people lived in Alaska at the time of the 1980 census, about 40 percent of them in or near Anchorage.

At the extreme northwest of the North American continent, Alaska embraces 586,400 square miles. It faces three seas: the Arctic on the north and northwest, the Bering on the west, and the Pacific on the south. The Ring of Fire slashes across Alaska's south face—one of the most active earthquake belts on earth.

Across the vast, ice-locked North Slope of Alaska, in the Land of Midnight Sun, Eskimos, Indians, and Aleuts share in the Native Claims Settlement Act of 1971, which placed 44 million acres and about $1 billion in trust for native-operated businesses. The North Slope oil field provided royalties that, among other things, erased Alaska's state income tax. About one-quarter of the state was set aside under the Alaska Lands Act in 1980, making a total of about 40 percent of Alaska conserved by state and federal agencies. The Lands Act tripled the United States' wilderness acreage, adding 56 million acres of Alaska land.

The popularity of pleasure cruising has brought many more visitors from the Lower 48 into Alaska's mainland Panhandle than into other areas of the state. The Panhandle includes a narrow, 400-mile-long archipelago that frames the Inside Passage, Alaska's heavily traveled Marine Highway, which snakes through narrow straits where mountain and forest close in from both sides. The closest habitation is sometimes 50 miles distant. Along its route are the capital city of Juneau, huddled like a giant's toe at the foot of precipitous 3,576-foot Mount Juneau; and the Mendenhall Glacier, an awesome prelude to the galaxy of 20 large glaciers within Glacier Bay National Monument. The bay itself is about 50 miles long, and the tongues of its glaciers reach out into the bay. A glacier named for the naturalist John Muir is among the most active. It is nearly two miles wide and has a face about 265 feet high. For those who visit Glacier Bay in summer, there is the memory of sound as well as sight: great hunks of bluish ice cracking off the glaciers and falling, with the reverberations of distant thunder, into the water.

Midway between Anchorage and Fairbanks, Mount McKinley, in Denali National Park, draws relatively heavy visitor traffic. At 20,320 feet, it is the highest peak in North America. Fewer Americans will see Gates of the Arctic National Park along the northern limit of wooded country. And it is a rare visitor who reaches Barrow, the northernmost of Alaska's towns, an Eskimo village with ice caves where Eskimo dances, carving, and blanket tossing are the major attractions. Barrow's brush with history occurred when Will Rogers and Wiley Post died in a plane crash nearby in 1935.

From Nome, an isolated town on Norton Sound in the far west, it is only about 120 miles across the Bering Strait to Siberia. No roads lead to Nome. Everything that does not

Above– CASCADE AT LOW WATER, ROGUE RIVER GORGE / OREGON

Right– PAINTED HILLS, JOHN DAY FOSSIL BEDS NATIONAL MONUMENT / OREGON

come by ship during the brief summer thaw must come by air. Fuel and supply ships unload a mile offshore and barge their cargo in; the sea is only three or four feet deep within a mile of Nome.

One day I flew north across the Arctic Circle from Nome to Kotzebue, an Eskimo town that extends like a fraying shoestring along a thin sandspit in Bering Strait. I wanted to see for myself this land that so few ever visit. Life here is harsh: In winter the trash is stacked out on the frozen sea, and in summer the permafrost melts just enough at the surface to make the land a quagmire. Along the beach in summer, wooden racks are laden with the black flesh of drying *oogruk* (seal) and strips of beluga (white) whale, which the Eskimos prize as food.

Yet not all is chill and harsh in Alaska. The permafrost-free, fertile soil of the Matanuska Valley, north of Anchorage, flourishes with grain, vegetable, and dairy farms, as does the farming area around Fairbanks, in the Tanana Valley. Here the land is still up for grabs. Homesteads of up to 160 acres can be acquired free from the U.S government, under certain conditions. The boom that accompanied the building of the Alaskan oil pipeline in the 1970s proved less than permanent, and vast areas of the state remain frontier.

Hawaii became the 50th of the United States within months after Alaska achieved statehood in 1959. Restless Americans who had westered across a continent now could leap by sea or air 2,397 miles beyond San Francisco and find themselves in a state capital. In land and climate, the two newest states dazzle by their contrasts. The stories of Jack London and the ballads of Robert Service tell of the bawdy Klondike gold diggers in Alaska; their tone is quite different from that of the enchanted Mark Twain, writing of what he called "the loveliest fleet of islands that lies anchored in any ocean."

The story of the creation of Hawaii brings us back to our Ring of Fire. The state is made up of the tops of submerged volcanic mountains; there are eight major islands. From west to east they are Niihau, Kauai, Oahu, Molokai, Lanai, Kahoolawe, Maui, and Hawaii. The volcanic eruptions that formed the islands have ceased on all but Hawaii, the easternmost and largest island. Volcanic activity is not uncommon on the highest Hawaiian mountains, Mauna Kea (13,796 feet above sea level) and Mauna Loa (13,680 feet). The repeated and dramatic eruptions of Kilauea in the winter of 1982-83 caused minimal damage but provided a veranda show for thousands of natives and visitors. It is the closest crater to Volcano House, a snug hostelry that draws thousands of thrillseekers. This island of Hawaii, known colloquially as the Big Island, is a wondrous volcanic triangle that soars out of the Pacific like an angry mastodon. Its old plantation towns, with their wood-frame churches, iron-roofed bungalows, and aging movie houses, seem to cry out of the 1930s. On the slopes of Mauna Kea, the venerable Parker Ranch claims

rank as the largest ranch under single ownership in the nation.

At Naalehu, the southernmost town of the United States, little meets the gaze but frame houses roofed in red iron, a schoolhouse in a playground that rambles to the edge of a sugar cane field, hedges of bougainvillea, a coffee shop and general store, small churches, and a monkey-pod tree that natives say was planted by Mark Twain. But there is a small road south from this southernmost town, and I turned down it one day with a native woman, Aala Akana. We drove through rolling grassland to Ka Lae (South Cape). Its ancient canoe moorings may mark the point where Maoris made first landfall after their heroic outrigger migrations, centuries ago, across 2,400 miles of sea from Tahiti. Shrines and temples of the ancient Hawaiians are being uncovered and restored near here. One built about 500 years ago by the Tahitian priest Paao has been stabilized as part of the Hawaii Volcanoes National Park.

The population of the state approaches one million, and almost seven of eight people live on the capital island of Oahu, where Honolulu and its fabled Waikiki Beach provide sybaritic symbols known around the world. Maui has become a bustling resort center, and so has Kauai, whose Na Pali Coast is one of the most idyllic in the world. It is an isolated 20-mile expanse of sheer drops, ribbon waterfalls, deep valleys, and overhanging cliffs. As with many of these islands' most stunning formations, the view of the land and sea from a helicopter is dazzling. A helicopter pilot once took me to the top of Kauai, not far from the Na Pali Coast. The restless white clouds that wrap mountain peaks here parted just long enough for us to swoop through, ducking around the edge of Waikoko Crater and landing atop 5,120-foot Mount Waialeale, the wettest spot on earth, getting an average of 472 inches of rain a year. Atop lonely Waialeale I saw a padlocked shack that housed the rain gauge. Nothing else. Lichens and stunted plants struggled in the volcanic soil against the wind and the deluge. The mountain is the source of all seven rivers of the island; they flow out to the sea like spokes of a wheel, forming the fertile valleys of the island where sugar cane, pineapple, and rice are grown.

We lifted off through the clouds and skimmed out over the same Pacific Ocean that I see from my study window in California at the foot of Devil's Slide. It surprises Americans of more traditional regions, but even across the great expanses of Pacific America, we feel a sense of neighborhood. Some think we live a bit dangerously along our Ring of Fire, but it is our own, and it is not dull.

STEPHEN HILSON / AlaskaPhoto

NANCY SIMMERMAN / AlaskaPhoto

NANCY SIMMERMAN / AlaskaPhoto

Left Top– SEASCAPE IN BEHM CANAL, NEAR
KETCHIKAN / ALASKA

Left Bottom– BLACK-LEGGED KITTIWAKES, NEAR
WHITTIER / ALASKA

Above– DISENCHANTMENT BAY AND HUBBARD
GLACIER / ALASKA

Above– HAENA POINT, NA PALI COAST, KAUAI / HAWAII

Right– CINDER CONES, HALEAKALA NATIONAL PARK / HAWAII

Maps of Pacific America

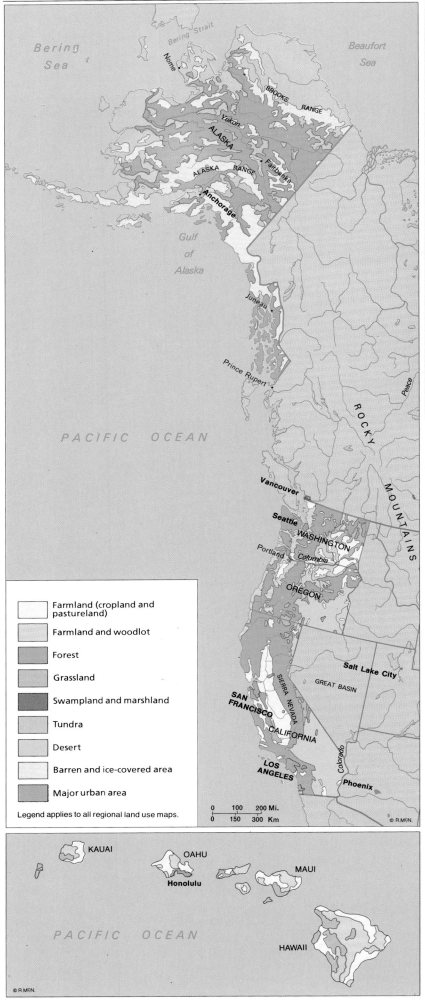

Rising steeply from the Pacific Ocean, Oregon's coast is typical of much of the region. Moisture from the Pacific drops here, promoting growth of the forests and allowing specialized agriculture on the coast's narrow strips of farmland. The irregular coastline adds to the region's beauty and has allowed protected harbor development of some of the country's major port cities.

The shores of the Pacific states are washed by a single ocean, but their regional identity is forged by the energetic outlook they hold in common. Yet these five states are so varied in environment, situation, and population that even this shared outlook is expressed differently by each. In other regions, bonds of environment, history, and resources usually compensate for intraregional differences, but the Pacific states are more difficult to characterize as a single region.

The same forces that act to unify other regions have conspired against the Pacific states; their histories and their resource endowments differ markedly. Alaska, often called the Last Frontier, is one of the final areas of the world to be explored and contains such great mineral wealth that its citizens have been paid dividends derived from taxes imposed upon its mineral industry. On the other hand, Hawaii is known as an island paradise, and the state was an independent non-Western kingdom before Europeans intervened. Today, Hawaii offers resources of a different type than does Alaska: a tropical climate and island beauty. Despite their differences, both Alaska and Hawaii promote themselves with the vigor characteristic of the Pacific region.

In their energetic approach, the Pacific states seem to imitate the geologic nature of their region. Located within the Pacific's Ring of

Land Use The diversity that characterizes the Pacific region can be traced in its land use. The area's widely separated farmlands are found in California's valley; the lowlands of Washington's Puget Sound, Oregon's Willamette Valley, and the states' eastern rolling hills; Alaska's Matanuska Valley; and Hawaii's coastal lowlands. Surrounding these rich regions are forests. The rugged terrain and arctic climate of Alaska are reflected in its barren land and tundra. Major urban areas in each state are principal ports, serving to link the region.

Outlook on the Pacific The Pacific states link America with the countries that rim the Pacific Ocean, and these states and nations have many common traits. They share a volcanic and tectonic history, and these forces continue to shape the physical environment of state and nation alike. Culturally, too, the region is affected by its position; its rich ethnic diversity results partly from exposure to the Asian continent. The Pacific region's role as a link between East and West has given this area a special character, added to by its past and present image as a new frontier.

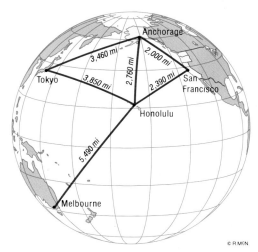

The great port cities of the Pacific region act as gateways to the countries of the Pacific and Asia. They owe their prosperity to protected harbors, a mild climate, access to the productive hinterlands of the western United States, and the industry of their people. San Francisco, shown here, exhibits all these traits, but the buildings spreading over the hills give the city a unique, unforgettable image.

Fire volcanic zone, Hawaii and the mainland Pacific states have all been directly affected by volcanism. Active volcanoes, lava, and ash beds dot the states. Faults in the earth's surface continue to shift, causing earthquakes.

The location of the Pacific states has had other effects on their development. Anglo settlement occurred relatively late in the country's history, and these states generally diversified into modern manufacturing directly from economies based on agriculture and extractive industries. Today, the Pacific states depend on light and high-technology industries, such as aerospace, electronics, and entertainment. Their lack of diversification means that economic downturns affect more of the population here than in the more industrially diversified eastern or midwestern states.

By facing west toward Asia and touching Mexico to the south, the Pacific states also exhibit an ethnic composition very different from their eastern counterparts. Hawaii is unique in that it is a melting pot of Pacific Basin peoples, and the Pacific region contains a significant number of people of Japanese, Chinese, and Hispanic heritage. It is unfortunate, however, that these groups have often had to pay a high price to prosper; discrimination is still a part of life.

In some ways, the country is fortunate that this region lies so far from America's eastern cultural and economic hearth. Not only were Americans inadvertently saving some of their important resources until last, but during the time it took for settlement, the nation was also developing the modern technology needed to effectively employ the Pacific states' resources. Washington and Oregon depend upon huge, sophisticated dams for necessary hydroelectric power and irrigation. Realization of California's extraordinary agricultural, industrial, and urban potential has required the development of one of the largest water-management systems in the world. Construction of the Trans-Alaska Pipeline would have been improbable in an earlier age. And Hawaii's tourist industry hinges upon a volume of air traffic that would have been impossible thirty years ago.

The use of today's technology to solve the demands of the Pacific region's economy has given the area a modern and forward-looking character unknown elsewhere in the country. This region is frequently regarded as the frontier of America's future.

People, Water, and Power   The contiguous Pacific states are characterized by contrasting landscapes. About eighty percent of the population lives in California, while the major water and hydroelectric resources are in Oregon and Washington. Thus, to meet the needs of cities and farms, states must transport water and power great distances. Solving the problems of resource sharing and developing new power sources are important to the future well-being of the region.

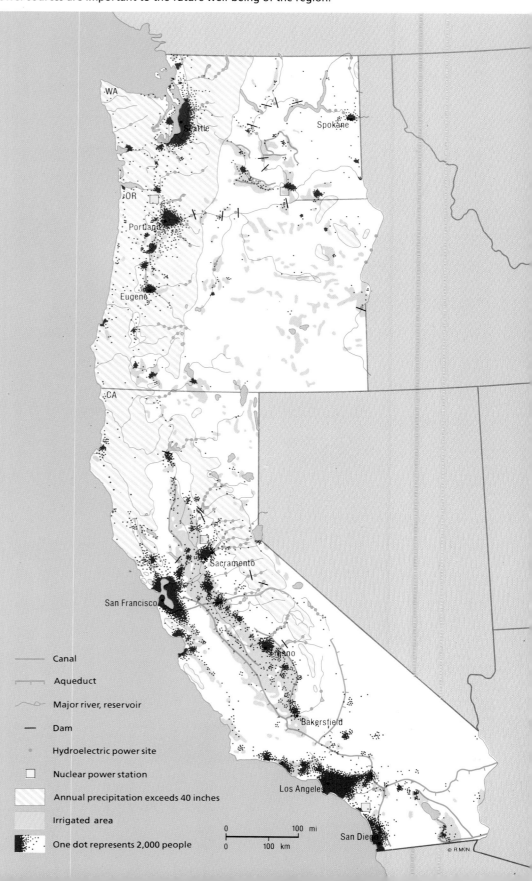

Canal

Aqueduct

Major river, reservoir

Dam

Hydroelectric power site

Nuclear power station

Annual precipitation exceeds 40 inches

Irrigated area

One dot represents 2,000 people

Hispanic Influence   Americans who share the rich heritage of Latin America make up a large proportion of the population in the southwestern United States. The effects of this are evident in the politics, art, architecture, food, music, and language of the area. The cultural diversity of the Pacific states, especially California, has benefited from this growing influence.

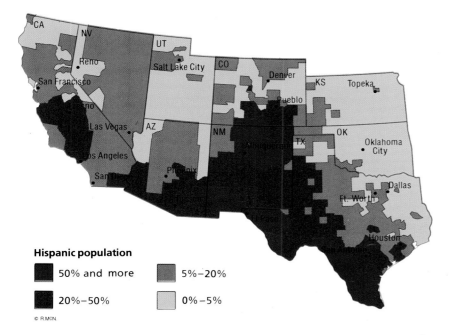

Hispanic population

50% and more

20%–50%

5%–20%

0%–5%

© R.McN

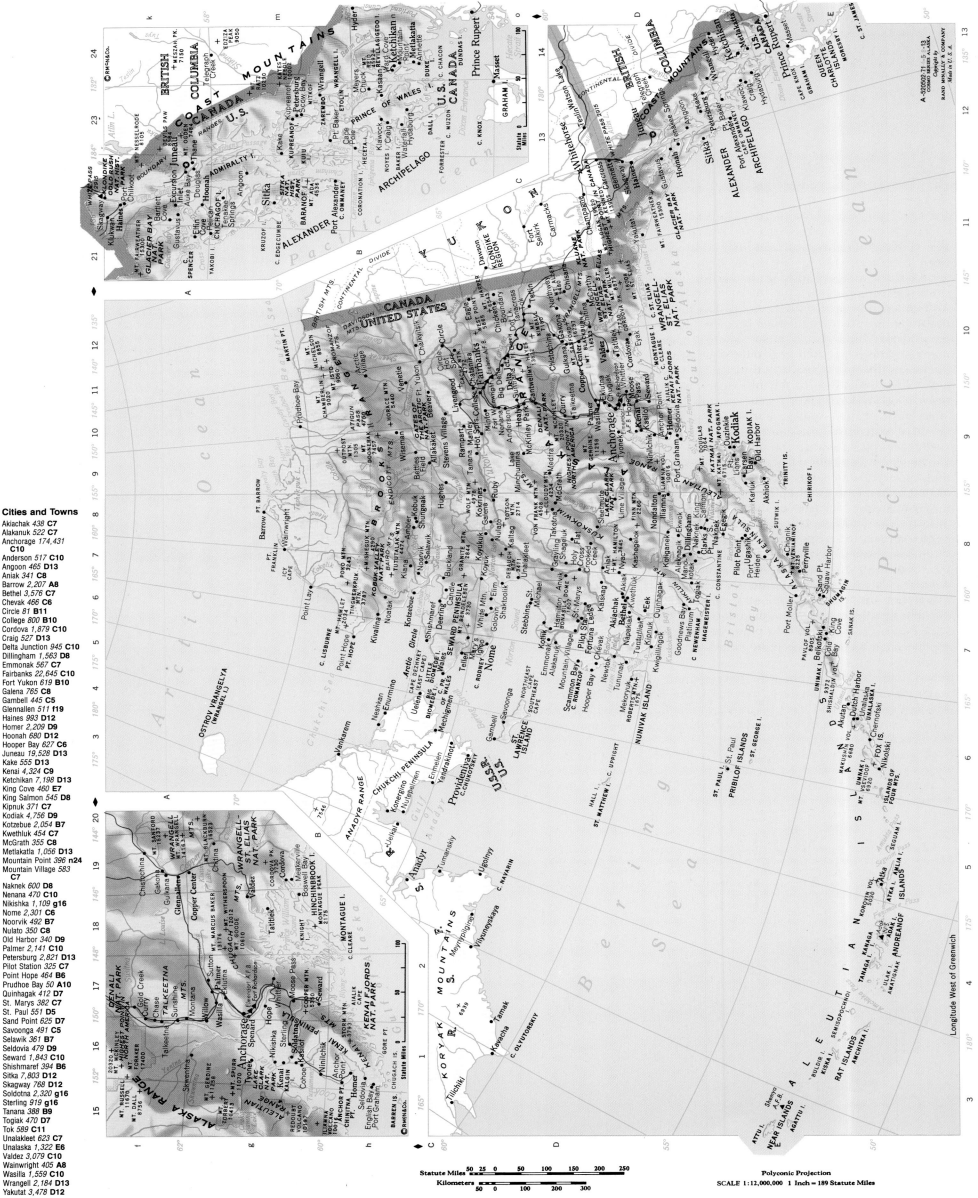

Cities and Towns

Akiachak 438 **C7**
Alakanuk 522 **C7**
Anchorage 174,431 **C10**
Anderson 517 **C10**
Angoon 465 **D13**
Aniak 341 **C8**
Barrow 2,207 **A8**
Bethel 3,576 **C7**
Chevak 466 **C6**
Circle 81 **B11**
College 800 **B10**
Cordova 1,879 **C10**
Craig 527 **D13**
Delta Junction 945 **C10**
Dillingham 1,563 **D8**
Emmonak 567 **C7**
Fairbanks 22,645 **C10**
Fort Yukon 619 **B10**
Galena 765 **C8**
Gambell 445 **C5**
Glennallen 511 **f19**
Haines 993 **D12**
Homer 2,209 **D9**
Hoonah 680 **D12**
Hooper Bay 627 **C6**
Juneau 19,528 **D13**
Kake 555 **D13**
Kenai 4,324 **C9**
Ketchikan 7,198 **D13**
King Cove 460 **E7**
King Salmon 545 **D8**
Kipnuk 371 **C7**
Kodiak 4,756 **D9**
Kotzebue 2,054 **B7**
Kwethluk 454 **C7**
McGrath 355 **C8**
Metlakatla 1,056 **D13**
Mountain Point 396 **n24**
Mountain Village 583 **C7**
Naknek 600 **D8**
Nenana 470 **C10**
Nikishka 1,109 **g16**
Nome 2,301 **C6**
Noorvik 492 **B7**
Nulato 350 **C8**
Old Harbor 340 **D9**
Palmer 2,141 **C10**
Petersburg 2,821 **D13**
Pilot Station 325 **C7**
Point Hope 464 **B6**
Prudhoe Bay 50 **A10**
Quinhagak 412 **D7**
St. Marys 382 **C7**
St. Paul 551 **D5**
Sand Point 625 **D7**
Savoonga 491 **C5**
Selawik 361 **B7**
Seldovia 479 **D9**
Seward 1,843 **C10**
Shishmaref 394 **B6**
Sitka 7,803 **D12**
Skagway 768 **D12**
Soldotna 2,320 **g16**
Sterling 919 **g16**
Tanana 388 **B9**
Togiak 470 **D7**
Tok 589 **C11**
Unalakleet 623 **C7**
Unalaska 1,322 **E6**
Valdez 3,079 **C10**
Wainwright 405 **A8**
Wasilla 1,559 **C10**
Wrangell 2,184 **D13**
Yakutat 3,478 **D12**

Statute Miles 50 25 0 50 100 150 200 250
Kilometers 50 0 100 200 300

Polyconic Projection
SCALE 1:12,000,000 1 Inch = 189 Statute Miles

Alaska

POPULATION 401,851.
  Rank: 50. *Density:* 0.7 people/mi²
  (0.3 people/km²). *Urban:* 64.3%.
  Rural: 35.7%.
AGE *<20:* 36%. *20–40:* 42%.
  40–65: 19%. *>65:* 3%.
ETHNIC GROUPS *White:* 77%.
  Black: 3.4%. *Spanish origin:*
  2.4%. *Native American:* 5.5%.
  Other: 14.1%.

INCOME/CAPITA $12,790. *Rank:* 1.
POLITICS 1960–1980 elections:
  President: 1 Dem., 5 Rep.
  Governor: 3 Dem., 3 Rep.
ENTERED UNION January 3, 1959,
  49th state.
CAPITAL Juneau, 19,528.
LARGEST CITY Anchorage, 174,431.

AREA 591,004 mi² (1,530,694 km²).
  Rank: 1. *Water area:* 20,171 mi²
  (52,243 km²).
ELEVATIONS *Highest:* Mt.
  McKinley, 20,320 ft (6,194 m).
  Lowest: Pacific Ocean shoreline,
  sea level.
CLIMATE Mild with heavy rain on
  panhandle; cold winters, cool
  summers, light rain inland.

Alaska is a land of extremes. It is the largest state, the northern-most, the westernmost, the most sparsely populated, and contains the nation's highest mountain peak. Approximately two miles of the Bering Strait separate Alaska's Little Diomede Island from Big Diomede Island of Russia, the state's former owner. Often called the Last Frontier, Alaska was not explored by white men until the 1700's, over two centuries after Columbus reached the New World.

Alaska is exceptionally rich in natural resources, a situation that often focuses national and international attention on the state's unique character and problems. The true extent of its natural wealth is not yet fully known. Timber is abundant, its fisheries are among the richest in the world, it possesses vast coal deposits and enormous hydroelectric power, and large oil and gas reserves have been discovered along the North Slope, in the Arctic coastal zone.

Many of Alaska's inhabitants have migrated from other states, drawn by the breathtaking beauty of its wilderness and the job opportunities created by its bountiful resources. But just as Native Americans in other states have valid claims to the land that once was theirs, so do the Eskimos and other Native Americans in Alaska. The state's native population has pressed for its right to traditional lands and resources with some success, as evidenced by the Alaska Native Claims Settlement Act of 1971.

Against the backdrop of its natural riches are the problems of Alaska's size and remoteness. Improved railways, roads, and coastal shipping and air transport routes have reduced the isolation that has often hampered development. But Alaska continues to challenge the efforts of its people to open its wilderness without destroying the delicate balance of its environment. The ways in which resources are discovered and used may well serve as a model for the development of other unspoiled regions of the nation and the world. Perhaps the Last Frontier will manage to preserve its wilderness beauty while becoming part of the modern industrialized world.

One of Alaska's oldest cities, Sitka gained early recognition as Russia's chief North American settlement and trade center. Its importance continued after the land changed ownership; under the American government, the city served as the capital of the territory until the early 1900's. Today, with access to the Pacific Ocean and the Inside Passage, it is one of the state's major ports—a role of great importance in a state with limited transportation routes. In addition, the city's fishing, canning, lumber, and wood-pulp industries contribute to the state's economy.

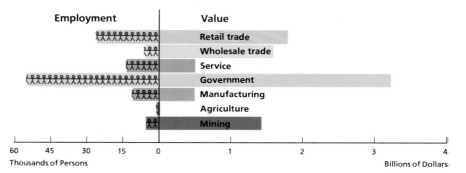

Economic Activities   Because of Alaska's large share of federally owned land, the state's economy depends greatly upon government commitment, in addition to productive mining, timber, fishing, and petroleum industries.

Land Use   Despite the great variety and wealth of Alaska's land, the state is not self-sufficient. Demanding climatic conditions, insufficient cropland, rugged terrain, and high costs of labor and supplies cause Alaska to specialize in resource extraction almost exclusively.

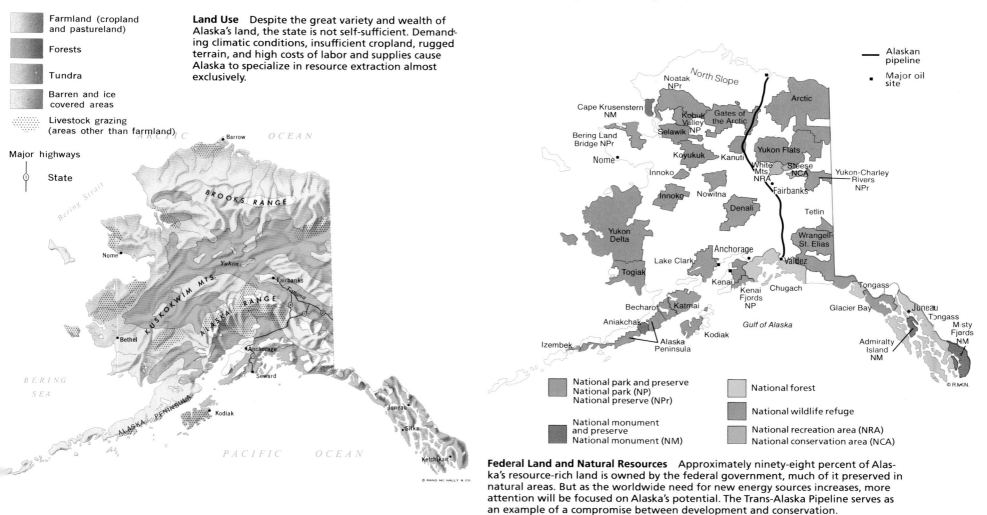

Federal Land and Natural Resources   Approximately ninety-eight percent of Alaska's resource-rich land is owned by the federal government, much of it preserved in natural areas. But as the worldwide need for new energy sources increases, more attention will be focused on Alaska's potential. The Trans-Alaska Pipeline serves as an example of a compromise between development and conservation.

Cities and Towns

Anaheim 219,494 **F5**
Antioch 42,683 **h9**
Bakersfield 105,735 **E4**
Berkeley 103,328 **D2**
Beverly Hills 32,367 **m12**
Burbank 84,625 **E4**
Calexico 14,412 **F6**
Chico 26,603 **C3**
Chula Vista 83,927 **F5**
Concord 103,255 **h8**
Costa Mesa 82,562 **n13**
Davis 36,640 **C3**
East Los Angeles 110,017 **m12**
El Cajon 73,892 **F5**
El Centro 23,996 **F6**
Escondido 64,355 **F5**
Eureka 24,153 **B1**
Fairfield 58,099 **C2**
Fremont 131,945 **D2**
Fresno 217,289 **D4**
Fullerton 102,034 **n13**
Garden Grove 123,307 **n13**
Glendale 139,060 **m12**
Hayward 94,342 **h8**
Huntington Beach 170,505 **F4**
Indio 21,611 **F5**
Lancaster 48,027 **E4**
Lompoc 26,267 **E3**
Long Beach 361,334 **F4**
Los Angeles 2,966,850 **E4**
Marysville 9,898 **C3**
Menlo Park 26,369 **k8**
Merced 36,499 **D3**
Modesto 106,602 **D3**
Monterey 27,558 **D3**
Napa 50,879 **C2**
Newport Beach 62,556 **n13**
Oakland 339,337 **D2**
Oceanside 76,698 **F5**
Ontario 88,820 **E5**
Oxnard 108,195 **E4**
Palm Springs 32,366 **F5**
Palo Alto 55,225 **D2**
Pasadena 118,072 **E4**
Pomona 92,742 **E5**
Redding 41,995 **B2**
Redwood City 54,951 **D2**
Richmond 74,676 **D2**
Riverside 170,591 **F5**
Sacramento 275,741 **C3**
Salinas 80,479 **D3**
San Bernardino 118,794 **E5**
San Clemente 27,325 **F5**
San Diego 875,538 **F5**
San Francisco 678,974 **D2**
San Jose 629,546 **D3**
San Juan Capistrano 18,959 **F5**
San Luis Obispo 34,252 **E3**
Santa Ana 204,023 **F5**
Santa Barbara 74,414 **E4**
Santa Cruz 41,483 **D2**
Santa Maria 39,685 **E3**
Santa Monica 88,314 **m12**
Santa Rosa 83,320 **C2**
South Lake Tahoe 20,681 **C4**
Stockton 149,779 **D3**
Sunnyvale 106,618 **k8**
Torrance 129,881 **n12**
Tulare 22,526 **D4**
Turlock 26,287 **D3**
Vallejo 80,303 **C2**
Ventura 74,393 **E4**
Visalia 49,729 **D4**
Yuba City 18,736 **C3**

Statute Miles

Kilometers

Lambert Conformal Conic Projection
SCALE 1:3,733,000 1 Inch = 59 Statute Miles

A-520505-71 -8 -16
COSMO SERIES CALIFORNIA
Copyright by
RAND MCNALLY & COMPANY
Made in U.S.A.

Longitude West of Greenwich

California

POPULATION 23,667,565.
Rank: 1. Density: 151 people/mi²
(58 people/km²). *Urban: 91.3%.*
Rural: 8.7%.
AGE *<20:* 31%. *20–40:* 34%. *40–65:*
25%. *>65:* 10%.
ETHNIC GROUPS *White:* 76.2%.
Black: 7.7%. *Spanish origin:*
19.2%. *Native American:* 0.8%.
Other: 15.3%.

INCOME/CAPITA $10,938. *Rank:* 3.
POLITICS 1948–1980 elections:
President: 2 Dem., 7 Rep.
Governor: 4 Dem., 4 Rep.
ENTERED UNION September 9, 1850,
31st state.
CAPITAL Sacramento, 275,741.
LARGEST CITY Los Angeles,
2,966,850.

AREA 158,706 mi² (411,047 km²).
Rank: 3. *Water area:* 2,407 mi²
(6,234 km²).
ELEVATIONS *Highest:* Mt. Whitney,
14,494 ft (4,418 m). *Lowest:* Death
Valley, 282 ft (86 m) below sea
level.
CLIMATE Cool, rainless summers,
mild winters on coast. Hot,
rainless summers inland.

From San Jose to Redwood City, high technology has replaced orchards in the area popularly known as Silicon Valley, center of semiconductor research and production. The area received its name from its products: minute silicon chips filled with transistors. Companies developed here because of nearby university research facilities and talent pools. As the technology grows, so does the area, expanding to other states and even countries to make California's influence international. And true to its status as a nation within a nation, California's major competitor in the industry is not another state, but Japan.

California is virtually a nation within a nation. Were it an independent country, its gross economic product would rank among the highest. Its riches lie both in the dramatic extremes of its human and natural resources and in the way these resources are employed to fuel a dynamic economy.

California is a leader in both agriculture and manufacturing. Farmers specialize in those crops best suited to the land and climate, maximizing the benefits of fertile soils and a long growing season. And lacking the resources needed for heavy manufacturing, the state sets standards for the country and the world by concentrating on the expanding high-technology industry. Through its new ideas and movements, California will lead America into the next century.

A key problem in maintaining this preeminence is water. California's agricultural, industrial, and urban growth is supported by the most extensive water-management system ever created. Because of this system, over half the state's population is able to live in the south, which contains only a fraction of the state's water supply. However, the full cost of this water-distribution system is only partially borne by the people who use the water directly, and this has created aggressive competition for water among northern cities, southern cities, agricultural interests, industrialists, and urban dwellers.

Population and economic growth also have exacted high costs. Urban expansion eats into valuable agricultural land. The automobile in the Los Angeles Basin and offshore oil wells in the Santa Barbara Channel threaten air and water quality. These problems, compounded by the high social and spatial mobility of the people, are not always debated in a stable political forum. Perhaps it is well, then, that California's politics so often extend beyond its borders; for as a nation within a nation, its problems and prospects require discussion in a national context.

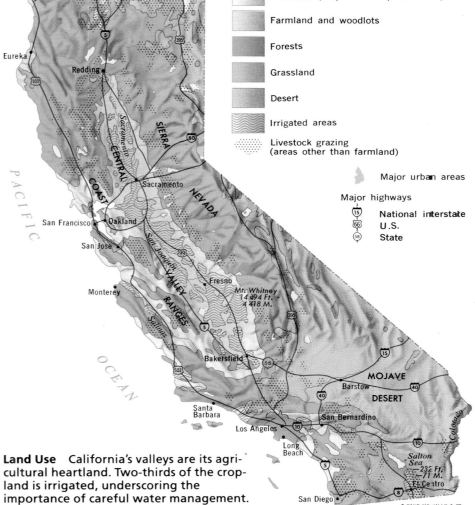

	Farmland (cropland and pastureland)
	Farmland and woodlots
	Forests
	Grassland
	Desert
	Irrigated areas
	Livestock grazing (areas other than farmland)

Major urban areas

Major highways
⑮ National interstate
⑯ U.S.
⑭ State

Land Use   California's valleys are its agricultural heartland. Two-thirds of the cropland is irrigated, underscoring the importance of careful water management.

San Andreas Fault   This fracture zone marks the boundary between two plates of the earth's crust. About twenty million people live over the zone, thus quake prediction is a most important challenge.

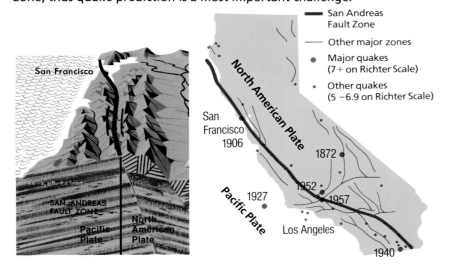

— San Andreas
   Fault Zone
— Other major zones
● Major quakes
   (7+ on Richter Scale)
● Other quakes
   (5 –6.9 on Richter Scale)

Economic Activities   California ranks first in the nation in agriculture and manufacturing. Because of the quantity and variety of goods produced, the state also leads the country in wholesale trade.

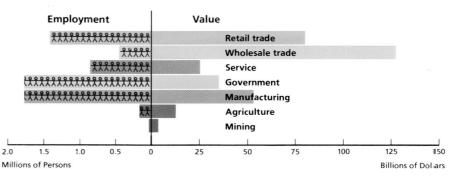

Employment		Value
	Retail trade	
	Wholesale trade	
	Service	
	Government	
	Manufacturing	
	Agriculture	
	Mining	

2.0   1.5   1.0   0.5   0   0   25   50   75   100   150
Millions of Persons   Billions of Dollars

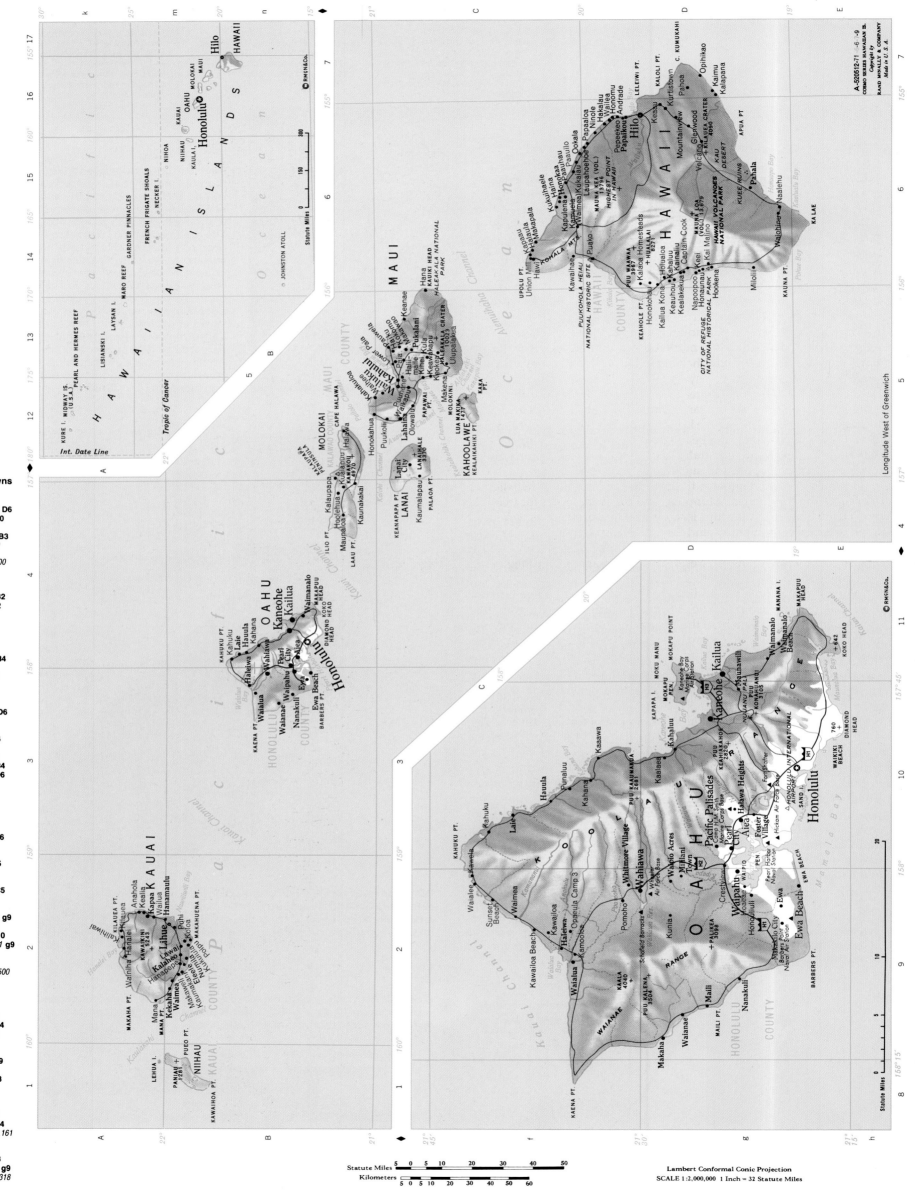

Cities and Towns

Aiea 15,200 **B4**
Anahola 915 **A2**
Captain Cook 2,008 **D6**
Crestview 1,000 **g10**
Ewa 2,637 **B3**
Ewa Beach 14,369 **B3**
Foster Village 3,700 **g10**
Halawa Heights 7,000 **g10**
Haleiwa 2,412 **B3**
Haliimaile 741 **C5**
Hanamaulu 3,227 **B2**
Hanapepe 1,417 **B2**
Hauula 2,997 **B4**
Hawi 795 **C6**
Hilo 35,269 **D6**
Holualoa 1,243 **D6**
Honokaa 1,936 **C6**
Honolulu 365,048 **B4**
Kaaawa 959 **f10**
Kahaluu 2,925 **g10**
Kahuku 935 **B4**
Kahului 12,978 **C5**
Kailua 35,812 **B4**
Kailua Kona 4,751 **D6**
Kalaheo 2,500 **B2**
Kamuela 1,179 **C6**
Kaneohe 29,919 **B4**
Kapaa 4,467 **A2**
Kaumakani 888 **B2**
Kaunakakai 2,231 **B4**
Kealakekua 1,033 **D6**
Kekaha 3,260 **B2**
Keokea 900 **C5**
Kihei 5,644 **C5**
Kilauea 895 **A2**
Koloa 1,457 **B2**
Kula 1,300 **C5**
Kurtistown 1,200 **D6**
Lahaina 6,095 **C5**
Laie 4,643 **B4**
Lanai City 2,092 **C5**
Lawai 950 **B2**
Lihue 4,000 **B2**
Lower Paia 1,500 **C5**
Maili 5,026 **g9**
Makaha 7,905 **g9**
Makakilo City 7,691 **g9**
Makawao 1,066 **C5**
Maunawili 2,200 **g10**
Mililani Town 20,351 **g9**
Naalehu 1,168 **D6**
Nanakuli 8,185 **B3**
Pacific Palisades 9,500 **g10**
Pahala 1,619 **D6**
Pahoa 923 **D7**
Paia 1,000 **C5**
Papaikou 1,567 **D6**
Pearl City 33,000 **B4**
Pepeekeo 1,800 **D6**
Puhi 991 **B2**
Pukalani 3,950 **C5**
Sunset Beach 800 **f9**
Volcano 900 **D6**
Wahiawa 16,911 **B3**
Waialua 4,051 **B3**
Waianae 5,000 **B3**
Wailua 1,587 **A2**
Wailuku 10,260 **C5**
Waimanalo 3,562 **B4**
Waimanalo Beach 4,161 **g11**
Waimea 1,569 **B2**
Waipahu 29,139 **B3**
Waipio Acres 4,091 **g9**
Whitmore Village 2,318 **f9**

Statute Miles 5 0 5 10 20 30 40 50
Kilometers 5 0 5 10 20 30 40 50 60

Lambert Conformal Conic Projection
SCALE 1:2,000,000 1 Inch = 32 Statute Miles

Hawaii

POPULATION 964,691.
  Rank: 39. *Density:* 150 people/
  mi² (58 people/km²). *Urban:*
  86.5%. *Rural:* 13.5%.
AGE *<20:* 33%. *20–40:* 36%.
  40–65: 23%. *>65:* 8%.
ETHNIC GROUPS *White:* 33%.
  Black: 1.8%. *Spanish origin:*
  7.4%. *Native American:* 0.3%.
  Other: 64.9%.

INCOME/CAPITA $10,101. *Rank:* 13.
POLITICS 1960–1980 elections:
  President: 5 Dem., 1 Rep.
  Governor: 5 Dem., 1 Rep.
ENTERED UNION August 21, 1959,
  50th state.
CAPITAL Honolulu, 365,048.
LARGEST CITY Honolulu.

AREA 6,471 mi² (16,760 km²).
  Rank: 47. *Water area:* 46 mi²
  (119 km²).
ELEVATIONS *Highest:* Mauna Kea,
  13,796 ft (4,205 m). *Lowest:*
  Pacific Ocean shoreline, sea level.
CLIMATE Rainfall varies, depending
  on trade winds. Mild
  temperatures.

The islands of Hawaii are more than America's tropical paradise; they serve as the crossroads of the Pacific, a slender bridge connecting East and West. The state's culture, its economy, and even its goals reflect this unique position.

A true melting pot, Hawaii has blended its cultural heritages into a plural society unrivaled in any state. Caucasians, native Hawaiians, Chinese, Japanese, Filipinos, Koreans, and Pacific Islanders live and work together with little of the tension common in states having fewer ethnic and racial groups. This cultural diversity is evident in Hawaii's many educational and scientific institutions that are international in scope and outlook, symbolized by the East-West Center, a federally created and supported research institute in Honolulu.

The state's crossroads position has also helped shape its economy. Hawaii serves as an attractive market for foreign investment, particularly from Japan. Its location has made it a strategic military outpost for America's Pacific defense system; Pearl Harbor, on the island of Oahu, is one of the world's great naval bases. Because of this, government expenditures make a large contribution to Hawaii's economy. Tourism, however, remains the largest source of revenue for the state. Hawaii's climate and natural beauty draw thousands of tourists each year from the mainland, Australia, and Japan. It is also famous for its rich harvest of pineapple and sugarcane.

Hawaii's immediate goal is to draw on the benefits of its position to become the commercial, shipping, and financial center for much of the Pacific. However, Hawaii's location can be a problem as well as an asset: distance from markets and raw materials is a handicap, and the high cost of imported goods may continue to rise. At present, the cost of living in the Honolulu metropolitan area is among the highest in the United States.

While many people are finding that it's expensive to live in paradise, Hawaii remains optimistic about its future—and with good reason. American commitment to the state will continue, and tourism can be expected to grow. As the crossroads of the Pacific, Hawaii offers abundant opportunity and unparalleled natural beauty.

Population   In the late 1700's, in-migrating Europeans brought Western diseases to which the Hawaiians had not yet developed immunities. Increased immunity and preventative medicine eventually helped to stabilize the population. After 1870, numerous ethnic groups were brought in to work on agricultural plantations, and their intermarriage with natives decreased the number of pure Hawaiians.

Hawaii's entry into the United States in 1959 and the start of jet travel in the 1950's helped bring mass tourism to the islands. Since that time Waikiki's extinct volcano, Diamond Head, has had to share the Honolulu skyline with increasing numbers of hotels and condominiums. Recently the state government has tried to help control the effects of Honolulu's rapid growth on the environment.

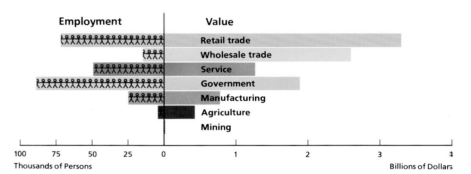

Economic Activities   Tourism and military expenditures are key components of Hawaii's economy. Although their contribution is not charted here directly, it can be seen in the value of the leading sectors of the state's economy: retail and wholesale trade, service industries, and government. Thus, changes in military programs or poor weather and a drop in tourism can have profound effects on Hawaii's economy.

Land Use   Perched on the peaks of mountains that rise from the ocean floor, Hawaii's land lies exposed to the changeable Pacific. In fair weather this makes Hawaii a tropical paradise of lush vegetation, suitable for agriculture and attractive for habitation and tourism. But unfortunately, this location also places Hawaii in the path of typhoons and tidal waves that can bring sudden devastation.

Ethnic groups

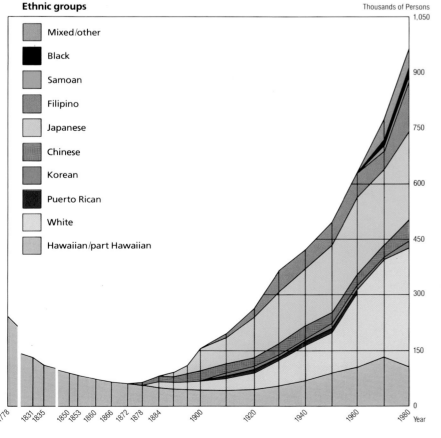

- Mixed/other
- Black
- Samoan
- Filipino
- Japanese
- Chinese
- Korean
- Puerto Rican
- White
- Hawaiian/part Hawaiian

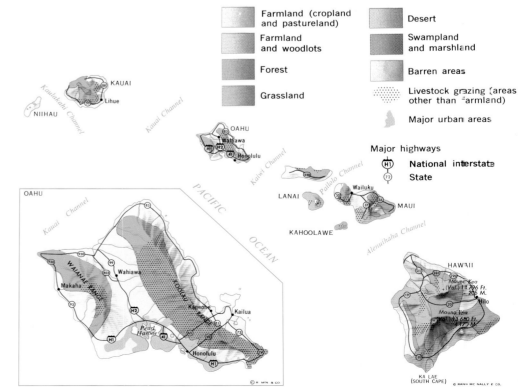

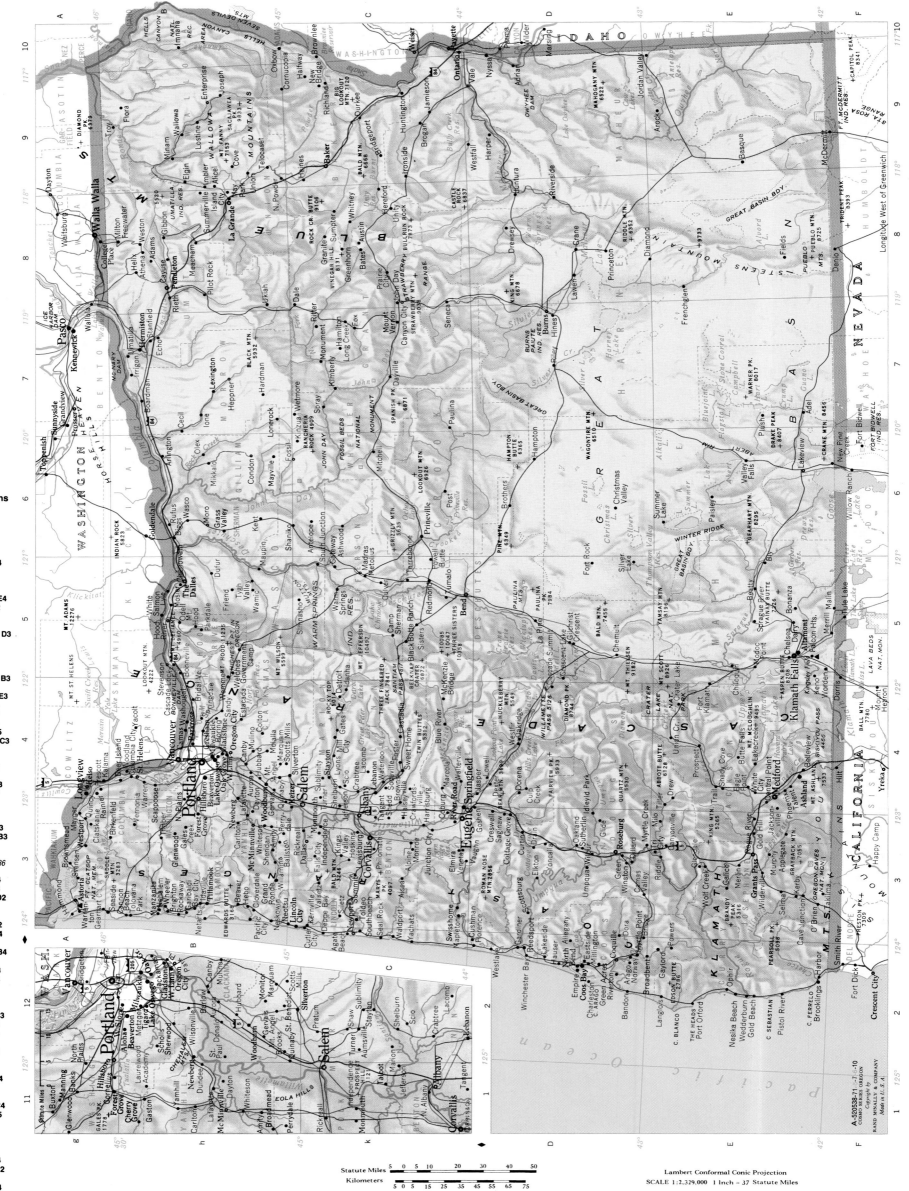

Cities and Towns

Albany 26,678 **C3**
Aloha 10,000 **h12**
Altamont 19,805 **E5**
Ashland 14,943 **E4**
Astoria 9,998 **A3**
Baker 9,471 **C9**
Beaverton 30,582 **B4**
Bend 17,263 **C5**
Burns 3,579 **D7**
Canby 7,659 **B4**
Central Point 6,357 **E4**
Coos Bay 14,424 **D2**
Coquille 4,481 **D2**
Corvallis 40,960 **C3**
Cottage Grove 7,148 **D3**
Crater Lake 25 **E4**
Dallas 8,530 **C3**
Eugene 105,624 **C3**
Florence 4,411 **D2**
Forest Grove 11,499 **B3**
Gladstone 9,500 **B4**
Grants Pass 15,032 **E3**
Gresham 33,005 **B4**
Hermiston 9,408 **B7**
Hillsboro 27,664 **B4**
Hood River 4,329 **B5**
Independence 4,024 **C3**
John Day 2,012 **C8**
Keizer 18,592 **C3**
Klamath Falls 16,661 **E5**
La Grande 11,354 **B8**
Lake Oswego 22,527 **B4**
Lakeview 2,770 **E6**
Lebanon 10,413 **C4**
Lincoln City 5,469 **C3**
McMinnville 14,080 **B3**
Medford 39,603 **E4**
Metzger 5,544 **h12**
Milton-Freewater 5,086 **B8**
Milwaukie 17,931 **B4**
Monmouth 5,594 **C3**
Myrtle Creek 3,365 **D2**
Newberg 10,394 **B4**
Newport 7,519 **C2**
North Bend 9,779 **D2**
Oak Grove 11,640 **B4**
Ontario 8,814 **C10**
Oregon City 14,673 **B4**
Parkrose 21,103 **B4**
Pendleton 14,521 **B8**
Portland 366,383 **B4**
Prineville 5,276 **C6**
Redmond 6,452 **C5**
Reedsport 4,984 **D2**
River Road 10,370 **C3**
Roseburg 16,644 **D3**
St. Helens 7,064 **B4**
Salem 89,233 **C4**
Scappoose 3,213 **B4**
Seaside 5,193 **B3**
Silverton 5,168 **C4**
Springfield 41,621 **C4**
Stayton 4,396 **C4**
Sutherlin 4,560 **D3**
Sweet Home 6,921 **C4**
The Dalles 10,820 **B5**
Tigard 14,286 **h12**
Tillamook 3,981 **B3**
Tri City 3,439 **E3**
Umatilla 3,199 **B7**
West Linn 12,956 **B4**
West Slope 5,364 **g12**
White City 5,445 **E4**
Woodburn 11,196 **B4**

Statute Miles 5 0 5 10 20 30 40 50
Kilometers 5 0 5 15 25 35 45 55 65 75

Lambert Conformal Conic Projection
SCALE 1:2,329,000 1 Inch = 37 Statute Miles

A-520536-71 -7; -10
COSMO SERIES OREGON
RAND MᶜNALLY & COMPANY
Copyright by
RAND MᶜNALLY & COMPANY
Made in U.S.A.

Oregon

POPULATION 2,633,149.
 Rank: 30. *Density:* 27 people/mi²
 (11 people/km²). *Urban:* 67.9%.
 Rural: 32.1%.
AGE *<20:* 31%. *20–40:* 34%.
 40–65: 24%. *>65:* 11%.
ETHNIC GROUPS *White:* 94.6%.
 Black: 1.4%. *Spanish origin:*
 2.5%. *Native American:* 1%.
 Other: 3%.

INCOME/CAPITA $9,317. *Rank:* 26.
POLITICS 1948–1980 elections:
 President: 1 Dem., 8 Rep.
 Governor: 2 Dem., 8 Rep.
ENTERED UNION February 14,
 1859, 33rd state.
CAPITAL Salem, 89,233.
LARGEST CITY Portland, 366,383.

AREA 97,073 mi² (251,417 km²).
 Rank: 10. *Water area:* 889 mi²
 (2,302 km²).
ELEVATIONS *Highest:* Mt. Hood,
 11,235 ft (3,424 m). *Lowest:*
 Pacific Ocean shoreline, sea level.
CLIMATE Cool summers, mild
 winters, heavy rain along coast.
 Hot summers, cold winters in
 drier east.

Within the golden chain of Pacific Coast states, Oregon has a distinctive identity, despite its close connection with its neighbors to the south and north. Although dominated by neither California nor Washington, it is linked to both by environment and occupation.

Oregon, like its northern neighbor, is divided by the Cascades into a humid, fertile west and a semiarid east. The volcanic upheavals that created these majestic peaks thousands of years ago also left large areas of eastern Oregon as a wasteland of volcanic lava beds. The state must look to the Pacific Ocean for the warm, moist air that bathes the western region and to the Columbia River for hydroelectric power, water for irrigation, and access to ocean transport.

Unlike its neighbors, however, Oregon is centered at a single valley—the Willamette. From here the state reaches out to marshall its impressive resources. Timber is prime among them, harvested from the Coastal Ranges, the Cascades, and the Columbia Plateau. Nearly half the state is covered with dense stands of forest, making Oregon a major source of lumber for national and foreign markets. The Willamette Valley farms supply produce, meat, and dairy products to regions up and down the Pacific Coast and send fruit and seed crops to more distant regions. The valley also serves as the center of Oregon's manufacturing and service industries. The hospitable climate and abundant labor supply make the valley an attractive site for high-technology business, particularly with California's vast markets and resources to the south. In eastern Oregon, contributors to the state's income include ranching, grazing, and—where irrigation is possible—several cash crops.

Oregon possesses a well-integrated economy, with an added boost from a strong tourist trade captivated by the state's scenic beauty and resort areas. Its resources and location allow Oregon to take advantage of new trends in the national economy. Because of its assets, Oregon is likely to remain a firm link in the chain of Pacific Coast states.

Clear-cutting is a method of harvesting timber in which intermittent blocks of trees are cut, leaving sunlit areas open to be reseeded by remaining trees. This conservation practice ensures future harvests and Oregon's continuing success in forestry.

Employment   **Value**

| Retail trade |
| Wholesale trade |
| Service |
| Government |
| Manufacturing |
| Agriculture |
| Mining |

250 200 150 100 50   0   5   10   15   20
Thousands of Persons   Billions of Dollars

Land Use   Oregon's lands range from some, on the west coast, that almost appear like rain forests, to others, in the eastern lava beds, that sometimes are compared to the moon's surface. Although these lands to the east and west are put to use for grazing and lumbering, respectively, Oregon's most productive land lies in the Willamette Valley, with its mild climate and fertile alluvial soils.

Economic Activities   Oregon's timber and fruit production has achieved national recognition and foreign customers. Recently, Oregon has benefited from the rapid growth experienced by its West Coast neighbors in high-technology, commercial, and service industries, since firms in these fields sometimes find it convenient to expand their facilities across state borders into Oregon.

Vegetation Zones   As moist, warm Pacific air rises over the mountains of Oregon, it cools and drops heavy rains on the western slopes. The air then descends the eastern slopes, warms, and holds its moisture, resulting in low rainfall in the east. Vegetation zones important to Oregon's forest-products industry develop mainly in the west, due to the plentiful moisture and mild West Coast climate.

			Farmland (cropland and pastureland)
			Farmland and woodlots
			Forests
			Grassland

| Desert |
| Irrigated areas |
| Barren and ice covered areas |
| Livestock grazing (areas other than farmland) |

Major urban areas

Major highways
 5 National interstate
 101 U.S.
 78 State

© RAND MC NALLY & CO.

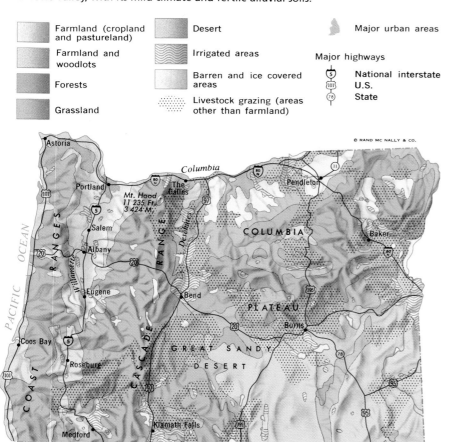

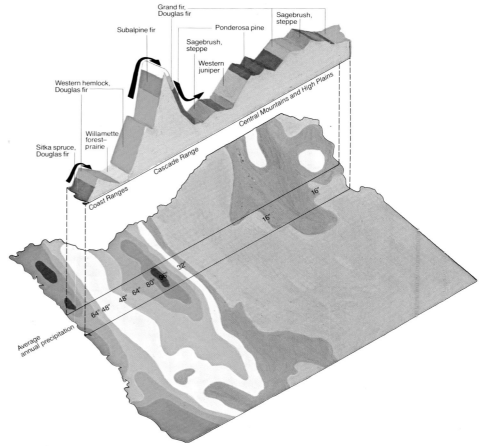

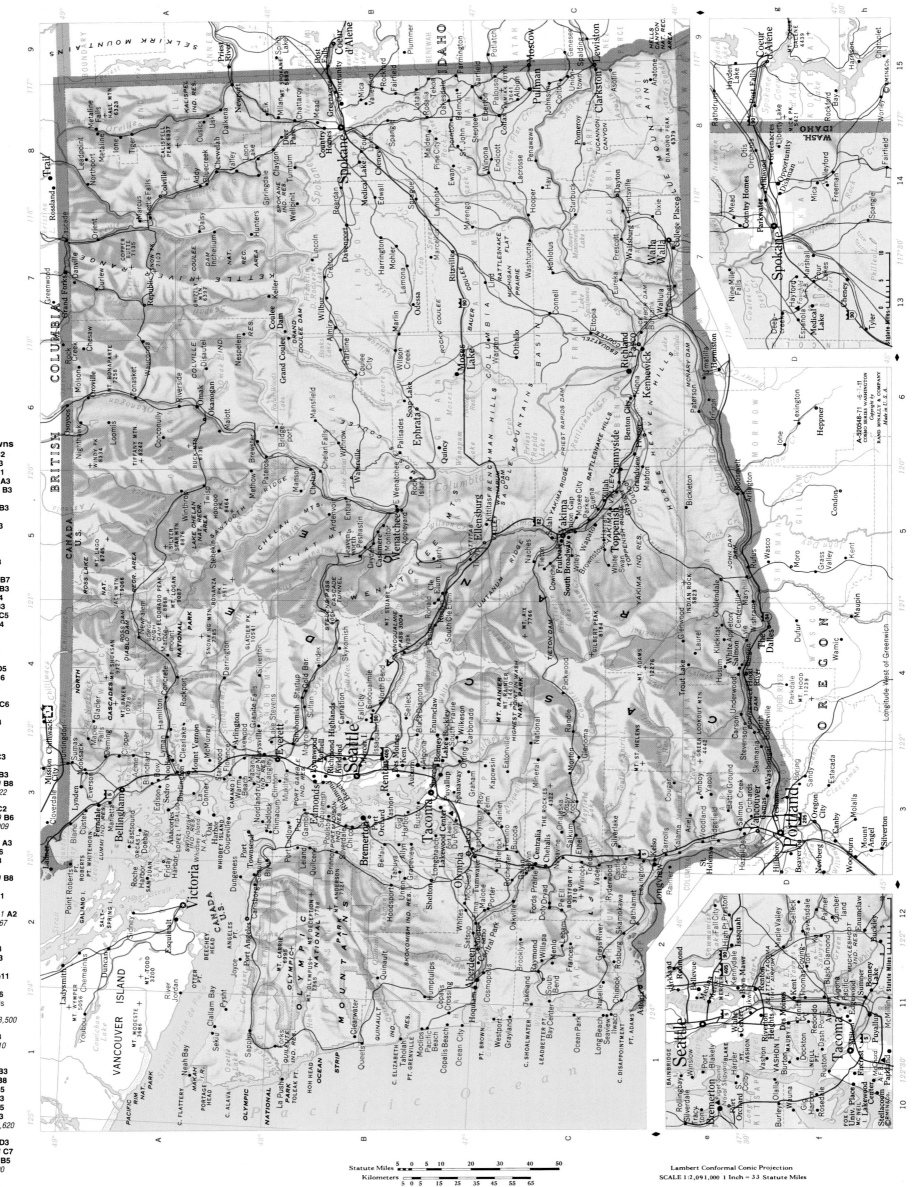

Statute Miles
Kilometers

Lambert Conformal Conic Projection
SCALE 1:2,091,000 1 Inch = 33 Statute Miles

Washington

POPULATION 4,132,180.
Rank: 20. *Density:* 62 people/mi²
(24 people/km²). *Urban:* 73.5%.
Rural: 26.5%.
AGE *< 20:* 31%. *20–40:* 34%.
40–65: 24%. *>65:* 11%.
ETHNIC GROUPS *White:* 91.5%.
Black: 2.6%. *Spanish origin:*
2.9%. *Native American:* 1.4%.
Other: 4.5%.

INCOME/CAPITA $10,309. *Rank:* 10.
POLITICS 1948–1980 elections:
President: 3 Dem., 6 Rep.
Governor: 3 Dem., 6 Rep.
ENTERED UNION November 11,
1889, 42nd state.
CAPITAL Olympia, 27,447.
LARGEST CITY Seattle, 493,846.

AREA 68,138 mi² (176,477 km²).
Rank: 20. *Water area:* 1,627 mi²
(4,214 km²).
ELEVATIONS *Highest:* Mt. Rainier,
14,410 ft (4,392 m). *Lowest:*
Pacific Ocean shoreline, sea level.
CLIMATE Cool summers, mild
winters along coast; hot
summers, cold winters, dry on
inland plateau.

Washington is a study in the interplay of geography and economy. Both its commerce and industry have been shaped by the state's far-northwest location and its endowment of natural resources.

Washington's location makes it a trade and transportation center whose influence extends far beyond its shores. In many ways, the state serves as Alaska's principal port of call, a harbor for northwest Canada, and an outpost for Japan and other Asian countries doing business with the United States.

Yet Washington's key resource is water—not only Puget Sound and the Pacific Ocean, but its many inland rivers. Both the Snake and the Columbia rivers are important sources of hydroelectric power and irrigation water, and because the Cascade Range divides Washington into wet and semiarid regions, geography determines how this water will be used. Hydroelectric power drives the major centers of industry along the western coastal areas while irrigation water is channeled to the croplands of the Columbia Plateau in the eastern regions. The state's water resources create an economy of unusual breadth and variety. Its production of aircraft and aerospace hardware in the west is as well known as its fruit and potato crops in the east. Inland wheat harvests are as important to national markets as the state's coastal shipbuilding.

Despite Washington's economic mastery of its geographical divisions, the state faces problems nearly as volatile as its Mount St. Helens. Markets for many of Washington's more important products—such as aircraft, ships, lumber and pulp, fruit, and grain—fluctuate widely from year to year, leaving the state vulnerable to forces outside its borders. Further, the federal government holds title to a major share of Washington's land and has invested heavily in irrigation, hydroelectric projects, the Hanford atomic energy facility, and the aerospace and shipbuilding industries. Changes in these commitments could affect Washington's control over its resources and its economy.

Yet even with these problems, Washington remains an important shipping center not only for the Pacific Coast but for countries halfway around the world. The state's rich industrial and natural resources will help it meet the many challenges of the future.

Mount Shuksan is typical of many mountains of the northern Cascades. The area's topography is often compared to that of the Alps, and the mountains are a major tourist attraction. But the high, rugged peaks affect more than Washington's beauty; they also act as an economic and climatic barrier, making transportation difficult and keeping moist Pacific winds from reaching the state's interior. On the positive side, the waterfalls and rivers provide water supplies and hydropower, and the tree-covered slopes are a source of timber.

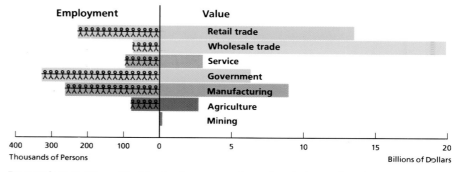

Employment		Value
		Retail trade
		Wholesale trade
		Service
		Government
		Manufacturing
		Agriculture
		Mining

400 300 200 100 0
Thousands of Persons

0 5 10 15 20
Billions of Dollars

Economic Activities   Washington's economy is modern in its outlines but still relies upon its basic endowment of natural resources for a large share of its income. Examples include wood production from timber, salmon and halibut supply from fisheries, and productive agriculture from good soil and precipitation.

Land Use   Although the farms of eastern Washington are blocked from much eastward-moving precipitation by the Cascades, the entire state is still influenced by the Pacific Ocean, which has a moderating effect on the climate.

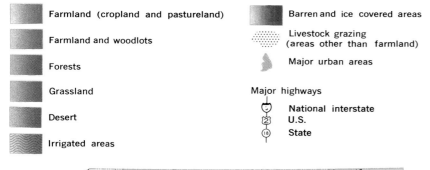

Farmland (cropland and pastureland)

Farmland and woodlots

Forests

Grassland

Desert

Irrigated areas

Barren and ice covered areas

Livestock grazing
(areas other than farmland)

Major urban areas

Major highways
National interstate
U.S.
State

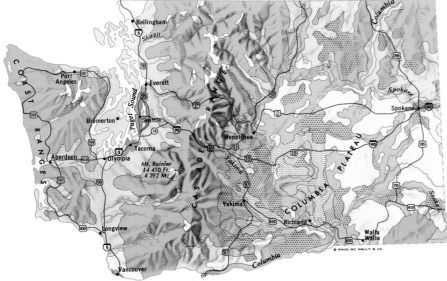

Volcanic Forces   The volcanic eruption of Mount St. Helens is a reminder of the forces affecting the lands circling the Pacific Ocean. Moving sections of the earth's crust called plates meet in these areas. At the zone of contact, the Pacific Plate is pushed into hotter depths and partly converted to melted rock, or magma. As magma rises, it erupts, and in time a series of volcanic mountains is formed.

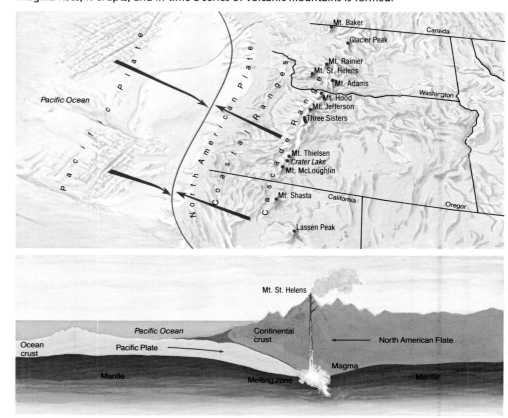

THE PEOPLE

STATE (abbreviation)	POPULATION (rank)	POPULATION CHANGE 1970-1980 (%)	PERSONS PER mi²	PERSONS PER km²	RESIDENCE (%) Urban	RESIDENCE (%) Rural	AGE <20	AGE 20-40	AGE 40-65	AGE >65	White	Black	Spanish Origin	Native American	Other	BIRTH RATE per 1,000	DEATH RATE per 1,000	AVERAGE LIFETIME (years)	NET MIGRATION	Elementary/Secondary Students	Teachers	Higher Education Students	High-School Graduates (%)	College Graduates (%)
Alabama (AL)	3,893,888 (22)	13.1	77	30	60.0	40.0	34	31	24	11	73.8	25.6	0.9	0.2	0.4	16.2	8.7	69.1	176,000	759,000	41,200	145,000	56	10
Alaska (AK)	401,851 (50)	32.8	0.7	0.3	64.3	35.7	36	42	19	3	77.0	3.4	2.4	5.5	14.1	22.5	4.0	69.3	36,000	87,000	5,200	24,000	80	18
Arizona (AZ)	2,718,425 (29)	53.1	24	9.2	83.8	16.2	33	32	24	11	82.4	2.8	16.2	5.6	9.2	17.7	7.4	70.6	712,000	514,000	26,200	196,000	73	16
Arkansas (AR)	2,286,435 (33)	18.9	44	17	51.6	48.4	33	29	24	14	82.7	16.3	0.8	0.4	0.6	16.0	9.5	70.7	232,000	448,000	24,100	65,000	56	9
California (CA)	23,667,565 (1)	18.5	151	58	91.3	8.7	31	34	25	10	76.2	7.7	19.2	0.8	15.3	16.3	7.6	71.7	2,078,000	4,118,000	175,500	1,691,000	74	17
Colorado (CO)	2,889,735 (28)	30.8	28	11	80.6	19.4	32	37	23	8	89.0	3.5	11.7	0.6	6.9	16.6	6.5	72.1	446,000	546,000	27,200	150,000	78	19
Connecticut (CT)	3,107,576 (25)	2.5	638	239	78.8	21.2	30	31	27	12	90.1	7.0	4.0	0.1	2.8	12.5	8.4	72.5	-52,000	531,000	33,900	100,000	70	18
Delaware (DE)	594,317 (47)	8.4	308	119	70.6	29.4	32	32	26	10	82.1	16.1	1.6	0.2	1.6	14.9	8.1	70.1	8,000	99,000	5,900	28,000	70	15
District of Columbia (DC)	638,432 (—)	-18.5	10,134	3,917	100.0	*	27	36	25	12	26.9	70.3	2.8	0.2	2.6	14.5	10.3	65.7	-151,000	100,000	5,200	14,000	66	23
Florida (FL)	9,746,342 (7)	43.5	180	69	84.3	15.7	28	28	27	17	84.0	13.8	8.8	0.2	2.0	12.8	10.4	70.7	2,716,000	1,510,000	78,300	346,000	65	14
Georgia (GA)	5,463,105 (13)	19.1	94	36	62.4	37.6	34	33	23	10	72.3	26.8	1.1	0.1	0.8	16.3	7.9	68.5	443,000	1,069,000	56,500	146,000	59	12
Hawaii (HI)	964,691 (39)	25.3	150	58	86.5	13.5	33	36	23	8	33.0	1.8	7.4	0.3	64.9	18.5	5.0	73.6	76,000	165,000	7,900	45,000	73	17
Idaho (ID)	944,038 (41)	32.4	11	4.4	54.0	46.0	36	32	22	11	95.5	0.3	3.9	1.1	3.1	21.5	6.8	71.9	130,000	203,000	9,900	34,000	72	14
Illinois (IL)	11,426,596 (5)	2.8	205	79	83.3	16.7	32	32	25	11	80.8	14.7	5.6	0.1	4.4	16.1	8.9	70.1	-410,000	1,983,000	105,700	504,000	66	14
Indiana (IN)	5,490,260 (12)	5.7	153	59	64.2	35.8	33	31	25	11	91.2	7.6	1.6	0.1	1.1	16.0	8.5	70.9	-87,000	1,056,000	53,800	193,000	67	11
Iowa (IA)	2,913,808 (27)	3.1	52	20	58.6	41.4	33	30	24	13	97.4	1.4	8.8	1.0	1.0	16.0	9.2	72.6	-58,000	534,000	32,400	100,000	72	13
Kansas (KS)	2,364,236 (32)	5.1	29	11	66.7	33.3	31	32	24	13	91.7	5.3	2.7	0.6	2.4	16.6	9.0	72.6	-19,000	415,000	26,200	124,000	73	15
Kentucky (KY)	3,660,257 (23)	13.6	92	36	50.9	49.1	32	31	24	11	92.3	7.1	0.7	0.1	0.5	16.2	8.9	70.1	209,000	670,000	33,400	116,000	53	10
Louisiana (LA)	4,206,312 (19)	15.4	94	36	68.6	31.4	36	32	23	9	69.2	29.4	2.4	0.3	1.1	19.1	8.4	68.8	188,000	778,000	42,700	151,000	58	12
Maine (ME)	1,125,027 (38)	13.2	36	14	47.5	52.5	32	31	25	12	98.7	0.3	0.4	0.4	0.6	14.5	9.1	70.9	76,000	222,000	10,200	32,000	68	14
Maryland (MD)	4,216,975 (18)	7.5	429	166	80.3	19.7	32	33	26	9	74.9	22.7	1.5	0.2	2.2	13.8	7.8	70.2	55,000	751,000	41,100	197,000	69	19
Massachusetts (MA)	5,737,037 (11)	0.8	733	283	83.8	16.2	30	36	25	13	93.5	3.9	2.5	0.1	2.5	12.3	9.0	71.8	-136,000	1,022,000	65,800	178,000	72	17
Michigan (MI)	9,262,078 (8)	4.3	163	63	70.7	29.3	34	32	24	10	85.0	12.9	1.8	0.4	1.7	15.6	7.9	70.6	-297,000	1,863,000	80,500	446,000	69	13
Minnesota (MN)	4,075,970 (21)	7.1	51	20	66.9	33.1	33	32	23	12	96.6	1.3	0.8	0.9	1.2	16.2	7.9	73.0	11,000	754,000	43,700	165,000	72	13
Mississippi (MS)	2,520,638 (31)	13.7	53	21	47.3	52.7	36	31	23	11	64.1	35.2	1.0	0.2	0.5	18.3	9.2	68.1	85,000	477,000	26,300	95,000	52	11
Missouri (MO)	4,916,759 (15)	5.1	71	28	68.1	31.9	32	30	25	13	88.4	10.5	1.1	0.2	0.9	15.6	9.7	70.7	16,000	845,000	48,800	173,000	64	12
Montana (MT)	786,690 (44)	13.3	5.4	2.1	52.9	47.1	33	31	24	11	94.1	0.2	1.3	4.7	1.0	17.8	8.2	70.6	33,000	155,000	9,300	32,000	73	14
Nebraska (NE)	1,569,825 (35)	5.7	20	7.9	62.9	37.1	32	31	24	13	94.9	3.1	1.8	0.6	1.4	16.8	9.1	72.6	-12,000	280,000	18,000	77,000	74	14
Nevada (NV)	800,493 (43)	63.8	7.3	2.8	85.3	14.7	30	35	27	8	87.5	6.4	6.7	1.7	4.4	16.2	7.0	69.0	257,000	149,000	7,100	40,000	76	13
New Hampshire (NH)	920,610 (42)	24.8	102	40	52.2	47.8	32	33	24	11	98.8	0.4	0.6	0.1	0.6	14.1	8.1	71.2	136,000	167,000	9,400	26,000	70	15
New Jersey (NJ)	7,364,823 (9)	2.7	986	381	89.0	11.0	31	30	27	12	83.2	12.6	6.7	0.1	4.1	13.1	8.9	70.9	-114,000	1,246,000	76,900	248,000	66	15
New Mexico (NM)	1,302,981 (37)	28.1	11	4.1	72.1	27.9	36	32	23	9	75.1	1.8	36.6	8.0	15.1	20.0	6.7	70.3	141,000	271,000	14,400	57,000	66	15
New York (NY)	17,558,372 (2)	-3.9	371	143	84.6	15.4	30	31	27	12	80.0	13.7	9.5	0.2	6.1	13.4	9.2	70.6	-1,543,000	2,871,000	169,300	572,000	66	16
North Carolina (NC)	5,881,813 (10)	15.7	120	46	48.0	52.0	32	33	25	10	75.8	22.4	1.0	1.1	0.7	14.5	8.0	69.2	395,000	1,129,000	55,300	236,000	55	12
North Dakota (ND)	652,717 (46)	5.7	9.4	3.6	48.8	51.2	34	29	22	12	95.8	0.4	0.6	3.1	0.7	18.1	8.2	72.8	-17,000	117,000	7,100	33,000	68	12
Ohio (OH)	10,797,624 (6)	1.3	263	102	73.3	26.7	31	31	26	11	88.9	10.0	1.1	0.1	1.0	15.5	8.8	70.8	-544,000	1,957,000	99,300	385,000	68	11
Oklahoma (OK)	3,025,290 (26)	18.2	44	17	67.3	32.7	31	31	25	13	85.9	6.8	1.9	5.6	1.7	16.5	9.3	71.4	295,000	578,000	34,400	140,000	66	12
Oregon (OR)	2,633,149 (30)	25.9	27	11	67.9	32.1	30	34	24	11	94.6	1.4	2.5	1.0	3.0	16.2	8.2	72.1	396,000	465,000	25,100	133,000	76	15
Pennsylvania (PA)	11,863,895 (4)	0.5	264	102	69.3	30.7	30	30	27	13	89.8	8.8	1.3	*	1.4	13.3	9.9	70.4	-289,000	1,909,000	109,500	293,000	65	12
Rhode Island (RI)	947,154 (40)	-0.3	898	347	87.0	13.0	30	33	26	13	94.7	2.9	2.1	0.3	2.1	12.4	9.5	71.9	-33,000	148,000	9,200	35,000	62	15
South Carolina (SC)	3,121,833 (24)	20.5	103	40	54.1	45.9	34	33	24	9	68.8	30.4	1.1	0.2	0.6	16.4	7.9	68.0	272,000	619,000	31,800	109,000	57	10
South Dakota (SD)	690,768 (45)	3.7	9.1	3.5	46.4	53.6	34	30	23	13	92.6	0.3	0.6	6.5	0.6	18.9	9.2	72.1	-26,000	129,000	8,100	26,000	69	11
Tennessee (TN)	4,591,120 (17)	16.9	112	43	60.4	39.6	32	32	26	11	83.5	15.8	0.7	0.1	0.6	15.1	8.5	70.1	394,000	854,000	41,300	153,000	55	11
Texas (TX)	14,229,288 (3)	27.1	54	21	79.6	20.4	34	33	23	10	78.7	12.0	21.0	0.3	9.0	18.3	7.5	70.9	1,779,000	2,900,000	163,100	626,000	65	14
Utah (UT)	1,461,037 (36)	37.9	18	6.9	84.4	15.6	41	33	19	7	94.6	0.6	4.1	1.3	3.5	29.0	5.6	72.9	149,000	344,000	14,800	62,000	80	18
Vermont (VT)	511,456 (48)	15.0	55	21	33.8	66.2	33	33	23	11	99.1	0.2	0.6	0.2	0.5	14.9	8.2	71.6	36,000	96,000	6,700	18,000	70	16
Virginia (VA)	5,346,818 (14)	14.9	135	52	66.0	34.0	32	35	25	9	79.1	18.9	1.5	0.2	1.8	14.5	7.7	70.1	353,000	1,010,000	58,200	251,000	64	16
Washington (WA)	4,132,180 (20)	21.1	62	24	73.5	26.5	31	34	24	11	91.5	2.6	2.9	1.4	4.5	16.0	7.6	71.7	474,000	758,000	35,700	250,000	76	16
West Virginia (WV)	1,950,279 (34)	11.8	81	31	36.2	63.8	32	31	24	12	96.2	3.3	0.7	0.1	0.4	15.4	9.2	69.5	113,000	384,000	22,200	71,000	53	9
Wisconsin (WI)	4,705,521 (16)	6.5	86	33	64.2	35.8	33	31	24	12	94.4	3.9	1.3	0.6	1.1	15.7	8.4	72.5	14,000	830,000	53,900	241,000	70	13
Wyoming (WY)	469,557 (49)	41.3	4.8	1.9	62.7	37.3	35	36	21	8	95.1	0.7	5.2	1.5	2.7	21.6	6.8	70.3	96,000	98,000	6,400	21,000	75	15
UNITED STATES	226,547,346 (—)	11.4	64	25	73.7	26.3	32	32	25	11	83.2	11.7	6.4	0.6	4.5	15.6	8.5	70.8	9,238,000	40,984,000	2,194,000	9,647,000	67	14

*Less than 1%

THE LAND

	AREA				LAND USE (%)					LAND OWNERSHIP (%)			TRANSPORTATION							WATER USE PER DAY		ENVIRONMENTAL-QUALITY EXPENDITURES (mil. of dollars)			
STATE	Total km²	Total mi²	Land km²	Land mi²	Urban	Crop-land	Range and Pasture	Forest	Other	State	Federal	Other	Highways 1,000 mi	Highways 1,000 km	Interstates mi	Interstates km	Railroads mi	Railroads km	Public Airports	Per Capita (gal)	Total (bil. gal)	Manufacturers	Local	State	Federal
Alabama	133,914	51,705	131,485	50,767	5	14	13	61	7	*	3	97	87.1	140.2	889	1,431	4,497	7,237	97	2,824	11.0	106	129	7	27
Alaska	1,530,694	591,004	1,478,451	570,833	*	*	2	2	96	1	96	3	9.9	15.9	—	—	550	885	477	546	0.2	4	44	13	5
Arizona	295,258	114,000	293,984	113,508	1	2	48	2	47	*	44	56	60.7	97.7	1,179	1,897	1,865	3,001	96	2,929	8.0	17	96	10	17
Arkansas	137,753	53,187	134,881	52,078	3	24	18	42	13	*	10	90	74.7	120.2	531	855	2,749	4,424	81	6,960	16.0	65	48	5	23
California	411,047	158,706	404,813	156,299	4	10	19	10	57	1	47	52	177.8	286.1	2,407	3,874	6,977	11,228	295	2,272	54.0	175	1,137	158	412
Colorado	269,595	104,091	268,310	103,595	1	17	38	5	39	*	36	64	88.4	142.3	939	1,511	3,413	5,493	90	5,512	16.0	△	130	15	19
Connecticut	12,999	5,019	12,618	4,872	31	6	4	45	14	6	*	94	19.3	31.1	337	542	664	1,069	15	1,188	3.7	20	202	18	69
Delaware	5,294	2,044	5,004	1,932	12	43	2	29	14	1	3	96	5.1	8.2	41	66	269	433	3	2,013	1.2	34	37	7	8
District of Columbia	179	69	163	63	67	—	—	—	33	—	33	67	1.1	1.8	22	35	52	84	7	534	0.3	△	72	—	11
Florida	151,939	58,664	140,256	54,153	12	9	25	35	19	1	12	87	96.3	155.0	1,506	2,424	3,698	5,951	132	2,127	21.0	63	575	17	126
Georgia	152,576	58,910	150,364	58,056	5	17	9	58	11	*	6	94	104.0	167.4	1,279	2,058	5,471	8,805	125	1,259	6.9	51	208	12	63
Hawaii	16,760	6,471	16,641	6,425	3	7	24	35	31	*	16	83	3.9	6.3	48	77	—	—	18	2,548	2.5	△	48	4	8
Idaho	216,435	83,566	213,449	82,413	1	12	14	8	65	*	64	36	66.5	107.0	613	987	2,567	4,131	126	19,007	18.0	28	22	5	8
Illinois	149,885	57,871	144,120	55,645	7	67	9	8	9	1	2	97	134.2	216.0	1,734	2,791	11,167	17,972	98	1,574	18.0	181	763	97	214
Indiana	94,309	36,413	93,063	35,932	8	58	9	15	10	1	2	98	91.1	146.6	1,102	1,773	5,896	9,489	78	2,551	14.0	228	213	21	109
Iowa	145,752	56,275	144,949	55,965	2	74	13	4	7	*	1	99	111.9	180.1	800	1,287	5,805	9,342	117	1,476	4.3	25	113	7	35
Kansas	213,104	82,280	211,812	81,781	1	55	36	2	6	*	1	99	135.0	217.3	800	1,287	6,699	10,781	129	2,788	6.6	113	74	5	32
Kentucky	104,659	40,409	102,742	39,669	5	21	23	42	9	*	6	94	69.0	111.0	741	1,193	3,572	5,749	62	1,311	4.8	48	161	12	43
Louisiana	123,675	47,751	115,309	44,521	3	21	11	44	21	*	4	96	55.8	89.8	861	1,386	3,452	5,555	74	3,079	13.0	221	136	7	26
Maine	86,156	33,265	80,277	30,995	2	5	1	83	9	*	1	99	22.2	35.7	314	505	1,727	2,779	45	1,421	1.6	37	40	9	25
Maryland	27,092	10,460	25,478	9,837	19	27	8	34	12	1	3	96	27.2	43.8	411	661	1,054	1,696	24	1,822	7.7	25	267	38	67
Massachusetts	21,455	8,284	20,264	7,824	25	6	2	55	12	5	2	93	33.6	54.1	512	824	1,462	2,353	35	1,027	5.9	32	315	64	153
Michigan	251,493	97,102	147,510	56,954	9	26	3	42	20	1	10	89	120.1	193.3	1,175	1,891	4,411	7,099	133	1,621	15.0	221	607	42	345
Minnesota	224,329	86,614	206,028	79,548	3	45	6	27	19	*	7	93	129.2	207.9	859	1,382	6,983	11,238	145	759	3.1	62	223	49	57
Mississippi	123,517	47,690	122,333	47,233	5	24	13	48	10	*	6	94	69.6	112.0	680	1,094	3,161	5,087	82	1,387	3.5	22	47	8	18
Missouri	180,515	69,697	178,567	68,945	3	33	29	25	10	*	5	95	117.9	189.7	1,124	1,809	5,902	9,498	118	1,401	6.9	37	173	17	52
Montana	380,856	147,049	376,564	145,392	*	16	45	7	32	1	30	70	77.2	124.2	1,194	1,922	4,660	7,500	118	13,959	11.0	12	27	5	6
Nebraska	200,348	77,355	198,507	76,644	1	42	51	1	5	*	1	99	96.5	155.3	485	781	4,903	7,891	94	7,634	12.0	△	58	6	18
Nevada	286,350	110,560	284,622	109,893	*	2	11	*	87	*	86	14	49.9	80.3	544	875	1,564	2,517	62	4,461	3.6	1	42	3	27
New Hampshire	24,033	9,279	23,292	8,993	6	5	2	69	18	1	13	86	15.7	25.3	226	364	617	993	15	1,083	1.0	△	20	21	35
New Jersey	20,168	7,787	19,342	7,468	24	16	3	41	16	5	3	92	33.4	53.8	375	604	1,576	2,536	35	1,356	10.0	87	532	111	187
New Mexico	314,924	121,593	314,256	121,335	1	3	55	4	37	*	33	67	72.0	115.9	1,000	1,609	1,964	3,161	66	2,989	3.9	4	55	5	389
New York	136,583	52,735	122,706	47,377	10	20	7	50	13	5	1	94	109.3	175.9	1,442	2,321	5,482	8,822	83	967	17.0	163	1,360	133	62
North Carolina	136,412	52,669	126,503	48,843	7	20	7	54	12	1	7	93	92.3	148.5	859	1,382	3,640	5,858	90	1,376	8.1	59	200	31	62
North Dakota	183,120	70,703	179,486	69,300	1	61	27	*	10	*	5	95	106.3	171.1	577	929	5,121	8,241	97	1,988	1.3	△	26	2	6
Ohio	115,995	44,786	106,200	41,004	13	45	10	22	10	1	4	95	111.6	179.6	1,544	2,485	7,320	11,780	133	1,296	14.0	211	556	226	221
Oklahoma	181,186	69,956	177,816	68,655	3	27	53	11	6	*	7	93	109.8	176.7	812	1,307	3,860	6,212	126	592	1.8	24	111	7	33
Oregon	251,417	97,073	249,115	96,184	1	8	19	16	56	1	52	48	123.3	198.4	723	1,164	2,957	4,759	96	2,578	6.8	54	124	22	45
Pennsylvania	119,251	46,043	116,259	44,888	12	20	6	50	12	1	3	96	117.5	189.1	1,500	2,414	7,248	11,665	77	1,347	16.0	286	623	53	227
Rhode Island	3,141	1,213	2,732	1,055	37	4	3	44	12	2	1	97	6.4	10.3	129	208	143	230	8	527	0.5	3	50	9	14
South Carolina	80,580	31,112	78,225	30,203	8	17	6	56	13	*	6	94	62.1	99.9	760	1,223	2,772	4,461	66	1,983	6.2	41	107	9	43
South Dakota	199,730	77,116	196,715	75,952	1	37	51	1	10	*	7	93	82.6	132.9	686	1,104	2,829	4,553	74	1,000	0.7	△	15	2	9
Tennessee	109,152	42,144	106,591	41,155	6	19	21	44	10	*	7	93	82.6	132.9	1,025	1,650	3,136	5,047	77	2,176	10.0	84	164	13	43
Texas	691,027	266,807	678,621	262,017	2	18	68	6	5	1	2	97	264.9	426.3	3,245	5,222	13,304	21,411	322	1,466	21.0	373	714	28	87
Utah	219,887	84,899	212,568	82,073	*	3	19	2	75	*	64	36	49.6	79.8	919	1,479	1,659	2,670	57	3,125	4.6	15	40	3	11
Vermont	24,900	9,614	24,017	9,273	5	10	9	66	10	3	5	92	14.0	22.5	309	497	384	618	20	664	0.3	△	11	6	16
Virginia	105,583	40,766	102,830	39,703	8	13	13	52	14	*	9	91	65.1	104.8	1,061	1,708	3,511	5,650	58	1,809	9.7	56	269	16	79
Washington	176,477	68,138	172,263	66,511	3	19	17	29	32	*	30	70	84.2	135.5	658	1,059	5,340	8,594	118	2,001	8.3	154	217	24	63
West Virginia	62,758	24,231	62,468	24,119	5	6	13	64	12	*	7	93	37.5	60.4	477	768	3,513	5,654	28	2,872	5.6	35	45	7	31
Wisconsin	171,496	66,215	140,963	54,426	5	34	8	38	15	*	5	95	106.7	171.7	523	842	5,653	9,098	102	1,227	5.8	3	249	22	87
Wyoming	253,324	97,809	251,200	96,989	*	5	43	2	50	*	49	51	35.7	57.5	922	1,484	1,985	3,195	44	11,368	5.4	△	15	2	2
UNITED STATES	9,529,081	3,679,201	9,166,732	3,539,295	3	18	24	17	38	*	34	66	3,917.8	6,305.1	42,899	69,039	188,304	303,046	4,768	1,953	451.0	3,602	11,513	1,411	3,723

* Less than 1%
△ Data not available

THE ECONOMY

Column groups: **CIVILIAN LABOR FORCE** (excluding agriculture) — *Total Labor Force (Rank)*, *Employment Rate (%)*, *Employment by Occupation (%)*: Government, Non-government, White Collar, Blue Collar, Other · **PERSONAL INCOME** (dollars): Per Capita, Per Family · **POPULATION BELOW POVERTY LEVEL (%)**: 1969, 1979 · **STATE GOVERNMENT REVENUE** (mil. of dollars): From State Taxes, From Federal Govt., From Other · **MAJOR PRODUCTS**: Agriculture, Industry, Mining

STATE	Total Labor Force (Rank)	Emp. Rate (%)	Govt.	Non-govt.	White Collar	Blue Collar	Other	Per Capita	Per Family	Pov. 1969	Pov. 1979	From State Taxes	From Federal Govt.	From Other	Agriculture	Industry	Mining
Alabama	1,642,000 (22)	91.2	22	78	43	41	16	7,488	16,602	25	19	1,857	1,232	1,065	Poultry, soybeans, cattle, eggs	Metal, paper, chemicals	Coal, petroleum, natural gas
Alaska	187,000 (50)	90.5	33	67	58	28	14	12,790	28,266	13	11	1,438	378	1,414	Greenhouse prod., dairy prod., potatoes	Food, chemicals, paper	Petroleum, natural gas, sand and gravel
Arizona	1,126,000 (31)	93.4	20	80	58	27	15	8,791	19,150	15	13	1,684	541	962	Cattle, cotton, dairy prod., hay	Elec. equip., machinery, trans. equip.	Copper, molybdenum, cement
Arkansas	972,000 (33)	92.4	19	81	43	37	20	7,268	14,356	28	19	1,161	715	419	Soybeans, poultry, rice, cattle	Electronics, food, paper	Petroleum, bromide, natural gas
California	11,203,000 (1)	93.2	18	82	58	28	14	10,938	21,479	11	11	19,367	7,079	9,641	Dairy prod., cattle, cotton, grapes	Trans. equip., elec. equip., food	Petroleum, cement, natural gas
Colorado	1,474,000 (25)	94.4	19	81	58	27	15	10,025	21,485	12	10	1,491	768	1,107	Cattle, wheat, corn, dairy prod.	Food, instruments, machinery	Petroleum, molybdenum, coal
Connecticut	1,616,000 (24)	94.1	13	87	59	29	12	11,720	23,038	7	8	1,840	804	828	Dairy prod., eggs, greenhouse prod.	Trans. equip., machinery, metal	Stone, sand and gravel, feldspar
Delaware	280,000 (47)	92.3	17	83	54	30	16	10,339	20,658	11	12	516	205	249	Poultry, soybeans, corn, dairy prod.	Chemicals, trans. equip., food	Sand and gravel, magnesium, clay
District of Columbia	317,000 (—)	92.8	46	54	67	16	17	12,039	18,839	17	19			—	—	Printing and publ., food, metal	—
Florida	3,925,000 (8)	94.0	17	83	52	30	18	8,996	17,558	16	13	4,804	1,742	1,677	Oranges, cattle, dairy prod.	Food, electrical equip., chemicals	Phosphate, petroleum, stone
Georgia	2,385,000 (15)	93.6	20	80	51	34	15	8,073	17,403	21	17	2,729	1,417	1,048	Poultry, eggs, soybeans, peanuts	Textiles, trans. equip., food	Clay, stone, cement
Hawaii	399,000 (42)	95.0	22	78	55	24	21	10,101	23,066	9	10	998	368	529	Sugarcane, pineapples, cattle	Food, petroleum, printing and publ.	Cement, stone, sand and gravel
Idaho	424,000 (41)	92.1	21	79	48	32	20	8,056	17,278	13	13	490	282	336	Cattle, wheat, potatoes, dairy prod.	Lumber, food, chemicals	Silver, phosphate, lead
Illinois	5,447,000 (4)	91.7	16	84	53	32	15	10,521	22,007	10	11	7,073	2,764	2,893	Corn, soybeans, hogs, cattle	Machinery, food, elec. equip.	Coal, petroleum, stone
Indiana	2,620,000 (12)	90.4	17	83	43	39	18	8,936	20,540	10	10	2,696	883	1,215	Corn, soybeans, hogs, cattle	Elec. equip., trans. equip., metal	Coal, petroleum, stone
Iowa	1,449,000 (26)	94.3	19	81	46	30	24	9,358	20,243	12	10	1,747	744	988	Cattle, corn, hogs, soybeans	Machinery, food, chemicals	Cement, stone, sand and gravel
Kansas	1,198,000 (30)	95.6	20	80	50	29	21	9,983	19,575	13	10	1,270	577	572	Cattle, wheat, corn, sorghum	Trans. equip., machinery, food	Petroleum, natural gas, cement
Kentucky	1,620,000 (23)	91.9	19	81	44	35	21	7,613	16,399	23	18	2,145	1,089	934	Tobacco, cattle, horses, soybeans	Machinery, food, elec. equip.	Coal, stone, petroleum
Louisiana	1,723,000 (21)	93.3	19	81	50	34	16	8,458	17,822	26	19	2,397	1,302	1,713	Soybeans, rice, cotton, cattle	Chemicals, petroleum, food	Natural gas, petroleum, sulphur
Maine	500,000 (38)	92.3	20	80	45	39	16	7,925	16,208	14	13	619	401	349	Eggs, dairy prod., potatoes, poultry	Paper, leather, lumber	Sand and gravel, cement, stone
Maryland	2,133,000 (17)	93.6	24	76	61	26	13	10,460	22,850	10	10	2,761	1,154	1,649	Poultry, dairy prod., corn, soybeans	Food, electronics, metal	Stone, cement, coal
Massachusetts	2,893,000 (10)	94.4	15	85	55	31	14	10,125	21,329	9	10	3,927	1,905	1,625	Greenhouse, dairy prod., cranberries	Machinery, elec. equip., instruments	Stone, sand and gravel, lime
Michigan	4,298,000 (7)	87.4	18	82	49	35	16	9,950	21,886	9	10	5,948	2,729	3,680	Dairy prod., corn, cattle, soybeans	Trans. equip., machinery, metal	Iron ore, petroleum, natural gas
Minnesota	2,116,000 (18)	94.3	17	83	51	26	23	9,724	21,217	11	10	3,203	1,223	1,274	Dairy prod., corn, cattle, soybeans	Machinery, food, metal	Iron ore, sand and gravel, stone
Mississippi	1,024,000 (32)	92.5	23	77	44	39	17	6,580	14,922	35	24	1,257	913	715	Soybeans, cotton, poultry, cattle	Petroleum, elec. equip., trans. equip.	Petroleum, natural gas, sand and gravel
Missouri	2,295,000 (16)	93.0	17	83	51	31	18	8,982	18,746	15	12	2,095	1,155	1,008	Soybeans, cattle, hogs, dairy prod.	Trans. equip., food, chemicals	Lead, cement, stone
Montana	374,000 (44)	94.0	25	75	46	27	27	8,536	18,839	14	12	436	364	353	Cattle, wheat, barley, dairy prod.	Metal, lumber, petroleum	Petroleum, coal, copper
Nebraska	776,000 (34)	96.0	21	79	46	28	26	9,365	19,110	13	11	817	361	328	Cattle, corn, hogs, wheat	Food, machinery, elec. equip.	Petroleum, cement, sand and gravel
Nevada	376,000 (43)	93.8	14	86	49	22	29	10,727	21,666	9	9	477	234	510	Cattle, hay, dairy prod., potatoes	Stone, clay, glass, print. and publ.	Gold, barite, sand and gravel
New Hampshire	461,000 (40)	95.3	15	85	50	31	19	9,131	19,796	9	9	267	241	386	Dairy prod., eggs, cattle	Elec. equip., machinery, paper	Sand and gravel, stone, clay
New Jersey	3,582,000 (9)	92.8	17	83	58	29	13	10,924	22,830	8	10	4,266	1,768	2,788	Greenhouse prod., dairy prod., peas	Chemicals, food, elec. equip.	Stone, sand and gravel, zinc
New Mexico	542,000 (37)	92.6	27	73	44	24	32	7,841	17,151	23	18	926	422	835	Cattle, dairy prod., hay, wheat	Metal, petroleum, food	Natural gas, petroleum, uranium
New York	7,992,000 (2)	92.5	18	82	57	27	16	10,260	20,385	11	13	12,716	6,574	7,909	Dairy prod., cattle, apples, corn	Instruments, print and publ., elec.	Cement, stone, salt
North Carolina	2,741,000 (11)	93.5	17	83	43	41	16	7,819	17,042	20	15	3,215	1,483	1,504	Tobacco, poultry, hogs, soybeans	Textiles, tobacco, chemicals	Stone, phosphate, sand and gravel
North Dakota	309,000 (46)	95.1	25	75	44	24	32	8,747	18,239	16	13	372	231	410	Wheat, cattle, sunflowers, dairy prod.	Machinery; food; petroleum, coal	Petroleum, coal, natural gas
Ohio	5,086,000 (6)	91.6	16	84	50	35	15	9,462	20,710	10	10	4,767	2,156	5,257	Soybeans, corn, dairy prod., cattle	Machinery, trans. equip., metal	Coal, petroleum, natural gas
Oklahoma	1,325,000 (27)	95.2	20	80	52	31	17	9,116	17,846	19	13	1,776	776	881	Cattle, wheat, dairy prod., cotton	Machinery, metal, petroleum	Petroleum, natural gas, coal
Oregon	1,271,000 (29)	91.8	19	81	54	31	15	9,317	19,837	12	11	1,455	927	1,659	Wheat, cattle, dairy prod.	Lumber, food, instruments	Stone, sand and gravel, cement
Pennsylvania	5,368,000 (5)	92.2	15	85	50	36	14	9,434	20,259	11	11	7,241	2,775	3,988	Dairy prod., cattle, corn, mushrooms	Metal, machinery, food	Coal, cement, stone
Rhode Island	462,000 (39)	92.8	15	85	49	38	13	9,444	19,441	11	10	551	355	487	Greenhouse prod., dairy prod., eggs	Misc. manufacturing, metal	Sand and gravel, stone, gems
South Carolina	1,306,000 (28)	93.1	20	80	45	39	16	7,266	17,340	24	17	1,678	817	989	Soybeans, tobacco, cattle, eggs	Textiles, chemicals, machinery	Cement, stone, sand and gravel
South Dakota	338,000 (45)	95.3	24	76	44	24	32	7,806	16,431	19	17	271	262	229	Cattle, hogs, wheat, dairy prod.	Machinery, food, petroleum and coal	Gold, cement, stone
Tennessee	2,015,000 (19)	92.8	18	82	45	39	16	7,720	16,245	22	16	1,887	1,208	933	Soybeans, cattle, dairy prod., tobacco	Chemicals, food, machinery	Coal, stone, zinc
Texas	6,412,000 (3)	94.8	17	83	52	33	15	9,545	19,372	19	15	6,759	2,898	3,267	Cattle, cotton, dairy prod., wheat	Chemicals, petroleum, machinery	Petroleum, natural gas, sulphur
Utah	607,000 (36)	93.8	23	77	55	31	14	7,649	20,035	11	10	786	497	606	Cattle, dairy prod., hay, wheat	Machinery, metal, trans. equip.	Copper, petroleum, coal
Vermont	245,000 (48)	93.6	19	81	49	31	20	7,827	17,549	12	12	267	242	202	Dairy prod., cattle, eggs, apples	Elec. equip., machinery, metal	Stone, asbestos, sand and gravel
Virginia	2,530,000 (13)	94.9	24	76	55	31	14	9,392	20,423	16	12	2,743	1,333	1,580	Cattle, dairy prod., tobacco, poultry	Chemicals, food, tobacco	Coal, stone, cement
Washington	1,907,000 (20)	92.5	21	79	55	30	15	10,309	21,635	10	10	2,917	1,153	2,254	Wheat, dairy prod., cattle, apples	Trans. equip., lumber, food	Cement, sand and gravel, stone
West Virginia	768,000 (35)	90.6	21	79	41	45	14	7,800	17,621	22	15	1,219	711	710	Cattle, dairy prod., apples, poultry	Chem.; metal; stone, clay, glass	Coal, natural gas, petroleum
Wisconsin	2,401,000 (14)	93.0	17	83	46	34	20	9,348	21,113	10	9	3,366	1,491	1,731	Dairy prod., cattle, corn, hogs	Machinery, food, paper	Sand and gravel, stone, iron ore
Wyoming	233,000 (49)	96.1	20	80	47	33	20	10,898	22,497	12	8	388	243	306	Cattle, sugar beets, wheat, sheep	Petroleum; chem.; stone, clay, glass	Petroleum, coal, sodium carbonate
UNITED STATES	104,719,000 (—)	92.9	18	82	52	32	16	9,521	19,908	14	12	137,075	61,892	78,035	Corn, soybeans, wheat, hay	Machinery, trans. equip., chemicals	Petroleum, natural gas, coal